For No One

by Alan Bradley

First Printing: 2013

ISBN: 978-1-63173-540-0

Laverna
Priestley Court, Staffordshire Technology Park
Staffordshire ST18 0LQ

http://www. for-no-one.com

enquiries@for-no-one.com

For No One

by

Alan Bradley

Laverna Group

Introduction

The Beatles were one of the most important musical phenomena of the twentieth century and ruled the musical world for much of the sixties. Together with the inspired management of Brian Epstein, they changed the world. Epstein found a rough-and-ready group playing small clubs in Liverpool. Within five years he developed them into the group chosen to represent the UK in the first ever satellite broadcast to the world!

But there were dark aspects to the Beatles story to go along with the million-sellers, and the record-breaking tours. Lost opportunities, millions of pounds squandered or stolen, and the involvement of some very unpleasant characters.

This book is an affectionate and penetrating retelling of that amazing story, laced with a huge amount of material never previously released. For the first time ever, this book tells the true and incredible story of Seltaeb, the company set up to sell Beatles merchandise around the world. As a result of dreadful errors, stupidity and arrogance, the deal which set up Seltaeb cost the Beatles a fortune.

And those mistakes and those lost millions led directly to problems and conflicts which caused the break-up of the Beatles. Along that painful road came the alleged death of Paul McCartney in November 1966 and the mysterious death of Brian Epstein in 1967

"For No One" is the story of the Beatles rise to super-stardom and their descent into a petty squabbling break-up, a process accelerated by two tragic events. The first was the alleged accidental death of Paul McCartney in a car crash in 1966. The second was the death of Brian Epstein, at the age of 32, just weeks after the release of “Sergeant Pepper” and 'All You Need is Love'. On top of the world, and then Epstein is dead. Accident? Suicide? Or something more sinister brought about by those dark elements that crawl all over the Beatles story? This new publication in novel form tells the full, eventful tale to enable readers to learn about these tragic and bizarre incidents, and readers will be left using one word to describe much of the sad, tumultuous Seltaeb story.

Curious!

Table of Contents

In Thanks

A book of this scale requires a great deal of work, but it is a task that cannot be achieved in isolation. Particularly in this case, for I am indebted to the support of family and friends during the long wearying months to get the manuscript completed.

More notably, I must express thanks to Bradley Reed for his constant encouragement, and also for his adroit design and formatting skills which have proved so helpful to the project.

And finally, it is imperative to express heartfelt thanks to two major characters in the book. John Fenton and Lord Peregrine Eliot were pivotal figures in the Seltaeb story but their significance has been largely forgotten. At the start of the project I knew very little about these men, largely because, like so many others I had swallowed the accepted myths about the overwhelming importance of Nicky Byrne.

Writing this book has been therapeutic for me in many ways, not least because I have been able to shatter some of those myths and restore John Fenton and Lord Eliot to the historic importance they deserve for their roles in the story of the Beatles and Brian Epstein.

Without their enthusiastic, considered and informative contributions, the book would have been much harder to write, and the process would have been much less enjoyable. My sincere thanks go out to both of them.

Finally, I must give thanks to, and clarify the existence of, Chrissie, who features so strongly in this book. Chrissie does not exist. However, she is an invented character who is an amalgam of two real women, one of whom lives in New York and one in Oxfordshire. Both were happy to speak to me, once I had proved that I could be trusted, but neither wished to be identified by name. Both had concerns about having their name attached to the book, and both were, perhaps surprisingly, worried about their safety. And this some fifty years after the events described in the book.

And surely any sensible person would regard that as curious.

Extremely curious.

"*The Beatles had to stop performing. The songs weren't theirs anymore. They belonged to everybody*"
- Elvis Costello

"*You can put a price on what Brian Epstein 'lost' for the Beatles. You can't put a price on what he gave them*" - Dennis O'Dell

"*I'd always felt that Brian was extremely efficient, but it soon became clear to me that while he was adept at arranging tours, he had no financial expertise of any kind.*" - James Isherwood

"*I have a box of evidence that's going to a certain person, should anything happen to me, so if you top me off it's still going to that person, and the truth will come out. I know everything and I know the truth*"
- Heather Mills

"*I am the last remaining Beatle*"
- Ringo Starr

A Hard Day's Night

It had been an extended, and generally painful process, but finally the edit was finished. We could turn the finished programme over to the Channel and let their Scheduling maestros get to work. Find the time when the most people could be induced to view my programme, but nobody, least of all me, expected that to be a large number.

"Pub?" enquired Jeff, the producer and console wizard, breezily as he wiped his right hand wearily across his eyes.

"Please!" I groaned. "I need to get out of here, get somewhere without glowing lights on a computer and banks of monitor screens."

"Sounds like the King's Head" he smiled. "Come on, I'm buying."

Twenty minutes later, after closing everything down and sending the hard disk off to the Production Company on a motorbike courier, we were drinking in the lager and the wild sights of Soho. It was a warm, perhaps unseasonably warm, night in May and the sudden end of the prolonged winter had brought out the scantily-clad peacocks of every brand and sexual persuasion.

"That's one edit I'm not sorry to see the back of!" remarked Jeff heavily.

"It's not been that bad" I replied, conscious that the workload had fallen much more heavily on him.

"They're squeezing all the time. Less time in pre-prod, less time for filming, and editing is becoming a real luxury. I had to fight for the time and the money for you to finish the voice-overs!"

I took a healthy swig of my lager, took off my glasses and rubbed my stinging eyes, which seemed to have been made worse by the bright early evening sunshine. I know it's not coalmining but editing tv shows can be really hard, intensive work, especially when you know that what you're editing is a heap of crap.

"Want to grab a bite to eat?" I asked. "There's a Pizza Hut round the corner, on Charlotte Street."

"I know!" laughed Jeff. "I've been there before - with you!"

"Sorry! I'm knackered. Can't think straight."

"Anyway, I can't. I'm meeting my brother - planning a birthday bash for my dad. Big birthday coming up, 60, so we need to do something special."

"Where are you meeting him?"

"Here. The King's Head" he admitted, more than a little shame-faced.

I saw the chance for a little malicious pleasure. "Oh, so you weren't really asking me to come for a drink? You were coming here anyway! I'm just filling the gap until your brother arrives!"

I sounded more outraged than I really was. Jeff knew that. The guy in the leathers sitting at the table to Jeff's left wasn't so sure. His startled reaction showed that he thought a major row was brewing. Anything but.

"Something like that," laughed Jeff, well accustomed to my sarcastic sense of humour, and never one to take offence anyway. "I texted him just before we finished the edit and told him I would meet him in here. You're just a welcome, famous extra."

That was a flash of gentle sarcasm aimed back at me. I made a reasonable living from writing stuff, and lately from churning out scripts for potboiler tv programmes, but famous? Hardly, and both Jeff and I knew it.

Perversely I had developed a bit of a side-line in voiceovers because my voice had a deep, grave tone which was in demand for various things, particularly toilet cleaners. Never on the level of Rob Bryden or Stephen Fry but it provided a welcome extra source of income, and, of course, for programmes like Hidden Conspiracies, the one we had just finished editing, I was a very cheap and convenient voiceover asset.

And it meant that on the very rare occasions that a member of the public showed any recognition of me it came as a result of something I said rather than from my scribblings or my minor tv shows.

Jeff and I continued talking through the pluses and minuses of the programme we had just finished and then indulged in a delightfully vicious disectment of the parlous state of the British television industry. This had taken in a second round of lagers and was still in full vitriolic flight when a shadow loomed over the table and interrupted the flow. It was created by a heavy featured man wearing a dark grey suit with an overly bright red tie.

Despite the visible difference in their ages the similarity in features made me realise immediately that this was Jeff's brother. He could have been anything up to twenty years older than Jeff but he had the same lopsided grin. And the huge ears, which Jeff tried so hard to hide, were clearly a family trait.

"Hiya kid" he started, dropping a large right hand on Jeff's shoulder. "How's it going?"

"Okay" replied Jeff, slightly reddening. "This is my brother, Tony" he said to me, a bit unnecessarily.

I held out my hand and shook his vigorously. He had a strong, physical grip suggesting someone used to either manual work or the gym. Judging by the suit and tie I suspected he was used to working out in controlled environments rather than lifting heavy weights in a work situation.

"So you're making programmes with Jeff, are you?" asked Tony, easing his big frame into the chair on the opposite side of the table. Jeff had shuffled off to the bar to get his brother a drink, without asking what he wanted. I surmised that their drinking sessions were quite frequent.

"Yes, we've just finished the final edit of the last programme of the series. We came out for a drink to celebrate."

"And what's it about?"

"It's called Hidden Conspiracies. Six programmes, each dealing with a different mystery or a conspiracy."

"Such as?" enquired Tony. He seemed interested but, like most people in the media, I needed little encouragement to talk about myself.

"Oh, leave it alone!" laughed Jeff, returning with his brother's pint.

"No, I'm interested. What's it about? The stories."

"It's fairly obvious stuff - Moon Landing, Twin Towers - things like that."

"And McCartney?"

Jeff and I exchanged slightly quizzical glances. It was clear that neither of us recognised the reference, though obviously we knew the name.

"McCartney?" I repeated. "What's that?"

"McCartney. Paul McCartney. The Beatles!" snapped Tony, wiping drops of bitter off his lips with the back of his right hand.

"Sorry Tony, you're rambling again" grinned Jeff, patting his brother sympathetically on the arm. "I've no idea what you're talking about."

"Me too," I added meekly.

"It's a story that McCartney was killed in some accident in the sixties and then replaced with a double or a look-a-like."

"What?" gasped Jeff. "What a load of bollocks! Where did you cook that one up?"

Tony was slightly hurt. "It isn't my story - it's quite well known."

"Well I've never heard of it!" stated Jeff firmly.

"Nor me!" I added.

"Well, I'm sure if you check on the Internet then-"

"The Internet?" Jeff scoffed. "Well that will confirm it then."

"After all, there's no idiots on the Internet, are there?" I commented sharply.

"Suit yourselves," Tony continued. "But it's not my story. I didn't make it up. There is a lot of background to it. I would have thought that if you are going to do a tv show on Conspiracies then Paul McCartney would be a prime target. And there was also some suspicion that the Beatles manager, Brian Epstein, had been bumped off."

I couldn't help laughing. It sounded like a bad outline for a Monty Python script. "Who's going to murder a pop manager? That's stupid! And as for swopping Paul McCartney with some robot - was it a robot? What was it?" I demanded, with a little too much acidity. One of my major faults, as a number of women have told me.

"I dunno," snapped Tony, a touch defensively. "I wasn't born for ten years after all that Beatles stuff finished. I don't know any more than I've told you." He sounded a bit hurt, and I felt bad, not least at the thought that I might have offended him and, even worse, his brother.

I thought I'd better try to be conciliatory, even though the story was obviously complete crap. "Well, we could look into it perhaps. What do you reckon, Jeff? Maybe in the next series?"

"Maybe" muttered Jeff, in a tone of voice which suggested that it was a topic that he wouldn't ever consider touching, and that he wasn't delighted about the way I had ridiculed his brother.

But that's how the seed was planted in my mind, no matter how ridiculous it all sounded, and I filed it away thinking I would look into the nonsensical story at some time in the future.

And that's how the whole thing started.

Tell Me What You See

I didn't start thinking about the McCartney stuff immediately, or even soon. It was so obviously ridiculous that I didn't feel inclined to waste time on it with other things to do.

Indeed it was almost a month after that casual meeting with Tony that it occurred to me to have a look into the tale. I'll confess that my early investigations or thoughts were entirely negative or sceptical. All I imagined was that it would provide a celebrity-packed storyline when …if we ever got a commission for series two.

I had reasonable expectations of a second series. Not because of the intrinsic value or quality of my work but at the dog-eared end of television - my natural habitat - the determining factors are price, price and price. The mantra in retail has always been Location, Location and Location, but at my end of television the only factor is Price.

There might have been, allegedly once was, a Golden Era where quality was not just the main factor, it was the only factor. When the BBC and companies like the original Granada Television prepared television programmes with a concentration on the quality of production rather than trying to squeeze every last drop from increasingly constricted budgets.

Sadly, those days are gone and the proliferation of Joke channels has led to the development of programming on Reality themes which achieve nothing more than filling time. As the great Danny Baker often comments, you think back fondly to those halcyon days where BBC Television would announce, "It's now Xpm and BBC Television is now closing down until Ypm."

A simple close-down. We've nothing of value to say or to transmit, so we are closing down until we do. Now, as an alternative, we infest the dozens of channels with nonsense and mindless, insulting pap, and, proud though I am of my work on Hidden Conspiracies, I can see how my stuff slips effortlessly into that grim category.

But despite that, or maybe because of it, Jeff got the word that our blessed Production Company had been advised by the channel that we were going to get a second series. I gave a silent prayer of thanks for the 500 or so viewers (At Least!) that formed our staple audience and started to think casually about likely topics for programmes.

JFK and Oswald and the Grassy Knoll was a certainty as was David Icke's Reptilian theories. I was also considering Jill Dando and the Slobodan Milosevic connection, and of course Roswell and the alien bodies was a must.

I started to sketch out various topic ideas on a chart which, besides the title and programme idea, also continued to a column indicating likely popularity and another column related to the availability, at an extravagantly cheap price, of the source material.

And it was the drawing up of that list that made me remember the crazy Paul McCartney story and one dull Tuesday evening I went on Google and typed in "Paul McCartney dead".

Given what Tony had said that night at the King's Arms I was expecting several sites to be listed. I was not expecting, was astonished by, the fact that dozens and hundreds of sites appeared. I started reading, clicking on links and found much later that more than four hours had passed and yet I had seemingly only scraped the surface.

Much, perhaps most, of it was garbage, but hugely entertaining. There were stories about Viv Stanshall, lead singer of the Bonzo Dog Doo Dah Band being involved, and a range of crazy stories about MI5 and an operative named Maxwell running an operation to replace McCartney to prevent mass suicides from young girls left distraught by their hero's death in a car crash. There was even one highly inventive story about McCartney not dying in a car accident but actually being assassinated in mid-1966 and replaced by an imposter who, the story goes, had been trained and readied for that eventuality.

There was even a diverting film produced by Highway 61 Entertainment who promoted an opus called Paul McCartney Really Is Dead: The Last Testament of George Harrison. The story was that George, racked by guilt and shame about his involvement in the conspiracy had put together a confession and sent it to those media titans, Highway 61 Entertainment.

It didn't seem to bother these conspiracy theorists that George hadn't thought to involve any of the major media outlets in the UK - The Times, Guardian, Telegraph - or their equivalents in the States - New York Times or L.A.Times - or any of the more significant television programmes.

The Highway 61 film purported to be a confession from George Harrison about the conspiracy to replace McCartney and that aspect of the nonsense even included the apparent suspicion from George Harrison that the man who attacked him and almost killed him in his home on December 30th 1999 had been sent by MI5 to finish him off!

I would be lying if I said that this aspect of the research was not hugely diverting and entertaining. I grew to love the wilder and wilder spins that were put on the story. I was particularly drawn to a story that the whole thing was actually a strange and bizarre plot created and orchestrated by John Lennon, who desired to found a new religion with himself as God and the "reborn" McCartney by his side as a Christ-like figure.

The only thing missing from the whole torrent of theories was an alien element, and I grew slightly disappointed that nobody had put forward the theory that McCartney had been abducted and replaced by some alien shape-shifter, able to mimic his every mannerism. Ludicrous? Obviously, but not much more viciously ridiculous than some of the other stuff being openly discussed on the web and in forums.

I was nauseated and affronted and bewildered by the information provided but most of all I was staggered that anybody would, ...could, believe such a crock!

And yet...

The more I read and researched, leaving aside the torrent of specious nonsense, the more I was struck by the thought that there were various elements - tiny elements admittedly - that didn't make sense.

I started making notes - always a bad sign because it was tangible evidence that I was being sucked in by the whole thing. I found that, no matter what other work requirements I had to deal with, I would be drawn every night to my notes. And every night the scribblings and the notes grew in both volume and also in complex detail.

After three weeks of this fairly unstructured activity I devoted a full weekend to an analysis of all the scribbled material which I sifted through a favourite computer programme called Mind Meld. This was superbly efficient at drawing out themes from a body of material and allowing me to find relationships and connections, and it made a significant difference to the way I looked at the McCartney material.

It teased out various names, various companies, various relationships that hadn't seemed so important when I was wading through the mass of material and so, on the Sunday evening, when I inspected the results of my Mind Meld activity that one name in particular leaped off the page.

SELTAEB

Before I started looking at the material the name meant nothing to me, and it was several days before it dawned on me that the word was actually BEATLES spelt backwards. More importantly Seltaeb was a company set up in the sixties to help the Beatles manager, Brian Epstein, administer the torrent of merchandising deals offered to him on behalf of the Beatles in America.

I read a lot about Seltaeb and related topics like Beatles Ltd, and Beatles & Co, and Apple and Stramsact, and began to see what a tangled web it became in the mid-sixties, particularly in the wake of the unprecedented torrent of money pouring into the coffers presided over by Brian Epstein.

So many facts. So much money.

And so much confusion.

I'd have to admit that the stories about the money, for the Beatles themselves and Seltaeb and Northern Songs and all the rest, made compelling reading. Over several weeks intensive Google reading I became quite proficient in the myriad aspects of the Beatles finances, and also in the small library of books that had been produced on the group and Epstein's empire.

Many of the books were a waste, mere pap and often regurgitated pap at that, but there were others which made interesting, and occasionally disturbing reading. The established bible was Philip Norman's opus, "Shout!" and I devoured the hundreds of pages without any great love for the text. It seemed more like an intelligent version of Smash Hits, a heavyweight bunch of anecdotes and rehashed stories.

Far more effective, and useful was Richard DiLello's famous treatise on the death of the group, "The Longest Cocktail Party". This contained more gritty material about the finances of the group and NEMS, and opened up new avenues of research for me.

The final two books which proved vital to the research campaign were "Apple to the Core" by Peter McCabe and "Many Years from Now" by Barry Miles, and I found myself scribbling copious remarks in the margins of all these books.

I also spent some time, too much time, wading in the reeking trough which was Albert Goldman's "The Lives of John Lennon". Over-the-top, inflated, grotesquely indiscreet, but massively entertaining, and, like the others, containing oblique references to the finances and the mess that the money and the contractual situations became.

Although there were books on Brian Epstein none were particularly helpful, and this situation even applied to his 1964 autobiography, "A Cellarful of Noise". Though ghost-written by sometime Assistant and later Beatles publicist Derek Taylor, the book provided little more than tantalising hints about the craziness of 1963-64, and yet again I found myself intrigued by the financial details.

I got a small insight into the nicer side of Epstein's personality when learning about the background to the book. I discovered that Epstein paid Taylor £900 with a £250 advance for his work on "A Cellarful of Noise". More significantly, once the book had been released Epstein spoke to Derek

Taylor and claimed that he thought that he had short-changed Taylor on the book deal.

To correct the imbalance Epstein took out his chequebook and wrote Taylor another cheque equal to the amount originally paid.

There were many disparaging remarks I came across about Epstein as part of the research, but that simple gesture towards Derek Taylor seemed to speak to a different, more pleasant, side of Epstein's character and his attitude to money.

Whatever I read, it seemed that my thoughts seemed drawn irrevocably to the money; not because of any particularly mercenary quality, but because it always seems such a compelling element of any story. And it was often over the following months that I remembered those compelling scenes in that great film “All the President's Men” when Robert Redford is meeting Deep Throat in the underground parking lot. All the chilling remarks coalesce into one grim piece of advice, "Follow the Money".

In that instance it was a helpful way for Deep Throat to keep Woodward and Bernstein on the right track, given that so much of the Watergate Conspiracy revolved around the massive amounts of monies raised by the Committee to Re-Elect the President.

But the more I read and learned about the Beatles and Epstein and NEMS and Seltaeb the more apposite Deep Throat's words seemed.

Follow the Money.

I did have the nagging, unsettling feeling that the phenomenal sums of money swirling around the Beatles organisation in the sixties opened the door to some very questionable practices. And there were questions being thrown up by those fortunes and the way they were handled because, from the early days of my interest in the McCartney and Epstein sagas, I was puzzled by various aspects of the story. Not the crazy things like assassinations or new religions, but the minutiae of contracts and payments and agreements. So much money; so many opportunities for graft, and corruption, and fraud.

Follow the Money.

Money, That's What I Want

There was a period of about nine months available to me for research purposes ahead of the filming of Series Two. I spoke frequently to Jeff about plans and kept him regularly updated about how things were going. Yet I found that, for reasons I didn't really understand, I was less than forthcoming about how fascinated I was becoming by the whole McCartney bewilderment.

It wasn't that I was embarrassed, or ashamed. That would have been too simplistic. Instead I had a sense of keeping my powder dry, of trying to sift through the torrent of facts and opinions and rumours, to get to the point where I was confident that there was a story that could be told.

I had a stroke of luck when the production company informed me that the filming of Series Two had been put back six months. No sensible reason was given, but logic has little relevance in the glittering world of television. There was clearly a financial imperative behind the decision, and I presumed that the channel would be able to save money by filming people looking at houses or baking cakes or cutting the lawn. I remain convinced that Celebrity Nose-Picking is only one good pitch away!

The reasons for the delay didn't matter. The important thing was that I was able to devote more time to the increasingly puzzling McCartney story because my pre-production responsibilities had been eased. I was able to persuade myself that my extra research into McCartney would help me deliver a killer script for one of the programmes in the series, but in hindsight I realise that even back then I was thinking of something bigger for the McCartney story than mere inclusion on a series.

And it was quite some time before I was able to admit, even to myself, that my original plan - to investigate the tale so that I could ridicule and destroy it and expose it as total nonsense - had been quietly abandoned.

With my unexpected holiday I began to get more and more immersed in the tale. I was amassing massive amounts of notes and hastily-compiled biographies of the major players. In this context the Mind Meld programme proved very useful in helping me to define and draw the connections between those major players. That process was critical in sorting out the roles that those major and minor players had played in the saga, because the cavalcade of characters had proved a real difficulty. I was fine with the names that everybody knows - Lennon, McCartney, Starr, Harrison, even George Martin, but the meat of the story, if it truly existed, would be found with the lesser-known names.

And so my notes and files began to swell with details of people like Alistair Taylor, Terry Doran, David Jacobs, Nicky Byrne, Mal Evans, Lord Peregrine

Eliot, Nat Weiss, Mark Warman, Geoffrey Ellis, Dick James, Simon Miller-Munday, Allen Klein, John Fenton, Walter Strach, Terry Knight. There were so many more, all of whom played a part in the Beatles saga to a greater or lesser extent, but I was intent on weeding out all the names of those characters not likely to have played a role in the bizarre McCartney and Epstein stories.

Because of the cascade of information I decided that it would make sense, and greatly help me, to create a schematic, a timeline of events. This was a device I had used with success in the past, with both books and with the tv stuff. The schematic is, put crudely, a skeleton of the main events, and onto that skeleton you drop more and more events and people and detail so that the skeleton eventually gets balls and starts walking.

From the start I had decided that the skeleton or timeline had to start with the first time Epstein and Beatles interacted. This momentous event came on November 9th 1961, a date that was to assume greater significance, albeit in a different year, later into my research. On that date Brian Epstein was working as Manager of the branch of NEMS at 12-14 Whitechapel. NEMS was the family store and Brian was in charge of the second in the chain. NEMS was an acronym for North End Road Music Stores.

Prior to that appointment Brian had been given responsibility for the operations on the ground floor at the NEMS store on Great Charlotte Street. At the start he was in charge of wireless sets and pianos, but this quickly expanded to gramophone records. He made such a success of the record department that when the family decided to open a second NEMS branch at 12-14 Whitechapel, Brian was placed in charge. Perhaps strangely, given the importance of the location, there's now nothing to mark that unassuming shop front on Whitechapel that was once North End Road Music Store, the record shop and appliance centre owned by Harry Epstein and his wife, Queenie.

One of the regular items on sale was the local music paper, Mersey Beat, which NEMS had promoted since its initial issue on July 6, 1961. Brian Epstein was astute enough to realise that the paper could become a useful promotional device for NEMS and so he had asked the editor Bill Harry if he, as the leading local record retailer, could provide a record column. Brian Epstein's first column appeared in the third issue of Mersey Beat on August 3, 1961 under the pithy by-line "Stop the World - And Listen To Everything in It: Brian Epstein of NEMS".

Three months later, on November 9th Brian Epstein, accompanied by Alistair Taylor, took the short walk from the NEMS store on Whitechapel in Liverpool to Matthew Street. There they had an unlikely appointment at the Cavern Club where they had arranged to see an unknown group called the Beatles.

The stimulus for the visit was the famous request by one Raymond Jones for a copy of 'My Bonnie' by the Beatles. That young man had wandered into NEMS on Saturday, October 28th 1961 and asked for the single which he had heard at a session at Hambleton Hall. NEMS didn't have it but Epstein's professional interest was raised, particularly when another request was made later that afternoon for the same unknown record, and then on the Monday two girls also asked for 'My Bonnie'.

Following the interest shown in the group, described by Raymond Jones to Epstein as the best group he had ever seen, the NEMS manager was intrigued, though it is clear that he was at least aware of the group by name before Jones spoke to him. It is also a matter of record that, as the professional record retailer, Epstein was curious to be asked for a disc which he couldn't find mentioned in the weekly industry bible, Record Retailer.

Epstein ensured that copies of the single were ordered to meet the local demand and two days after the girls had asked for the single, Epstein rang Bill Harry at Mersey Beat and asked him to sort out a visit to the Cavern. Bill made the arrangements with Ray McFall and crucially with Paddy Delaney, the imposing presence on the door.

It's likely that Epstein's request attracted some amusement or even scorn. The Cavern was a sweat-soaked cellar, not the sort of venue to which an immaculately dressed businessman like Brian Epstein would venture, let alone order advance tickets. The pair were ushered in without the ignominy of queuing, but any attempt at anonymity was ruined when Brian Epstein was welcomed over the Cavern's PA system by the resident DJ, Bob Wooler.

He arrived for that lunchtime appearance on November 9th, accompanied by his assistant, Alistair Taylor who would subsequently achieve notoriety by claiming that Raymond Jones didn't exist and that he, Taylor, had invented the name and the story to justify the order of the first copies of the single.

They stood at the back of the rough enclosure to catch the Beatles lunchtime show. Taylor was not impressed, horrified by the surroundings not least because in their white shirts and dark business suits they stood out completely from the rest of the crowd.

But though he felt very uncomfortable in that environment, Taylor was impressed by the music and the stagecraft of the Beatles, but his enthusiasm was nothing compared to Brian Epstein. His remarks at the time, confirmed later in “A Cellarful of Noise”, were explicit in his surprise and joy at the impression the four Beatles made on him. He spoke warmly of their music, their beat and their sense of humour, but the impression wasn't limited to the onstage action.

One of the important aspects of NEMS to the Beatles story which is often overlooked is the part the shop's record booths played in building up the group's set-list in the early performance years. Both Brian Epstein and Alistair Taylor admitted that they recognised the individual members of the Beatles from visits to the store. Requesting and then listening to obscure B-sides in the cramped booths enabled the members of the Beatles to choose to feature in later performances tracks like 'Chains', and 'Boys' and many others.

After the lunchtime show on the 9th, Epstein and Taylor entered the sparse dressing room and spoke to the group, with Epstein commenting later that he was taken by their personal charm. So much so that Epstein made the effort to view the group perform a number of times during the next few weeks. There were also meetings at the NEMS premises, most significantly a no-holds-barred discussion involving Bob Woolmer on December 3rd when Brian Epstein first suggested that the group would benefit if he were to become their manager, a meeting slightly complicated by Lennon introducing Woolmer as "me dad!". Those benefits, if Epstein could be believed, were tangible. He told the four Beatles that he could double their fee for performances, get them released from their existing recording contract with Polydor, and, critically, get them a record deal with a London company. The Beatles, both individually and collectively, needed little persuading.

Further meetings took place at NEMS on December 6th, and then at Mona Best's Casbah Club on December 10th, and Epstein carried on attending various performances in and around Liverpool.

During those first few days in December Epstein took the opportunity to discuss his commercial interest in the Beatles with a friend and colleague named Rex Makin. He was then a family solicitor with a relationship with the Epstein family as their neighbour on Queens Drive. They were associates rather than close friends but Epstein took the opportunity to tell Makin about his new venture and the group who he was sure would go on to dominate the world. Makin readily admitted a healthy scepticism about Brian's latest claims but his lack of enthusiasm didn't dissuade Epstein on that occasion or, months later, trying to bring Makin's legal skills into the NEMS family. Makin was to resist those offers and go on to establish a laudable reputation inside Liverpool as legal representative to the rich and famous and, critically, many, many others more needing, but less able to pay for, his help and tireless expertise.

Another instrumental conversation took place with Allan Williams, sometime manager and promoter. Epstein needed to be reassured that Williams had no existing contractual links to the group, but the ebullient Williams also warned Epstein to keep well clear of the Beatles. A long-standing disagreement about a non-paid Hamburg percentage was the main cause for

Williams' ire but he pulled no punches in advising Epstein not to get involved with the group.

Despite such interventions the momentum was moving remorselessly towards an agreement, aided by the substantial moves Epstein was making on the group's behalf even without the security of a contract. In mid November he had started to use his power, via NEMS, as a major record retailer to pressure Dick Rowe to get someone from Decca to come to see the group. The link to Rowe was a tortuous one and initially involved a chap from Liverpool who had moved to London for work reasons. His name was Tony Barrow and late in 1961 he was writing a column called *Off the Record* for the main Liverpool paper, the Liverpool Echo, under the by-line Disker.

Barrow had been providing the record review column for the newspaper since the mid-fifties and would continue for several years until his Press Officer duties for the group proved too onerous. As part of his early onslaught on the record industry, Epstein wrote to Disker with a view to getting some publicity for the Beatles. He was naturally expecting a reply from Liverpool, from the Echo offices, and hence his surprise at receiving a response from London.

Barrow explained the circumstances plus the fact that his "day-job" was as a sleeve writer for Decca Records. That led to the meeting at Decca headquarters in Barrow's cubicle within the Sleeve Department, where Epstein, apart from strongly impressing Barrow with his appearance and demeanour, played a disc representing the Beatles in performance. It wasn't an official recording from Decca or EMI - they hadn't yet happened. It wasn't even the Polydor record backing Tony Sheridan. Instead it was an acetate recorded by Epstein from a Cavern performance by the group. Lacking the benefits of mixing and professional recording the result was a mess, with nothing to commend the group to Barrow or his colleagues. He ushered Epstein gently out of the building after informing him that the constraints of the Off the Record column meant that Barrow, or Disker, simply couldn't write about the Beatles until they had a record on release. Instead Barrow offered the helpful suggestion that Epstein should approach the Liverpool Echo for some general coverage recommending the possible services of an Echo staffer, curiously named George Harrison.

Epstein left Decca, tail firmly between his legs, but to his great credit, Tony Barrow didn't forget him or the Beatles. He rang a colleague in Decca Marketing and told the tale of the visit from Epstein and his appeal on behalf of his new group. The reaction wasn't warm, until that is, Barrow revealed the link between Epstein and NEMS, the important retailer in the north of England. That piece of information got the immediate attention of the marketing department, which presumably led to a conversation with the A&R department.

It cannot be proved that Barrow's intervention was pivotal; more likely that Barrow's call added to the momentum caused by Epstein's meetings with Decca management, and also to his constant hectoring of the Decca representatives who visited NEMS. The result was that someone inside the A&R department decided to take action, and the eventual outcome was Mike Smith's trip to the Cavern in mid-December.

In the sixties Decca, fresh from their days as a Radar company, had become a major record company. Given the period, it was mostly classical and Edmundo Ros or Mantovani-led orchestral music, although steps were being taken to dip a company toe into this new thing called beat music.

On Friday December 1st, Epstein made a trip to London to meet with Colin Borland and Beecher Stevens of Decca Records at their London office to discuss a recording contract. His entreaties fell on deaf ears but NEMS was too big to offend and so Decca promised to send someone to Liverpool to see Epstein's new protégés.

That promise was realised in the appearance in Liverpool by Mike Smith but even before that Epstein had made further representations to Deutsche Grammophone, the English company representing the German recording of 'My Bonnie', and also to the mighty EMI.

In the first week of December the German company sent representatives to Liverpool to meet Epstein to discuss the possible release of the single in the UK. A couple of days later Epstein wrote to Ron White, who was with the sales department at EMI, to try to get the group an EMI contract. Ron White had already been provided with a copy of 'My Bonnie', and, given his role in the EMI Sales department, Ron White was also totally aware of the importance of NEMS to EMI sales, particularly in the north of England.

Given the stature of NEMS in the industry at that time, it was obviously deemed inadvisable to annoy the Epstein family and so Decca A&R man Mike Smith was delegated to travel up to Liverpool to view the group in action. This show took place on December13th and led directly to the infamous Decca audition early the following year.

Indeed Smith had already established a link with Liverpool by being involved in recordings by Billy Fury, then and now one of the city's favourite sons.

Epstein was also hard at work with other record companies, using the NEMS name as leverage, but Decca was the first British company to bite. Mike Smith was quite impressed but didn't feel that the performance was sufficiently strong to warrant the immediate offer of a contract. Covering his back, Smith recommended that Decca should offer the Beatles a session at the West Hampstead Studios at 165 Broadhurst Gardens. He made the recommendation to Dick Rowe to take the next step and so Epstein was invited to make the group available at the Decca Studios.

He made the necessary arrangements and Neil Aspinall drove the group down to London on New Year's Eve in 1961, for the audition. Unfortunately he got lost en route near Wolverhampton, partly due to snow. This, of course, was long before the comparative luxury of a three-lane motorway run from Liverpool to London. The journey lasted just over ten hours with the result that they didn't reach London until 10 o'clock that night.

Epstein had made a booking for the group and Neil Aspinall at the Royal Hotel on Woburn Place, near to Euston and the British Museum. Perhaps surprisingly Epstein didn't join them in London that night, but not because the draw of spending New Year's Eve at home was too strong. Instead he travelled down to London on the afternoon of New Year's Eve by train, and stayed that night with a family member.

Although New Year's Day was traditionally a public holiday in Scotland this was not the case south of the border. New Year's Day did not become a Bank Holiday in England until the mid-Seventies which meant that the Beatles audition at Decca took place on an ordinary working day. This after what was by popular custom the biggest drinking night of the year. Even the Beatles and Neil Aspinall shared a glass or two in the hotel whiling away the hours and dreaming of what lay in store at Decca.

There was very possibly some animated conversation about the gigs and the money they had missed by travelling down to London. Even at that time, New Year's Eve was one of the primary entertainment nights of the year and any group, or individual entertainer, would have been entitled to expect a good payday from working that night. To pass up the chance of such a decent return is an indication of how determined the group must have been to get the elusive recording contract, and how persuasive Epstein must have been to sell the proposition to them.

Unfortunately what awaited them at Decca, at least initially, was disappointment. Mike Smith, having seen the group at the Cavern almost three weeks earlier, had been delegated to run the session but he had partied a little too hard or a little too well the night before.

He was late for the session. The Beatles were unimpressed; Brian Epstein was incandescent, taking Smith's tardiness as a slur on the Beatles and a real indication that Decca were not wholly committed to the arrangement.

The urbane Smith managed to smooth the ruffled feathers when he finally arrived but the audition clearly didn't go well. The gap between Smith's expectations and the capabilities of the group and their battered equipment was too large, and there was another issue of which the group and Epstein were unaware. And that issue came in the unlikely form of Brian Poole and the Tremeloes.

Unbeknownst to the group and their near manager, Decca were auditioning both groups that day and in the end the choice was dictated by geography, not musical ability or even potential sales. The Beatles and their urbane manager were based two hundred miles to the North West. Brian Poole and the Tremeloes were originally from Essex and, even at the time of the Decca audition, were largely considered as a London band. As such they were a much more practical commercial proposition than a group from the wilds of Merseyside.

Nobody said that. NEMS was too important a customer to offend flippantly and so the group and their manager said goodbye to Mike Smith and left Decca thinking that they were in a good position to achieve the holy grail, a recording contract.

None of them noticed, or paid any attention to the other group sitting in the reception area, and it would be many months before the relevance of Brian Poole and the Tremeloes became clear. At that time it was far more important to put some miles between London and themselves.

The group loaded their equipment and themselves back into the van with Aspinall and began the long journey back north. Epstein took a taxi back into London to catch the train back from Euston.

On one wet Wednesday many years later I went out to the West Hampstead studios as part of my supposed research for the tv programme. It had not been a recording studio for quite some time but the music connection has been retained because the building is now the headquarters of English Opera. I didn't go in. There was no point, but after a few minutes drinking in the atmosphere outside I hailed a cab to get me back to Soho.

The driver's conversation wandered from immigration to football and back again, but I was dimly aware of his mentioning that a traffic accident meant that Finchley Road was closed and so he would take a slight detour. It meant nothing to me. I was busy scanning emails on my phone and only distantly aware of the big, grand houses on either side of the road. In fact I didn't notice anything until the taxi squealed to a sudden halt. "Bloody idiots!" snarled the driver, a mixture of anger and disdain.

I looked up absently and saw a bunch of obviously Asian, perhaps Japanese, youths laughing as they paraded their way across the road.

Across a zebra crossing, near a wall covered in scribbles and messages.

Abbey Road. It was Abbey Road, with the EMI studios off to the right, and I couldn't help a little tingle wondering if Epstein's taxi journey all those years earlier might have taken the same route from the failure at Decca past the overwhelming future promise of EMI and Abbey Road.

The artists and the manager made their way back to Liverpool and the Beatles were back on the Cavern whirlwind on January 3rd. Refreshed by the apparent success with Decca there was a surge of activity from Epstein in the build-up to the contract signing on the 24th. His enthusiasm was aided by the result of the Poll in Mersey Beat for Most Popular Group which was released on January 4th. The Beatles were clear winners over competitors like Johnny Sandon and the Searchers, Gerry and the Pacemakers, Rory Storm and the Hurricanes, and the Remo Four.

The following day, largely as a result of his tireless lobbying of Deutsche Grammophone, their British arm, Polydor Records, released 'My Bonnie' in the UK. It was most unlikely to become a hit. Everybody, including Epstein, knew that, but there was a more subtle strategy at work. The release of the single allowed Epstein to start advertising the Beatles as Polydor Recording Stars, and he wasted no time in exploiting this marketing advantage.

So, as January ran down, the group continued their remorseless appearance schedule while Epstein maintained the standard at NEMS and carried on his struggle to become the greatest pop manager the world had ever known.

He took the apparent success of the Decca audition as the chance to start to enforce his vision of what the group should be and, more importantly, what they could become. Almost immediately he persuaded Ray McFall from the Cavern to double their pay to £15 per show, and he also managed to increase their pay for the forthcoming Hamburg trip by an extra £10 a week. There was an outstanding debt at Frank Hessy's music shop for their various instruments and Epstein cleared the £200, which in modern currency would have been thousands of pounds.

At that stage the contentious aspect, the grooming, began. The first step was to get the group to abandon their trademark black leather suits and use the grey mohair suits, originally a German design, which became so recognisable over the next couple of years, and also have their hair styled at Horne Brothers, his personal barbers in Lord Street. Epstein was also insistent on a draconian set of rules for stage performances: No swearing - either at the audience or each other, no taking audience requests, and no more eating and smoking on stage, and finally a synchronised bow at the end of the number. It was a long way from the unfettered mayhem of Hamburg and the early days at the Cavern.

Another tangible symbol of the changes being inflicted on the previously-chaotic Beatles by their ambitious new manager was documentation. Each week the four members of the group, plus road manager Neil Aspinall, were supplied with itemised statements of accounts which listed exact details of the bookings over the previous seven days showing all fees, expenses and management commission. The document also contained a schedule and relevant instructions for the shows during the coming week, and such attention to detail was a revelation to the Beatles and light years ahead of the standards being followed by any of the other Liverpool groups.

Epstein's various involvements with EMI, Deutsche Grammophone and Decca didn't stop, because the recording contract was the next major element in his campaign to prove himself to the group as their manager. And that was the deal. The Beatles reluctantly put up with Epstein's changes - the styling, the onstage rules and, most painfully, the switch from sweaty black leather into smart stage suits. In exchange the group wanted....demanded a recording contract, and that was the next, and possibly the most important link in that chain. Epstein gave no indication of preference and it's a reasonable assumption that he didn't care. The contract - any contract - was all.

There had been letters exchanged with Ron White from EMI before Christmas which culminated in a letter from him on December 18th turning down the chance of representing the group. Later events showed that Ron White had approached several EMI staff producers to discuss the possibility of the Beatles with them. Various luminaries like Norman Newell, Norrie Paramor and Walter Ridley were offered the chance to take the Beatles but turned the group down. A further EMI staff producer, albeit much lowlier than the others, didn't turn the group down, simply because he was away. That simple accident of fate and timing, a holiday, was one of the primary reasons that George Martin eventually became the producer of the Beatles.

The rejection by EMI was frustrating but hardly a disaster. At that time, though important, they were hardly the monolith that the unparalleled success in the sixties would produce. The company had been founded in 1931 and its main fame lay in the manufacture of televisions and electronic equipment. It was then revitalized by Joseph Lockwood who assiduously purchased several record companies and their pressing plants for EMI during the first half of the fifties. For the next few years the principal labels were HMV, Columbia and Capitol, with Parlophone, a small German company which had been purchased before the war, remaining very much the poor relation.

However, at the start of the sixties Decca was still a major force in entertainment, certainly compared to EMI. Though further triumphs lay ahead through the likes of the Rolling Stones and the Moody Blues, the decline of Decca, when it came, would be sudden and dramatic.

That though was far in the future as Epstein eagerly awaited the response - obviously the triumphant response - from Decca. It couldn't fail. Their man, Mike Smith, had watched the group in action at the Cavern in front of the adulation of the home crowd, and he had then brought them down for a studio audition on January 1st. Though the group, particularly John Lennon, was not happy with the set that they had been compelled to play for the audition, the reaction at Decca was such that all the Beatles and Brian Epstein were fairly certain that an offer of a contract would be forthcoming.

It was in that spirit of optimism that the initial Management Contract between Epstein and the group was signed on January 24th. Given the work he had already done on behalf of the group before that date, particularly in dealing with EMI, Decca and Deutsche Grammophone, it was difficult to dispute the validity of the contract. Not least because, three weeks before the 24th, Epstein had managed to get the group their first "audition" for a British recording company, that infamous Decca audition.

On any practical or reasonable basis it was hard to defend any opposition to the new manager, the efforts he was putting into the group, and the percentage required in return for his work and support. The arguments, the suspicions, came later, but they were all a legacy of that initial contract and its timing.

The document contracted the group to Epstein while he worked on putting together their first record deal, and contains the signatures of all four group members, as well as the respective fathers or mothers of Paul McCartney, George Harrison and Pete Best, given that the trio were still under 21.

The successful signing was aided in no small part to Epstein's intensive wooing of the various families. He visited both Paul's father, Jim, and also the forbidding Mimi, who was John's legendary Aunt, but perhaps most time was spent on Pete's mother, Mona, who had been acting as de facto manager.

The deed was done and a five-year management contract signed, without any great ceremony, on Wednesday January 24th. The one oddity about the agreement was that, although it was witnessed by Alistair Taylor, it was not signed by Epstein.

When I saw a copy of this original contract some time ago the absence of Epstein's signature seemed really startling, although his justification at the time seemed quite plausible. He claimed that he wanted the group to have the power to walk away from the arrangement if they were not happy with it. This was a perfectly laudable intention although, as I was to discover over and over again, the contract situation was never, ever quite what it seemed.

And when I looked back over the Beatles story and the whole bewilderment of the McCartney replacement story it was clear that it all emanated from that first contract, and its October replacement, however noble or principled were the motives.

Epstein followed up his sparkling managerial performance during December and January by arranging a second meeting in London with Decca. This meeting was arranged for February 6th but a number of significant events took place before that.

February 1st saw the start of Brian Epstein's contractual period with the Beatles and after the regular lunchtime Cavern gig they appeared that night, at the delightfully-named Thistle Café, out on The Wirral. This was the first time Epstein took a formal commission from the show at the Grand Opening of the temporarily renamed The Beatle Club, which was normally a dance instruction venue above the Thistle Café in West Kirby.

The next night saw the group's first official appearance outside Liverpool, down the East Lancashire Road in Manchester. They had been booked into the Oasis Club, another subterranean venue similar to the Cavern, and the owner, Hugh Goodwin was well placed to create a site to capitalise on the growing interest in pop or beat music. He had appeared at the Cavern as trombonist and leader of a jazz group called the Sunset Seven and his local music connections had brought him into contact with Brian Epstein.

Hugh Goodwin held onto a copy of the receipt signed by Brian Epstein for a series of Beatles appearances at the Oasis for the princely sum of £25. He remained impressed by an aspect of Epstein's management which received little credit. The venue was sent some advance publicity for the Beatles and, according to Goodwin, the Beatles, via Epstein, were the only group that ever bothered with such advance promotion.

And surviving posters for the Oasis appearance clearly demonstrate the value that Epstein was extracting from that brief skirting with recording fame with Tony Sheridan.

For the First Time in Manchester
POLYDOR RECORDING STARS

Three days later, back in Liverpool, came an unplanned appearance by the group in the form which was to sweep the world. A stomach upset left Pete Best unable to perform and so the group pulled in the Hurricanes drummer, Ringo Starr, to deputize for the lunchtime show at the Cavern and then that night in the refined spaces of the Kingsway Club in Southport.

This wasn't the first time Starr had sat in with the group. One pill-fuelled evening in Hamburg had seen him filling the gap temporarily left by Pete Best on a selection of mainly rock standards. That show didn't count.

Nobody could really remember it, but the two shows on February 5th were different. The first formal appearances by the four Beatles as the world would shortly come to know them. February 5th, 1962.

And then the following day came the first major disappointment of Epstein's career as Beatles manager. He took a call from Dick Rowe at Decca quietly informing him that Decca would not be signing the Beatles. This was the conversation which contained the immortal mistake "Guitar groups are on the way out, Mr. Epstein!"

To his great credit Epstein refused to take this rejection. He rang Decca and arranged a meeting at Decca headquarters for Tuesday, February 6th and it was there on the Embankment that Epstein was left in no doubt that any possibility with Decca had been extinguished.

He met Dick Rowe and Sidney Arthur Beecher-Stevens, Decca's sales manager, for lunch and tried, very hard, to persuade them to reverse their decision. It didn't work. They patronised him about his group and his pretentions; airily declaring their view that they would struggle to market a Liverpool group to a national audience. They also advised Epstein to return to Liverpool and to stick to retailing. The depth of his anger isn't difficult to imagine and in return Epstein snootily lambasted their lack of vision, warning them that his group was going to be as big as Elvis.

The session didn't end well and Epstein left, viciously disappointed that his main opportunity to secure a recording contract had vanished. But, by one of those strokes of good fortune which coloured those early years of the Beatles, Epstein came away from the meeting with a priceless trophy. He left Decca carrying a precious copy of the Beatles' Decca audition on two large reel-to-reel tapes.

There was one other possible small advantage from the abortive conversation. Dick Rowe made the offer that he would arrange for Tony Meehan, ex-drummer with the Shadows, to produce the Beatles at Decca - if Epstein agreed to cover the expenses, estimated at £100.

This was not the kind of triumphant arrangement that he was seeking but he was in no position to refuse any option. The result was that he extended his stay in London and made an appointment for the following day, February 7th, to meet Meehan. This meant a return to the Decca Studios in Hampstead where Epstein was kept waiting while Meehan and Dick Rowe worked on a session. Eventually, after some thirty minutes, Meehan took Epstein into another room for the discussion.

If Epstein had returned to Decca in any spirit of optimism his mood was dispelled by Meehan's attitude which reflected and echoed the patronising disdain showed by Rowe and Beecher-Stevens the previous day. Epstein, too urbane to display his anger and despair, cut the discussion short and left the building, and never went back to Decca.

Events were moving fast and Epstein decided to stay down in London to try to get some progress on the recording contract front. It would also be realistic to believe that he was not anxious to return to Liverpool and face the disappointment of the group, and the scorn of Lennon who was still seething about the set they had been forced to perform in the New Year's Day audition.

Once again it is difficult now, in a world of social media and mobile communications, to understand how easy it was then to avoid contact if that was your intention or desire. Staying in London gave Epstein the chance to pursue other opportunities for a contract, but it also allowed him to postpone the inevitable disappointment and confrontation with the Beatles. He had grown to relish the chance to be welcomed by one or more Beatles at Lime Street Station when he returned from London trips, but he really wouldn't have looked forward to having to pass on the bad news from Decca.

Grasping at the diminishing number of straws in London, Epstein set up meetings with Pye Records, then the third largest label in the country, and also with Oriole Records but the responses were completely negative. Similar approaches to Phillips Records also proved futile and it was clear on the evening of February 7th that his options had narrowed substantially.

Thursday February 8th 1962 was scheduled as Epstein's last day in London. He couldn't stay away from NEMS indefinitely and he was gloomily aware that he would have to meet the group and endure a searching conversation very soon after he arrived back in Liverpool.

In that mood of gloom and perhaps impending disaster, he took the chance for a moment of light relief by calling to see an old friend from the record retail industry. He had met Bob Boast, the manager of the flagship HMV store at 363 Oxford Street, some months earlier. The occasion was a seminar on record retailing staged in Hamburg under the auspices of Deutsche Grammophone, and the pair had a number of shared experiences in the world of record retailing to unite them. It's also quite likely that Epstein wanted to see if Bob Boast could open any doors for the Beatles but, once again, he was doomed to disappointment. Although Bob Boast had a prominent role in HMV it was purely on the retailing side of that branch of the EMI operation. He was not able to make any practical suggestions which would get Epstein nearer to the mystical contract.

However, hearing the story of Epstein's travails with the various record company meetings, Boast was able to offer one vital suggestion. He warned Epstein that dragging the rather dog-eared Decca master tapes around the meetings would inevitably create the wrong, entirely negative impression. The prominent Decca labelling would tell anybody in a meeting that the group had been auditioned by Decca and had been rejected. But Boast wasn't just being critical or negative. On the contrary, for he suggested to Epstein that he should avail himself of a unique facility within the HMV building.

For many years that HMV flagship building had included a small recording studio which also had a small cutting room for transferring music from tape to 78-rpm discs. Bob Boast recommended Epstein to use the service, on the entirely reasonable basis that the finished discs would look and sound more professional, and would sever the unavoidable visual ties with Decca.

Epstein eagerly agreed to the suggestion and so Bob Boast took him to the studio and introduced Epstein to Jim Foy, the disc-cutter, who worked in the studio. Epstein explained what he needed and Jim Foy set about the task.

On listening to the playback of the finished discs Foy was impressed by what he heard and engaged Epstein in conversation about the group playing on the discs. He was particularly taken by the fact that three of the songs included in the session material were original compositions. Although commonplace today it was then very unusual and certainly enough to catch the interest of someone in the business like Jim Foy.

To Epstein's surprise the conversation went in an unexpected direction. Foy asked him about music publishing, but Epstein readily conceded that it was a subject about which he knew little. In a laudable attempt to help the new boy, Jim Foy suggested that Epstein should meet the music publisher Sid Coleman, head of EMI's record publishing company, Ardmore & Beechwood, which coincidentally was located on the top floor of the imposing building.

With Epstein's permission Foy rang Coleman who happened to be in his office and not in a meeting, and so was able to walk downstairs to the cutting room.

He was introduced to Epstein and listened to a few tracks on the discs while Foy animatedly conveyed the fact that three of the tracks were written by two young men in the group, named John Lennon and Paul McCartney.

Coleman was clearly impressed by the quality of the tracks, and obviously alive to the music publishing opportunities. Epstein was invited back up to Coleman's office for a discussion but Epstein, though definitely flattered by some interest after so much negativity, was at pains to impress on Coleman that his main priority was to secure a recording contract for the Beatles.

To his eternal credit Coleman understood the situation and made an immediate, world-altering move. He made a call to the offices of EMI records located just a few hundred yards away in Manchester Square and spoke to Judy

Lockhart-Smith, the secretary to one of EMI's younger record producers. Her boss wasn't there at the time but she made an appointment for Epstein to come to meet her boss the following Tuesday, February 13th.

Her boss, and future husband, George Henry Martin.

George Martin had joined EMI in 1950 as an assistant and became head of the Parlophone label when Joseph Lockwood took over in 1954. A management shakeup then led to the retirement of the head of the label. Martin was just 29 at the time but was promoted to the role making him the youngest head of a label within EMI.

Martin was head of A&R at Parlophone, then one of EMI's minor labels. It had a reputation for quirky or comedy records, and Martin had little daily involvement with pop music, though responsible for minor hits by the likes of the Temperance Seven, Matt Monro and Shane Fenton. There was even a constant rumour in the recording industry in the early sixties that Parlophone was in danger of closure and that George Martin's job was at risk.

Coleman wandered over to Manchester Square the following day for a coffee with George Martin, and part of their conversation was occupied by Coleman's story about the elegant record manager and his song-writing group.

Martin's interest was piqued but he had to wait several days for Epstein to return to London. Before that the Beatles manager had the not inconsiderable duty of reporting back to the group on his trip to London to court the record companies.

A testy and fairly acerbic meeting took place at NEMS before the end of the week. It fell to Epstein to justify the failure with Decca, but this was helped by the residual annoyance about the way the session on January 1st had gone. Epstein somehow forgot to mention the abortive approaches to Pye and Oriole, concentrating instead on the positive conversation at HMV and the strong interest in the music publishing. The forthcoming meeting with George Martin cut no ice - nobody had heard of him - but Epstein was able to massively win the day because of the prize he had brought back from London with him, the discs which Jim Foy had cut upstairs at HMV.

Those discs made a return trip to London three days later, taken by Brian Epstein to his first meeting with George Martin. Before that he had put pen to paper to sever all ties with Decca, taking the chance to decline the offer of Tony Meehan's services and to claim, disingenuously, that since the meeting with Rowe a recording contract from another company had been offered to the group.

Economical with the truth, or prescient? It's hard to tell all these years later but it cannot be disputed that the course of the Beatles history, and possibly music history, was changed completely by Bob Boast and Jim Foy and those 78rpm discs.

But years after the event, in the days when he was regularly lampooned as the man who gave away the Beatles, Dick Rowe would state firmly that, if the stories were true that Epstein had guaranteed to buy through NEMS 3,000 copies of any single Decca released by the Beatles, there was no way he would have turned them down. Harsh economics of the record business at that period would have forced him to sign the group, indeed any group or artist with that kind of guarantee.

The meeting with George Martin took place at Manchester Square on Tuesday, February 13th and it was clear that Epstein found George Martin a more agreeable companion than many of the other rougher, sweatier types he had encountered on the quest for a recording contract. Martin, though from working-class origins, was charming and urbane and cultured, and Epstein clearly felt an empathy with him.

But that first meeting was a sales operation, nothing more or less. Epstein's job was to sell the group to George Martin and Parlophone, stressing the huge importance of the group on Merseyside and beyond, using the recent Mersey Beat issue and the just-past appearance at the Oasis in Manchester as evidence. But inevitably it was the discs recorded at HMV which had the biggest impact. Martin would always afterwards decry the quality of the performance of the material as represented on the discs, whilst maintaining that there was something, some quality, he heard in the music which made him think it might be worth pursuing.

He made no promises to Epstein but the reaction was sufficiently warm to encourage Epstein on his journey back north, especially as Epstein had to mull over another potential obstacle.

The interaction with Ron White before Christmas had thrown up the existence of a German contract which bound the Beatles to the company which released 'My Bonnie'. It was clear that before any contract with George Martin could be contemplated, a release from the German contract had to be negotiated. A week after the meeting at Manchester Square a letter was sent from NEMS to Bert Kaempfert in his role as A&R manager at Polydor in Germany, asking him formally to dissolve the contract. In fact, it still had four months to run but Epstein was anxious that no obstacle should come in the way of the possible Parlophone deal. Bert Kaempfert replied within ten days on Saturday March 3rd 1962. His charming and businesslike letter effectively agreed to the release of the group with the request to keep recording options open during the Hamburg trip which was coming up for the Beatles before the end of June.

Brian Epstein answered his letter shortly before the end of March giving Kaempfert formal notice of his intention to run the contract down to its natural expiry at the end of June. More pleasantly, he also offered to meet Kaempfert in Hamburg when he arrived there in advance of the Beatles period in the city, and Epstein sugared the pill of the contract termination with the offer to discuss possible fresh recordings before the June 30th deadline.

The relationship between Bert Kaempfert and the Beatles was a curious one. They had been hired by him in Hamburg as little more than session musicians and back-up singers. At that time the German band-leader and record producer was interested only in Sheridan as a solo recording artist. He went to a show at the Top Ten Club and decided the Beatles would fit the bill as Sheridan's backing band at his forthcoming Polydor recording sessions. It was clear that Kaempfert wasn't concerned what the band were called, and there was even confusion over whether the record label for the single should credit them as The Beat Boys or The Beatles.

They recorded Sheridan's arrangement of 'My Bonnie', plus the old standards 'Ain't She Sweet' and 'The Saints' and finally a George Harrison instrumental called 'Cry For A Shadow', recorded as a weak pun on the material played by Cliff Richard's then backing group, The Shadows.

The material The Beatles recorded for Polydor was poor, and significantly inferior to the test material tape produced in West Hampstead with Mike Smith on New Year's Day, but it did provide an extra headache which Epstein steadfastly kept away from everybody else - particularly the members of the Beatles. However good or bad the Polydor material was, it resulted from a binding contract between the Beatles and Polydor, and Epstein knew that it was essential that he negotiate his way out of the unexpired Polydor recording contract, before even thinking of new contracts with EMI or anybody else

Nevertheless, all the pieces in Epstein's mental chessboard were being moved into place and his grand plan was approaching lift-off, even though less than six months had passed since he first met the group at the Cavern.

The next landmark would be reached in the April-May engagements in Hamburg which had been negotiated with Peter Eckhorn in December. This was the first substantial contract which Epstein handled on behalf of the group and it was the first opportunity for him to demonstrate his capacity to charm, or chisel, a larger payment for the group. Despite refusing the terms originally offered, Epstein was confident that an improved offer would appear, and he was correct. Three weeks after negotiations were broken off, the Germans returned with a contract agreeing to the financial terms demanded by Epstein. The second meeting also provided the first manifestation of another financial quirk which would dog Epstein's management of the group.

This was the "brown bag", an under the counter payment, inevitably undeclared, which would come in cash, always separate from any taxable income, and would be made available after Hamburg in places all over the world. Epstein wasn't the first, nor the last, rock or pop manager to expect or even demand such brown bag payments but few of his peers elevated it to such a slick operation.

The Beatles left for Hamburg, for their third session in the city, on April 11th but the involvement with Epstein meant that the long journey by train and ferry was a thing of the past. He flew them out of Manchester but only John, Paul and Pete took the flight. A delayed recovery from German measles meant that George Harrison flew out the following day accompanied by Epstein and the mother of the late Stuart Sutcliffe who had died from a brain aneurism on the 10th. Lennon, McCartney and Best had been met at the airport by Astrid Kirchherr who gave them the dreadful news of the death of their friend.

Epstein flew in with Harrison and busied himself confirming details for their season at the Star Club. He also took care, in his usual ethical way, to ensure that he kept his promise to Kaempfert and so a final recording session to meet the terms of the Polydor contract was arranged for Thursday, May 24th. The expectation on both sides was that this engagement would effectively terminate the contract, and this arrangement allowed Epstein to remove one of the last restrictions on the group and his complete control of their destiny.

Having overseen the first few appearances at the Star Club it was time for Epstein to head back to Britain. His charges didn't need him as a babysitter and in any case there were far more important topics to pursue back at home.

Several weeks had gone by since that initial meeting with George Martin and there had been no follow-up, no contact. It wasn't an obvious cause for concern but the recent example of the apparent promise with Decca followed suddenly by the painful disillusionment was still too vivid.

He flew back determined to make the final step towards the recording contract before the group returned from Germany. He couldn't risk another failure or the vicious embarrassment of having to explain to the group, especially Lennon, why the contract still hadn't materialised.

The result was that Epstein travelled back to EMI on May 9th to meet with George Martin for the second time. The major difference this time was the venue. Instead of the antiseptic surroundings of Manchester Square the meeting was set for a place Epstein had never visited before, the EMI recording studios at Abbey Road.

In the intervening period Martin had been subjected to some unsubtle lobbying from Sid Colman, the person who had set up the introduction to

Epstein. He subsequently admitted that, to preserve the advantage for Ardmore & Beechwood, he fully intended directing Epstein and his group towards Philips Records if the Parlophone possibility wasn't realised. And, as a partial result of Sid Colman's machinations, George Martin met Brian Epstein for the second time at 11.30 am on Wednesday May 9th.

On that day Epstein met with Martin at EMI's studios in Abbey Road, St.John's Wood, London. Martin must have been doing some research in the three months since his previous meeting with Epstein, because at that meeting, he immediately offered Epstein a recording contract for The Beatles, subject to meeting them and hearing them play. A date was set: Wednesday June 6th.

To Epstein's surprise and delight George Martin declared that he was willing to offer the Beatles a recording contract - even though he hadn't seen them in person. This wasn't quite as radical as it sounded. The politics of the situation were that Martin could offer a contract which would remain unsigned and unratified by EMI until he had seen and approved the group. But there were politics at play on the other side of the equation and the fact that Epstein was able to state, with a degree of conviction, that he had secured a contract with EMI certainly gave his reputation a boost with the group and even more widely back in Liverpool.

Consequently, upon leaving the studios, Epstein walked immediately from Abbey Road and onto Circus Road, travelling the few hundred yards to the nearest main Post Office which was located on Wellington Road. He needed the Post Office to enable him to communicate with people and pass on the fantastic news, but again it's difficult to comprehend such a process from a modern perspective of mobile phones and social media.

Epstein naturally wanted to pass on the good news about the contract to his parents, and obviously wanted to let the group know as soon as possible. His parents had a conventional, landline phone in their home in Queens Drive in Liverpool so a call directly to them was relatively straightforward. Communications with the Beatles in Hamburg were far less certain or reliable, and so the only recourse was the then safe fall-back, the telegram.

For a set fee per word, a person could dictate a message which would be printed and then delivered by hand to the intended recipient. For generations, indeed for most of the 20th century, if it was impossible to deliver news of significance in person, then the main alternative was to send a telegram, and that was the primary reason that Brian Epstein rushed to the Post Office that blustery day.

He rang his parents from one of the telephone kiosks outside the building, then entered to compose, pay for and send two telegrams announcing the securing of the contract with EMI.

The first telegram was to the Beatles in Hamburg, and would be opened the following day by George Harrison. The second was to Bill Harry, editor of Mersey Beat, a friend and supporter of the group. Ever the professional, Epstein knew the value of allowing Mersey Beat to provide the news about the contract to Liverpool and to a wider world.

And, as another demonstration of how different communications were back then, the responses from the Beatles to Epstein's great news came in the form of postcards in which Lennon demanded to know how quickly they would be millionaires, McCartney requested an advance of £10,000, while George Harrison suggested ordering four new guitars.

George Martin was busy with various EMI matters after Epstein left but eventually he turned to the administrative aspects of the proposed contract with the Beatles. He had made an arrangement with Epstein to bring the group to Abbey Road on Wednesday June 6th for what would effectively be another audition. He had expressly not signed the contract and he would not sign it and formalise it until he had heard the audition material. As such there was nothing legally binding on EMI or Martin, but it was quite ironic that within five months both Martin and Epstein created contracts with the Beatles but didn't sign the documents, albeit for different reasons. At that time in his career George Martin was keen, if not desperate, to widen his career into the pop sphere. Although his label, Parlophone, had enjoyed minor success in that area, it was far better known for different material. Martin's reputation by 1962 had been largely founded on classical music and cast recordings of theatrical shows. In addition he was justly renowned for his involvement with comedy, and his productions of Flanders and Swann, Beyond the Fringe, and the Goons gave him great kudos in the industry and substantial success for Parlophone and EMI. The close involvement with people like Spike Milligan and the Goons would also do Martin no harm at all in the subsequent conversations with John Lennon and Paul McCartney, both real fans of that anarchic style of comedy.

But the comedy content in the Parlophone portfolio was something of a straightjacket, and Martin was clearly seeking some means to break free and possibly challenge the supremacy within EMI of his fellow producer Norrie Paramor who had achieved massive success with Cliff Richard and the Shadows.

Giving an unknown group from Liverpool an audition on the back of an unsigned contract was a gamble but not a major one, but in a major organisation like EMI there were various administrative duties to be performed. On Friday, May 18th 1962, George Martin despatched the standard "Application for Artiste Contract" to EMI's administration department. In return, a contract, which was post-dated June 4th, was sent back to Martin six days later. It was then delivered to NEMS, to Epstein, for him to secure the various signatures of the group members. This took place when the group returned from Hamburg on Saturday June 2nd, and the signed contract was dispatched to EMI by Epstein on Tuesday June 5th 1962. This auspicious document was signed by Brian Epstein and witnessed by Bob Wooler, the DJ at the Cavern.

The timing was important. The contract was sent on the 5th and then on the following day came the first-ever appearance by the Beatles at Abbey Road studios.

They were ushered into the studio and ran through four songs under the control of Martin's assistant, Ron Richards, later to achieve great success with the Hollies. The engineer at the session was Norman Smith who would go on to engineer all the Beatles' sessions up to and including Rubber Soul.

George Martin wasn't present. That was not unusual. Auditions were never taken by the producer; invariably by his assistant, and that's why Richards was in control. The session acted as both audition and formal recording session and so the group were able to run through their first four songs, 'Besame Mucho', 'Love Me Do', 'PS I Love You' and 'Ask Me Why' in true studio conditions. The impression made wasn't great, not least because of the problems caused by the group's equipment. The reservations expressed by Mike Smith at Decca several months earlier were repeated by Norman Smith, and various hasty changes to equipment had to be made to allow the group to give of their best.

Nevertheless, it wasn't an auspicious start though Smith recalls being taken by 'Love Me Do', especially given that it was self-written. At some point during the session, George Martin entered the control room which, in the circumstances of an audition for an unknown group, was in itself unusual. He was no more impressed than his colleagues, but in his usual cultured way was measured in his judgement and remarks when he invited the group into the control room to listen to the playback.

As ever Martin was considered and constructive, dissecting the songs, the group's performance and their equipment in some detail. It was more of a lecture than a conversation and Martin was quite surprised by the lack of reaction. But that was the famous occasion when, in response to Martin's gentle enquiry to the individual group members if there was anything they didn't like, George Harrison told him that he didn't like his tie!

George Martin detected something in the music, in the performance, that he could work with, but the greatest impression was made on a personal basis by the four individuals. One point which would assume greater importance in the near future was the dissatisfaction felt by many, particularly Martin, with the drumming of Pete Best. Nothing was said at the time but a note had been made of a potential weakness. More important was the fact that the chat in the control room, and the subsequent discussion with his colleagues like Norman Smith, convinced Martin to go ahead with the contract for the Beatles.

This wasn't prescience or brilliance on Martin's part. Instead it was cold pragmatism for, as he correctly calculated, EMI could hardly lose. The deal to which the company were committed was as parsimonious as it could be to the new group, who would receive one penny for each record sold, with that single penny to be split among the four members of the group. That tiny royalty rate was further reduced for all singles sold outside the UK, on which the group received half of one penny per single, which again would be divided among the whole band.

Even worse, Parlophone was contractually bound to record only four sides, or two double-sided singles, in a one-year period. It was just about the lowest possible offer a record company could put forward, but, given the number of earlier rejections, it's clear that Brian Epstein did not feel exploited, at least at that point.

But the rise in popularity and sales for the group after the release of 'Please Please Me' in 1963 was so meteoric that Martin would be moved to suggest to EMI that the agreed initial royalty rate of one penny should be doubled, at no penalty to the group. His suggestion was dismissed and the situation even led to certain members of the EMI hierarchy describing George Martin as a traitor inside EMI.

Such extravagance was in the future though. The next step after that audition or test session on June 6th was the finalisation of the legal agreement. Martin made the necessary moves with his colleagues at EMI, and the result was that on June 18th Brian Epstein received a fully signed, authorised and legal contract between the Beatles and EMI.

The derisory royalty rate - provided without any advance - didn't raise any objection from group members or manager; none of them knew enough to query, and in any case it was the classic, cliché situation of the cynical company exploiting the gullible naïve newcomers. It might have been expected that the manager would have been a little wiser to the game and might have fought rather harder for his charges but, not for the last time in this saga, Epstein did not know any better.

For the moment that didn't matter, but it was another seemingly minor matter which would come back to haunt him in the future.

Like so many others.

But as June 1962 crawled towards its conclusion, it seemed that all the pieces in Epstein's grand master plan were coming together. Given that he had a contract with the group, albeit unsigned by him, and a recording contract with EMI for the group, and an increasingly lucrative set of dates for the Beatles, it seemed it would be hard to argue with his view. To cement that progression it was time to form a company which would manage all his various activities.

NEMS Enterprises was formed on June 26th 1962 with Brian and his brother Clive as Directors and shareholders, and a share capital of £100. Brian had chosen to keep the name NEMS to continue the link with his family's North End Road Music Stores, and the name NEMS was to play a prominent role in the evolution of the Beatles up to and even beyond Brian's death.

There was a flurry of correspondence in June relating to the various dealings with EMI around the contract. Copies of the contract were passed between George Martin and EMI administration in the first half of the month including one memo mentioning Musicians Union payments. This would later cause uncertainty about whether the Abbey Road encounter on June 6th was an audition, a trial, or a recording session.

There was also a refined exchange of letters between Ron White and Epstein in which White wrote to NEMS on June 26th, explaining the apparent anomaly in which the EMI recording managers had, through White, passed on the chance of recording the Beatles. He finished by mentioning George Martin and the expectations for the contract. The ever-diligent Epstein replied four days later thanking White and stating Epstein's expectation that the first disc from the group would be released "towards the end of August".

Such a timescale was tight, but achievable. However, there was one major problem which had to be dealt with before the momentum could be resumed, and that problem was the group's drummer, Pete Best. At the session on June 6th, among the various criticisms of equipment and songs, there were remarks made by Martin to the group and to Epstein about the perceived weakness of Pete's drumming. This issue was hinted at in a remark in Ron White's recent letter, "George Martin has made certain suggestions which may improve them still further".

These criticisms planted doubts in the minds of McCartney, Lennon and Harrison about the future viability of the recording contract if their drummer was an obvious weakness. This, added to the existing minor issues where Best was seen as having a different sense of humour to the others and, critically, refused to adopt the same hairstyle as the others, had just one result. He had to go. There were already signs of the coming schism. Pete Best did not learn of the failure of the Decca approach for quite some time after Messrs'. Lennon, McCartney and Harrison knew, and while they may not have been actively looking for a reason to dispense with his services, they didn't resist when the chance presented itself.

But despite the fact that the other three Beatles had known Best for some two years while Epstein had known him for just a few months, there was no question of their handling the knife. It was passed to Epstein with a request, if not instructions, on how to use it.

Pete Best was summoned to a meeting with Epstein at NEMS on Thursday August 16th and summarily dismissed from the band. He had no idea that was why he was being called to the meeting, nor did he know that two days earlier John Lennon had phoned Ringo Star offering him the gig with the Beatles.

At that point Ringo was on the east coast, at Skegness, appearing in a summer residency with Rory Storm and the Hurricanes at Butlins holiday camp. There was an existing relationship between Starr and the three surviving Beatles based on shared times in Hamburg and the general Liverpool musical fraternity, and Starr had been unhappy with the Hurricanes for some time.

For all those reasons he didn't need to be asked twice. He gave Rory Storm three days notice and left Skegness that Friday night. And on Saturday August 18th he appeared for the first time as a member of the complete group in their show at Hulme Hall in Port Sunlight, near Birkenhead.

As a bizarre follow-up to the story, Pete Best would eventually record for Decca, and would also be produced by Mike Smith, under the name of his subsequent group, Lee Curtis & the All Stars, and then as part of the Pete Best Four on their June 1964 single 'I'm Gonna Knock on Your Door'/'Why Did I Fall in Love With You?', but this was long after the Beatles had begun their dominance with EMI.

August 11th produced another development which would have a monumental impact on the Beatles history and the story I was hoping to tell. Brian Epstein engaged the services of a bouncer at the Cavern, Mal Evans, to act as Road Manager for the group. At the time, the duties seemed straightforward but as the fame of the group, and the demands on the four Beatles grew unimaginably over the next three years, Mal Evans was to become a vital, trusted member of the inner circle. And, as I was to learn, he was to play a critical role in the events surrounding the disintegration of the group.

August also saw another event which has become part of Beatles folklore. The only piece of film of the group in performance prior to the breakthrough at the end of that year, appeared on August 22nd with a short, grainy black and white piece of footage of the Beatles on the tiny Cavern stage performing the Leiber and Stoller and Richard Barrett classic, 'Some Other Guy'. This became the only ever piece of film of the group playing live in the Cavern, and yet, despite all the grandiose claims in the years since, it was entirely fortuitous. Granada Television would go on to have a more prestigious role in the emergence of the Beatles but the 'Some Other Guy' filming was a happy accident of timing despite the fact that the quality was poor. But it was film of the Beatles playing on stage at the Cavern.

Timeless. Historic. It happened just once, and would never, could never happen again.

Despite Epstein's optimism about the release of the first single, none of the tracks recorded on June 6th were considered good enough for release. Another session had to be organised and so the group were brought back to EMI on Tuesday September 4th for a session overseen by Ron Richards, which was dominated by recordings of two songs, 'Love Me Do' and 'How Do You Do It'. The former was a Lennon and McCartney original, whereas the other song was a bright, ordinary pop song which came to George Martin via a traditional Tin Pan Alley route.

It had been written by Mitch Murray and supplied to Ron Richards who liked the song and recommended it to a struggling music publisher named Dick James, who took the song. Ron Richards filed it away and, in one of the meetings after the initial Beatles session on June 6th when Martin, Richards and others were debating what song should appear as the Beatles first single, Richards remembered and introduced 'How Do You Do It'. Martin thought it would be a perfect choice, believing it to be a number one record, and sent a copy to Liverpool for the group to rehearse ahead of the next recording session.

Martin clearly wasn't expecting or prepared for the obstinacy of the group. They hated the song, and were intent on recording their own material but once again, given modern conditions, it is very difficult to understand just how radical or revolutionary this stance was.

But they played the game and prepared the song and turned up at Abbey Road ready to record it. However, it wasn't total capitulation. They insisted on playing that song as the first one at the session, and dashed through it to allow more time on their own material, particularly 'Love Me Do'.

A couple of versions of 'How Do You Do It' were taped as well as more than a dozen takes of 'Love Me Do', and it was one of those takes which was later mixed down to mono and pressed onto an acetate disc. This was then the subject of a meeting the following day between Martin and Epstein to discuss the all-important first release.

Perhaps surprisingly, Martin again expressed dissatisfaction about the drumming on the track. This though was a comment on Ringo Starr's timing on the track and not his basic competency, which had been the complaint against the unfortunate Pete Best. And there was general acceptance that Starr's problems on the session were a reflection on how little time he had been given to rehearse, rather than any inability to handle the material.

However, Martin was in no position, or mood, to allow time for Starr to come up to speed and so he told Epstein that a second session would be arranged for the following week to re-record 'Love Me Do', this time using a session drummer. He didn't ask Epstein - he told him. The days when the Beatles were all-powerful and so powerful that EMI danced to their tune on recording time lay in the future, but Epstein left the meeting on September 5th knowing that he had to bring the Beatles back several days later, but this time it was expressly, solely to record their own material.

The session was under the control of Ron Richards who had booked Andy White to provide the drumming. Ringo was relegated to provide tambourine and maracas at various points in the session, creating a sense of resentment which took quite some time to dispel. In the grand scheme of things, though, that didn't really matter. The vital thing was that the single, the critical first single, had been recorded and would be scheduled shortly for release.

George Martin had clearly accepted that the group had some possibilities in terms of writing their own material, and both of these developments represented major breakthroughs for the Beatles and Brian Epstein.

In those quieter, simpler times it wasn't difficult to schedule a release quickly, especially for a record which wasn't expected to be a major hit. 'Love Me Do' was scheduled for release on October 5th backed by another Lennon-McCartney original, 'PS I Love You'.

That single was arguably the Beatles first step on the road to the domination of music that they would achieve in the next few years, but the days before the release of the single would see Epstein take two further steps which would play a big part in the catastrophes to come.

Conscious of the weakness in the original contract with the Beatles, albeit not signed by him, and knowing that a fresh contract removing Best and replacing him with Ringo Starr was necessary, Epstein had a new NEMS contract prepared which was signed by him and the four members of the group. This contract was for a five-year period and made Epstein the manager of the group until 1967. That document became almost a sacred tract and came to public attention in 2004 when it was sold at Christies auction house in London for £125,000.

With the signing of the contract, trust in Epstein was unqualified especially after the fantastic triumphs since Christmas. Perhaps that was the reason that nobody read, or perhaps to be fair questioned, the terms of that five year contract which later managed to shock no less a person than James Trevor Isherwood, who achieved prominence as Epstein's accountant at Bryce-Hamner.

The contract of October 1st allowed Epstein, through NEMS Enterprises, to take 25 per cent of the gross income, rather than the 10 or even 12.5 per cent normally taken by managers. In addition all of Brian Epstein's expenses were to be deducted from the gross income, and this involved office rental, staff salaries or wages, travel, telephone costs, and entertaining. The net effect was that Brian Epstein would receive substantially more from the Beatles activities than each of the individuals in the group, and the effects of that contract and its various ramifications would be a ticking time bomb for the next five years.

And those problems were made far, far worse because of his ignorance, though totally understandable ignorance, of the finer commercial points of music publishing.

Following the helpful intervention of Syd Coleman in the introduction to George Martin earlier in the year Epstein casually gave the publishing rights on that first single, 'Love Me Do'/'PS. I Love You', to the EMI publishing company that Syd Coleman ran, Ardmore and Beechwood.

The ownership of these tracks would become an intractable nightmare in future years made immeasurably worse by Epstein's cavalier handling of the music publishing issues on the next single release which, among other disasters, would ultimately lose John Lennon and Paul McCartney ownership of their songs.

On October 5th 1962 such disasters were in the distant future and, for the Beatles and for Brian Epstein, almost unimaginable. There were much happier matters to consider. Their first proper single, the first to be released in England under the name The Beatles was released as Parlophone R4949.

On the night of the 5th, EMI played the song on its own London-produced weekly radio program Friday Spectacular, which was broadcast on the hugely popular Radio Luxembourg. The first ever radio play for a Beatles record, the first of many.

They were on their way.

Tomorrow Never Knows

For thirty minutes on the afternoon of Saturday, October 6th 1962 the Beatles stepped nervously into a new world, giving them the briefest taste of just how the world had changed for them, and how it would never be the same again.

It was a small-scale, relatively inauspicious Signing Session at Dawson's Music Store in Widnes, a satellite town southeast of Liverpool. The group were there from 4pm to sign copies of their new single, 'Love Me Do', released just twenty-four hours earlier.

It was still a year away from million copy advance orders and frenzy at the mere mention of the name, Beatles, but it was their first official signing session and notable just for that.

The session lasted just over thirty minutes and each copy of the silver and red label single bearing all four signatures is very valuable property. As with any major event there are thousands who claim to have been present but the facts indicate otherwise.

A small scale, relatively trivial event on Church Street in Widnes, but a fleeting glimpse of the madness which awaited them.

That was a first and from that point it was a dizzying series of firsts for the group and their increasingly impressive manager.

It was this period which saw one of the mythical events which coloured the history of the Beatles. Allegedly the NEMS organisation ordered some 10,000 copies of 'Love Me Do' which would have provided a massive slice of the disc's initial sales. Although this story has often been denied, it is a matter of record that representatives of both Decca and EMI recall being told that Epstein had guaranteed to order some 3,000 copies of the first single released by the Beatles on their label. In the wild excitement of that initial release it is conceivable that such an order might have been placed not least because, as possibly the leading record outlet in the north-west, NEMS would certainly have been listed as a Chart Return shop. And that's the scenario which often found aunties and brothers and friends going into Chart Return shops and "purchasing" 5, 10 even 20 copies of a single which were then logged up as legitimate sales thus increasing the chance of a climb up the charts.

Whatever the circumstances, the following week saw the first appearance by 'Love Me Do' in a UK chart, with Record Retailer showing the single for the first time. Less than a week later came the first official, publicised appearance on British television when People and Places, an early-evening magazine programme on Granada Television, featured the Beatles in a studio setting for the first time. They went to Studio Four in the Quay Street headquarters of Granada and performed 'Love Me Do' and, with a nod to the past, 'Some Other Guy'.

This was to be the first of many appearances on Granada over the next two years before the crush of fame took them out of the North West forever, and many of those appearances were prompted by the brilliance of Granada's Head of Entertainment, an unsung genius named Johnny Hamp.

A week later 'Love Me Do' entered the charts for the first time though the group were hardly in a position to capitalise on the success as Epstein had committed them to yet another Hamburg trip with appearances at the Star Club that would occupy most of November.

Johnny Hamp brought the group back into Granada shortly before they left for Germany to record another mimed session to be broadcast while they were out of the country. This time, although 'Love Me Do' was repeated, the second number was 'A Taste of Honey'. Granada broadcast the brief session, again in People and Places, on November 2nd.

This time the Hamburg trip would be a much more acceptable fourteen days although they still managed to cram in almost fifty performances. Though this meant that they managed to further improve their stage performance the absence from the UK effectively crippled the chance of capitalising on 'Love Me Do'.

The return to the UK saw them jumping onto a familiar treadmill of performance, on a basis increasingly distant from Liverpool, plus promotion to spread the name of the group to a rapidly widening audience. So the second half of November 1962 found the group performing in the usual venues around Liverpool but also in the Midlands, at Coventry and also at West Bromwich. In addition they made a second appearance on Radio Luxembourg and their first recording for BBC radio performing 'Love Me Do', 'PS I Love You', plus the Cavern favourite, 'Twist and Shout'.

Sandwiched between the two radio recordings came a highly important engagement. Monday November 26th saw the group back at Abbey Road to record their next single to follow on the limited success of 'Love Me Do'.

This would prove to be 'Please Please Me', although the version released to the public in 1963 was markedly different to the original version presented to George Martin in September. He was clearly unhappy with the original tempo of the song and the instrumentation, leading him to make various constructive suggestions, such as speeding up the tempo, which transformed the song. At the start of the session on November 26th Martin was still inclined towards persuading the group to go back to 'How Do You Do It' but the differences he heard in the revitalised 'Please Please Me' made him believe their protestations about being able to write their own material were likely to bear fruit.

The session delivered some eighteen takes of 'Please Please Me' plus several versions of the planned B-side 'Ask Me Why'. In addition, the group worked on another new song, 'Tip of my Tongue', but Martin didn't really like it and the song was abandoned for another day, although the group would never formally record it. The song would be handed on to another of Epstein's discoveries, a young man named Tommy Quickly, who would become part of the NEMS stable during the massive expansion in the second half of 1963.

It was George Martin who had suggested that the song be speeded up from the maudlin ballad which he had heard in September. Clearly Martin also played a part in Lennon introducing the song with the strident harmonica solo but, however the elements were gathered together, the result was, to everybody's ears, a genuine hit.

That opinion was endorsed enthusiastically to Epstein in a meeting the following day. While the group were at the BBC's Paris Studio in central London recording three songs for later transmission on The Talent Spot on the Light Programme, their manager was away attending meetings. His first scheduled meeting was at Manchester Square with an EMI executive who made the fatal mistake of being late. Epstein waited twenty minutes beyond the appointed time, decided he was not being treated correctly, and walked out.

The stroll across Soho to the office occupied by Dick James on Charing Cross Rd was a short one. Epstein introduced himself to the receptionist and apologised for being very early but the receptionist buzzed through for James who came bounding out to greet the Beatles manager.

It is hard, in retrospect, to understand the bond that grew up between the two men. Both were Jewish but there was little to connect them socially, although Dick James had a genuine history in the music industry. Indeed almost forty years before 'Everything I Do I Do It for You' dominated the charts in 1991, Dick James had recorded the hit version of perhaps the definitive Robin Hood theme, 'The Adventures of Robin Hood'. He also had some credence within the industry for being involved in the writing of a popular novelty hit for Max Bygraves in 1960, 'You're a Pink Toothbrush'. Most men of Epstein's age would have known the songs and quite possibly the name, Dick James, but the biggest factor in his favour was the whole-hearted support of George Martin.

He had recorded the Robin Hood theme with Dick James for Parlophone in 1956, and watched it become very popular and even climb into the top twenty. That was the summit of its chart popularity but the name, Dick James, carried a certain weight in musical circles for a number of years. He had retained the friendship of George Martin ever since the recording in the mid-fifties, and, as James' recording career fizzled away, Martin encouraged him into other areas of the music industry.

Tin Pan Alley was a natural destination and so, in the early years of the sixties, Dick James was active as a song-plugger and music publisher. Active, but not wildly successful. He entertained high hopes for a song called 'How Do You Do It' which he had brought to George Martin earlier in 1962, but he had enjoyed virtually no success as a music publisher.

Until the day that Brian Epstein played him a disc by a group called the Beatles, an acetate of their new single, 'Please Please Me', and told Dick James that he was seeking a music publisher.

When his singing career effectively disappeared, Dick James joined the well-established firm, Sidney Bron Music, as a song-plugger but, after three years with that company, he decided to go on his own and so Dick James Music opened in 1961. On the day that Epstein appeared in the office of Dick James Music the company had been in existence barely a year.

When Epstein made the appointment to see him it was more a courtesy to Martin than a real commitment to go with Dick James. His unhappiness with the way 'Love Me Do' had been handled had caused him to look at alternatives. With his instinctive move towards quality he had researched and considered an American company called Hill & Range who were the publishers of Elvis Presley's material. Martin, possibly anticipating troubles ahead, suggested a more local option, naming three possible organisations including a company which would be hungry and small and keen, and this was Dick James Music.

And in all this interplay it mustn't be forgotten that the song 'How Do You Do It', which George Martin had been so keen to be recorded by the Beatles, had been provided to Martin by his friend, Dick James.

In my later research for the tv programme, in various places I saw the interplay between Epstein and Dick James compared to a hopeless person being handed a winning lottery ticket. That seems ungracious and unfair on James. Although he was undeniably the man in the right place at the right time, it seemed and seems a little cruel to blame him for that.

The meeting in his office overlooking Denmark Street was relatively brief. Both men were prepared to vest more faith in the other because of the recommendation of George Martin, but Epstein was clearly encouraged by the enthusiasm and energy displayed by Dick James. For his part James was impressed, as so many others were, by the cool civility of Brian Epstein, but for James the clincher was the acetate.

James clearly recognised some quality in the performance, but he was mainly interested in the song and the publishing options. As part of the verbal sparring Epstein raised the perfectly reasonable question of what James could provide for the Beatles that the EMI publicity machine couldn't.

In classic huckster mode James didn't answer the question. Instead he picked up the phone and dialled the number of Philip Jones who was then the producer of the ABC show Thank Your Lucky Stars. At that time, ahead of the advent of Top of the Pops and Ready Steady Go a couple of years later, Thank Your Lucky Stars was the only national show featuring pop music in the UK, and the importance of the programme wasn't lost on Epstein.

Nor was the ease with which James called the producer direct, and explained about this new disc 'Please Please Me' which was a certain hit.

He played the disc, holding the phone over the tinny speakers and, despite the sound quality issues, Philip Jones took Dick James' recommendation and guaranteed the group an appearance on release of the single early in the New Year. There was no need for further discussion. Epstein was impressed, and convinced, and Dick James was granted the publishing rights to 'Please Please Me'.

The call to Philip Jones wasn't mere chance. Dick James had known him for several years ever since they had come across each other while Jones was in a senior position at Radio Luxembourg. Curiously he left Luxembourg in 1955 to join the new Granada Television in the role of light entertainment producer in which he proved so successful that he was head-hunted by Tyne Tees Television to join their new operation as a producer/director in Light Entertainment. His success in television continued and so in 1961 he was enticed away from Tyne Tees to take up a senior position with the London and Midlands network, ATV.

It's all hypothetical, of course, but had Philip Jones remained at Granada rather than moving to Tyne Tees and ATV then he might have sanctioned those first People and Places appearances by the Beatles rather than Johnny Hamp.

Instead Philip Jones took the call from Dick James, agreed the booking for Thank Your Lucky Stars, and thereby cemented James into a life of riches that he could hardly have imagined.

Given the impressive performance by James in securing the tv appearance Epstein had no doubt that he was the man to choose, despite his reservations about the shabbiness of James' office. There was an implicit understanding that James would continue to publish music from the Beatles beyond 'Please Please

Me', and the meeting ended with both men agreeing to meet up again and give some thought to future possibilities.

Epstein returned to Liverpool, as did the group and resumed their hectic schedules, taking in the Cavern and other venues around the country. Nobody gave any thought to the music publishing situation. It was not that important, at least compared to the joy of performing and the thrill of the new single to come out.

Over the weekend of December 8th and 9th the group returned to the Oasis club in Manchester, and also welcomed George Martin to the Cavern to see them perform. The Oasis performance was their penultimate show at the prestige Manchester club and their second appearance there in four months. There was one major difference. On the previous appearance in September the group were proudly introducing their new record. This time they were playing their hit record, 'Love Me Do', and the approval and the reaction of the audience reflected the change. On the first Oasis appearance just ten months earlier there had been a sparse crowd in the club, several of whom were slightly jaundiced or cynical Manchester group members dismissively eager to see what the fuss was about this group from Liverpool.

By December, with a record in the charts, and radio and tv appearances, and a definite buzz about the group, things were different. The Oasis was packed, as was the Cavern on the following evening when Brian Epstein had the pleasure of taking George Martin and Judy Lockhart-Smith to the club to see the group perform in its natural habitat. And ironically, that visit came almost a year to the day after the trip to the Cavern by Decca A&R man, Mike Smith. Whilst there, the party were introduced to the young cloakroom attendant, Priscilla White who, within a few months, was to change her name to Cilla Black and start a meteoric journey of her own.

Just ten days after Martin's visit to the Cavern, the group, extremely reluctantly, had to leave England again for a Hamburg booking, although this would be the final one. It was increased money, and a short, 13-day engagement, but there was clear resentment at having to abandon the growing excitement back at home.

There were no surprises, no disasters, in Hamburg on that final trip, just a growing sense that the days at the Star Club and the Indra, the Kaiserkeller and the Top Ten were ending, and that the bright, bright promises offered by Epstein in the contract which they had signed in January 1962 were being realised.

And so they entered 1963, the year when they would achieve their first Number One record, and several others, and the year when the term Beatlemania came into common currency. If there was a year when the swinging sixties began, when the old order was overthrown, and when Britain was changed irrevocably, then it was 1963.

But that was also the year when the second contractual time bomb, Northern Songs, was introduced, with painful, costly and wounding consequences for the principals for many, many years.

Although, as ever, it didn't seem like that at the start. Somehow with Brian Epstein's endeavours it never did.

The year started auspiciously with the release of the second single from the group, 'Please Please Me' on January 11th. George Martin had stated publicly that he thought this release would bring the group their first Number One.

Once again a number of unrelated factors conspired to help the group. The day the single was released was deep into one of the coldest winters ever recorded. Indeed that January was the coldest month of the 20th century. Heavy snowfalls which had started across the country just after Christmas had drifted and frozen, making roads impassable and many communities isolated.

One of the consequences of this was that many people across Britain became almost housebound, only venturing out for essential purposes.

Once again this was a period long before multiple sources of in-home entertainment. Not every home possessed one television set let alone two, and there were no digital entertainment devices like X-boxes or Playstations or the Wii.

The result was that television, and, to a somewhat lesser extent, radio was the major entertainment outlet for people across Britain. And so, in the midst of the blizzards and the snowdrifts and the plummeting temperatures, the broadcast of Thank Your Lucky Stars on Saturday January 19th was seen by a larger audience than usual. Because of the exclusively pop content the audience was primarily young and, critically, for most of them, this would be their first sight of the Beatles.

The show featured acts miming to their current single and so the Beatles, thanks to Dick James' inspired call in November, were there to mime to 'Please Please Me'. The rest of the bill demonstrates just what a turning point this was. Chris Barber's Jazz Band, Mike Berry, Acker Bilk, The Brook Brothers, Petula Clark, Alma Cogan, David McBeth, Frankie Vaughan and Mark Wynter with Sam Costa appearing as guest DJ. It was a line-up that creaked of the late fifties with only the Beatles as a name to represent the imminent changes.

The show was recorded on the previous Sunday at the ABC studios in Aston, Birmingham with the Beatles, clearly bottom of the bill, miming to the new record, 'Please Please Me', to close the first segment of the programme and lead into the commercial break.

The broadcast lasted from 5.50pm to 6.30pm on the Saturday evening on a day which had seen the winter bite even more fiercely. All football games on that day were cancelled because of the weather, leading to the introduction of the Pools Panel, a novel format which has remained in place ever since.

So that first broadcast on Thank Your Lucky Stars came on a bitterly cold night with most of the potential audience not able to get out, or cosily disinclined to leave home. It was a perfect captive audience, and the Beatles made the most of it.

Philip Jones, the tv producer persuaded by Dick James to take a chance on the Beatles, was impressed by the impact the group made that winter night. So much so that, besides their other individual performances on the programme, Jones compiled a special under the Summer Spin banner which totally involved Liverpool acts.

Headlined by the Beatles the show, broadcast on June 29th, showcased Gerry and the Pacemakers, the Searchers, Billy J. Kramer and the Dakotas, Lee Curtis, the Big Three, Kenneth Cope and the Breakaways, and the Vernon Girls, and attracted more than six million viewers.

By then though, the role and status of the Beatles in the national consciousness had changed. Not as massively or comprehensively as it would by the end of the year, but the summer of 1963 saw the beginning of the real madness.

Thanks in no small part to the developments during the early months of the year. 'Please Please Me' rapidly became a major hit, number one in many UK charts but only number two in the prestigious Record Retailer chart.

But the success of the single, and the increasingly frantic reaction to live performances around the country, persuaded EMI and George Martin to make a dramatic move. After a hit single, especially in an environment where record companies wanted to make a killing on short-term pop success, the imperative was to get an album released. George Martin had already been considering such a move and indeed his trip to the Cavern in December been with half a mind to recording the group live in their natural habitat.

That idea was rejected and so Martin summoned the group back to Abbey Road on Monday, February 11th where, in three sessions over that single day, the group recorded what was to all intents and purposes their live act. In less than ten hours they managed to produce what is, fifty years later, still one of the most energetic, effervescent and exciting debut albums ever.

Naturally the album climbed to the top of the LP charts by May and stayed at the top for almost eight months until it was replaced by the Beatles next LP. Such chart domination was surprising and unexpected, because in those days the album chart was invariably dominated by film soundtracks like "West Side Story" and easy-listening material from the likes of the George Mitchell Minstrels. In January and February there were several events which were to impact on the group in the future. In late January an obscure American label, Vee-Jay, was given permission to release Beatles records in America, while back in the UK the group's live performances were now restricted almost entirely to theatres and cinemas. The small clubs were rapidly being phased out and it is a matter of record that the group made six appearances at the Cavern in January, just three in February and then none at all in March.

Those intimate, sweaty club shows had been replaced by major theatre tours organised by Epstein in conjunction with significant industry figures like Arthur Howe. This move up the performance food chain was another demonstration of Epstein's growing influence and the increasing importance of the Beatles. The sequence started with a tour headlined by Helen Shapiro, also featuring Danny Williams, Kenny Lynch, the Kestrels, and the Red Price Orchestra, and it was while they were on that initial tour that news of their first number one came through.

It was during that period that Epstein received an important phone call at the family home in Liverpool. His mother, Queenie, took the call and spent a couple of minutes speaking to the stranger on the other end of the call. Then she called her son who was upstairs. When he got to the phone, the call turned out to be overseas, from America, from somebody called Sid Bernstein.

To Epstein's amazement Sid Bernstein was offering to stage the Beatles in New York, in the august surroundings of Carnegie Hall. It isn't difficult to imagine the tremendous sense of vindication that Epstein must have felt to have even an enquiry being made about putting his group on in America - and in Carnegie Hall, of all places. He learned a lot about Bernstein in that brief conversation, about his period in England during the Second World War, about his love for Britain and everything British, and about the fact that he picked up English papers every week from a pavement seller in New York.

It was reading those English newspapers that made Bernstein first recognise the name of the Beatles, and then increasing mentions made him suspect that something significant was happening. And that realisation led him to make the call to Brian Epstein. There was a real irony in the way Bernstein had got hold of Epstein's number. On one of his walks around New York he had bumped into an old associate named Bud Halliwell who was then engaged as an independent trying to get radio airplay for a new group called the Beatles. He told Bernstein what a fruitless task it was, but Bernstein took the opportunity to work through Halliwell's contacts - Transglobal then EMI then NEMS - until he got the number of the Epstein family home.

Despite his surprise and delight at even speaking to someone from New York about the Beatles, it is a matter of fact that Epstein was initially suspicious if not dismissive about Bernstein's offer. Not because of any animosity between the men, for, as most of his associates would confirm, it was very, very difficult to dislike Sid Bernstein. No, the concern in Epstein's mind was simple and very pragmatic. He was struggling and failing to get any interest in the group in America with EMI's affiliate, Capitol, turning down each release from the Beatles.

That was the reality. And yet this American, this thoroughly engaging American, was offering to put on the group at possibly the most prestigious venue in America.

It was nonsense, delirious, exciting nonsense, but not something Epstein intended to allow as a diversion. He concluded the call in his usual charming way but not until he had yielded to Bernstein's pressure about the American date. Epstein agreed that if and when the Beatles ever made it to America then Bernstein would have sole rights to promote a concert by the group at Carnegie Hall. In response to Bernstein's gentle urgings Epstein agreed to a date in the following year, February 12th 1964, Lincoln's birthday, with Bernstein reasoning that the public holiday would mean that all the kids would be out of school.

No contract for, as Bernstein would discover, there was no need for a written contract with Brian Epstein in such situations. His word truly was his bond, but once the call finished Epstein forgot about the engaging American. There were much bigger matters to handle.

Sometime in February 1963 Epstein and Dick James had a conversation about a new business venture which had painful ramifications that are still being felt and suffered today.

As ever, it started innocently and with the best of intentions. The idea was to create a structure which would protect the Beatles, primarily John Lennon and Paul McCartney's, songs in terms of music publishing. The result was the suggestion of forming a separate company to handle those song publishing issues.

Although song publishing had always been a very lucrative aspect of the music industry it was a source of mystery to most people. Indeed when McCartney and Lennon were first confronted by the machinations of song publishing, McCartney expressed bewilderment that money could be obtained from a song, as opposed to a record. He believed that music, in the form of songs, was free and that it was impossible for somebody - individual or company - to own music. He was wrong and it was a bitter and expensive lesson to be learned.

Much as I searched, there was no proof, nothing to indicate who, Epstein or James, first suggested the forming of a company to handle the Beatles song publishing. Most likely it emerged from a succession of phone calls and meetings following on the release and success of 'Please Please Me', with the critical meeting taking place on Sunday, February 17th at Teddington where the Beatles were recording another session for Thank Your Lucky Stars.

This, the group's second appearance on the show in just over a month, featured them miming again to 'Please Please Me' in an edition broadcast the following weekend, February 19th.

The backstage discussions about music publishing took place in a very convivial atmosphere. Philip Jones, the producer, was delighted by the excitement created around his programme by the Beatles who had been suggested to him by his friend, Dick James. In turn James was very happy because the single 'Please Please Me' was already a hit, there was an album on the way, and the rights to the music publishing granted to him by Epstein in November promised to do quite well for him.

And, yet again, Brian Epstein had every reason to be thrilled. His group, his boys, had recorded a song which was threatening to be a sizeable hit, and just five days earlier they had recorded a remarkable debut LP in one day at Abbey Road. They were now moved onto a fresh performance level, appearing mainly at concert halls and city centre cinemas, and they were making frequent appearances on television and radio, promoting the name of the group without the need for arduous, time-consuming and costly personal appearances.

From Epstein's perspective, everything he had contemplated a year earlier when discussing a contract with the Beatles was being triumphantly realised. And now his new associate, Dick James was suggesting a venture which would cement Epstein even more permanently in the regard and the unquestioned debt of his boys. A company to administer the music publishing for the group; security, control and, critically, a step which few songwriters other than the legendary Irving Berlin had contemplated, let alone achieved.

I knew a few horror stories about music publishing, such as all the hit songs Elvis Presley allegedly co-wrote, but it wasn't until I embarked on that element of the research that I realised what a venomous snake-pit music publishing could be.

From the earliest days of rock 'n' roll there were instances of young enthusiasm being cynically exploited by businessmen. One of Chuck Berry's earliest hits, 'Maybellene', bore the names of Alan Freed and Russ Fratto as well as Berry's as writers. This was a legal as well as a creative nonsense, but that was, quite simply and cynically, the way things were done.

Perhaps the best example of how tawdry these affairs could become comes in the story of Morris Levy. He was the classic example of a New York businessman with close ties to the Mob, closely linked to Gaetano 'Tommy the Big Guy' Vastola, a brutal member of the DeCavalcante Mafia family. Levy had also grown up with Vincent "the Chin" Gigante, who would eventually power his way to becoming the head of the Genovese family.

Levy ran Roulette Records and the famous Birdland club, and conned and cheated and extorted money from hundreds in the entertainment industry. There were dozens of examples but perhaps the most scandalous involved the hit record, 'Why Do Fools Fall in Love'. This record, the lasting memorial to Frankie Lymon and the Teenagers, was number one in both the R&B and the pop charts, and was a million-seller in 1956. Though written collectively by Lymon and group members Herman Santiago and Jimmy Merchant, the writing of the song was credited to Frankie Lymon and Morris Levy and Allan Freed.

Although Frankie Lymon & The Teenagers did get paid pittances for their stage appearances, Frankie and the members of the group never saw a penny from record sales, juke box or radio plays, nor publishing shares, which were owned by Freed and Levy, who would eventually be indicted by the Federal Authorities on charges of racketeering and tax evasion.

It is a matter of fact that neither of these gentlemen wrote a note of the melody or a word of the lyric. The whole song, still played on radio and featuring in compilations to this day, was created by Frankie Lymon, Herman Santiago and Jimmy Merchant.

But a man who would copyright the term "rock and roll" and then charge record companies a fee for using it, was not a man to be lightly challenged. The mob background of many characters in the East Coast music industry in the fifties and early sixties meant that organised crime was drawn to the entertainment world as a source of glamour, excitement and, most critically, huge revenues. Music publishing was just one of the most attractive areas and so the mob families placed a stranglehold around many entertainment activities. As far back as the mid-Forties Meyer Lansky was in charge of the Emby Distributing Co., which controlled every Wurlitzer jukebox in the New York area, a nickel-in-the-slot empire he divided among the henchmen of Luciano, Joe Adonis, Longie Zwillman and others. For his part Lansky was a notorious figure in the world of organized crime, reputed to be the mob's chief banker and the man who had helped to create the mob's assassination department Murder Inc. He had seen the potential for rich returns from the music industry, and those lessons were eagerly learned by younger followers like Morris Levy.

While running the famous Birdland club in New York, Levy had been outraged then angered and finally fascinated by repeated demands from ASCAP representatives for royalties to be paid for the music played at the club. Once he had been assured that this wasn't a scam or a shakedown but was a legitimate feature of the music industry he became greedily captivated by the revenue potential of music publishing.

That interest led to a series of ventures which made Levy an immensely powerful name in the music industry particularly on the East Coast. He started a publishing company called Patricia Music, and rapidly secured the rights to all the songs first performed in the Birdland club, with this catalogue including the venue's soon-to-be-famous 'Lullaby of Birdland'. His music publishing interests grew considerably when he acquired the Big Seven Music catalogue which included more than 30,000 titles including 'The Yellow Rose Of Texas'.

Levy salted away his royalties and negotiated a substantial loan from Thomas Eboli of the Genovese crime family. He used the money to start a vinyl label called Roulette Records with George Goldner and Joe Kolsky in 1957. Some of the stories about Levy's activities at Roulette are truly horrific. The violence - baseball bat beatings and murders were commonplace as were savage attacks like the one inflicted on recording star Jimmie Rodgers in 1957. And Rodgers' crime which resulted in his being left for dead by the side of the road in the San Fernando Valley? He chose to take himself off the Roulette label at the end of his contract and go elsewhere.

Other of Morris Levy's actions were less gruesome and more amusing. When the same Jimmy Rodgers released an album of seasonal songs in 1959 titled "It's Christmas Once Again" the album included among its mix of secular and sacred the timeless 'Silent Night'. Early releases of the album betrayed the startling news that the composer of this Christmas perennial was one Morris Levy!

Levy's involvement in the seedier side of the music business ran through the sixties, but I came across one interesting titbit of information which got me thinking. Levy and Roulette were subjected to an inventory by an aggressive young accountant who was trying to retrieve monies allegedly owed to two of his clients, Jimmy Bowen and Buddy Knox. The accountant's name was Allen Klein and the bravado he showed in standing up to the fearsome Levy got him at least part of the royalties he was seeking for Bowen and Knox. Besides the 25% off the top which Klein freely admitted was his commission, the story of the young accountant who had entered the lion's den, challenged the lion and emerged semi-victorious and, crucially, with all his limbs intact, made Klein's reputation in New York music circles. Before long he was acting for names like Bobby Darin, Lloyd Price and Bobby Vinton as well as the Shirelles' label, Scepter Records, and those successes led directly to his acting in a management capacity for Sam Cooke.

Besides his minor role in launching the career of Allen Klein, it is clear that Levy was involved in a number of other dubious and shady activities involving music and the music industry. The most famous tax scam label, Tiger Lily, was a subsidiary of Roulette, and the federal authorities reckon conservatively that millions of dollars were siphoned away from legitimacy via these shadowy non-releases. This, of course, doesn't include the revenues lost by artists, rock, pop and even comedy, who invariably had no idea that they had an album on release on Roulette or one of its murky subsidiaries.

Morris Levy came to impact on the Beatles' story long after the break-up of the group when he sued John Lennon in 1973 for plagiarism of part of the lyric in 'Come Together'. The contention of the lawsuit was that Lennon had used two lines from Chuck Berry's 'You Can't Catch Me' as part of the lyric on his song which opened the album, "Abbey Road".

The case was rapidly settled out of court by Lennon's representatives, but the settlement moved into very strange territory. Rather than demand the usual capital amount Levy insisted that Lennon should record three more songs from the Big Seven Music catalogue. It was this unusual agreement that prompted Lennon to produce his "Rock 'n' Roll" album in 1975. This album, a nostalgic re-working of rock numbers important to Lennon in his youth, was intended to honour the agreement with Levy but problems arose when the album's producer, Phil Spector, had one of his spurts of irrational behaviour and kidnapped the master tapes.

Without the completed masters Lennon's record company, Capitol, were in no position to release the "Rock 'n' Roll" album and so it was delayed. To such an extent that Lennon released another album, "Walls and Bridges", in the interim but during that period the enterprising Levy had obtained demo tapes recorded by Lennon of some of the "Rock 'n' Roll" material and he proceeded to issue a completely illegal album under the title, "Roots".

This concoction was advertised as a mail order tv compilation and rapidly attracted counter law suits from Capitol and from Lennon. The result was an unseemly mess which gave none of the parties any complete satisfaction or comfort, but this was evidence of yet another link between Levy and the Beatles. This link was made even more vibrant given that part of Levy's evidence supporting his claim to be allowed to issue the "Roots" album came from a lengthy interview given by Allen Klein.

I started thinking about Morris Levy purely in terms of music publishing when I was researching the genesis of Northern Songs, and stumbled across that early connection with Allen Klein, but it was quite some time later, and several New York visits, before I began to understand the grim significance of the mafia connection to Brian Epstein, and the lasting significance of names like Morris Levy and Salvatore James Pisello and Stan Polley.

That lay in the future. At that time I was far more concerned to understand what had happened at the birth of Northern Songs especially given the rancour and viciousness which lay in the future for the participants.

It's hard to imagine that the initial idea for a publishing company didn't come from Dick James. After all he was the man directly involved in that side of the business with the kind of intimate insider's knowledge denied to Brian Epstein. Whatever the circumstances it is a reasonable conclusion to draw that the substantive discussions about the new venture took place in the studio complex at Teddington where Thank Your Lucky Stars was being recorded. The timing is relevant because five days later, on February 22nd 1963 John Lennon and Paul McCartney met Epstein and his lawyer in Liverpool to sign the documents which effectively set up Northern Songs. As ever they didn't read the legal documents. There was no need to - Brian Epstein was their manager working on their behalf. Their interests were obviously being protected!

And so, innocently and naively, they signed a document, a legally-binding document, which gave 49% of the new company to Lennon, McCartney and Epstein with the remaining, the critical 51% majority shareholding, in the hands of Dick James and his somewhat mysterious business partner, Charles Silver.

At the start the initial share capital for Northern Songs was £100 in £1 shares. Dick James received 25 per cent of the shares, with an equal amount taken by accountant and financial partner, Silver. Of the remaining 50% shareholding Lennon and McCartney were each given 20%, and Epstein received 10%. Northern Songs was to be administered by the company Dick James Music, with directors Brian Epstein and Dick James, and, not surprisingly, a hefty administration fee was to be charged by Dick James Music.

At the start of the process both George Harrison and Ringo Starr were also contracted to Northern Songs. As the Epstein empire expanded, Dick James also began to separately handle music publishing for other NEMS acts like Gerry and the Pacemakers and Billy J Kramer and the Dakotas. And, knowing how successful that NEMS stable was during those frantic middle years of the sixties, it isn't difficult to imagine what success, what prestige, what wealth that association brought to Dick James. Truly the proverbial lottery winner!

Yet the amount of work he put into the Beatles and Epstein's other acts can't be denied, and during 1963 and 1964 James became accepted and trusted by the Beatles and Brian Epstein. He created a publicity wave behind the songs which in turn helped Lennon and McCartney achieve one of their ambitions by seeing established stars recording their songs. James was also meticulous and invaluable in the administration of the process, ensuring that over-recording of specific numbers didn't happen whilst carefully controlling the observance of embargoes on the playing of new releases.

The Beatles couldn't and wouldn't have concerned themselves with these tasks; Brian Epstein couldn't and wouldn't have tried to do it, and so Dick James performed an essential, invaluable service, particularly during those frantic, frenzied years in the mid-sixties.

In addition, it is clear that James also acted in the capacity of a business advisor to Epstein, particularly as his interest in America grew. James provided an introduction for Epstein to the New York attorney Walter Hofer, who would play a major role in the development of the Beatles links in the US.

But the critical importance of Dick James lay in his involvement with the Lennon-McCartney catalogue. Even a cursory glance at the way that Beatles songs became accepted into the mainstream of both performance and recordings during the sixties show how successful Dick James was at getting the bandwagon moving. So, for every example of a crassly-commercial cashing-in on the new phenomenon from England, for example "The Chipmunks Sing The Beatles Hits", which appeared in 1964, there came in the same year the seminal Ella Fitzgerald swing version of 'Can't Buy Me Love'; and there were a host of recordings from established names, artists like Sammy Davis Jnr., and Petula Clark and the Beach Boys - none of whom needed to jump on any short-lived bandwagon.

Of course the major factor was, and would always be, the quality of the songs, but it took the dogged skills of someone versed in the music publishing world to alert the world to the riches of the Lennon-McCartney catalogue and, for a brief, lucrative period, Dick James was that man.

Sadly though for his colleagues in the music publishing world the success of Dick James with the Beatles catalogue also contributed largely to the destruction of that world. Of course, music publishing continued after Dick James, and indeed music publishing flourishes to this day, but it is a very different animal to the time when Northern Songs was born.

But it is very difficult to recognise the range of services Dick James performed and simultaneously accept that these services were worth 50% of the shareholding in Northern Songs, let alone the countless millions that his work for Northern Songs delivered.

And yet, as I came to discover in so many instances of Epstein's business practices, it is all too easy to be smug, to be all-seeing, in hindsight. In the case of the Dick James involvement whatever the genesis of Northern Songs it can't be denied that Dick James was, for whatever motive, trying to be fair towards the group at least from his perspective and according to the standard practices of the time. On the basis of a standard song-writing contract, Dick James Music could expect to receive 10% of the retail price of sheet music, which was still a valuable entity at that time, plus up to 50% of the royalty on cover versions of all songs.

Instead he set up with Epstein a company into which all revenue from the Lennon-McCartney song-writing would go. And the percentages were determined as 50% to Dick James, 20% each to John Lennon and Paul McCartney and the remaining 10% to Brian Epstein.

Looked at coldly, without the knowledge of what lay ahead for the Lennon-McCartney catalogue, this was a creative and not ungenerous proposition. Dick James was agreeing to take a chance, to work effectively for nothing, in the hope that this relatively unknown group would turn into something special.

And it has to be recognised that most artists desperately needed the expert services of someone versed in the business of music publishing. In the fifties and the early sixties it was song publishing, not records, where songwriters made a lot of their revenue, but anybody who wrote songs for a living needed a good publisher. The alternative was to get screwed.

The publisher would oversee getting the song publicized, printed and sold - which meant a lot of money in the days when the home parlour piano was still serious competition to records and record players, and sheet music sales were still considerable. In addition, the publisher would market the song around to any recording artists, who might cover it, via contacts like George Martin, and this made the song an even more lucrative proposition. And finally the publisher would oversee the bothersome job of collecting all royalties from sales of sheet music, other artists' cover versions, and any other income that a song might generate - apart from the actual sale of records.

These were skills which Dick James palpably displayed, and he had come with the inestimable recommendation of George Martin.

One of Brian Epstein's most commendable qualities was his ability to recognise areas in which he had little or no expertise, and to delegate authority for these tasks to trusted others. In truth, this often involved areas in which he had little or no interest, but the result was that people like Dick James were granted entry to the inner circle and significant power simply because they were liked and trusted by Epstein.

In years to come, the Northern Songs situation would become vicious when characters like Lew Grade and Michael Jackson and Rupert Holmes á Court entered the story, but such disasters weren't envisaged when Northern Songs was first set up. Like so many ventures it began with high hopes and arguably the best of intentions, but the two major parties in the transaction, John Lennon and Paul McCartney, were trustingly and naively unaware of the ramifications of the contract they signed.

The company's shares were to be owned for a period of 10 years. There was a commitment to expand the catalogue annually, and a minimum of six new songs were to be written each year by Lennon and McCartney. The monies which would be gathered by Northern Songs were to be channelled into a second company, Lenmac Enterprises with an ownership roster of 40% each for Lennon and McCartney with NEMS having the remaining 20%. Crucially the company would only collect profits from the UK, and a separate company, Maclen Music, was set up subsequently to handle the publishing in the US.

Maclen was a vehicle to publish songs written by John Lennon and Paul McCartney and for the whole of its existence that was all the company did - with one exception. As I was to learn later in my investigations Maclen would publish just one song not written by Lennon and McCartney, and that song, for various reasons, would add to the mystery surrounding the reputed death of McCartney.

Maclen and Northern Songs were administered by Dick James Music for a healthy administration fee, and these monies became part of the open wound which would fester and then explode so spectacularly five years later.

In essence, despite the intricacies of the legal scaffolding which was erected around the Beatles in the form of a myriad of companies the important relationship in terms of music publishing was between Northern Songs and Maclen. And, stripping away all the verbiage and the personality disputes, the simple fact was that Northern was nothing more than a simple distributor for Maclen (Music) Ltd., and that company would continue to provide the Beatles with an income from songs regardless of which entity controlled Northern.

The other critical legal venture in 1963 was the formation of the first Beatles company, Beatles Ltd, which was formed in June 1963 with a minimal share capital of £100 which was split equally between the four members of the group.

The Beatles Limited, the company, was established by Epstein to handle the group's business and legal affairs. This inadvertently created a new, and extra, layer of complexity given that NEMS Enterprises, Epstein's own company, was already providing a number of those functions.

Nevertheless, as with everything in that extraordinary period, the move was made with the best of intentions. The new company was to be a simple partnership which allowed each of the members of the group to have a defined stake in their future success. The agreement also provided a planned future benefit in that it would ensure that each Beatle would enjoy tax benefits commensurate with a directorship in a limited company.

The company, The Beatles Ltd, would last almost four years before being replaced by The Beatles & Co, which in turn transformed into Apple Corps., but this was many millions and many heartaches later.

But during those frenetic months in the middle of 1963 there were no clouds capable of blotting out the Beatles sunshine. Two massively prestigious shows in April demonstrated the incredible development. On April 18th the group made their first appearance on a big show at the Royal Albert Hall, on a bill which resembled the last stirrings of a Variety edge to showbiz which only had a few months of life left. Del Shannon and the Springfields shared the famous stage with Rolf Harris and Lance Percival with the whole mish-mash, including the Beatles, introduced by George Melly. The show was a BBC broadcast under the ungainly title of "Swinging Sound '63" and, apart from the glamour of the location was largely unremarkable but for two small meetings after the show.

Del Shannon was introduced to John Lennon in the dressing rooms and told Lennon that he was going to cover 'From Me to You' to give the Beatles some exposure in America. Although Lennon rapidly cooled on the advisability of such promotion, Del Shannon recorded and released the track on Bigtop Records, and achieved the distinction of taking the very first Lennon-McCartney composition into the US charts.

The second casual meeting would prove to be even more significant as that was the first time that Paul McCartney met Jane Asher, the young actress who would play such a prominent part in his life for the next five years. She was attending the concert with a representative of Radio Times, reporter Tony Aspler, to provide first-hand impressions of the show. She performed a similar "voice of the younger set" role in several appearances on Juke Box Jury in the early sixties.

Three days after the Albert Hall the group took part in a mammoth show which in many ways came to symbolise the innocence and grandeur of the sixties. The New Musical Express staged their 1962–63 Annual Poll-Winners' All-Star Concert at the Empire Pool, Wembley, with Cliff Richard and The Shadows topping the bill.

This was truly the peak of the popularity of Cliff and the Shadows with the Wembley concert coming on the back of the release, just three months earlier, of the seminal film "Summer Holiday", which represented innocent, virginal pop in a way that the Beatles were shortly to grind into dust.

For their part, the Beatles were second on the bill despite their glaring absence from the poll results, but their rise was, and continued to be, so meteoric that it was genuinely difficult for the media to keep up.

In mid-May the group embarked on their third national tour, this time headlined by the peerless Roy Orbison. Also on the bill were Gerry and the Pacemakers, David Macbeth and Louise Cordet, and, though Orbison rightly started out closing the shows, the growing clamour for the Beatles meant that that positions on the bill had to be changed, if only to cope with the building frenzy provided by the audiences, mainly female, who came for the Beatles.

It was that tour which first alerted Fleet Street to the new phenomena. The first pictures of screaming girls and prostrate Beatles fans began to appear on front pages of newspapers but the first documented use of the term "Beatlemania" was several months away. But nobody who witnessed any of those spring concerts, least of all the laconic Roy Orbison, could be in any doubt that something extraordinary was happening.

These shows were invariably in major cinemas in the centre of large towns and these Gaumonts, Odeons and Granadas provided a degree of opulence far away from the sweaty underground rooms in which the group had honed their craft. Another demonstration of the rocketing pace underneath the group came on the afternoon of May 24th, a few hours before their appearance on the Roy Orbison bill at the Gaumont in Walthamstow.

The setting was the charming Aeolian Hall in central London which had been a BBC studio from the war years, and would continue in this vein for another twelve years. In May 1963 the Beatles embarked on their own radio series, Pop Go the Beatles, a massive step for a group with scarcely a handful of major media performances. Yet this once again demonstrated the way things were going for the group and particularly for their astute manager.

And as I was researching this amazing period in British history and marvelling at the sheer vibrancy of life at the time, I was struck by the surprising relevance of the political situation in the country to the emergence and development of the Beatles. My first point of contact was obviously in the UK, but a very similar point and set of circumstances would emerge a few months later in America, albeit in much more tragic circumstances.

The British political dimension was opened, at least to the public, on March 22nd 1963. On that day the Minister for War, a Conservative grandee named John Profumo, stood up in the House of Commons and denied that he had enjoyed a relationship with a known call girl, Christine Keeler.

This was untrue. Many people in the media knew it, and also many Members of Parliament. The denial in March set Profumo on an inevitable slippery slope to exposure and disgrace. That came effectively with his admission in early June to lying in and to the House of Commons which brought his resignation as Minister for War and also from the Commons. The disgrace and the ending of a highly promising political career were the public-facing face of a malaise which had afflicted Britain through the fifties and early sixties. The sense of a ruling class, with little or no understanding of how most of the country lived or thought. Of landed gentries and old people like SuperMac and Sir Alec Douglas-Home. Of grand country houses and outdoor pools and people well outside the remit of the ordinary person in Britain.

It would be untrue to state that the Profumo affair cast a shadow over the country. Instead there was a sniggering distaste at the toffs and the way they behaved, a realisation that there were two worlds in operation in Britain, where the main one, the important one, the overwhelming one, was populated and dominated by old, grey men.

That was the fact, the undeniable fact. But then came the Beatles. And in a wave of colourful, irreverent but above all youthful endeavour much of the mustiness exposed by the Profumo affair was swept aside. And it was darkly ironic that two years later, in the filming of "Help" the group would come to use Cliveden, location for Profumo's ominous first encounter with Christine Keeler, as the replacement for Buckingham Palace.

And this demonstration of the irresistible capacity of the group to lift the mood of a nation would be demonstrated again in less than a year on a different continent, and in much more sombre circumstances.

But before that, Epstein's plan for the Beatles still had several stages to run. An important milestone came in May when the debut album, "Please Please Me" went to the top of the charts in the UK. This in itself was auspicious. A first album by a new group reaching the top of the charts was an unprecedented event, made even more remarkable when that same album stayed in the number one position for the following thirty weeks.

At the same time that the "Please Please Me" album reached the top of the album chart the group's third single, 'From Me To You' hit the top of the singles chart, and with a sweet irony displaced their NEMS stable mates, Gerry and the Pacemakers from the top spot. The Pacemakers were enjoying their first number one, and this was with 'How Do You Do It?', the same song that George Martin had been so keen for the Beatles to record as their first single.

And the singles chart on June 15th 1963 was able to feature three acts managed by Brian Epstein occupying the top three positions. Below 'From Me To You' came Gerry and the Pacemakers with their second disc, 'I Like It', which was destined to reach the top the following week. The third position was taken by Billy J. Kramer and the Dakotas with the Lennon and McCartney number, 'Do You Want to Know a Secret'.

This was a remarkable feat for any manager, let alone one as new to the game as Brian Epstein. This was the week when attention began to turn to the quiet northerner, to the impressive stable of acts he was building, and to the dramatic impact he was having on the worlds of pop and entertainment.

He continued working his major charges hard throughout that summer, believing that extensive exposure would lock the group in the national consciousness. That was certainly happening, thanks to the frantic touring, interspersed with regular tv and radio broadcasts.

But maintaining the commercial momentum meant regular single releases and, once 'From Me To You' had peaked in early June, thoughts turned inevitably to the next single which would be scheduled for late summer or early autumn release. And so, in the wearying hours before a concert at the Majestic Ballroom in Newcastle upon Tyne on June 26th, John Lennon and Paul McCartney took up their acoustic guitars and put together the song which came to identify and personify the early years of the Beatles. 'She Loves You' was more than a pop record and its success on many different levels utterly transcended its simple life as a pop record.

Not least for the press, now starting to realise that something remarkable was beginning to happen around the UK, prompted by the musical talents of the Merseyside group. The hook line from 'She Loves You', 'Yeah, Yeah, Yeah' was to become shorthand for a lifestyle, for a mentality that grew up in the second half of 1963, all still under the careful control of Brian Epstein who was already looking for greater challenges than just chart domination in the UK.

July 1963 was the month that things began to seriously change. On the 1st of the month the group returned to Abbey Road to record 'She Loves You' along with 'Get You In The End', later to become better known and loved as 'I'll Get You', the b-side of 'She Loves You'.

The 1st of July was a Monday. The song had only been written five days earlier yet such was the frantic pressure on their schedule that it had become a pragmatic question of fitting things in whenever time allowed. It is a matter of record that George Martin wasn't overly impressed with 'She Loves You' thinking it slightly hackneyed and corny. Fortunately for the Beatles and for pop history both Lennon and particularly Paul McCartney disagreed and won the day.

July 22nd should have seen the release of the first ever Beatles album in the States. The Vee-Jay label, exercising their rights to distribute Beatles material in the States were preparing and intending to put out an album entitled

"Introducing the Beatles", which would have been exactly the same as the "Please Please Me" album in the UK but for the fact that two tracks were omitted. To maintain the American practice of having twelve tracks on an album, two of the original fourteen tracks had to go and 'Please Please Me' and 'Ask Me Why' were chosen. This was the start of an ungainly process in which every Beatles album in the States was different from the equivalent release in America up to Sergeant Pepper in 1967.

Popular mythology now has Vee-Jay as a novelty, unimportant label, and yet one of the most surprising and gratifying aspects of my research into the Beatles history was to learn how unfairly Vee-Jay has been treated. Far from an insignificant label, Vee-Jay was for a number of years one of the most significant independent labels in America. Any label promoting artists like Jimmy Reed, Jerry Butler, John Lee Hooker and the Four Seasons cannot be described as insignificant.

The group arrived on Vee-Jay as a result of record company politics. EMI's label in the States was Capitol but they had regularly turned down the Beatles. In the end, Sir Joseph Lockwood and L. G. Wood sent EMI staffer, Roland Rennie, over to the States to see if anything could be done. In New York he met up with Paul Marshall, the entertainment lawyer who represented EMI in America. Rennie and Marshall made the painful rounds of the Capitol people, the men like Dave Dexter, who had rejected the Beatles, but realised with painful certainty that there was no way forward with Capitol.

Rennie flew back to London and reported the gloomy conclusions to Lockwood, but to everyone's surprise Lockwood decided that the best way forward was for Rennie to base himself in the States, work with Paul Marshall, and handle the distribution problems at source.

The result was that Rennie moved to the States in the summer of 1963 with his wife and child and various pieces of furniture and, with the priceless help of Paul Marshall, expanded the activities of Trans-Global Music.

And so EMI subsequently asked their affiliate agency Transglobal to find an American label prepared to release the Beatles material. 'Please Please Me' was the first title offered and Transglobal, whose role was simply to place UK master recordings with American labels, began to offer the Beatles to record labels in an uncomfortable echo of Epstein's courting of UK labels in the previous year.

Atlantic turned down 'Please Please Me' and there are rumours that other labels like Columbia also passed on the opportunity. The result was that the deal was done with Vee-Jay on a simply expedient basis. They were available, and keen, unlike the giants of the American music industry.

Ironically the Beatles came to Vee-Jay as a throwaway, an add-on to sweeten the main part of the deal which allowed Vee-Jay to market a record which had recently gone to the top of the charts in Britain, the yodelling epic 'I Remember You' by Frank Ifield.

So little importance was attached to the group or the release that when 'Please Please Me' was released in America on VJ 498 in February the label even spelt the name of the group wrongly, inserting an extra "t" into the name as "The Beattles". More importantly the song did attract some local attention in the Chicago area, particularly on the top-40 station WLS, and even appeared on their top-40 charts for two weeks. This was therefore the first ever top-40 appearance, albeit strictly local, for the Beatles in the US.

That set the tone and so, when the first album material was available from the UK, the label quite properly took the chance to market the album. Pressing information, including an acetate produced by URC in Chicago, suggests an initial plan to release the album exactly following the number and order of tracks on the UK release.

For some reason that plan was abandoned and the album didn't formally appear until the following year when knowledge of and feelings about the Beatles were somewhat different in America.

Then the commercial problems which were swirling around the label came to the fore. During the spring and summer a series of rumours suggested that the label was suffering financial troubles, largely exacerbated by their deal with the Four Seasons.

It emerged that the deal left Vee-Jay losing a small, but appreciable, amount on every Four Seasons track that they sold. Given that the first three Four Seasons releases on Vee-Jay were million sellers it isn't difficult to imagine the scale of the problems.

Management shakeups followed rapidly, plus the departure of several artists. In the midst of this chaos EMI requested the release of Frank Ifield, fresh from his fourth UK number one, 'I'm Confessin', which had reached the top of the UK charts on July 13th.

Even though the release was granted, the administrative chaos at Vee-Jay meant that both they, and Capitol, released 'I'm Confessin', albeit with different b-sides. More significantly for the Beatles, the new Vee-Jay management team, now ensconced in some luxury in Los Angeles rather than Chicago, believed that the release of Frank Ifield also meant the release of the Beatles.

Whilst this would not have had serious repercussions for the label, at least from the perspective in August 1963, it was in this climate that "Introducing the Beatles" was scheduled and then cancelled.

The malaise at Vee-Jay deepened when they were effectively sued by the Four Seasons, the start of a depressing sequence during which, at one point, the label was involved in fighting and defending more than sixty lawsuits.

August in the UK was as frantic as ever for the group. On the first of the month came the publication of the first issue of the Beatles Monthly, an increasingly important publication for Beatles fans over the following five or six years. The idea of such a regular publication had been proposed to Epstein by a young publisher named Sean Mahoney, who was already responsible for another magazine called Beat Instrumental.

Epstein liked the idea and the magazine was commissioned with Mahoney acting as editor under the pseudonym of Johnny Dean. The launch on August 1st was for 80,000 copies; by the end of the year the print run had grown to 330,000 copies a month. Interestingly, and ominously, the magazine also included an advertisement, sanctioned by Brian Epstein, for the sale of official Beatles merchandise.

August 3rd represented a sad landmark, generally unnoticed at the time. On that date came the final Beatles appearance at the Cavern, after 291 previous shows of varying quality and growing importance. Bob Wooler, the Compere at the Cavern, claimed to remember Brian Epstein promising that the group would return to the Cavern, but it never happened.

In truth the group had simply outgrown the Cavern and indeed all of their traditional club circuit, and it is quite likely that Epstein was already aware that they had outgrown Liverpool as well.

The first manifestation of this change was a relocation to new premises in Liverpool at 24 Moonfields. Epstein took a staff of three to the new offices which were dedicated solely to NEMS activities, and had nothing whatsoever to do with the record shops which were rapidly receding in importance in Brian Epstein's life.

One of the first things they had to deal with was the distribution to the press the incredible news that the new Beatles single, 'She Loves You', had achieved advance orders ahead of release in excess of half a million!

By the 4th of September 'She Loves You' was at the top of the charts while the album, "Please Please Me", was enjoying its 24th consecutive week at the top of the album charts. This was timely as, during July and August, the group had been recording tracks for their second album, "With the Beatles".

Epstein kept the group to a punishing schedule which was a mixture of concert appearances, radio and tv recordings, and crucially Abbey Road recordings. Even for young men in their prime this was gruelling but they were sustained by the taste of immense popularity and success, plus the promise by Epstein of a guaranteed holiday period from the middle of September.

Before that Epstein managed another couple of major steps forward. On September 6th 1963 he announced the first Beatles Christmas show which would be staged at the Astoria, Finsbury Park with a bill comprising almost entirely NEMS acts. Such a show for a mere pop group was virtually unheard-of. There was a tradition of pop groups appearing in Christmas shows but these were almost always nothing but pantomimes, and indeed Epstein had already contracted for Gerry and the Pacemakers to appear in the pantomime "Babes in the Wood" at Stoke-on-Trent starting on Christmas Eve 1963.

On the same day that he announced the Beatles Christmas show, Brian Epstein added another talent to the NEMS roster in the form of Tommy Quickly, but still NEMS had no females. This prominent gap was filled when Epstein signed Priscilla White and persuaded her and her father that Cilla Black would indeed be a better stage name.

She obviously knew the Beatles and Gerry and the others from her time working at the Cavern, and so she was rapidly assimilated into the Epstein family. A Lennon-McCartney song, 'Love of the Loved', was quickly chosen for her first single, and she was rapidly added to the bill for the forthcoming Beatles Christmas Show. Of course, after a year managing the Beatles and taking them through the minefields of record companies and media access, it was much easier for Epstein to guide newcomers like Cilla Black and help them avoid some of the pitfalls which the Beatles had encountered during 1962. Inevitably the incredible success that Epstein's acts had enjoyed over the past year made it very difficult for anybody to turn him down, and thus doors were opened more quickly and easily for the likes of Cilla Black because of what Epstein had done before she emerged.

There was an urgent need to secure an American release for 'She Loves You' but the contractual problems with Vee-Jay ruled them out of consideration. Epstein asked Transglobal to source another label for him, and the result was Swan Records. The contract with Swan only entitled them to release that one single, and the period of the contract was limited to two years.

'She Loves You' was released in America on September 16th but attracted little attention. Radio airplay, still a major element in the success of a record at that time, was severely limited and the record lay dormant for several months until the explosion in interest in the group in America in the spring of 1964.

The final two weeks of September had been allocated as holidays for the group and they dispersed to various parts of the globe to enjoy their period away from the barrage of publicity. This period of tranquillity was not open to Epstein though. He stayed in Britain, still building the empire. One of the last things the group did collectively before departing was, however unlikely it sounds, to record four messages for broadcast by Australian DJs on stations around Australia. This process was a good example of Epstein's forward-thinking attitude to promotion and to the expansion of the group's international popularity.

As far back as early July 1963 Epstein had verbally committed to a concert tour of Australia in June 1964, and though the contract would not be formally signed until early December the recordings in September were intended to stoke up interest in the group in Australia before their arrival.

It was during this September period that the first rumours were heard about a move by the NEMS organisation from Liverpool to London and, though hastily denied, there were many who saw it as an inevitable step.

Late September also brought a rejection from Epstein of an offer to purchase NEMS. Though the bidder was never formally revealed it became clear in succeeding years that avaricious eyes were being turned toward Epstein's creation. Figures released at the end of September demonstrated why there should be such interest. The trade publication Record Retailer revealed that the Beatles had the largest-selling album - "Please Please Me", EP - 'Twist and Shout', and single – 'She Loves You' that year. The sales figures were extremely large and on the verge of becoming astronomic. It was no wonder that covetous eyes were turned in Epstein's direction.

Three of the Beatles returned from holiday on October 2nd with George Harrison coming back to London from his sister's home in America on the following day. They were stepping back into a bedlam which, over the following three months, would elevate the four members of the Beatles to the position of probably the most famous four men in Britain and possibly the most famous people on the planet.

Three months. Just three months.

It started on October 13th with an appearance on the top television show in the UK at the time. Sunday Night at the London Palladium was an old style variety show often featuring major American stars like Judy Garland, Bob Hope and Sammy Davis, Jr. who shared the stage with a mix of novelty acts, games and up-and-coming British acts. The show was compered by a succession of leading British comics, names like Tommy Trinder, Norman Vaughan, Jimmy Tarbuck and Bruce Forsyth, and it was the redoubtable Forsyth, still a staple on British television decades later, who acted as compere on the October 13th show when the Beatles made their first appearance.

And that was the night that the press and the media really grasped that something remarkable was happening. Not because of what took place on the stage. That was a fairly standard rendition of four songs from their current act. The eye-catching events took place in the streets around the Palladium, in Argyll Street and the surroundings, where thousands of youngsters, mostly female, laid siege to the theatre in scenes of uncontrolled hysteria which delighted the press, radio and television. It was as a result of the bedlam in and around the Palladium that the national ITN news covered both the pandemonium and the tv appearance itself.

One totally unexpected outcome of the Palladium triumph was a huge upsurge in approaches to NEMS on the part of manufacturers to produce merchandise and memorabilia emblazoned with the name and/or the image of the Beatles. There had been a number of such approaches since the spring but October, and the Argyle Street excitement, caused a huge jump in interest. Sticks of rock, lunch boxes, balloons, pillow-cases - the range and number of enquiries was suddenly overwhelming.

Prior to October 1963 all such enquiries were handled internally at NEMS, and on a fairly amateur basis, but now it became a major problem. In desperation Epstein asked his lawyer, David Jacobs, for help, and Jacobs promised to find somebody who could assist them with the growing problem.

But, as ever, Epstein took steps to deal with one problem only to find that the chosen solution created another, even greater problem. In this instance that greater problem was to prove the most painful and brutally damaging aspect of Epstein's glittering career.

Most of the remainder of October was taken up with a brief tour of Sweden, their first notable excursion overseas since Hamburg had been left behind. The return to England on October 31st presented them with their first airport frenzy scenes, the first of many over the next few years. The scenes at Heathrow were so chaotic that other people passing through the airport were caught up in it all.

Contestants in the imminent Miss World contest were evidently quite excited by the noise and the excitement: the new Prime Minister, Sir Alec Douglas-Home seemed momentarily baffled by it, but the most lasting impression was made on an American tv host named Ed Sullivan who was passing through the airport.

Sullivan and his wife Sylvia were at the airport after flying in from America, but were prevented from landing for several minutes. When they finally got down onto British soil Sullivan and his wife were surprised by the commotion created by the thousands of screaming fans. They were met by a chap called by the name of Bob Goldstein who besides being a personal friend of Sullivan's was also a locally-based publicist for United Artists. Though the Beatles were not involved with United Artists it was impossible for most people in Britain, especially someone involved in the entertainment industry, not to know all about them. Bob Goldstein was totally aware of who the Beatles were and why there were so many people at the Airport to greet them. The shrewd Sullivan gathered the desired information from his friend, and added to his knowledge later that day at his London hotel.

He stored the information about the Beatles away in case they ever had a relevance to his show but, although on his arrival in London the name of the Beatles meant nothing to him, crucially the growing importance of the Beatles was known to others in the senior management of the Ed Sullivan Show.

The programme employed a man named Jack Babb as talent coordinator, and Babb spent most summers in Europe investigating potential talent and acts for the show. In this European role he was ably assisted by a London-based agent named Peter Prichard, who was also contracted to the Sullivan show as European talent coordinator. In that role Pritchard was totally aware of the Beatles and the way their profile and national importance had grown during the year. Indeed Pritchard had already had a handful of brief·contacts with Brian Epstein, long before Epstein and Sullivan met.

When Sullivan saw and heard the bedlam at Heathrow on October 31st the cause was unknown to him but that situation wouldn't prevail for long.

Sullivan was still in the country when, just four days after the return from Sweden, the group made a stunning appearance on the Royal Command Performance at the Prince of Wales Theatre in London. This was the famous occasion when Lennon invited the audience to "rattle your jewellery".

If the press had woken up to the impact that the group was making on the night of Sunday Night at the London Palladium they were jolted into overdrive by the Royal Command Performance. And two days before that Prince of Wales show in front of the Queen Mother and Princess Margaret, the Daily Mirror produced a headline which encapsulated the mood in a single word.

Beatlemania.

The fact that the Mirror used the word in a headline in the newspaper just two days earlier was a telling sign of the growing interest in this phenomenon created by the Liverpool group. That the frenzy which prompted the Mirror headline was created by a Beatles performance at the Odeon in Cheltenham, Gloucestershire was eye-catching.

In the minds of most British people Cheltenham was traditionally the home of twin-set and pearls, and retired colonels and quiet discreet suburban lives. To find Cheltenham being brought to national attention by scenes of frantic screaming at a pop group was startling, far more so than had the same scenes been found in Manchester or London or Newcastle. As the Daily Mirror so graphically put it, "Beatlemania! It's happening everywhere. . . even in sedate Cheltenham."

Although there is a credible story that the word was actually first coined several hundred of miles further north some days earlier. Scottish concert promoter Andi Lothian had booked the group for a show in January, but that was in the throes of the Big Freeze and only fifteen people turned up for the show. He rebooked them for Glasgow on October 5th and inevitably, in the wake of hit singles and hit albums and much better weather, the situation was vastly different.

The night was the usual Beatles bedlam, made worse because the bouncers Lothian had booked for the hall were still in the pub when the crowd were filling the hall. The local police, unused to this kind of frenzy, insisted that Lothian bring the Beatles on early to calm the situation. He summoned the bouncers back who raced into the hall and down to the front like a troop of cavalry in a John Ford western. A Radio Scotland broadcaster standing beside Lothian asked him what was happening and he came back with the impromptu, timeless quip, "Don't worry, it's only... Beatlemania."

Beatlemania. It was. All over the country, but it was that Royal Command Performance that escalated the Beatles onto a new plateau beyond their contemporaries and even their envious NEMS stable-mates. In its story of the show, and the scenes surrounding the Prince of Wales theatre, The Mirror repeated the use of "Beatlemania". Now though, the same term appeared widely in the press and across the copious coverage on radio and television.

The uniformly astonishing press coverage on the morning after the Royal Command Performance proved a timely godsend for Brian Epstein. He was already booked on a transatlantic flight to New York, going out to discuss possible appearances by the Beatles in the States, and to try to get a cabaret career moving for his travelling companion, NEMS artist Billy J. Kramer. The main priority for the journey though was to try to sort out the slight mystery over the Beatles releases in America. The massive sales for Beatles records in the UK were a triumph, but the meagre sales via Swan and Vee-Jay were frankly pathetic. More disturbing for Epstein was the complete indifference shown by Capitol and their four rejections of Beatles material over the year. Given their relationship with EMI Records in the UK, and the growing importance of the Beatles to EMI, Brian Epstein had leverage to use with the moguls at Capitol.

He also had a swathe of very recent press reports, from the Royal Command Performance and the Sunday Night at the Palladium shows, to demonstrate to the people he was meeting that he was representing a rather special act.

Among those people were representatives of Liberty records with whom he wanted to place Billy J. Kramer. More importantly he had an arrangement to go to the imposing Delmonico Hotel on Monday November 11th to meet Ed Sullivan to discuss possible appearances by the Beatles on the famous show.

The meeting at the Delmonico was eventually extended to a second meeting on the following day. Part of this was caused by an unusual degree of respect between the two men. Sullivan was an icon of the American entertainment industry with an importance emanating from the place that the Ed Sullivan Show held in American life through the fifties and early sixties.

Even in the days when regular showing of American tv shows on British television was very rare, the name and reputation of Ed Sullivan was well known in the entertainment industry in Britain. For any act hoping to establish a presence in America, a slot on the Ed Sullivan Show was a major step.

Epstein's courting of Ed Sullivan was yet another example of his careful and meticulous planning, an aspect of his managerial style which is often overlooked. In making his plans to get the Beatles established in America he had concluded that an appearance on the Ed Sullivan show would be highly beneficial.

Once again fate stepped in and gave Epstein a hand. He wasn't aware when he shook hands with Sullivan at the Delmonico about Sullivan's chance encounter with the returning Beatles at Heathrow just two weeks earlier. Nor did Epstein know that Jack Babb had been lauding the group to the show's management in New York, but Epstein did know of the connections between Peter Pritchard and Jack Babb and Sullivan. He did not, had not made the connections but the fates were moving firmly in his favour.

Sullivan started the conversation with the idea of using the Beatles just once as a virtual novelty act but in his usual charming but relentless manner Epstein would not agree. Eventually a settlement was reached under which the Beatles would appear three times for Sullivan, live from the theatre in New York for the first and then a remote broadcast from the Deauville Hotel in Miami Beach. A third show was to be recorded on the day of the first live show but held back for later broadcast.

The Sullivan Show normally paid up to $10,000 for the headline acts, but these would have been major, invariably American stars. Not an almost unknown pop group from the other side of the Atlantic with silly haircuts and strange accents from somewhere that most people hadn't heard of called Liverpool. Given Epstein's determination to get the Beatles on the programme, he agreed at that first meeting to the three suggested appearances with the fees to be decided and confirmed at a dinner meeting on the following evening.

Having concluded his business at the Delmonico he spent a short time sight-seeing, including some very specific areas of Central Park to which London friends had directed him, before heading back to his hotel to prepare for the evening. He was booked into the Regency Hotel on Park Avenue, a selection made by an old friend from Liverpool named Geoffrey Ellis.

As arranged, Ellis came to the Regency at 7pm to meet him and they spent a wonderfully nostalgic evening in a restaurant off Lincoln Square, talking over mutual friends and old times in Liverpool. Ellis was clearly taken by the assurance being shown by his old friend. For his part, Epstein was very impressed at how much his friend had grown, not physically but in poise and self-assurance. Ellis just thought Epstein was showing an interest in the way his career had developed and so he told Epstein possibly a little more about his work for the Royal Insurance Company than was either prudent or required. Ellis didn't understand the true basis for Epstein's interest and it wouldn't become clear for several months.

They concluded their evening on East 55th Street at the legendary Blue Angel nightclub. In a bizarre twist the cabaret that evening was provided by Rolf Harris, who was genuinely relieved and pleased to get some response in the relatively thin audience from two Liverpudlians so far from home.

They parted after they had left the Blue Angel. Ellis was returning to his apartment. Epstein was, he told Ellis, returning to the Regency to get some rest before his important meetings the following day. But Ellis knew that his friend might be returning to the hotel but that it wouldn't be happening for at least a couple of hours. Prior to that, Epstein would be prowling the gay clubs round Times Square or the less salubrious areas inside Central Park. Ellis knew about his friend's private lifestyle, didn't share his tastes or inclinations, and so they parted, with Ellis making a vague promise to keep in touch. He didn't realise, and couldn't have imagined, the plans that Epstein was already concocting for the future of Geoffrey Ellis.

During the afternoon of the 12th, Epstein had a chance meeting with another old acquaintance from England. Bess Coleman was a bubbly girl from Leicestershire, who had graduated from a junior reporter on the Leicester Mercury to a PR post at EMI in the early sixties. This required her to arrange press coverage for artists but, given her age and lowly status with EMI, she had only been allowed to deal with the newest or least important of artists.

Into that category came a group from Liverpool called the Beatles, with whom she got associated in September 1962, at the time of their first release. She left EMI the following year on a whim, and travelled to New York. No job, no firm prospects, until a chance meeting led her to a secretarial job at United Artists offices in New York City.

Even that wasn't going so well until November 12th 1963, when into the UA office came one Brian Epstein for a pre-arranged meeting to discuss the planned Beatles film the following year. Epstein recognised her and remembered her work on behalf of the group a year earlier. The conversation developed and eventually he asked her to work for him in New York. The fact that he was on the point of signing a deal with Ed Sullivan convinced Bess that it was a step worth taking. She had been present at the press meetings at EMI when the Beatles were initially dismissed, and then lauded, and Epstein remembered and valued her loyalty back in those difficult early days.

Epstein had his meeting with the United Artists people about the film deal, and then met Sullivan for the second time at an early evening dinner at the restaurant in the hotel. This time the pair were joined by Sullivan's son-in-law, Bob Precht, who was also a producer on the show, and the three of them concluded the deal which, in Epstein's usual and creditable way, was sealed on a handshake.

The deal that was agreed gave the Beatles $3,500 for the initial performance plus a similar fee for the second live performance in Miami. At the suggestion of Bob Precht, Epstein agreed that the group should record several more songs whilst at the studios in New York, and these would be held back for future broadcast. Epstein accepted a lower fee for the taped segment and the figure of $3000 was agreed making a total of $10,000 for the three Sullivan shows.

Sullivan sweetened the pill by agreeing to pay transport and hotel costs for the group and the negotiations were concluded. Epstein's agreement was based on his belief that the Beatles would be top of the bill on the shows. He stated that this was the case when he returned to England but it seems very likely that his conviction, like his statement eighteen months earlier to Decca that that the Beatles already had a contract with another label, was based on his rather biased interpretation of events.

Although no paperwork records appear to have survived, it seems inconceivable that the shrewd and battle-hardened Sullivan would have granted top billing to a new pop group from England, without any success whatsoever in the States.

With some history of chart sales in America the picture might have been different, but the Beatles had no such basis to influence Sullivan. In the absence of anything tangible to make him change his mind it seems likely that Sullivan did nothing more than agree to consider putting the Beatles at the top of the bill - and that is a long way from actually doing it.

Real, tangible record sales success could transform the situation and once again in the early story of the Beatles and Epstein, circumstances, some fortuitous and others eminently tragic, would change things in their favour.

In the conversation with Sullivan at the first meeting, in an effort to impress the tv mogul, Epstein casually mentioned the likelihood that the Beatles would be appearing in their first feature film during the following year. Meetings had taken place in October with representatives of United Artists in the UK, and they had expressed interest in such a film.

In truth the idea at the time in the heads of the United Artists people was simple; quick exploitation of a hot resource which would inevitably cool, and lose its commercial potential, very quickly.

The impetus for the film had come from Noel Rodgers, who was the UK representative for United Artists Records. Like his colleague, Peter Pritchard, in the UA operation in 1963, Rodgers had been astounded by the growth in popularity of the Beatles. He recognised that the success of the EMI contract meant that there were no openings for United Artists in terms of normal record releases, but, unlike EMI, United Artists was a large and successful film company. Perhaps not as prestigious as when it was formed in 1919 by D. W. Griffith, Charlie Chaplin, Mary Pickford and Douglas Fairbanks; but still an important film company. And film companies which produced films were also able to release film soundtracks…

Rodgers made some discreet enquiries and discovered that the very basic contract the Beatles had signed with EMI did not cover film soundtracks. Sensing a real opportunity, Rodgers approached and made a proposition to George "Bud" Ornstein who was then the Production Head of UA's European Film Division. The accountants looked at the proposition and gave it their tacit approval, and early meetings with Epstein in October had been positive.

But even those meetings threw up another glaring example of Epstein's ignorance at the level he was now operating. The meeting with Walter Shenson, who had been appointed producer of the as-yet untitled film, found Epstein taking a firm line with the film company. He stated strongly but politely that he would not accept less than 7.5% of film income as payment for the participation of the Beatles.

This was a massive shock to Walter Shenson, and also to the UA management. They had sent Shenson to the meeting prepared to go up to 25% income for the Beatles, and perhaps unsurprisingly Shenson didn't bother explaining this glaring, basic error to Epstein.

Epstein then met UK film director, Michael Winner, for dinner in London at the Empress on October 14th just after the Sunday Night at The London Palladium show, and a few days after Epstein's eventful first meeting with Walter Shenson. The meeting had been suggested by Winner who, also conscious of the commercial possibilities of a film involving the Beatles, was keen to discuss a possible deal with Brian Epstein.

Winner had enjoyed some minor success with films like "Play It Cool" and "The Cool Mikado" although more substantial success would come later in the sixties with films like "The Jokers" in 1967 and then in the seventies and eighties with films like "Cato's Land" and the various "Death Wish" epics.

At the meeting with Epstein though, Winner had no leverage, particularly in the face of the existing interest from United Artists. All he could do was offer advice which Epstein was unusually happy to receive, given that he and Winner had realised their families had a connection via shared summer holidays in Cornwall in the fifties. Indeed Epstein and Winner had enjoyed a modicum of success on those holidays, imitating the Ink Spots in the hotel cabaret sessions.

Epstein described the basic United Artists offer to Winner. On a three-film deal, for the first film £5,000, for the second £10,000 and the third £15,000. And, crucially, United Artists had the sole rights to release the soundtrack records.

Winner was not wholly impressed. He had £40,000 available from his associate Lewis Gilbert, one of the truly great figures in British, if not world cinema. Gilbert had been responsible for directing films like "Reach for the Sky" and "Carve Her Name with Pride". Later he would direct films like "Alfie", and "Educating Rita", and even three Bond films, "You Only Live Twice", "The Spy Who Loved Me" and "Moonraker".

Winner's borrowed £40,000 wasn't of interest to Epstein; he had already reached an agreement, albeit not yet contractual, with United Artists, and Brian Epstein was one of those rare men for whom his word and a handshake were his bond.

Undeterred, Winner didn't panic. He approached Bud Ornstein and offered to direct the eventual film. Ornstein had to knock him back by stating that Dick Lester had already been engaged as director, but the conversation ended with Ornstein expressing surprise that Winner would want to be involved in what was so obviously a "low-budget quickie".

Confident that the film would be produced in 1964, Epstein was relaxed in mentioning it to Sullivan, although it clearly didn't factor in the negotiations. To the Sullivan camp, a British pop group, however successful in the UK, would be little more than a novelty attraction in America, and a film featuring that group was certain to be of minimal interest in America. It was just commercial reality.

Just four days before the meeting with Ed Sullivan, the first significant steps on the road to the Beatles first film were taken. The group were booked on

November 7th to make their first, and only, appearance in Ireland at the Adelphi Cinema in Dublin. It was their usual show, current for that stage of their career, with the usual bedlam and the inevitable pandemonium surrounding their every move. The one significant addition was the heavily-built man in the dark suit standing in the wings, watching the show intently beside Mal Evans.

The man was Alun Owen, who had been commissioned by Dick Lester, director of the untitled film, to produce a script. The choice of Owen had met with the approval of the Beatles, all of whom remembered his play, No Trams to Lime Street, which appeared in the Armchair Theatre series in 1959. Though this was the days of small black and white television sets, the play had enjoyed a remarkable success in the Liverpool area, not least because of Owen's sympathetic use of Liverpool speech patterns and vernacular.

When the possibility of a film was first mooted to the group, and the question of a scriptwriter was raised, Lennon was quick to mention Owen as a favoured contact. The fact that Owen had worked successfully with Dick Lester was another point in his favour, and so he was engaged to spend several days with the group, following and observing them. Much of the authenticity of what appeared in the eventual "A Hard Day's Night" was prompted by Owen's observations over those three days.

Before Epstein left America he had one other task to achieve. He had to deal with the Capitol problem, the baffling and increasingly infuriating mystery of why they refused consistently to release Beatles product. 'Love Me Do', 'Please Please Me', 'From Me To You' and then 'She Loves You' had been spurned and, to Epstein and other interested parties like George Martin, the continued resistance was hard to understand.

Fortunately for Epstein his new position of importance in the UK meant that he was given telephone access to the Capitol Records president, Alan W. Livingston, a privilege which would have been denied him just a few months earlier. On the phone to Livingston the persuasive Epstein played all his trump cards, massive and growing sales in Britain, a film to be released by United Artists, and three appearances as headliners on the Sullivan show. In addition he dropped in the politically valuable note that, because of the growing sales importance of the group, he and they had been invited to a reception with Sir Joseph Lockwood and other EMI executives in the boardroom at Manchester Square on November 18th. This was to celebrate an amazing year, one in which EMI's American arm, Capitol, had played no part whatsoever.

Livingston had enjoyed a multi-faceted career before he ever came into contact with Brian Epstein. Before taking up a management role, he had created the Bozo the Clown character in America and overseen its highly profitable merchandising. He also wrote 'I Tawt I Taw A Puddy Tat' for Mel Blanc, or maybe for Tweety Pie, and he was also responsible for the launch of the tv series, Bonanza. In the music world he was in charge of Capitol when the company took a huge gamble and re-launched the career of the largely washed-up Frank Sinatra leading to his spate of timeless classic albums on Capitol in the mid-fifties. Some years later, it was Capitol, still under his management, that launched the career of a new group from Hawthorne, California called the Beach Boys.

The result was that when he took the call from Brian Epstein in mid-November 1963 Alan W. Livingstone was not some nervous middle manager, unsure of which way to go. Instead he was a proven executive with a glittering career already to his name. But crucially he was also somebody who recognised commercial and political realities. At that time, as President of Capitol, he also had a board position with EMI, and Capitol was owned by EMI. In those circumstances, even without the massive sales in the UK, and the promised film, and the Sullivan appearances, it was politically dangerous to continue to refuse to release Beatles product without startlingly good reasons.

And as Brian Epstein delicately, politely but forcibly put it, by November 1963 such reasons simply didn't exist any longer - if they ever had.

Epstein had with him acetate of the new Beatles single, 'I Want To Hold Your Hand', which was scheduled for release in the UK at the end of November. This record, as Epstein casually informed Livingston, was on schedule to have over one million advance sales before release - the first time such a feat had been achieved in the UK.

Epstein played the acetate to Livingston over the crackling phone line but it was clearly unnecessary. Despite the gentle pressure from London, and the refined arguments of Epstein, it's clear that Livingston was mildly surprised that until November 1963 he had heard nothing internally about this group. The decision to reject each of the four singles had been taken much lower down the food chain at Capitol.

Livingston took the arbitrary decision to overrule his people and sign the Beatles. Epstein's final triumph was to persuade Livingston to commit to a promotional budget to launch the group in 1964, and Livingston agreed to spend $40,000 for promotion - a colossal amount at that time, possibly worth some $300,000 today.

Livingstone, and thereby Capitol, was committed to the release and he agreed to schedule the release for mid-January 1964 to take advantage of the Sullivan shows.

Epstein was able to return to England to inform the group that they had a major American release plus a series of top-of-the-bill appearances on the biggest tv show in America.

Just over a year had passed since the group, including Ringo Starr, had signed the revised contract and now they stood on the verge of undreamed-of success. Before the end of November the group were scheduled to release their second album "With The Beatles" and also their fifth single, 'I Want To Hold Your Hand'. The album had advance sales of some three hundred thousand and the single would reach one million advance sales before release day.

Totally unrelated to the Livingston-Epstein conversations, Time magazine took note of the Beatlemania phenomena in England in an article on November 15th and coverage in such a prestigious journal could only have soothed any doubts being expressed about Livingston's boldness. On the same day as the Time magazine article, all three major American networks, CBS, ABC and NBC, independently sent crews to the UK to film a story about the Beatlemania phenomena.

All three units were on hand to film parts of the Beatles performance on November 16th at the Winter Gardens Theatre in Bournemouth. Scenes of audience frenzy appeared in sporadic news broadcasts during the third week in November but these were just fillers, used to occupy space in the absence of anything more important. The CBS piece would prove to be particularly relevant. The Head of the CBS News London Bureau, Alexander Kendrick, was sent to handle the filming, and his distaste is evident in every patronising word of his voiceover. But it was to be several days before it would be heard.

On November 18th the NBC broadcast of the Huntley-Brinkley Report included a four-minute segment which showed footage from the Bournemouth show, with the footage dominated by screaming, uncontrollable girls, because, as far as America was concerned, that was the story - not the warblings of four young men with strange hairstyles.

However, the first significant use of the footage from Bournemouth, and interviews with the Beatles, would not appear on American screens until December 10th, but that would air in a transformed country.

Friday November 22nd was an important day in the history of the Beatles. Their crucial second album, "With The Beatles", was scheduled for release, coincidentally on the same day as another album which has gone on to become a timeless classic, "A Christmas Gift For You" (more often known as the Phil Spector Christmas Album).

From the Beatles perspective, critical acclaim was more important than commercial success. With more than 300,000 advance orders for the album it was a guaranteed best-seller and, given the amazing responses their every move produced, there was little doubt that it would only further strengthen their reputation.

On a different basis Phil Spector had every reason to expect his seasonal album to be a massive hit. He had enjoyed substantial worldwide success with his production of singles like 'He's a Rebel', 'Zip-a-Dee-Doo-Dah' and 'Be My Baby', among many others, but "A Christmas Gift For You" was the first time he had thrown the same amount of energy and commitment into a full album. Using the peerless musicianship of the Wrecking Crew, allied to the vocal talents of names like Darlene Love and Ronnie Spector, he chose a number of Christmas standards, plus one new number 'Christmas (Baby Please Come Home)', to update in his trademark production style.

It should have been a massive success but fate intervened in the most painful way.

It was standard practice in those pre-digital days, that television news divisions would spread their costs, get more bang for their buck, by showing various pieces of news footage in more than one programme in the schedule. In the case of CBS their usual pattern was to use a story, or part of the footage, on the CBS Morning News in mid-morning, and then show it again as part of the evening schedule for the different audience that came in from work and watched the CBS Evening News.

I read about this as part of the background research into the events of November 1963 and, wearing my jaundiced television head again, thought back longingly to those days before Rolling 24 Hour News.

The Alexander Kendrick story from Bournemouth was shown in the Morning show, hosted by Bob Wallace, and that time the intention was to re-show in the evening show.

Two hours later bullets in Dallas killed President John F. Kennedy and changed the world totally and irrevocably.

Naturally the normal television programme considerations for CBS and indeed most tv networks around the world were scrapped. All normal programming was suspended indefinitely.

The CBS Evening News did not appear, superseded by a marathon of improvisation started with Cronkite's voiced segments, superimposed on top of the current programming until Cronkite was hurriedly dropped on air, his lack of jacket emphasizing the drama and the seriousness of the moment.

And that instant when Cronkite in mid-sentence is handed a sheet of paper on which is written the official confirmation of Kennedy's death, information that Cronkite has to impart to a disbelieving America - that moment when he has to fight back his own emotions and conquer the catch in his throat - that moment is breathtakingly painful and powerful.

Walter Cronkite would become the most trusted man in America and cover scores of major stories including Neil Armstrong's walk on the moon but it is arguable that he never surpassed the journalistic mastery he displayed on November 22nd.

CBS didn't return to anything like formal programming until later in the weekend but with the succeeding calamities of the shooting of Lee Harvey Oswald and then the sombre grandeur of the Kennedy funeral it would be December before CBS and other American tv stations returned to anything like normal.

A similar distaste for frivolity, for anything approaching normal life, afflicted much of America, and the scale of the mood of national grief and disbelief is perhaps difficult to understand now. Since then there has been a coarsening of daily and political life, and a series of agonies and humiliations - Watergate, Vietnam, 9/11, Iraq, Afghanistan - and against that bitter backdrop the mood of national grief so prevalent in much of America in December 1963 seems almost unbelievable.

But normal life slowly, perhaps reluctantly, resumed.

Many things happened quietly, almost apologetically, and this was the case with an unobtrusive press release from Capitol Records on Wednesday December 4th in which the signing of the Beatles was announced. The release date of the first single, 'I Want To Hold Your Hand' was revealed as Monday January 13th, just three weeks before the planned first Sullivan appearance.

On strictly commercial terms there was no point in Capitol releasing the single any earlier. Most record sales take place in the approach to Christmas, and sales over the actual holiday period traditionally slump. Delaying the release until later in January made sense, but events, and the gods, smiled on Brian Epstein.

In every area of American life people were wondering how soon they could or should begin to put the grief to one side. Television executives were no different and even the tv stars were conscious of the need to balance respect with an attempt to slightly lighten the mood. Walter Cronkite, still guiding America through the gloom via his role at CBS, remembered the light-hearted piece from England which had been dropped from the evening programme on November 22nd because of the Dallas tragedy.

He decided that the evening show on December 10th might prove a suitable moment, perhaps a gentle diversion from the general misery.

That piece introduced by Cronkite on December 10th was seen by a large CBS audience across America, including a 15-year-old schoolgirl called Marsha Albert who was living in Silver Spring in Maryland. On the following day she wrote a letter to her favourite DJ at the local radio station, WWDC in Washington, and again the media interactions show just how long ago it all was. Marsha Albert, of Sligo Junior High School, wrote a letter. No email, or Facebook, or Tweet; she wrote a letter and the DJ, Carroll James (CJ the DJ) responded to it. He too had seen the piece on the CBS Evening News, but he had never heard of the Beatles, and he had no knowledge that Capitol was planning a release in January, and equally he had no way of knowing what the Sullivan Show was planning.

In her letter the priceless Marsha Albert asked, "why can't we have music like that here in America?" Carroll James spoke to one of the station management and rang a friend who worked for BOAC, the British national airline which flew regularly into New York and Washington. A stewardess was persuaded to purchase a copy of the new single, 'I Want To Hold Your Hand' and bring it in her hand luggage on her next transatlantic flight a couple of days later. Curiously, 'I Want To Hold Your Hand' didn't feature in the CBS footage introduced by Cronkite. The segment began with truncated footage of 'She Loves You' and comprised mostly of interview footage, screaming audience reaction shots and mostly sarcastic remarks from Alexander Kendrick.

As such, the disc received by Carroll James on December 17th was a brand new song to him. He played it for the first time on his show that day and, in a suitably fitting touch, got the young Marsha Albert into the studio to introduce the first play in America of the record which would break the Beatles there.

Her introduction is faltering and stumbling, but the impact was almost instantaneous. Carroll asked his audience for their reactions and, in his words, the "switchboard lit up like a Christmas tree". The reaction was so overwhelming that Carroll took the extreme measure of playing 'I Want To Hold Your Hand' for a second time later in the show and as he mischievously admitted, there was a strict WWDC rule against repeating records in the same show.

But those were unusual times, unusual circumstances. Carroll James and his fellow DJs at the station reacted to the unprecedented interest by putting their sole copy of the record on a constant rotation through virtually every programme in heavy repetition. The frequent plays of the record created even more listener interest which created more calls, and on it went.

Carroll James was contacted by a fellow DJ, a friend in Chicago, who had heard about the situation, and James provided a professionally taped copy of the single to him. This created a similar firestorm in the mid-west.

The Chicago DJ duplicated the tape and passed it on to another DJ operating in St. Louis who created similar levels of interest in the Beatles and their new record in St. Louis.

Almost unnoticed in the midst of this madness, the PR people working for the Sullivan show released the announcement that the English group, the Beatles, would be appearing on the show in February.

As a result of the initiative shown by Marsha Albert and by Carroll James, record shops in the Washington area began to be bombarded by requests for a record that none of the shops had heard of, and information about a group that was even more a mystery.

By this time Brian Epstein was busy at work in England preparing for the first ever Beatles Christmas show. He certainly didn't know anything about Marsha Albert or Carroll James at that moment, nor was he aware of the scenes at the Washington record shops. Had he known about it then very likely the irony of the situation would not have been lost on him, because only two years earlier his involvement with the Beatles had started with Raymond Jones coming into NEMS and asking for a record that Epstein didn't know, by a group that was a mystery to him.

Two years later the same scenario was being played out on a much larger, more explosive scale. Three thousand miles away; a different record and the same group, albeit a vastly changed group - one whose lives were about to be changed completely.

Following the pressure on the Washington record shops, word fed back to Capitol Records in Los Angeles that an important Washington radio station was providing significant airplay to an illegally imported copy of a record not due for release for several weeks. This threatened to disrupt the marketing plans and so the initial reaction was to ask WWDC to stop playing the record. When Capitol were made aware that bootleg copies of the imported disc were being played on a number of other stations, the lawyers got involved.

Capitol hired New York entertainment attorney Walter Hofer, who later represented Epstein, The Beatles and Northern Songs, to threaten to issue a "cease and desist" order on WWDC, and Carroll James was even warned that he might be mentioned in the proceedings.

Fortunately, on December 20th common sense, and the sound commercial sense of Alan Livingston, came to the fore. Discussions within Capitol revolved around the simple point that invariably record companies are desperate to get radio stations to play their product, but here was a situation where the stations were playing the product, albeit imported, and getting fantastic interest, and yet the record company were threatening the stations!

As another casual demonstration of something massively unusual taking place, there was a surprise dedication made on WINS on Monday, December 23rd on the Stan Z Burns show. He played a record after providing a dedication to the dock workers on the west side of Manhattan who were in the city from London and Liverpool. He finished by saying that those English visitors wanted to hear their British Number One. And that record, inevitably, was 'I Want To Hold Your Hand'.

The interest in the Beatles being communicated to Capitol was becoming a storm, and so, in conjunction with some of his chastened executives, Livingston came to a shock conclusion. In the unprecedented circumstances the best solution was to advance the release of the disc to capitalise on the huge, and growing, interest.

Despite the normal refusal of record companies to release anything between Christmas and New Year, Livingston rationalised that the best commercial advantage would be obtained by getting the disc out as soon as possible. He gave instructions that 'I Want To Hold Your Hand' should be rush-released as soon as possible, and Christmas leave was cancelled for large numbers of staff to cope with the unexpected pressing demands.

The release date was brought forward to December 26th, that date not being a public holiday as it is in the UK. Capitol also quickly appreciated that its initial factory order of 200,000 units would be insufficient to meet the growing demand. Instructions were issued to the Capitol pressing plants in Scranton and Los Angeles to substantially increase production by having all pressing machines concentrate exclusively on the Beatles single. In addition, Capitol took out subcontract agreements with other companies, such as RCA and Decca, to press additional copies of the single if necessary.

Again good fortune smiled on Epstein and the Beatles. Because the decision had been taken some weeks earlier to release the record on January 13th, and because of the Christmas-New Year holiday, and because of the danger of delays caused by bad weather in early January, all the necessary stocks of vinyl had already been shipped to the relevant pressing plants. On the day that Livingston issued his emergency pressing order for 'I Want To Hold Your Hand' all the physical elements necessary to meet such an emergency pressing demand were in place. There was no hiatus, no delay, as would normally be the case in those circumstances.

The pressing order was issued to Capitol plants around the country on December 20th and on the day before Christmas Eve 1963 Capitol issued an internal memo to sales people and regional managers across America, outlining an extensive "Beatles Campaign" on the basis of the $40,000 budget Livingstone agreed with Epstein just a few weeks earlier.

The campaign involved a range of promotional items which would swamp the country in the coming weeks. Besides a fake Beatles tabloid newspaper, which appeared as thousands of copies, there were huge numbers of Beatle buttons, wigs, stickers plus an amusing battery-powered, "Beatles-in-motion," head-shaking window display for record stores.

On a more conventional basis, Capitol had created a massive trade advertisement campaign for all the major American music trade ads. As Christmas Day 1963 dawned the number of Americans who genuinely knew that "The Beatles Are Coming!" was relatively few, but the change was imminent.

On overtime rates, the pressing plants worked through Christmas Eve and Christmas Day so that by the day after Christmas, December 26th, promotion men working for Capitol were furnished with plentiful copies of the single for delivery to radio stations. The impact was instantaneous and became almost legendary. Deliveries of the disc in the greater New York area took place around 9am and by lunchtime the three major stations in New York, WINS, WABC and WMCA, had put the disc on constant replay. The pattern was followed in other major cities as the promotion men made their deliveries.

And at this point, good fortune, or those gods who smiled so warmly on Brian Epstein in those early years, stepped in again.

As in the instance in England in January 1963 when the snows meant that kids could not get out, thus boosting the audience for the Beatles' initial national tv broadcast on Thank Your Lucky Stars, the advance of the release of 'I Want To Hold Your Hand' worked out perfectly for the group. Because the release came during the school Christmas holidays most kids were either at home or at least available to listen to the radio, something that would not have happened had the record been released as scheduled on January 13th. Most American schools did not resume until Monday January 6th and so those kids, the target audience, were subjected to blanket Beatles coverage for almost ten days.

The results were incredible. In New York City, 10,000 copies of the single were sold every hour over the first few days. Similar results were reported from other areas, and in the period before New Year's Day over a quarter of a million copies were sold. As a result, Capitol was severely stretched and had to do a quick deal with RCA and also with Columbia Records to help with extra pressings.

Although the Beatles and, more importantly, Epstein were kept informed at certain points, much of what was happening passed them by. Again, communications at the time played a major part. Telegrams or long-distance telephone calls were the only reliable forms of international communications, and at the time of the release of 'I Want To Hold Your Hand' the first-ever transatlantic television broadcast via satellite had been only six months earlier.

Constant contact between the States and England on a level we now take for granted was unknown, the stuff of science fiction. As such Epstein would have known the headlines about what was happening in the States but the detail, the fantastic, mind-boggling detail, would have eluded him.

Over Christmas, he was far too pre-occupied with the Beatles Christmas Show at the Astoria, Finsbury Park. This was almost entirely a NEMS bill with Tommy Quickly, the Fourmost, Billy J. Kramer and the Dakotas and Cilla Black being complemented by the Barron Knights and Rolf Harris. The show involved music and comedy and gave full vent to Epstein's theatrical flair. It opened on Christmas Eve and ran for sixteen nights with nights off for the holidays of Christmas Day and New Year's Eve.

After the single show on December 24th Epstein ferried all his Liverpool acts, who wanted to be home for Christmas, back via private jet, but that was a gesture which, though typical of the innate thoughtfulness of the man, was rapidly becoming redundant.

They returned on the morning of Boxing Day, December 26th, oblivious to the firestorm which was erupting in America over the Beatles.

That firestorm got hotter on January 3rd when The Jack Paar Program, entirely without permission, ran the full clip of the Beatles performing 'She Loves You' on stage in Bournemouth in November. This was the footage which had been shot by the networks who went in search of a novelty story in England some weeks earlier, similar footage to that shown so movingly by Cronkite on CBS in December.

Neither Paar nor his network, NBC, had formal permission to film the musical clip and when he learned about it Epstein was incandescent with rage. However, as The Jack Paar Program was a major chat show of the period this was the first chance many people had been given to see the Beatles in action. As such it largely added to the torrent of news and information about the group, but Paar wasn't showing the footage to steal a march on Sullivan, although that was clearly a benefit. Instead he used the Bournemouth footage to indulge himself with jokes about the group, their appearance, and the behaviour of the fans.

That didn't matter to Epstein. He was furious that the BBC had apparently done a deal with NBC to make the footage available to them. He threatened to remove the Beatles from all future BBC broadcasts if they did not rescind the agreement with Paar but NBC, and Paar, refused to budge. Epstein wasn't worried about Paar or NBC or the BBC. His concern, totally justified, was that

Sullivan would cancel their contract because he would be so angered by Paar's transmission of Beatles footage a month before the Sullivan show. That was exactly Sullivan's reaction. He contacted Peter Pritchard and ordered him to cancel the booking for the Beatles, but the canny Pritchard decided to wait a few days and see what happened.

Those few days took in the period when Capitol was swamped with demands for 'I Want To Hold Your Hand', when sales climbed remorselessly towards one million. In the face of such unprecedented interest, the ever-pragmatic Sullivan changed his mind, Pritchard was asked to put it right, and Epstein didn't hear about the near-cancellation for over a year.

In England, besides concluding the Christmas Show season in London, the group were preparing for a short series of concerts in Paris before the long-awaited trip to America. They completed another triumphant Sunday Night at the London Palladium show on January 12th, this time starring old friends Dave Allen and also Alma Cogan with whom Brian Epstein would be close until her premature death in 1966. The concerts in Paris were not especially happy; the general reaction to the group in France seemed cooler and more reserved than they had become used to, and the longing to get back to London and on the flight to New York was tangible across the group and Aspinall and Evans.

Epstein, while in Paris, met with Nat Weiss, who was to become a life-long friend and colleague. Weiss was involved with Sid Bernstein at GAC, and Weiss had been asked by Bernstein to conclude the contractual arrangements for the planned Carnegie Hall concerts in February 1964. Weiss also reached agreement with Epstein for another show, the Beatles first ever concert on American soil, to be staged between the first Sullivan show and Carnegie Hall.

Epstein was conscious of the commercial significance of the Beatles appearing at Carnegie Hall, and he was keen for the group to have another show prior to Carnegie. Not exactly as a rehearsal for the New York shows but certainly as a full run-through for the group and the equipment. It was also a consideration, at that early stage in the group's American career, that recouping some of the extra costs of the trip could be helpful. Sullivan had offered to cover air fares and hotel accommodation, but the group weren't to grow rich on Ed Sullivan.

Epstein discussed with Nat Weiss a range of possible locations for that warm-up show. The host city was a major consideration, as was the weather on the east coast which could be expected, in early February, to have an impact on travelling.

Cities like Boston were considered but eventually and quickly the pair settled on Washington DC which, as the nation's capital, had a symbolic importance for Brian Epstein. GAC signed the contract with Epstein for a single show to take place in Washington on February 11th.

One further housekeeping chore remained. To enter and work in America the group and their extended party needed visas and so they visited the American Embassy in Paris on February 3rd to complete the necessary paperwork. This was another piece of good fortune in terms of timing. The relative indifference of the French towards the group at that time meant that they could make the trip to the American Embassy in relative calm. Had they tried to make the same trip to Grosvenor Square, to the American Embassy in London, the result would have been bedlam, the kind of scenes which were to be so faithfully recreated in the film which they were due to start in just a couple of months.

A mini-version of that bedlam was seen on January 15th when Lennon and Harrison took advantage of a brief gap in the Paris schedule by returning to London. A small group of just over a hundred schoolgirls greeted them at Heathrow with their frenzied volume making up for the unusually limited numbers. The pair went their separate ways before returning to Paris, with Harrison enjoying dinner that evening with Phil Spector and his protégées, The Ronettes, who were on tour in England.

Several days later Spector would join the Beatles party on the historic flight to New York, although, with his customary chivalry and obsession with self-publicity, he forbade the three girls to take the same flight.

Much of the intensive scripting work which would illuminate the film "A Hard Day's Night" a few months later was done in the hotel rooms in Paris as Alun Owen and Dick Lester sat and watched and listened to the interplay between the Beatles.

And on January 15th a quiet announcement in London signified a major change in the lives of Brian Epstein and the Beatles, and a sea-change in the evolution of the group.

NEMS Enterprises announced formal plans to move from its original Liverpool base to offices in Sutherland House in Argyll Street, London.

Liverpool to London, and the complete divorce from the leather-clad Cavern group was almost complete.

Yet, over the latter part of the group's stay in Paris, Epstein was slightly less troubled than usual, partly because he reacted well to the sophistication of Paris, and because he was carrying a secret from the group.

That secret broke the night they returned to their hotel room at the George V after another less than satisfactory concert in Paris. Epstein was handed a telegram which informed him that the following week's Cashbox chart would show 'I Want To Hold Your Hand' at Number 1.

It had entered at 80 on January 11th, jumped to 43 a week later and then, on January 25th, hit the top of the American charts.

Top of the charts in America? The home of all their heroes? Elvis... Buddy Holly... Little Richard? The excitement in that hotel room that night can only be imagined, and the sense of accomplishment, of dreams realised, by Brian Epstein must have been equally vast. In less than two years he had taken a scarcely-known group from a provincial city in England to a position of power in America, but he and they would not realise just how massive they had become until they travelled across the Atlantic in early February.

Pan Am flight 101, a scheduled Boeing 707, took off from Heathrow early on Friday, February 7th. It was an airport under siege from literally thousands of tearful young girls many of whom seemed strangely distraught, perhaps fearing that they were on the verge of losing the Beatles forever.

For the group it was just wildly exciting, the culmination of a collective dream, and for Epstein vindication for his belief in the group, and perhaps just a small rebuff to all those who had doubted him over the years.

On the long flight across the Atlantic the excitement slightly waned as they began to wonder what kind of reception they might receive. Epstein clearly was untroubled by such doubts. He had supreme confidence in the ability of Alan Livingstone and his staff to deliver the promotional onslaught that his $40,000 budget promised.

In the event Epstein was proved gloriously correct.

Media reports later claimed that Capitol promised that every single person who turned up at JFK would be given a dollar bill and a t-shirt. As ever with the press this was a convenient story, but not entirely accurate. What actually happened was that the various receptionists at Capitol Records had been told to answer every call from December 20th with the message, "Capitol Records - The Beatles are coming".

That mantra, "The Beatles are coming!" was constantly intoned on the various radio stations as well, but the free t-shirt copy came via Seltaeb, the Beatles' American merchandising operation, and not from Capitol. Seltaeb had done a deal with the main radio stations, WINS and WMCA, under which every fan arriving at JFK would be given the free Beatles t-shirt plus a dollar bill.

The t-shirts were ordered from Jerry Rubin, a substantial t-shirt manufacturer, who would become a major supplier of goods to Seltaeb.

The DJ, Murray the K, who became internationally famous because of his association with the Beatles, was working for 1010 WINS, and he repeatedly announced the full details of the Beatles' flight number and time of arrival. That information was gleefully repeated by rival stations, WABC and WMCA which only helped to build up the crowd and inflame the feverish anticipation.

Posters and car stickers, bearing the legend "The Beatles are coming", were plastered all over the airport and in thousands of prominent locations across New York City.

The plane touched down at the newly-renamed JFK Airport at 1.20pm. Idlewild Airport had been renamed in honour of the late President on Christmas Eve, 1963, and already New Yorkers and visitors had grown used to the snappy acronym, JFK, to identify the airport.

The party flew into an airport and a city awash with Beatles memorabilia, and Beatles souvenirs and sheer Beatles bedlam. It is reckoned that over five thousand kids were at the airport to greet their arrival and the noise created by the teenage fans was clearly sufficient to convince the group, if any doubts remained, that they were on safe ground.

After running the gauntlet of the noisy welcome the first endurance test for the group was the famously vicious New York press pack in the Press Conference. However, once again it could hardly have gone better and the pressmen, used to single syllable, moronic replies from pop stars were amused and charmed and delighted by the sardonic, self-deprecating replies to the questions thrown at them.

From that moment, any reservations America had about the Beatles were dispelled and the Fourth Estate largely fell in love with the group.

The acid test remained though. The Sullivan show on February 9th. For the intervening two days the group, apart from rehearsals at the Sullivan studios on Broadway, were imprisoned in the Plaza Hotel, holding court to a succession of visitors. Epstein was constantly busy, discussing plans for the subsequent events on the tour including a series of meetings arranged for the Monday, the day after the Sullivan show.

The itinerary allowed the group to rehearse at the studio, a session which proved difficult when George suffered a short-run illness. For camera rehearsal purposes Neil Aspinall initially stood in for the absent George but he was called away to deal with a temporary crisis when the police refused to allow George's sister access to the Plaza to see him. Given that there were probably five thousand females outside the Plaza claiming admission on the basis of some relationship with one or other of the Beatles, the reticence of New York's finest is perhaps understandable.

Aspinall slipped away to provide the necessary identification and his place as temporary replacement for George Harrison was taken by Sullivan staffer, Vince Calandra.

By Sunday February 7th George Harrison had recovered. Inevitably. Anything else, after coming so far from sweaty underground cellars, and vans on the M1 with a hole in the windscreen, and rejections from virtually every record company in Britain was inconceivable.

They recorded a whole show before the live show. That recorded show would thus become their third appearance on the Sullivan Show but it was the first one, the live one that was important, the one that made television history in the United States.

Because on virtually any level that mattered it was an unqualified triumph. Over 73 million viewers, almost 40% of the population of the country, and the police reckoned that the night in question showed the lowest crime figures for over a century!

And it is clear that not only the country was captivated by that magical hour of television. A whole industry, the all-dominant American rock and pop industry of the sixties, seventies and eighties was largely conceived during the hour of the Sullivan show. A host of stellar names from Bruce Springsteen to Stephen Stills to Billy Joel to Carl Giammarese and many, many others testified that their lives were utterly transformed by the events in the Ed Sullivan Theatre.

Epstein had given the group the following day off for rest and recreation, to wallow in their immense triumph. He, as ever, didn't stop to rest. He had arranged meetings at the Delmonico and, thinking it a lucky charm after the Sullivan meetings there in November, he went back there at 10am on Monday February 8th accompanied by the ever-reliable Mal Evans.

Mal was there as a kind of bodyguard, to steer Epstein clear of unwanted attention not least because, after the huge press coverage of the past month, his face was getting almost as well known as those of the group. Mal Evans was also present to act as a sort of secretary, getting the people who turned up early for the meetings to wait patiently. Epstein still put great store by punctuality as many people had found to their cost.

In my research I read the details about the Sullivan shows and that first visit to America with a sense of disbelief and wonder. To come so far, and to accomplish so much in just two years? It truly was miraculous.

And on one later research visit to New York I walked past the Delmonico, much changed from those days but now transformed by its conversion into part of the Trump empire.

Past the hotel where the climactic meetings between Sullivan and Epstein took place. There was little visible to suggest how it must have looked all those years ago in the high promise of February 1964.

And on that visit, when I returned later to The Plaza where the Beatles had been imprisoned by the excited clamour in the streets on that first visit, I stood and I imagined the scene on that fateful day as Brian Epstein sat back, resplendent in his position as King of the World after a scarcely-imaginable two years. Courtiers, and media, and acolytes scurried around trying to please him and meet his every need.

And then the imposing figure of Mal Evans brought across a tall, thin figure with a foppish mop of chestnut brown hair.

Unusually for young people coming to meet Epstein the young man didn't appear nervous. Instead he grinned broadly, thrust out a manicured right hand and said confidently, "Good morning, Mr.Epstein. I'm Nicky Byrne."

In my severely unremarkable career in television I've always looked for the key moment, the single event on which the story turns or hangs. A wizened BBC producer once, very irreverently and drunkenly, described it to me as the 'Gethsemane moment', meaning the encounter in the Garden of Gethsemane when Judas Iscariot betrayed Jesus to the Roman soldiers with a kiss.

Now, clearly, my brand of cheap television cannot be compared or linked to events of some monumental or historic significance. But the comparison still holds in terms of the pivotal importance of a dramatic moment. And that's why that first meeting between Brian Epstein and Nicky Byrne had such long-lasting and devastating consequences for both men and indeed for the Beatles.

I didn't know anything about Nicky Byrne. I don't think I'd even heard the name, apart from the Westlife guy, before I started on the research quest on the McCartney project, and many of the initial sources I used barely mentioned him at all. That wasn't surprising. He seemed to be more directly connected to Brian Epstein and the solicitor, David Jacobs, than to the group, and as such he didn't feature prominently in the libraries of books about the Beatles.

And yet, as my research and, it must be admitted, my fascination with the story grew in intensity I found that Nicky Byrne became an ever more compelling figure. Not because of crimes or villainy. Unusually for people associated with Brian Epstein it was difficult to fault the behaviour of Nicky Byrne. He had an opportunity offered to him, and he took it. That's all. Nothing more vicious or venal or outrageous than that.

But what an opportunity!

He met Brian Epstein for the first time while Epstein was basking in the reflected and wholly deserved glory from the Sullivan appearance. The Nicky Byrne meeting wasn't the only one facing Epstein that day, and on paper it was far from the most important one. The astonishing impact made by the Beatles on that American tv programme on February 9th meant that Epstein was under siege from people and companies offering propositions for his urgent consideration, and many of those proposals involved merchandise.

It was a fact that a number of the seats on the plane that brought Epstein and the Beatles and Phil Spector from London to New York on February 7th were occupied by American businessmen. Many of them were there just by coincidence, but others had booked the flights very deliberately in a calculated attempt to get close to the Beatles manager. He had been accosted by men trying to get his signature on a deal, generally for Beatles related merchandise. In every instance Epstein charmingly, but firmly, rebuffed the offers. He had bigger and better things to concern him.

Fortunately the days when Epstein had to consider such matters personally were long past. In late 1963, aware that these demands were threatening to swamp the tiny NEMS operation, Epstein had asked one of his trusted inner circle, solicitor David Jacobs, for help.

In legal circles at that time Jacobs was an undeniable star. For much of the late fifties and the early sixties David Jacobs was unquestionably the leading show business lawyer in the country, with a glittering list of clients. Household names like Judy Garland and Laurence Olivier were represented by him, as also was Brian Epstein. On a wider front Jacobs had also been involved in the Profumo case, and, in addition, on behalf of John Vassall, the Admiralty civil servant who was convicted of spying for the Russians after being blackmailed over his homosexuality.

That wasn't the case that made his name. Instead it was the organisation of the libel case mounted by the American entertainer, Liberace, that made his reputation as the go-to man for high profile cases. The Daily Mirror columnist, Cassandra, had published a column in 1956 which comprised an astonishing attack on Liberace and, without using the word, was clearly implying that he was homosexual. Liberace had come into England on the Queen Mary via Southampton, to appear at a series of concerts in the country including the Palladium, the Royal Festival Hall, and the Palace Theatre, Manchester. Cassandra performed his attack during that 1956 tour but, given the painful progress of the British legal system, the case didn't reach the court until 1959.

In terms of the homosexual allegation, with modern sensibilities most people would think, "So What?", but the fifties were very different, darker times. Homosexuality was a crime, prosecuted with vigour by the authorities as brilliant men like Alan Turing had discovered to their cost. Public figures like Liberace, David Jacobs and even Brian Epstein lived in constant fear of disclosure, or blackmail or worse. It was illegal to be a practising homosexual or rather a practising male homosexual. The reluctance or inability of Queen Victoria to countenance the context of female homosexuality meant that it did not feature as a criminal offence during the whole of the first half of the twentieth century in England.

The Sexual Offences Act of 1967 removed the stigma of criminality from male homosexuals; thanks to Queen Victoria, women in the UK had never lived under that specific legal cloud.

Cassandra's article in the Daily Mirror oozed with florid expressions like "the summit of sex - the pinnacle of masculine, feminine, and neuter. Everything that he, she, and it can ever want… a deadly, winking, sniggering, snuggling, chromium-plated, scent-impregnated, luminous, quivering, giggling, fruit-flavoured, mincing, ice-covered heap of mother love".

Leaving aside the question of whether there might have been just the slightest hint of accuracy in Cassandra's charges, Liberace decided to sue the Mirror and Jacobs was engaged to conduct the case. In English High Court proceedings, a solicitor conducts the management of a case, but the physical and verbal presentation of the case in the court is in the hands of a barrister.

The masterstroke performed by Jacobs came in his choice of barrister. Ignoring the claims of other, seemingly more appropriate or capable figures, Jacobs chose Sir Gilbert Beyfus QC, a barrister who was then well past seventy years of age and also visibly suffering from terminal cancer.

The initial meeting between Liberace and Beyfus must have been a pantomime. The American star was clearly horrified and alarmed at the prospect of being defended by this septuagenarian relic, whilst the ancient Beyfus was far too polite to evidence an opinion on Liberace's gold and bracelets and rings.

In the trial, thanks to the brilliance and foresight of David Jacobs, the peculiarities and mannerisms of Beyfus, even the physical impact of his illness, became a strength for the Liberace defence. Beyfus had always displayed a number of affectations and mannerisms, particularly in court, and invariably behaved like a throwback to the Edwardian age.

He quite often displayed a disconcerting twitch and a constant habit of cupping his hand over his deaf ear when he apparently or allegedly could not hear what was being said in the witness box. His frequent entreaties or demands that testimony be repeated meant that much of the testimony from Mirror journalists, including Cassandra, created problems for their side. Perhaps curiously Beyfus didn't seem to suffer the deafness problems when a statement was made which was damaging to his client.

Once judgement was given in Liberace's favour, David Jacobs' reputation as the premier celebrity lawyer in the country was secured, and he remained in that position of eminence until his mysterious death several years later.

And Liberace was able to leave the court head held high, with record damages, luxuriating in the fact that he was not, in the precious words of Mr. Justice Salmon, a 'homosexualist'.

Brian Epstein and Jacobs had met in the early sixties when Epstein's trips to London, for commercial and sexual reasons, brought him into the circles frequented by the glamorous Jacobs. As the importance of the Beatles grew through 1963 it was perhaps inevitable that Epstein would start to use Jacobs' legal services on an increasing basis, part business and part personal. Jacobs, given his own homosexuality, was in a unique position to understand the strains impacting on Brian Epstein.

There were a number of instances in the mid-sixties when Jacobs was able to use his legal knowledge and contacts to extricate Epstein from situations created by his increasingly dangerous personal life.

By 1963 Epstein and Jacobs had become close and familiar friends, which wasn't strange as the two men had much in common. There was the basic religious link with both men coming from Jewish stock, but in addition, their respective families were both connected with the retail end of the furniture business. The Epstein family's involvement via their local furniture store was rather less imposing than that of the Jacobs family. David Jacobs' grandfather, John Jacobs, had founded the major home furnishing chain, Times Furnishings, which had grown into a substantial concern well before the Second World War.

Both Epstein and Jacobs were habitual and regular users of uppers and downers, and through the sixties Brian Epstein became a frequent visitor to the Jacobs retreat in Hove. His trust in Jacobs and the solicitor's judgement became total, although the two men differed greatly in the way they presented their personal selves to the world.

Epstein was always the immaculately dressed, reserved, conservative businessman, nervous of public shows of emotion. That was the reason that the picture of him with a chamber pot on his head in the hotel room at the George Cinq caused such a stir. It was so uncharacteristic of the shy Epstein. The fact that the photograph was taken in the midst of the wild celebrations after receiving the telegram confirming that the Beatles were Number 1 on the Cashbox chart seemed a perfect excuse for what was for him unrestrained and almost wild behaviour.

David Jacobs, the solicitor, was very different. A large man, some 6' 3", he had a bearing which greatly resembled the theatricals and entertainment figures who were his major clients. His greying hair was invariably dyed jet black which was often offset by the makeup that he wore, even in court.

Clothes were a major consideration and he shared the same personal tailor as Grace Kelly's husband, Prince Rainier of Monaco. His vehicle of choice was a twin tone maroon and pink Rolls, with a chauffeur kept on hand permanently in case he needed transporting to another appointment or court engagement.

His homosexuality was not a secret but in the climate of the times he could not afford to advertise or broadcast it. Instead he relied on the discretion of friends and clients with whom he shared interests and a particular lifestyle. That group included people like Larry Parnes, Gilbert Harding and Lionel Bart. It was perhaps inevitable that Bart, the tragic composer of classics like the musical Oliver, also became a close friend of Brian Epstein. And in that list of associates of David Jacobs would also be included the Kray twins, particularly

Ronnie whose homosexual lifestyle led him into a number of savage encounters in London in the mid-sixties.

David Jacobs was a highly personable and popular figure in London in the sixties, the host of huge parties at his opulent Chelsea home which would be attended by many members of London society and the more glittering end of the show business spectrum. Away from London he was keen to maintain a substantial family home on the coast in Hove, and kept his mother there in some considerable style and comfort. He loaned the house to Ringo Starr in 1965 when he married Maureen Cox and they enjoyed their honeymoon there.

On a number of levels, it was obvious and natural that Epstein and Jacobs should become friends and enjoy a relationship wider than that of simple solicitor and client. Jacobs was allowed into the inner sanctum, people Epstein trusted implicitly, and to whom he would allocate tasks and duties based simply on the fact that he valued the person rather than any natural or discernable ability to fulfil the task at hand.

As a direct result, Epstein's relationship with David Jacobs involved him in a major project which developed over a period of years into a substantial crisis. The situation with Seltaeb was ultimately the responsibility of David Jacobs, but in turn the fault could be justifiably laid at the door of Brian Epstein who glibly and casually passed over responsibility for merchandising of the Beatles to David Jacobs.

It started very quietly and simply in early 1963 when NEMS were made aware that a company in Blackpool were producing cheap and tacky Beatles souvenirs and selling them to the unaware. Epstein wasn't certain what steps to take but a conversation with Jacobs put his mind at rest.

The matter was dealt with and the irritation in Blackpool disappeared.

Many concerns for Epstein vanished as a result of Jacobs' interventions. There were two outcomes to this efficient piece of legal work from Jacobs. In a half-hearted attempt to provide some more creditable souvenir material for the Beatles fans who started requesting such items in the middle of 1963 Epstein persuaded family members to produce a very limited range of sweaters and badges, initially just to members of the official Beatles Fan Club.

This was via a firm called Weldons of Peckham based in Rye Lane in London. They produced a fetching two-tone Beatles badge embroidered in gold and red. This was then stitched onto a black polo neck sweater which was made of 100% Botany wool.

As Epstein decreed, it was a quality product and became the only item which was ever sold directly through the Official Fan Club. Mail order price for Christmas 1963 was £1-15-00 (£1-75), a price which also included postage and packing. In the advertisements the garment was modelled by fan club assistant, Mary Cockram, but the caption beneath credited the appearance as, "Anne Collingham wears the Official Sweater in the picture above."

Anne Collingham was an invented name. She didn't exist, but most of the enquiries to the Fan Club, which didn't mention people like Bettina Rose or the redoubtable Freda Kelly by name, were invariably directed to the invisible Anne Collingham.

The sheer numbers joining the fan club, plus the huge numbers who liked the group without bothering to join the fan club, quickly made such limited efforts redundant. At the time that the badges started appearing during 1963 the Beatles Fan Club numbered around 2,000; well before the end of that tumultuous year the number of Fan Club members had grown to more than 30,000, and that number would more than double during the following year, and carry on increasing in subsequent years.

Various events in the second half of 1963 turned the flood of requests for Beatles merchandise, and particularly for applications for a licence to produce such items, into a torrent; one that was well beyond the capacity of Epstein or his family or the staff of NEMS to handle.

His remedy was to ask David Jacobs for assistance. This was a fairly reasonable outcome given their friendship; Jacobs' proven capability for handling complex situations, and the adroit way he had dealt with the Blackpool problem with the minimum of fuss were his credentials.

The first issue of the Beatles Monthly magazine had appeared in August 1963 and Epstein had consented to the publication advertising the Beatles jumpers and badges as a mail order purchase. He and the publishers and the NEMS staff were staggered by the response. Almost 25,000 jumpers and more than 50,000 badges were sold in a week, but the NEMS organisation lacked the resources to deal with this volume of interest, particularly when the huge sales via the Beatles Monthly prompted a fresh wave of enquiries and offers from merchandising companies, keen to jump on this lucrative but inevitably short-lived bandwagon.

Epstein had a strict policy which he maintained despite all the pressure and the offers. He refused to allow the Beatles, individually or collectively, to endorse any product directly, but using NEMS Enterprises he would allow a series of discretionary licenses to companies which, in Epstein's eyes, were able to produce a quality product at a fair price. As ever, it was a decent policy created by a manifestly decent man. The deluge of interest rendered such a policy almost unworkable, not least because the trickle of unlicensed products that started in Blackpool had already become a tidal wave by late 1963, and the massive sales demand would reach tsunami proportions within months.

Epstein asked David Jacobs to handle the merchandising issues for him but at the time that request was made two things were very clear. One was that Epstein clearly didn't expect the merchandising demands to expand greatly, and the other was that, for the best of reasons, he gave no consideration whatsoever to the possibilities of merchandising demands, from customers or suppliers, from overseas.

For those reasons the merchandising was a small, local problem - one best dealt with by David Jacobs and his people. And for Brian Epstein, questions of badges and pillowcases and calendars were inconsequential next to the recordings and the tours and the tv shows. Small beer, particularly to a man becoming accustomed to the very finest of wines.

Jacobs took over the daily responsibility for the merchandising requests, with a particular emphasis on dealing with the requests to produce merchandise, but even those applications proliferated at an alarming rate following the release of 'She Loves You' and "With The Beatles" plus the twin explosions of Sunday Night at the London Palladium and then the Royal Command Performance. More than seventy thousand applications for merchandising licenses were received in October and early November, and even the urbane Jacobs was nonplussed.

That was the background to Epstein's approach to David Jacobs about merchandising. It was part lofty disinterest and part desperation because of the scale of the enquiries. Quite reasonably, he calculated that Jacobs would be able to handle these matters far better, and if Jacobs couldn't or wouldn't do the job himself he was bound to know someone who could.

In his first attempt, Jacobs turned to Edward Marke, the senior clerk in his practice in London, but Marke allegedly quickly informed Jacobs that he would not be competent to deal with Epstein's merchandising problems.

This left Jacobs in a dilemma. On a personal level he didn't want to disappoint his friend Brian Epstein. On a business level the work coming in from NEMS was extremely lucrative as was the more private and discreet work he did for Brian. And there was the extremely glamorous extra benefit afforded by being, and remaining, in the Beatles circle. Jacobs had a number of very telling reasons to want to solve the merchandising problem for Epstein.

The solution he chose was apparently bizarre. All the books, all the internet sites, state unequivocally that Jacobs made contact with a man named Nicky Byrne, leader of a group allegedly named 'the Kings Road Rats' and Jacobs and Byrne negotiated and signed the contract.

Wrong. Incorrect. Lazy lies, which have taken on the power of solid fact as a result of constant repetition. As I was to discover months later, from conversations with people much more intimately and directly involved with

Seltaeb than the journalists and assorted Wikipedia contributors, the real architect of Seltaeb was not Nicky Byrne - it was John Fenton.

And so, for decades afterwards people read about the slightly seedy Chelsea man-about-town, a frequenter of the Chelsea party scene, named Nicky Byrne. About Jacobs happening to bump into him at the party of a friend of Lionel Bart's, and the way that Jacobs, not for the first time, wasn't slow to lace the conversations with hints of how close he was to the group. The stories then claim that that Jacobs started describing in some detail the merchandising problems being suffered by Epstein. He allegedly told Byrne about the terrible mess that Brian had made of the situation, with the net result that Jacobs offered Byrne the chance of running the merchandising operation on behalf of Epstein and NEMS. Not surprisingly, were any of this true, Nicky Byrne accepted the offer.

Untrue. Inaccurate. Misleading. Byrne was not involved until much later, after the deal had been thought up, negotiated and sealed by John Fenton.

The tales of what the 37-year-old Byrne did in London to pull off the deal have become legendary, but, as my research and my conversations were to reveal, the truth was often rather different. Often no less interesting or remarkable, but invariably different. In so many instances of the Beatles story during the sixties I was to learn that maybe history has been wrong all along.

The simple fact is that because of certain legal difficulties relating to earlier failed business ventures Byrne was not even legally allowed to sign such a contract, even if he had thought up the Seltaeb venture in the first place.

But he didn't even think it up. The impetus came entirely from John Fenton thanks to family connections and a very sharp mind.

The real and lasting impact Nicky Byrne had on the Seltaeb situation came after he had left London for New York. Those activities would cost many, many people a lot of money, with the most substantial loss, in pain and money, being endured by Brian Epstein.

In London Nicky Byrne had led several ventures that had failed or stalled, such as involvements in theatre production and clothing design. He had been more successful in a stint as manager of the Condor Club at which he came to the attention of frequent visitor, Lionel Bart. It was while Byrne was managing the Condor Club that Bart had recommended that his friend Larry Parnes should go to the club to see a singer called Reg Smith for whom Bart expected a bright future. Reg Smith would change his name to Marty Wilde and went on to become one of the real stars of the UK's early rock 'n' roll days, and later a songwriter of some repute. Many years later that same Reg Smith fathered a daughter who, as Kim Wilde, had substantial chart success of her own.

The prevailing wisdom claims that Jacobs was also aware that Byrne was involved with a group of youngish people in west London who called themselves "the King's Road Rats". Sadly it now emerges that the members of this group not only did not use this group name about themselves, it is a title they do not even recognise.

The story which has sustained for half a century claims that Jacobs took a call from Nicky Byrne confirming that he had met with his friends, explained what was on offer, and the responses were very positive. The group had decided to form a limited company called Stramsact, bought off-the-shelf for less than £100, which would act as sole agent for merchandising approaches and deals in the UK. The funding for the creation of the company was to come from Byrne's partners including Lord Peregrine Eliot, Mark Warman, John Fenton, Simon Miller-Munday, and Malcolm Evans, and each contributed the 1963 equivalent of £5,500 to the fund.

By the time Nicky Byrne allegedly met David Jacobs for the second time everything was in place. Indeed the conversations among the King's Road Rats had confirmed the tremendous possibilities in the offer. The connections in London and in the general entertainment industry had alerted them to the fact that things were starting to happen in America for the Beatles and one of the group, who had a family connection to Jane Asher, was able to pass on the priceless advance information about the Sullivan appearances early the following year.

For those reasons Jacobs was offered a superb proposition. Not only would Byrne and his colleagues sort out the merchandising mess, they would do this via one company in the UK, named Stramsact Ltd, and a separate company overseas to be called Seltaeb Inc.

As ever, it is easy to be critical of Epstein and Jacobs but in this instance it is difficult to be hypercritical of Jacobs' reaction to the proposition presented. A growing problem, merchandising, would be handled by a group of dedicated professionals including a man who was a Lord and heir to a magnificent 6000-acre estate in Cornwall.

A merchandising contract was prepared covering all the points discussed, and the important meeting took place on Wednesday December 4th 1963 in Jacobs' London office. All the relevant sections of the contract had been completed, bar one - the column dictating the percentages of revenue to be taken by the two sides. When Jacobs queried the gap and asked what figure should be inserted Byrne apparently, allegedly airily replied "Oh, just put in 10%".

Jacobs obliged and that was the contract which was eventually taken to Brian Epstein and then returned with the pages initialled, demonstrating that

Epstein had read it. The Beatles manager had then signed it and had the contract witnessed by Jacobs.

On the strength of that legal agreement, Byrne and his colleagues set about the task of rationalising and then exploiting the massive merchandising opportunities, which included a rapid decampment to New York early in 1964 to take advantage of the situation there. And it was as a result of the way that he and his colleagues had dealt with the American opportunities that Nicky Byrne was ushered into Epstein's regal presence on that bleak February morning.

They hadn't met before. All the discussions, all the negotiations, such as they were, had taken place between Jacobs and Fenton face to face.

Epstein had never been involved and that was why Nicky Byrne had to introduce himself at the Delmonico.

Byrne gave a measured explanation of who he was, and how he was involved with Seltaeb. Epstein by this point was becoming quite the politician, never giving away the fact in a business situation that he didn't know what was going on, or that he wasn't fully briefed. That kind of glassy control wasn't necessary in this situation though. Epstein had only read and signed the contract a few weeks earlier and he had discussed the merchandising situation with Jacobs by phone while Epstein was in Paris with the Beatles before leaving for America.

Epstein hadn't asked Jacobs for details, merely for reassurance, and Jacobs provided it.

So the meeting in the Delmonico started in a convivial spirit and continued in that vein as Byrne described to Epstein the huge interest in the Beatles that was being shown by American companies. As a demonstration of that incredible level of interest he was able to hand Epstein a Seltaeb check for merchandising royalties for activity which pre-dated the Sullivan show. Both men dreamily conjectured on what the upsurge in interest and sales might be once the impact of the Sullivan show was felt across America.

And then Epstein looked at the cheque.

$9,700.

A very tidy sum, particularly given that the Beatles were only being paid $10,000 for three Ed Sullivan appearances. Epstein was grateful, and impressed, and then asked Byrne "How much of this amount do we owe you, Nicky?"

It was an innocent, genuine question created from the understandable assumption that Byrne was handing over all the Seltaeb takings from which

Epstein or NEMS would keep their share before handing the residue back to Seltaeb.

Sadly, Epstein was mistaken. Without any hint of triumphalism Byrne calmly replied, "Nothing, Brian. That's your 10%!"

Byrne carried on talking about the incredible offers that were being received and accepted, but in truth Epstein was barely taking in the words.

$9,700.

10%?

That meant that Seltaeb or Stramsact or whatever had taken just short of $100,000, and kept, totally legally and legitimately, almost $90,000!

It was a shocking, staggering development, and it was truly the first moment when Brian Epstein felt his position of supremacy in the world of the Beatles to be under threat. And events were to prove him painfully, bitterly, fatally correct.

But the furore surrounding Epstein didn't allow him to dwell on that astonishing development, or to wallow in the intense misery it caused him.

Once again the simplicity of the then-current technology hampered his actions. If the same conversation happened today Epstein would clearly have been able to ring Jacobs immediately on his mobile, or cell phone, to discover what was happening. In those days he was restricted to landline calls which could be intermittently difficult for transatlantic communications.

More significantly, it was a call and a conversation that Epstein didn't want to have in public, in the lounge of the Delmonico. He had chosen that venue very deliberately. He wanted some peace, a little tranquillity, away from the continuous bedlam in and around the Plaza, where it seemed that every American boy and girl below twenty were laying siege to the venerable hotel. Epstein was also coming under sustained pressure from the management of the hotel who had innocently accepted bookings in December for a Mr. Lennon, a Mr. Starr, a Mr. McCartney and a Mr. Harrison, plus sundry others. At the time it was just another booking for the hotel.

Nothing either remarkable or out of the ordinary. The names didn't register or cause any eyebrows to be raised but that is hardly surprising. At the start of December 1963, few people in America had heard of the Beatles, let alone being able to name the individual members of the group.

For that reason when it was leaked to the radio stations that the Beatles would be staying at the Plaza for the duration of their period in New York the wonderful hotel on Central Park South became a magnet and place of pilgrimage for thousands of kids as well as massive amounts of media, press, television and radio. The four Beatles were marooned in their suite, content to stare out of the windows at the frenzy in the streets below, frenzy that moved up several notches when one of the four stood by the window and waved. The thousands of kids down by the fountain were just overcome with joy whenever there was a sign of movement from one of the windows on the Beatles floor. As visitors like Geoffrey Ellis and Sid Bernstein confirmed, the Beatles couldn't resist going to the windows to gaze out at New York but principally to view the bedlam being caused by the thousands of fans who had turned out in the cold just to be near the Beatles.

The other members of the party - Mal Evans, Neil Aspinall and so on - could come and go unmolested and largely unrecognised. Even Brian Epstein was an unknown character in the drama. All the media attention had focussed on the four Beatles, not least because of their cheeky, irreverent personalities. The four individuals were already winning over large sections of the American public who loved the group but adored a particular individual Beatle.

Scant attention was paid to other people and nobody probably noticed the greying middle-aged man who stood by the Pulitzer Fountain watching the crowds and the pandemonium caused when a small English arm waved from a distant window.

The man walked over to the entrance to the Plaza and, giving the appropriate credentials, was escorted up to the suites containing the Beatles and their retinue. But, however the situation was considered from the street, it was obvious that Sid Bernstein was going to have an important impact on events. Strangely, he had only met Epstein once before the Plaza. On one of the days in November while Epstein was waiting for the dinner appointment with Sullivan and his son-in-law, Bernstein and Epstein had met for coffee, and to strike up a friendship which was to last until Epstein's untimely death.

Going up into the heavily protected suite of rooms occupied by the Beatles party was a privilege during the days that the Beatles were at the Plaza.

Many, many tried to gain admittance; very few managed it.

Bernstein and Epstein greeted each other like old friends which, given the number of transatlantic calls over the previous few months, was quite accurate. In addition, in response to a remark made by Epstein's mother during that first call several months earlier, Bernstein had dutifully posted every issue of the New York Review of Books to her. Such gestures, such thoughtfulness, resonated with Epstein but above all he valued the fact that Bernstein had shown such total faith in the Beatles all those months earlier.

There was one oasis of calm in the hotel suites. A beautifully spoken woman from Yorkshire, who had arrived as Brian Epstein's guardian angel not via Leeds but via Los Angeles. Wendy Hanson had been sent by Capitol to act temporarily as Epstein's secretary and, crucially, to filter his calls. The calm, self-possessed Hanson proved a godsend in the madness in the Plaza to such effect that Epstein insisted on taking her with him as his assistant when they all returned to London.

She had brought Bernstein in to meet Epstein and left them alone in the comparative quiet of Brian's bedroom, wisely on a separate floor to the Beatles suite, to discuss the situation and to marvel at what had happened.

Those days were well before the modern sophistication of Neilsen ratings and instant social media verdicts, but by any measure something quite remarkable had happened the previous evening. In coming days it would be realised that the audience for the Sullivan show was some 73 million Americans, the largest television audience in the United States for any one show up to that time. Among the many people and organisations delighted by this, perhaps the happiest were those companies with advertisements running on either side of the two sets by the Beatles on the show, names that included Anacin, Aero Shave, Pillsbury and Kent.

In their conversation, Bernstein was keen to confirm the arrangements for the Carnegie Hall concert with Epstein, and he also wanted to make another suggestion.

That meant leaving the Plaza so the two men walked out, again totally unrecognised, and took a yellow cab across to Madison Square Gardens.

They went a rather unusual route, even by the standards of New York cabbies, so that they went past Carnegie Hall to allow Epstein to see the venue. The cab slowed on 57th street as it approached Seventh Avenue so that both Bernstein and Epstein could savour the moment, and then the cab moved southwest to reach what was actually the third incarnation of Madison Square Gardens. That particular building had enjoyed a forty-year lifespan and featured in some of New York's most glittering occasions, mainly sporting, with New York Rangers and New York Knicks having long-standing residencies at the Gardens. Other more social events also featured in the story of the venue, and the Barnum & Bailey Circus was a major attraction for many years. But perhaps the most famous incident in the decades that building was open, came in May 1962 when a birthday party was held there for President John F. Kennedy. Leaving aside the incongruity of a birthday party being held in an arena like that for the Leader of the Free World, the event is timeless because of the cameo of Marilyn Monroe in a breathlessly tight shimmering dress singing “Happy Birthday Mr.President” to the glowing JFK.

Bernstein didn't want to show the Gardens to Epstein as a history lesson. Instead he wanted to interest the Beatles manager in the prospect of a concert there to follow on from the imminent shows at Carnegie Hall. The tickets had been taken for the two performances at Carnegie Hall at a phenomenal rate. In the cab as they were passing Carnegie Hall, Bernstein told Epstein that the Hall Manager at Carnegie, a venerable chap named Matt Posnak, had told him that demand at Carnegie was so great that he reckoned that Carnegie Hall had turned down around 100,000 applications for tickets!

Even in a world where everything around the Beatles was becoming telephone numbers, the details being imparted by the gregarious Bernstein took Epstein by surprise, as did the proposition made by the New Yorker when they arrived at the Gardens a few minutes later.

Bernstein had arranged to meet his cousin at the entrance and he was waiting there for them. The three men walked into the old building which, though imposing, was starting to look its age by then. Indeed it would close just four years later to be replaced, on February 11, 1968, by the current Madison Square Garden located above Penn Station after the Pennsylvania Railroad pulled down the ground-level parts of the old Pennsylvania Station.

Bernstein proudly showed Epstein the cavernous layout and explained his grand plan. The tickets had sold so well at Carnegie Hall that he had tried to arrange another date there, but they had no other free dates during the Beatles brief visit. As an alternative, a huge alternative, Bernstein had approached the booker for the Garden, John Goldner, for possible dates around the Sullivan shows. By happy coincidence, the Garden did have dates free and Bernstein reckoned that selling out the 17,000 seat Garden would not be a problem.

To his surprise Epstein, though clearly captivated by the prospect, rejected it, using the reasoning that the Beatles could and should leave the New York fans wanting more. But he gave Bernstein the promise that they would be back, and that any future New York appearances by the Beatles would be the sole prerogative of Sid Bernstein. No contract, no involvement from lawyers, just the word of an honourable man, and Bernstein never would have cause to doubt or criticize Epstein.

And the small temporary disappointment of the polite rejection of the Garden offer was the cause of the creation of a small idea in Bernstein's mind, an idea which would result a year later in the largest pop concert in history.

Epstein returned to the chaos at the Plaza to deal with more complaints from the management about the way their refined, dignified establishment had been damaged by the scenes outside, and indeed inside. The exterior of the hotel looked like the setting for a major police drama with dozens of police cars and horses patrolling the 58th and 59th streets area in front of the hotel around a series of police barricades. Fifth Avenue was virtually impassable and the statue and the fountain were swarming with kids desperate to get a view of their heroes.

The more daring tried to find a way into the hotel and the staff were hard-pressed to keep the intruders out. Very, very few got anywhere near the Beatles on the fifteenth floor but just in case extra police security had been stationed by the lift and the stairs.

The final barrier was presented by the intrepid Wendy Hanson, who had proved her total value to Brian Epstein in those first few hours at the Plaza. She took the brunt of the complaints from the hotel management about the alleged subterfuge which had been used to make the original bookings for Messrs. Starkey, Lennon, McCartney and Harrison. In response to one particularly bitter complaint from a member of the hotel management, the shrewd Hanson showed the man the news footage on CBS, NBC and ABC plus front-page stories on a number of the major newspapers. In every case the Beatles stay in New York was the main story, and in many instances the image of the exterior of the Plaza along with the distinctive livery was clearly visible. "Now how much would advertising like that cost - normally?" asked Hanson sweetly. The topic was not raised again, but the Beatles would never be allowed to return to the Plaza after that initial trip in February 1964.

The main event on February 10th was a Press Conference at the hotel, one of a swathe of press and PR events which dominated the group's time during those first few days in America. At all those events the glowering presence behind the group, beside the group, alongside the massed reporters was Beatles PR Manager, Brian Sommerville who had only been employed by Epstein for a short time before the trip to the States.

For many observers the Beatles first visit to the States was a Public Relations triumph and much of that was down to the nervous, acerbic Sommerville, but the major praise, inevitably, must go to the group themselves who repeatedly managed to charm one of the most cynical and jaded press contingents in the world.

Once the Plaza press conference on the 10th concluded the group were left to their own devices in the hotel, preparing to leave New York the following day for their first-ever concert on American soil in Washington DC. They tried to get out of the hotel but the hordes surrounding the Plaza on all sides made escape difficult, but constant practice in England over the previous two years had made the group skilled in escape methods.

In this they were also greatly aided by the compliance of Mal Evans and Neil Aspinall, and that pair were crucial in enabling the four Beatles to get out of the Plaza for a couple of trips to the Playboy Club which was handily located not far from the hotel.

Mal Evans, in particular, thrived on the sheer exuberance of life in New York, starting a love for the city which lasted the rest of his short life. He was treated badly by the group in America, but that was the normal situation. To many observers Mal Evans, even more than Neil Aspinall, was regarded and often treated as a lackey, as a mere servant and for much of the time in New York he was engaged in cleaning up after the group. In the suite at the Plaza, the four Beatles went slightly wild, indulging themselves with the assorted pleasures of American room service. Obviously they had already spent huge periods in hotels in Britain, France and Sweden, but this was the States!

Massive amounts of French fries, and rum and coke, and steak platters were ordered and largely untouched, leaving an impression for first-time visitors of a slovenly mess. Evans was instructed by several members of the party to clean up the mess, a job which might have been left more properly to the totally competent Plaza staff, but the diligent Evans had a fierce devotion to the image of the Beatles. That, and the snide instructions from various people, brought Evans to a self-imposed cleaning routine in the hotel rooms, gathering up discarded plates and glasses and abandoned food and placing them in one of the anterooms. It was necessary, but dispiriting work. Necessary - because of the huge amount of rubbish accumulating in the rooms in such a short time. Dispiriting - because Mal Evans was not a cleaner, not there to move rubbish around, even if that was something he had to do for the Beatles all too often.

And it was on the Monday evening that Mal Evans was called into action to clean up another mess, one which could have totally derailed the remorseless Beatles conquest of America. He had not gone out that evening. The combination of excitement and drudgery was tiring. He opted for a night spent quietly in the hotel, content that Aspinall and Sommerville were sufficient for all the baby-sitting duties at the Playboy Club and elsewhere.

Evans was channel hopping on the tv set, marvelling at a world that offered so many different channels. He was prone on the bed accompanied by two strange bedfellows. They were the two gold discs which had been presented to the group earlier that day by Alan Livingstone of Capitol. One gold disc marked the sale of a million copies of 'I Want To Hold Your Hand', and the other represented a million dollars in sales of the album "Meet The Beatles".

The casual positioning of such trophies on Evans' bed demonstrated just how blasé the Beatles were becoming about such trinkets, even though the first gold discs from America were priceless.

Leaving such things with Mal Evans was eminently sensible. Of all the Beatles party he was the most physically capable if trouble started, and thefts or robberies, even from a well-protected area like the suite at the Plaza, was never far from their minds.

The ringing of the phone in the room was a surprise. He didn't expect to get calls. A muttered "Hello? Mal Evans?" was sufficient to get the caller talking, with a message that Evans didn't want to hear.

The caller was a stranger, a guttural American accent, talking of a problem, a problem that had been negotiated, a problem caused by naughty Mr. Epstein that had been handled. The questions were obvious - who, what, where, when? Most of all - who are you - but the caller wouldn't provide responses or information, except to say that the problem had been negotiated. Evans tried three, four times to get the mysterious caller to give a name, or to confirm what the problem was, or to explain what "negotiated" meant, or how it involved Brian, but he got nowhere.

The call was over in less than two minutes. Evans was puzzled not just about the confusing, strange message but why he should have received the call. He wondered who to ask. Brian was the obvious one but he was out. The group, particularly Paul, would have been the next choice, but Mal Evans' chosen role was to protect the various Beatles from problems. If the phone call represented anything it was likely to be trouble and the group could not, should not be subjected to problems - not with everything they had worked for now in their grasp.

So he took the pragmatic decision to say nothing and keep his eyes open, particularly around Brian, But Mal Evans could only keep his eyes open inside the Plaza, not in Central Park.

The following day saw the Beatles party leaving the Plaza, with the hotel management breathing a sigh of relief at the sudden calm and freedom. The group were due to return on the 12th for a one-night stay after their shows at Carnegie Hall, but that would be the end of it.

The Beatles were heading for Washington D.C. to play a concert which had been arranged by Epstein to allow them some warm-up time before the Carnegie Hall shows. The easiest and quickest way to get from New York to Washington was by plane but the group, particularly George, were slightly nervous and apprehensive about internal American flights. All of them were still big fans of Buddy Holly who had made a particular impact on the song writing of the young John Lennon and Paul McCartney. Each of the four Beatles had been deeply upset, like millions of young people around the world, by Holly's premature death just over five years earlier.

A death in a plane, on an internal flight. In the snow.

The five inches of snow overnight in New York convinced the party that perhaps George Harrison's nervousness was wise, but the weather had caused flights to be cancelled anyway. As a precaution, Epstein booked a sleeper compartment and had it hitched to the train from Penn Station southwest to

Washington DC. The carriage, an old Richmond, Fredericksburg and Potomac Railroad sleeper car called The King George, was unfortunately crammed with excited press when the Beatles party arrived at the Pennsylvania Railroad express. The journey of just over two hundred miles should have enabled the trip to be enjoyed in some comfort and a great deal less stress than the plane journey might have caused, but, at every stop on the journey, press photographers appeared and another bunch of lenses were thrust against the carriage windows.

However, one benefit of the train was the relative freedom to move around, and the extended party of journalists, media people and general hangers-on who had latched onto the Beatles found the train journey gave many opportunities to pursue their particular objectives.

Al Aronowitz was there on the train, researching the material which would form his record-breaking Life magazine article. Murray the K was there, creating a mythology which would sustain him for decades into the future.

Members of the Seltaeb group were also present, trying to grab the opportunity to discuss fresh projects with Epstein. Given his abject shock at realising what the $9,700 represented, Epstein wasn't rushing to speak to anybody representing Seltaeb. Instead he was keeping his counsel until he got back to London and was able to have a longer conversation with David Jacobs than the crackling transatlantic line had allowed.

Another huge crowd, in excess of two thousand kids, was waiting at Union Station in the bitter cold to greet them, the near-blizzard conditions barely calming the excitement. Hotel space had been booked at the Shoreham Hotel in which the Beatles party were taking the complete seventh floor. A group of limousines was on hand to transport the party to the hotel from the station and the party was swelled by the addition of Carroll James of WWDC, the Washington DJ who had started the avalanche of interest by having a copy of 'I Want To Hold Your Hand' flown from England.

Accompanying James, in an unusually sweet touch, was Marsha Albert, the young girl whose letter to James about the Beatles had been the catalyst back in December.

She was able to ride in one of the limousines to the hotel accompanied by Cynthia Lennon and George Harrison's sister who were also in the party. The booking at the Shoreham demanded complete security, and so the floor was completely sealed off from the clamouring fans. One unfortunate family had, despite appeals and offers of compensation, refused to leave their room on the Beatles floor. Unfortunately, the electricity, then the central heating and even the hot water all failed in their room leaving the family in a desperate situation. Officially it was an accident which the Shoreham management blamed on a power failure, but the family demanded and received a move to other rooms in the hotel.

Curiously, and most fortunately, electricity, central heating and hot water were all working perfectly in the replacement rooms on the fifth floor. The disgruntled family were happier, and warmer, and the privacy of the Beatles was secure.

After a brief stop at the hotel, they all climbed back into the limousines which transported them to the Coliseum. Prior to the show Carroll James was able to conduct an interview with the Beatles, just reward for the remarkable and wholly unplanned part he performed in that initial American success. And Carroll James played his role perfectly by bringing the young Marsha Albert in to meet her heroes.

The concert at the Washington Coliseum was only a filler, and the facilities demonstrated that. The stage was tiny and was actually a barely converted boxing ring, and surviving long-range photographs look like prize fights from the fifties or sixties.

There was barely room for the Beatles and their equipment which was hardly lavish anyway. In order to maximise the experience for the crowd the group stopped playing three times and physically manhandled the equipment, particularly Ringo's drum kit, round to face a different direction.

The movement of equipment had a damaging effect on their level of performance. The microphones in particular suffered, and there was a strange intermittent problem with Paul's amplifier but hardly anybody, apart from the group themselves, noticed. There were more than 8,000 people in the crowd, their largest audience to date, and the reaction was as wild as ever.

Washington Coliseum had engaged almost four hundred police officers to keep order, and the local press made great play of one of the policemen who was so affected by the volume of the fans that he placed a bullet in each ear and used the bullets as ear plugs.

The incessant screaming meant that most of the audience could scarcely hear a note while the Beatles, pleasant and professional and smiling as ever, knew that the performance was poor - but did it matter when nobody could hear anyway? The seeds of the disillusionment which would cause their retirement from live performance after a future American show were sown in the enjoyable shambles of shows like the one at Washington.

And as if to emphasize the problems, the whole concert was filmed and then later transmitted as a closed-circuit broadcast to cinemas in March.

The support acts at Washington were the Caravelles, Tommy Roe, and the Chiffons, performing to a largely female audience paying $2-$4 per ticket, and reactions from the audience were completely positive about the British group.

They returned to the Shoreham to change for a function the group had been committed to at the British Embassy, part of Epstein's regular PR onslaught. It was only meant to be a light-hearted, press the flesh evening, but it turned into a painful and humiliating evening for all four Beatles, particularly Ringo Starr who had to suffer a hideous unnamed woman snipping a lock of his hair off with nail scissors without his permission or even knowledge.

The return to New York the following morning was welcomed by the whole party because a real warmth had developed for the city thanks to their reception there since arriving on February 7th. More importantly, the return to New York signified the imminence of the two Carnegie Hall shows. These were taking place on February 12th, a public holiday in America, Lincoln's Birthday, and the day that Sid Bernstein had pitched to Epstein in 1963.

One of the reasons Bernstein had opted for that date was because the kids would be off school, and his premonitions proved correct. The crowds were so huge around Penn Station that the limousines chartered for the Beatles couldn't move, and so a pragmatic decision was made to grab a series of taxis to move the party back to the Plaza. At the hotel another quick change of clothes was followed by a hurried escape through the cavernous kitchens, and back into the cars.

The Carnegie Hall shows were meant to be recorded by George Martin for future broadcast or release, but objections from the American Federation of Musicians thwarted that plan. Instead, the Beatles delivered their usual set to two separate audiences of almost three thousand people who had sold out the box office quota of tickets in less than a day.

Carnegie Hall was definitely a venue to attract the great and the good, and the backstage area was crowded with show business personalities, politicians, sports stars and the usual flotsam and jetsam which clung to the Beatles. Among the large contingent was a full group from Seltaeb who were already raking in a considerable fortune thanks to the impact the Beatles had made over the previous week. Sid Bernstein was obviously there, exulting in his modest way about the brilliant way his plan had worked out, not least because when his contact at Carnegie first heard Bernstein's proposition in 1963 she had assumed that by Lennon, McCartney, Starr and Harrison he was referring to a British string quartet.

The date was symbolic because, forty years earlier to the day, came the inaugural performance of George Gershwin's timeless "Rhapsody In Blue" which was premiered less than a mile away at the Aeolian Hall.

Bernstein's history with the Carnegie hall organisation was considerable. This included a legendary concert in June 1962 when Tony Bennett took to the famous stage supported by some of the top musicians of the time, including the Ralph Sharon Trio, Kenny Burrell and Al Cohn. That concert took place at a low point in Bennett's career, and, despite Bernstein's faith in the singer and his innovative ideas for promoting the event, Tony Bennett had to put up a substantial sum from his own funds to secure the booking.

The night was a triumph, thanks in no small part to some of the tactics Bernstein used to publicise and promote the show, methods he would polish and re-use for Beatles appearances in the next couple of years. But Tony Bennett's success at Carnegie in June 1962 revitalised his career with Columbia Records and also established an ongoing relationship between Sid Bernstein and the staff at the Hall.

One small but significant milestone was achieved backstage at the Beatles concert with the presentation to the group of a gold disc for selling one million copies of 'She Loves You'.

But this presentation came not from Capitol Records, flushed from the success of 'I Want To Hold Your Hand'. Instead it was awarded by Swan Records as the company which had tried to market and sell 'She Loves You' back in the autumn when nobody cared about the Beatles or wanted to hear their music. The Ed Sullivan show, and the torrent of publicity, had changed the situation and Swan had not been slow to re-issue the disc and capitalise on their advance, much to the annoyance and frustration of the sales team at Capitol.

The situation would get much worse in the coming weeks as various labels with any claim on Beatles material sought to make some money from the sudden interest. Chief among these were Vee-Jay, plus their subsidiary, Tollie Records, and Swan - they being the two companies which had tried to market the Beatles in 1963 in the midst of Capitol's massive disinterest.

Now though, in settings like the Carnegie Hall backstage area, the Capitol staff were intent on establishing their dominance over the situation, and there were a number of testy conversations between representatives of Capitol and Swan. The numbers didn't lie, and the Swan people had a gold record to prove their success with the Beatles.

And a similar, more contentious problem for Capitol was looming in the form of Vee-Jay and the assorted Beatles material they had been handling since the spring of 1963. The label's attempts to promote Beatles material during that period had been bedevilled by the indifference of American record buyers and also by the financial problems besetting the label.

By early 1964 the indifference had clearly been replaced by a mad passion for anything Beatles related; the money problems hadn't disappeared at Vee-Jay, but suddenly the reservoir of Beatles material offered a potential way out of the mess, and, not unreasonably, the Vee-Jay people grabbed the lifeline.

So 'Please Please Me' was released as a single on February 1st, with 'From Me To You' following later in the month. There would be further single releases over following months as Vee-Jay sought to squeeze every ounce of profit from its unexpected musical harvest, but the real problems came when Vee-Jay sought to re-release the one Beatles album in its catalogue. "Introducing the Beatles" had originally been intended as a release in the States in the summer of 1963 but was cancelled despite very advanced preparations for the release.

As the news about the Capitol promotion and the forthcoming Sullivan and Carnegie shows became public knowledge it is not surprising that the beleaguered management at Vee-Jay sought some financial return on their work in 1963. Besides the Beatles singles, the label naturally wanted to market the album and so it came out in early January, ten short days before Capitol was hurriedly scheduling the release of their first official Beatles album, "Meet the Beatles".

The decision to release "Introducing The Beatles" was taken in full expectation that legal problems would follow, but financial imperatives were more important, though the financial difficulties had a marked physical impact on the release. Money was so short at the label that though it still had 6,000 front covers printed and stockpiled from the aborted 1963 release Vee-Jay could not afford to design and print brand new back covers for "Introducing The Beatles".

As a stop-gap, emergency measure the label used a print from their standard inner sleeve which showed nothing other than small reproductions of other albums on the label under the clarion call "other fine albums of significant interest".

Interest in the trade was so strong that Vee-Jay had to rapidly commission another pressing of the album but by this point, given that the company had not yet received any money from sales, they couldn't even afford to run copies with the 25 album promotion on the back. Fevered discussions in Los Angeles, and attempts to raise money, produced no tangible outcome. The result was that this second pressing of the album was released with a completely blank white back cover.

The third and final version appeared with the official back cover and this remained in place for the lifetime of the album, but all three of these prints of the album appeared within days of the release on January 10th.

And then, just as the Vee-Jay management must have thought that fortune was favouring them, came another disaster. On January 16th the label was served with a restraining order compelling them to cease distribution.

The music publishing subsidiary of Capitol was a company named Beechwood Music Inc. and they owned the copyright to both 'Love Me Do' and 'PS I Love You'. Given the fact that neither song had been formally released in the States, Beechwood refused to grant a licence for Vee-Jay to release the songs.

Both tracks were included on "Introducing The Beatles", among the album's twelve tracks, and so the release, as originally planned, was crippled.

In this context, it is ironic to realise that it was the same Beechwood Music, as part of Ardmore & Beechwood, which had lamentably failed to promote the British release of 'Love Me Do', the situation which had effectively driven Epstein and Lennon and McCartney into the waiting arms of Dick James.

By the time Beechwood served the restraining order, close to 100,000 copies of "Introducing The Beatles" were on release, and Vee-Jay were facing yet another crisis. Their remedy was inventive. They took the two offending tracks off the album and replaced them with the two tracks which they had deleted from their Americanised version of the British album, 'Ask Me Why' and 'Please Please Me'.

The new versions of the album were pressed in the last few days of January and hit the record stores around the time of the first Sullivan show, although, to add to the general chaos, many copies with the revised tracks on the disc still showed the original, pre-Beechwood track listing.

The net effect of the delay was that, even though "Introducing the Beatles" was originally released ten days before the Capitol release of "Meet The Beatles", it did not reach the charts until three weeks after the Capitol album.

The delays, and concerns about covers and track listings had no impact on sales. It would reach the number two position on both Cashbox and Billboard, staying there for almost two months.

The restraining order imposed by Beechwood created, or possibly inflamed, the relationship between Capitol and Vee-Jay, and that acerbic situation would pertain for several months, and even slightly poison the atmosphere backstage at the Carnegie Hall concert. At that moment the object of the Capitol employees wrath was Swan Records and their gold record for 'She Loves You' but the Capitol resentment, however unreasonable, would extend to Vee-Jay, Tollie, MGM and even Decca in the remaining months of 1964.

The two shows at Carnegie Hall effectively ended the professional part of the Beatles first visit to New York. After a few hours relaxing at a club, they returned to the Plaza for the final time for more partying, some sleep, and a departure for Miami on the following day on National Airlines flight 11 at 1.30pm EST.

The arrival at Miami airport had again been orchestrated by the Seltaeb people using the model already used so successfully in New York. The local radio stations, WQAM and WFUN, had been primed with the details of the flight times, and offers of free badges and t-shirts, though present, were far less plentiful than in New York. It was not that Seltaeb couldn't afford the promotional budget. Instead they simply didn't need to spend it. Interest in the Beatles and their activities had grown so massively over the previous few days that merely mentioning the time of arrival was sufficient to guarantee thousands of kids arriving to greet the group.

In the event, several thousand were at the airport to watch the now well-practiced routine of the wave from the top of the airplane steps, the waves from the tarmac, and then the departure in a fleet of limousines. But the scenes at the airport in Miami got slightly more riotous than expected. A large plate-glass door was smashed, several windows were shattered, a group of chairs were broken apart, and a number of large sand-filled ashtrays were tipped over.

Airport authorities reckoned that over $2000 in damage was done to the airport, and this was just a minor taste of what was to come when the Beatles returned for their first full tour during the summer.

The presence of a dozen police outriders surrounding the Miami convoy gave the journey an extra edge of excitement for the Beatles, as did the profusion of palm trees - an exotic species that their journeying so far hadn't made available to them.

The performance in Miami was the second live show for Ed Sullivan. Apart from that, the group were committed to a couple of rehearsals in the hotel and a lot of highly welcome leisure time. On the first night in Miami the party went out to a couple of clubs, the Miami Peppermint Lounge and the Mau Mau Lounge to see groups whose names and music the Beatles knew but had never been able to see in person, the Coasters and Hank Ballard and the Midnighters.

The following day included a short rehearsal plus a photo-session for Life magazine, and a trip round Miami Harbour on a boat owned by furniture multi-millionaire, Bernard Castro, the inventor of the fold-down sofa bed. Succeeding days were taken up mainly by relaxation in the warmth of what must have seemed like a tropical paradise, with time spent water-skiing and fishing and swimming in the beautiful waters around Miami.

A couple of minor rehearsals culminated in a full dress rehearsal on the 15th in front of almost two thousand people, on a day when the Billboard chart showed 'I Want To Hold Your Hand' still at the top of the chart for the third consecutive week. This was the chart which, for the first time ever, showed one act, the Beatles, with five songs in the US Hot 100.

The second live Sullivan was shown at 8pm on Sunday February 16th. CBS Television had given out tickets for the show, and the hotel also distributed free passes to guests. The result was that more than a thousand additional people turned up for the show. Extra police had to be called in, and some ugly fights broke out between disappointed fans and security staff.

Perhaps remarkably, given the impact made in the previous Sullivan show, the Beatles were not headlining at the Deauville. The headline act was Mitzi Gaynor but she, and the other acts on the bill, were simply consumed by the noise made by the crowd in anticipation of the Beatles appearance. Subsequent ratings showed that, for the second time in eight days, the Beatles had attracted more than seventy million people to watch the Sullivan show.

If there were any lingering doubts about the importance of the Beatles or the impact they had made in their short trip to America, that Miami appearance on Ed Sullivan dispelled them. A second audience of seventy million couldn't be ignored or dismissed as a fluke or a fad.

The remaining few days in Miami were dominated by recreation with just a single day, February 18th, occupied by the kind of PR nonsense that Lennon in particular resented and hated. The group and their associates were taken out to the training camp at the Fifth Street gym being used by Cassius Clay to prepare for his forthcoming fight with Sonny Liston on February 25th. The visit involved the usual round of questions and a raft of photographs involving members of the group and Clay, who was then at the height of his physical prowess. He was only days away from this first meeting with the fearsome Liston and still some way from becoming the worldwide embodiment of a professional sportsman. But the staged meeting at the Fifth Street gym was symbolic in putting together the two forces which would dominate sport and music worldwide for the rest of the decade.

And that ceremonial, PR function with the soon-to-be World Boxing Champion finished their work in America. One final night in the hotel, and then an internal flight to New York the following afternoon to catch the overnight flight to London.

They arrived back at Heathrow not quite as conquering heroes but certainly on a new level of fame. Thousands more fans at the airport, and press requirements which demonstrated the change brought about by the astonishing developments in America. The customary press conference took place at a suite in the airport, disrupted slightly by a telephone interview between the Beatles and Brian Matthew broadcast live on Saturday Club that morning.

There was also a special piece filmed by the iconic Pathé News who took footage on the runway and also in the press conference, and built it into a short feature called "Beatles Welcome Home". The narration was provided by Bob Danvers-Walker, whose voice had enlivened Pathé News films since 1940, and "Beatles Welcome Home" was subsequently shown in cinemas - another sign of how important an event it was considered to be.

Footage from the press conference was even shown during that afternoon's Grandstand programme including an interview with the host of the programme, David Coleman. Grandstand was the flagship sports programme broadcast live every Saturday afternoon on the BBC. Its regular diet of sports results, horse racing and general outdoor pursuits would only ever be interrupted by major international news, and information about a mere pop group would never fit into that category.

But events in America, if not what had gone before, had elevated the Beatles to a new eminence, one that would take many years to fade.

But before that there were other mountains to climb, with the first coming in the form of the group's first film. Negotiations had been concluded well before Christmas with United Artist Films on a three-film deal, and since his days in Ireland and France observing the group in action, Alun Owen had been busily preparing a shooting script. Various important steps had been taken while the group were in America, which meant that the framework to support a major enterprise like a feature film was already being assembled.

United Artists had appointed Walter Shenson as producer and Dick Lester as Director, and provided the film with the relatively modest budget of £200,000. Lester was known to the Beatles through his work on "The Running Jumping Standing Still Film" which starred Spike Milligan and Peter Sellers, and had long been a collective favourite.

Lester had decided to make the film in black and white, largely because the United Artists budget precluded colour. He also adopted a cinema verite, semi-documentary style. Several leading British actors had already been hired for major parts in the as yet untitled film, including Victor Spinetti, Eleanor Bron, Norman Rossington and Wilfred Brambell who had appeared with the Beatles on the Royal Command Variety Performance in the previous November.

Although the working title of the film was "The Beatles", those words are never mentioned in the final screenplay.

Shooting was set to begin on March 2nd 1964, just a week after the group returned from America. Because of the budget restrictions, and principally because of other demands on the time of the Beatles, the shooting schedule was limited to two months.

Recording for what was intended to be the soundtrack to the film, plus additional music, began on February 26th at Abbey Road with early takes of 'And I Love Her' and 'I Should Have Known Better' being completed, both of which would feature prominently in "A Hard Day's Night". It was clear that, despite the amazing triumphs in America, Epstein had no intention of allowing them to rest on their laurels or ease their punishing schedule.

He had concerns of his own. The intense worries created by the conversation in New York with Nicky Byrne about the $9,700 had been deepened by Epstein's subsequent conversation with David Jacobs via the transatlantic call late on Monday. It was clear to both men that this crisis needed urgent handling and that had to be done face to face, and so Epstein flew back early from America on the day after the Cassius Clay session. He left the group to make their triumphant flight back without him although he made sure that he was present at London Airport when their plane touched down thirty minutes late on February 23rd.

He needed to go through the paperwork with David Jacobs, to make certain what had been agreed, and signed with regard to Stramsact and Seltaeb.

More urgently, he also needed to discuss with Jacobs the latest disaster, albeit only a potential one, in his troubled personal life. During the flight down to Miami, Epstein had endured a strange conversation with Mal Evans in which the roadie had described the disturbing phone call he had received in his room at the Plaza. In itself, the story wasn't deeply troubling, although slightly worrying - especially as Mal Evans wasn't given to flights of fancy. The unfortunate aspect of what Mal Evans told him was that it fitted unhappily with another story told to him, in disturbing circumstances and detail, just after he arrived in Miami.

One of the accursed Seltaeb people, an overbearing man although Epstein didn't know most of their names, climbed into the limousine taking them to the Deauville after ensuring that Epstein's other intended travelling companion took a different car. On the journey he told Epstein the gruesome story of how an enterprising press photographer had obtained various compromising shots in New York. The man didn't explain whether the shots in question were from the hotel or elsewhere in New York.

It didn't matter. The photographer was probably looking for nothing more than a couple of exclusive shots of the Beatles but, according to the Seltaeb story told to Epstein, the photographer got far more than expected.

The man didn't look at Epstein as he told the story of the photographer getting several brutally candid shots of a member of the Beatles party naked in acts of sodomy with another naked man.

The Seltaeb representative would only state and repeat, in a voice devoid of all emotion, that it wasn't one of the Beatles.

Epstein didn't need to be told that detail. He knew who the member of the Beatles party was.

Himself.

An abandoned night in the freedom of Central Park had culminated in Epstein sneaking one of the rent boys he had met there back to his room at the Plaza. It was a risk, he had known that, but far less dangerous than something similar in England. And in some respects the danger was part of the attraction.

The Seltaeb man kept respectfully silent after describing the shots the photographer had taken. The silence only served to concentrate Epstein's mind on the gravity of the situation. It was a disaster, and potentially the end of everything the Beatles had achieved in America.

While these thoughts coursed through Epstein's mind his companion stared silently out of the window, clearly confident that the silence would be far more telling than any words.

Finally, he spoke again, telling the dry-mouthed Epstein that the situation had been negotiated. That was the moment, the use of the word "negotiated", that Epstein made the link to the weird story told to him earlier that afternoon by Mal Evans.

Epstein's companion told him that certain people - he didn't specify and Epstein didn't ask - had heard about the photographs and, aware of the gravity of the situation, had taken steps to ensure that the photographs never saw the light of day.

Epstein didn't ask what those steps were. He didn't want to know. He just wanted the horror of the conversation and the journey to end. Fortunately the journey to the Deauville wasn't long and Epstein was able to get away from his unwelcome companion quite quickly. No mention had been made of who the mysterious member of the Beatles party was but Epstein was painfully aware that the man knew perfectly well.

The only consolation was that the man seemed painfully embarrassed by the conversation. There was no sniggering, nor veiled hints about blackmail, a nightmare that had afflicted Brian Epstein several times in the past, and a problem from which Jacobs had often extricated him..

But whatever it meant, such a cataclysmic situation could only be discussed with someone like David Jacobs, and so Epstein had really pressing reasons to want… to need to have a private conversation with the lawyer.

He had warned Jacobs that he needed to meet with him as soon as he returned from America and so, having cancelled his usual driver, Epstein took a cab from Heathrow to the Jacobs family home at Brighton, arriving there on the afternoon on the 23rd.

As it was a Thursday, Jacobs would normally have been in London but Epstein had stressed the urgency of the situation and particularly the need to have a conversation away from inquisitive ears. He was tired after the journey but euphoric. Mainly he was keen to get these two minor crises resolved quickly.

The beach in Brighton in February is many things. Private, sometimes even desolate, is one, and so it was there, walking along those wet sands, that Epstein was able to describe the twin problems in graphic detail to Jacobs.

The lawyer obviously knew all about the Seltaeb merchandising matter, given that he had conducted the negotiations with John Fenton. However, he refused to back down to Epstein's waspish remarks about the ludicrous percentages that had been agreed. To endorse his position he produced, there in the sand and the wind and the rain, his copy of the merchandising contract embroidered on every page with Epstein's initials and signed with the fully legal signature of Brian Epstein.

Jacobs didn't seem as worried by the Seltaeb dilemma as Epstein was. His view was clearly that 10% is better than nothing. Unlike Epstein he wasn't able to make the calculation, bearing in mind what Epstein had seen in America over the previous week, what that 10% might amount to.

Or, more importantly and painfully, how much the lost 90% might total.

Running through Epstein's mind was the fear, if not the terror, that if the Beatles were deprived of millions of pounds in merchandising returns they would inevitably blame him. And blaming him for that error might cause them to look critically at his management, however unfair that might be.

There was no suspicion of illegality in anything that had been done under Epstein's management. Rather it was the suspicion of incompetence, and Brian Epstein's pride could not countenance anybody, least of all the Beatles, thinking of him that way.

The result of the discussion about the Seltaeb problem was an offer by Jacobs to explore the situation, and, because of Epstein's insistence that 10% being returned to the group was unacceptable, the clear understanding was that between them the two men would have to find a more equitable return on the merchandising.

The problem of the New York photographs was far less clear-cut. In discussing what had happened, and what to do next, Epstein was in a much less awkward position than had he been speaking to virtually anybody else. David Jacobs had been a confidant for many months and, thanks to his own sexual history, Jacobs understood Brian Epstein far better than most other people could have done.

There had been other, earlier problems which had dogged Epstein, difficulties which Jacob had quietly, smoothly and very discreetly handled. A particularly florid incident involving an ex-Coldstream Guard had threatened to explode in mid 1963 but Jacobs interceded and with soothing words, and a substantial cheque the problem had quietly disappeared. Epstein clearly hoped that Jacobs would be able to work similar magic with regard to the incident in New York, but Jacobs was privately worried because the American aspect put another dimension on things. And this strange, mysterious business about the problem being "negotiated"? What did that mean?

Negotiated? By who? And how?

Jacobs didn't voice his concerns to Epstein. It wasn't his role, and, knowing Brian so well, he knew that candour would not help the situation. He had always been slightly highly-strung but the pressures of running NEMS had increased his nervousness. Added to that he shared with Jacobs a delight in the power of pills, uppers and downers, and they had impacted severely on his equilibrium.

In those circumstances it made sense for Jacobs to soothe Epstein's concerns about New York and reassure him that once again, as usual, David Jacobs would make the problem disappear. Epstein seemed consoled but, as they left that wind-swept beach, David Jacobs was perturbed about how he would handle this particular problem. And he was also struck by the thought that it was extremely sad that this disaster should fall on Epstein's head at the moment of his greatest triumph.

Sad. Very sad.

But, ever the pragmatist, Epstein was able to compartmentalise things and move the Seltaeb and New York problems to the back of his mind to concentrate on the next major project - the first Beatles film.

February 1964 ended; probably the most tumultuous month in pop music history, and certainly the peak of the many achievements in the Beatles short history. As ever, the last week in the month, as the group prepared to start work on their first film, was a heady mix of the exciting and the mundane. The final Ed Sullivan performance was broadcast in America, this being the set they had pre-recorded before the initial performance on February 9th. Once again it attracted a colossal television audience and represented the first time that an artist had appeared three times on this, the most prestigious American television programme. A Newsweek article in the same week, featuring the group on the cover of the magazine, only provided further proof of how totally the Beatles had won over America.

A party at the London home of Alma Cogan in Kensington provided some light relief and respite from all the attention, but also threw an unexpected focus on Epstein who just a few days later was to be named as one of Britain's most eligible bachelors by the Daily Mail. A relationship between Epstein and the delicious Alma Cogan on any level but close friends and soul mates was obviously never on the cards, but for many months the gossip columnists speculated endlessly on the chance of a pop music royal marriage involving Brian Epstein and Alma Cogan.

Sadly, for many reasons it didn't happen… couldn't happen, and the pair were to die, in sad circumstances, within a year of each other in the mid-sixties.

More important things than parties happened. Recording continued for the music which would feature in the film and on the next Beatles album, and to swell his growing portfolio of directorships Epstein took his place on the board of The Beatles Film Production Limited which was incorporated on February 25th.

The following day saw the latest, and probably most desperate attempt for Vee-Jay to mine their reserves of Beatles material. The album, "Jolly What! The Beatles And Frank Ifield On Stage" released as VJLP 1085, featured material from the Beatles and also the Australian singing star, though only four Beatles tracks were included, all were studio recordings and hence not "on stage", and all four tracks had been previously released.

In time-honoured Vee-Jay tradition, the album appeared in a variety of sleeves and label configurations, with some pressings bearing the immortal message "It is with a good deal of pride and pleasure that this copulation has been presented".

To many purchasers it probably did seem like a real copulation-up.

But Vee-Jay could not be faulted on their efforts to maximise the return on the Beatles material they had received, thanks to Roland Rennie's efforts, in 1963. During 1964, until Capitol pulled the plug in October, Vee-Jay managed to release five albums, six singles, four reissued singles, and one EP, and all these releases came from just fourteen Beatles songs - effectively the material which comprised the "Please Please Me" album in England.

And Vee-Jay would further muddy the waters in March providing more rich pickings for the lawyers by releasing 'Twist and Shout' on a single, but this time on the Vee-Jay subsidiary label, Tollie Records. This label had only been formed in February and would last little more than a year before the legal storms afflicting Vee-Jay utterly consumed the subsidiary label.

But back in England, the Beatles were largely oblivious to these relatively minor events back in America. Their new toy, the filming, was totally preoccupying them. The first scenes were to be shot at Paddington Station but shooting was delayed by an embarrassing legal technicality. To appear in the film all four Beatles had to be members of the Actors' Union, Equity.

In their meteoric career up to that point Equity membership had never been necessary but, to ensure shooting could begin on time, the individual Beatles had to be proposed for membership by Wilfred Brambell and then seconded by Norman Rossington, both of whom had significant support roles in the film.

The schedule called for several days filming on a train and so Walter Shenson, through the production company, had hired a train which was to feature some of the most memorable scenes in the film. Shenson had also played a minor, but significant role in formulating the plotline, input which greatly added to the overall appeal of the film, especially to young girls.

When visiting a friend shortly before filming started, the friend's daughter, a fervent Beatles fan, told him of her earnest hope that none of the Beatles had any love interest in the film. Shenson took the point and ensured that there were no romantic developments for any of the Beatles in "A Hard Day's Night".

As filming got started, space had been cleared on the British Rail network for the train to trundle southwest towards Minehead, and then, after several days on that line, the train moved on to Taunton and Newton Abbot.

The opening scenes of the film did not feature Paddington. Instead, in the fragmented style beloved of filmmakers, the opening scenes were shot at a different station, Marylebone, several weeks later.

The film was to be a strange experience for Epstein. Though he had signed all the contracts for the film, he would have little daily involvement. In essence, he was going to turn his Beatles over to someone else for several weeks, the first time of such physical separation since he had signed the management contract in January 1962.

Dick Lester took temporary charge of the Beatles on March 2nd and set off on the road which would deliver perhaps the best pop film that has ever been made. He was an inspired choice as director. A background in advertising and an interest in French New Wave, laced with the indispensible flavour of Goon Show visual and verbal gags made Lester the ideal choice. He was also pragmatic enough to admit later that the film had been put together so quickly because so many people at the head of the record and film companies simply didn't expect the group to last.

The film was a quick, cynical exploitation of an asset with a very short shelf life. As such, it was imperative to get the product out earning as quickly as possible, before the inevitable boredom set in among the public.

Perhaps that attitude is partially responsible for the breathless pace of the action. The film was shot on the run and many of the scenes mirror the techniques of French New-Wave filmmakers, but the pace was relentless. The opening shot sets the tone. A breathless chase along London streets with the hounds, the fans, in pursuit of the prey, the Beatles. The chaos, the panic, is cut against a series of non-verbal gags and, set against the strident chords of A Hard Day's Night', it is a superbly executed opening to the film.

All the street scene shots had to be filmed surreptitiously and completed very rapidly, given that crowds would quickly appear whenever the Beatles were on the streets. In that distinctive opening sequence the fans chasing the group are real fans, not extras, and the enthusiasm is genuine not fabricated.

The filming was completed in a mere eight weeks, with United Artists retaining an amount of footage which never made it through the final edit. Throughout the course of the filming there were a number of days, or periods, when not all four Beatles were present. Epstein had carefully tried to manage their time to provide the best value for both the filming but also various ancillary activities. In the main, this process worked very well but there were occasional discrepancies.

On April 23rd the group were summoned to Thornburg Playing Fields in Isleworth to complete the filming of the sequence in the film when the helicopter lands and the Beatles disembark to the strains of 'Can't Buy Me Love'. Filming was scheduled to last into the afternoon but John Lennon had to leave early to fulfil an engagement at a literary luncheon which was being held in his honour at the Dorchester Hotel. The filming continued after his departure with the result that the sequence in the actual film ends with just the three other Beatles in the shot.

For most practical purposes, for the duration of the two-month shoot, Epstein was largely absent from the Beatles daily lives.

The final day of location filming, March 9th, found Epstein taking charge of the relocation of the NEMS offices anticipated by the casual announcement back in January. The organisation took up its base on the 5th floor at Sutherland House, just a few yards from the heart of British showbiz, the London Palladium. The Press Office which had been located across Soho on Monmouth Street was also brought into Sutherland House and suddenly

NEMS took on the appearance of a much more intense, professional organisation.

The Press release issued on that date listed the NEMS management as Alistair Taylor, General Manager, J.B.Montgomery, Accounts, Tony Barrow, Press officer, Brian Sommerville, Beatles Personal Press representative, and finally Wendy Hanson, Personal Assistant to Brian Epstein.

Under NEMS management at that time were the Beatles, Gerry & The Pacemakers, Billy J. Kramer, The Dakotas, Cilla Black, the Fourmost, Tommy Quickly, Sounds Incorporated, and The Remo Four, and Epstein clearly took advantage of the relative downtime with the Beatles, caused by the filming, to advance things for the other NEMS acts.

His main involvement with the Beatles during the filming period came on March 19th when he accompanied the group to the prestigious Variety Club of Great Britain Annual Show Business Awards. This ceremony, the twelfth such event, took place at a lavish luncheon at the Dorchester Hotel where Harold Wilson, then Leader of the Opposition, presented the Beatles with the award for "Show Business Personalities of 1963". The event, and the award, was captured forever with the timeless images of the shrewd Wilson standing beside the Beatles and having a number of pictures taken with them. In his remarks after the presentation, Lennon even mentioned the need to get back to the film because of the cost of their being absent.

No sign of Epstein in the background but he was there, quietly exultant about this latest tribute to his group.

The end-of-production party for the film took place in Twickenham on Friday, April 23rd, and, though there was general delight at what had been achieved during the previous two months, nobody - least of all Dick Lester or Brian Epstein - expected the film to have the impact it did. Yet that spring had displayed more figures to prove the world domination being achieved by the group.

The top six records in the Australian charts, nine records in the Canadian top 100, an announcement that the Capitol album, "Meet The Beatles", had sold 3,650,000 copies.

Another, less immediately commercial milestone came towards the end of March when Madame Tussauds, the famous waxwork museum in central London, put effigies of all four Beatles on display. Those original models appeared several years later on the cover of Sergeant Pepper, although the museum were compelled to slightly alter the appearance of the models at various times during the decade to reflect the obvious changes in the appearance of the Beatles.

However, whilst the length of hair, and amount of facial hair, and the flamboyance of clothing might change, basic factors like height and type of ears and shape of jaw do not change unless major illness becomes a factor, and to my real astonishment the various measurements taken by Madame Tussauds in the early months of 1964 would later emerge as a real bone of contention in the McCartney story.

One of those significant moments in the history of the group came on April 4th 1964; an incident so rare that it is unlikely ever to be repeated. In the Billboard Hot 100 chart for that week the Beatles occupied the top five places, and a further seven places further down the list.

'Can't Buy Me Love' was top, with 'Twist And Shout' next, then 'She Loves You' at number 3, 'I Want To Hold Your Hand' at number 4, with 'Please Please Me' at number five.

The remaining places in this historic chart comprised 'I Saw Her Standing There' at number 31, 'From Me To You' at 41, then 'Do You Want To Know A Secret' at number 46, 'All My Loving' at number 58, 'You Can't Do That' at 65, 'Roll Over Beethoven' at number 68, and finally 'Thank You Girl' at number 79. As if that wasn't enough two more singles slipped into the chart one week later, with 'There's A Place' entering at number 74 and 'Love Me Do' appearing at 81.

April also saw the release of "The Beatles Second Album" on Capitol, representing the high point of the massive confusion caused by the release of different albums on different labels with all of them differing markedly from the equivalent UK release. In most respects that Capitol album is a strange mish-mash of material; five tracks from the UK release, "With The Beatles" supplemented by singles, b sides and EP tracks.

Despite its given American title, the album was actually the group's third album release in the US, though only their second long-player release on Capitol.

A couple of days later the missing element from the film, the title, was discovered from, allegedly a chance remark from Ringo Starr, although there are two or three alternative tales. In the first book from John Lennon, "In His Own Write", published in March 1964, there appears a story called "Sad Michael" in which Lennon wrote: "He'd had a hard day's night that day, for Michael was a Cocky Watchtower".

Perhaps astonishingly Lennon, on hearing the chosen title of "A Hard Day's Night" declared that he would write the title song, and he returned the following day to the shoot with a near-complete song. A little polishing from McCartney and the finished article was presented to Walter Shenson and Dick Lester, and recorded two days later.

Perhaps surprisingly there was resistance to the proposed title. Walter Shenson called United Artists to run it by his bosses but his suggestion was not well received. In response Shenson suggested that they ask the secretaries and other young employees at United Artists, who might now be fans of the Beatles, for their thoughts about the suggested title. His idea worked and the title was enthusiastically and obviously accepted.

With the film nearing completion, Epstein brought an old friend back into the picture. Ed Sullivan appeared on St.Patrick's Day to interview the group in the garden of the Les Ambassadeurs club where the Beatles were filming interior scenes for the film.

Sullivan had flown in two days earlier expecting to film the interview on the Thursday, but the schedule for the Beatles on that day was so intensive that even the great Ed Sullivan had to wait. The interview had hurriedly been pushed back 24 hours which meant that the reunion between the Beatles and Ed Sullivan took place on the Friday afternoon. Time pressures - on the Beatles not Sullivan - were so great that there was only enough time available for a very brief interview.

The finished piece was finally shown in the Ed Sullivan show on May 24th, but the actual interview only lasted 1 minute 34 seconds - barely worth the flight across the Atlantic and back!

The saving grace was that to compensate for the disappointment and the severe inconvenience, United Artists provided the Sullivan show with a clip from the still-unreleased film. The piece was taken from the footage shot at the Scala Theatre which simulated the tv studio footage in the film using an audience of 350 fans who, by union rules, were paid for the privilege of watching and screaming at the Beatles. In that crowd was a young Phil Collins, years before his success with Genesis and as a solo performer.

The piece of performance footage proved to be very special. It showed the group onstage at the Scala miming to 'You Can't Do That' which was ultimately a victim of the editing process and was cut from the film. Although he was unaware of it as he flew back across the Atlantic with his 1 minute 34 second interview, Sullivan also had the consolation of an exclusive piece of performance of the Beatles.

Following the end of their active participation in the filming, the Beatles returned to live performance for the first time in almost four months with a return appearance at the New Musical Express Poll-Winners' All-Star Concert. This time the group returned triumphant, repeating their 1963 victory in the Outstanding vocal group and British vocal group categories, and they were handed their prizes by film star, Roger Moore. Less pleasing was the involvement yet again of the self-styled Fifth Beatle, Murray the K, whose presence had been mildly amusing in New York, less so in Miami, and was now exasperating many in the Beatles entourage, with George Harrison being the most conspicuous in his growing distaste.

Late in April 1964, the affable Derek Taylor was taken on board the NEMS juggernaut. His involvement with the group had started modestly. A staff newspaperman with the Daily Express, he had been sent to review a Beatles concert at the Odeon Cinema in Manchester on Thursday, May 30th 1963, and the expectation was clear that he would deliver a damning, cynical review. Instead, he found himself captivated by the energy and style of the group, and his copy reflected that view. That initial article led to a number of similar complimentary reviews and articles, and some time later he was invited to a meeting with Brian Epstein in Liverpool. That initial contact established a respect and the basis for a long-term friendship between the two men. The first manifestation of that came when his editor engineered an approach for Taylor to provide a ghosted column on behalf of George Harrison. That material developed into a valuable outlet for the Beatle and a solid career boost for Taylor. It also gave Brian Epstein the chance to observe Taylor's laconic personality and his undoubted writing abilities at close hand.

The relationship developed during the early months of 1964 to such an extent that Epstein was moved to ask Taylor to join his team. By that time it was obvious to anybody that being involved with the Beatles was likely to present some amazing adventures, and so Taylor accepted the offer. The announcement that he had become Epstein's personal assistant was made in late April, but the duties were later refined to make him press liaison for both Brian Epstein and the Beatles

One of the most immediate tangible results came when Epstein asked Taylor to ghost-write his autobiography. The pair worked on the project intermittently during the middle months of 1964, with particularly intensive sessions taking place on certain days while the Beatles were away filming.

There was a definite bond between Epstein and Derek Taylor which did not involve Epstein's sexual preferences. Taylor was a confirmed heterosexual, but that didn't influence or affect the relationship between the two men, founded very much on their mutual love for literature and the arts.

For the book, Taylor conducted a series of interviews, transcribed the material, with help from Diana Vero, and produced a manuscript to which Epstein contributed, and over which he retained copy control. Given the potential sensitivity about certain areas of Epstein's personal life there were definitely topics that Taylor had to avoid, and the result was a masterpiece of information and delicate issue evasion.

But Epstein was pleased with the results and delighted by the way Taylor had handled the project, and his satisfaction was recorded in a very tangible form. Before the work commenced he had agreed a fee for the work with Taylor, a substantial figure of £750, but when the book was a bigger success than Epstein had expected he insisted on giving Taylor another cheque to the same value, asserting that Taylor deserved more than he had been paid originally. In his role as press liaison for Epstein and the Beatles Taylor was primed to play a significant part in the planning for the major world tour to be launched during the summer. But, during the early part of the summer, Epstein was content for the enthusiastic Taylor to find his feet at NEMS whilst working a couple of days a week on "A Cellarful of Noise".

Epstein was trying to build on the tv interest in the group, and another major tv event took place before the end of April. The television special, Around the Beatles, was recorded in front of a studio audience at the Wembley studios of Associated Rediffusion. This was a classic spectacular with a host of established stars on the bill including Cilla Black, Long John Baldry, and P.J. Proby, but in time-honoured tradition Epstein had squeezed some radio interviews for Swedish radio in between the final rehearsal and the taping.

Continuing his assiduous manipulation of American media, Epstein encouraged the major US channels to bid against each other for the transmission rights which were finally won by ABC, who then showed the programme in America in mid-November.

Two long-standing Scottish dates completed the workload at the end of April and then came holidays. The pressure on the group during the first four months of the year had been intense. A season in Paris, then the shimmering brilliance of America, and then filming "A Hard Day's Night", and interspersed with these major events were the intermittent recording sessions at Abbey Road to keep the momentum going forward.

The end-of-production party took place in Twickenham on Friday, April 23rd, and, though there was general delight at what had been achieved during the previous two months, nobody - least of all Lester or Epstein - expected the film to have the impact it did. Yet that spring had displayed more figures to prove the world domination being achieved by the group.

The top six records in the Australian charts, nine records in the Canadian top 100, an announcement that the Capitol album, "Meet The Beatles", had sold 3,650,000 copies.

Yet Epstein had concerns. Not least, because he had the background concern about the alleged photographs in New York, and there was the related worry about the on-going Seltaeb problem. Since Epstein had returned from New York in February and turned the two matters over to David Jacobs, the lawyer had worked very diligently to sort out the two issues. He had made two trips to New York to speak to the Seltaeb people, and reported back in person to Epstein after each visit.

The news wasn't good. In fact, it was disastrous.

Jacobs had described to Epstein his first visit to the offices on 5th Avenue being shared by Seltaeb. Inside the office appeared to be two, or possibly three of the original group that had formed Seltaeb back in England. He had spotted Lord Eliot and also Malcolm Evans, and he thought he spotted Nicky Byrne but he was just leaving the premises in a limousine accompanied by a stunning redhead.

Jacobs hadn't gone into the office on that occasion. As he ruefully confessed to Brian Epstein he hadn't been able to go into the office. There was a queue of people, mostly men, waiting in line to gain admittance, and Jacobs later discovered that all these people were waiting to buy a licence to produce Beatles merchandise through Seltaeb.

None of them were there to negotiate a licence. It was a redundant exercise. Seltaeb had been totally upfront about the terms of the licence. $25,000 as a one-off licence fee, and then 10% of the turnover from sales of the item in question. That was it, brutally simple, yet, as Nicky Byrne had gleefully admitted, the Seltaeb people couldn't keep up with the demand.

And hence, on the day that Jacobs first turned up at the Seltaeb office on 5th Avenue, he had been confronted by the amazing sight of American businessmen and women queuing out of the door, out onto the opulence of 5th Avenue, queuing for the privilege of giving Seltaeb $25,000 plus 10% of turnover!

And, Byrne demonstrated, there had been hundreds of such deals since January with thousands more to come.

That news in itself rocked Jacobs back on his heels. His mood was not improved when he learned from one of Byrne's less than happy colleagues about the lavishness of the lifestyle being enjoyed by Byrne on the back of the massive Seltaeb takings.

Massive, but as Jacobs bitterly reflected, the Beatles, and Brian Epstein, and NEMS would only get a small fraction of those sums. The vast majority would go to Seltaeb, and he feared that legally there would be no way back. Despite his show business affectations, and despite the degree to which many people in the legal profession loathed him, there were few people who would dispute that David Jacobs was an extremely efficient lawyer. He wasn't given to making expensive errors in drawing up contracts. His work for clients like NEMS, and his opulent lifestyle, wouldn't permit such mistakes.

He knew that Epstein would clutch at that particular straw. He feared that it would be a futile gesture and scanning the Seltaeb contract that night in his hotel room convinced him that, in terms of the original agreement, Seltaeb, or rather John Fenton, had done a first-class job. It appeared to be watertight but Jacobs had the hope that, once he returned to London, a discussion in Chambers with Edward Marke might tease out some tiny route of escape.

The problem presented by the secret photographs was more intractable. Not because it involved Brian Epstein and behaviour which was outside the sexual norms of the times. That had happened previously, and Jacobs was well used to picking up the pieces and dealing with the debris caused by Epstein's occasionally reckless lifestyle.

The New York situation was different, and not just because of geography.

The extra factor was the mysterious person or persons that had negotiated the problem photographs away. It was almost impossible to get to the bottom of things in New York. Although the other Seltaeb people appeared to know that something had happened, both Eliot and Evans seemed to be unaware of the details. Byrne was too far off his head on drink and drugs and lavish living to want to discuss any serious situation with Jacobs, and, perhaps surprisingly, that was the aspect - wanton excess - that formed the bedrock of his report back in London to Brian Epstein.

It was perhaps a demonstration of Epstein's concern that he had gone out to Heathrow with his driver to pick up Jacobs. This gave Epstein the chance to quiz the lawyer immediately, and it was a demonstration of his anxiety that the chauffeur had hardly pulled off the airport concourse before Epstein was asking about the meetings in New York. Jacobs couldn't reassure him or console him on either front, just able to offer the crumb of comfort that Jacobs would track down John Fenton in London and try to sort out both matters with him.

Fenton was key to both issues. Despite the widespread misconception, largely fuelled by his own admirable talent for self-promotion, it wasn't Nicky Byrne who had set up and concluded the deals which resulted in Stramsact and Seltaeb and the fortune being amassed in New York. John Fenton was the key man in terms of those initial negotiations. It was also Fenton who then brought in the other members of the group which the media labelled the Kings Road Rats, although the members of the group laughed at the use of the absurd title.

And the New York discussions suggested that Fenton might prove to be the important Seltaeb man in connection with the mysterious photographs. Eliot and Evans seemed too busy working to make a success of the new venture, and enjoying life in New York to provide tangible details of what had actually happened. Conversely, Nicky Byrne was just too busy enjoying life to be concerned about trivial matters like contracts and potential blackmail.

No, the answers, Jacobs hoped and finally persuaded Epstein, the answers lay with John Fenton.

But three long days passed before David Jacobs was able to track down the elusive Fenton. Once again, by modern standards this seems an eternity and I found myself having to reject the idea that they should simply pick up the mobile. Different times, different technologies. Simpler times.

Jacobs had to resort to leaving word at the single address Fenton had given him, and then messages with a couple of mutual friends to ask him to phone the lawyer's office as soon as possible.

In the end that didn't happen.

By pure good fortune Jacobs was out for dinner with a client and somebody that knew both Jacobs and Fenton wandered into the restaurant. Jacobs shared greetings with the man and enquired casually about the whereabouts of Fenton. To his shock the chap was able to pass on the surprising news that he had seen Fenton just an hour earlier holding court at the Ad Lib club. Jacobs knew that the Ad Lib had been a popular staging ground for the Byrne, Fenton and Eliot group.

Jacobs left his dinner companion hurriedly and took a cab the short distance to the Ad Lib in Leicester Place. He was a regular and very welcome patron. The club in the mid-sixties was a retreat for the rich and famous, albeit just for a limited time. It would soon be dropped in favour of other places like Scotch of St James but in the summer of 1964 the club on the top floor of 7 Leicester Place was at the height of its fame. A regular haunt of London's beautiful people, it frequently welcomed names like Terry Stamp, Mary Quant and Julie Christie while pop stars like sundry Beatles, Stones and Kinks would also be regulars.

On the night that David Jacobs hurried into the club via the escalator from the Prince Charles Theatre looking for John Fenton he was in luck. The club was relatively quiet which meant that he didn't need to search for Fenton. The club wasn't massive but when there were a number of people present, and they were milling about under the influence of drink or substances, it could be difficult to find someone in a hurry.

Not this night. He spotted John Fenton standing talking to another man. Jacobs recognised the man as a member of a Birmingham group called the Moody Blues, which were still some months away from their later huge success with 'Go Now'. Jacobs asked for a word in private and the Moody Blue, recognising David Jacobs, as most people in the club did, gracefully withdrew.

Fenton was surprised to see Jacobs there, but not astonished. Word had reached him from New York that Jacobs had been over there investigating. Given that fact, it was fairly obvious that Jacobs would return and would be keen, if not anxious, for a word.

John Fenton wasn't concerned. He had done nothing wrong and, apart from the crazy excesses of Nicky Byrne in New York, neither had Seltaeb.

And, as Fenton knew very well, had it not been for the intercession of him on behalf of Seltaeb, and the co-operation of certain New York figures he had got to know through Seltaeb, the fate of Brian Epstein could have been very, very different.

No. John Fenton had no reason to fear a conversation with David Jacobs. The club system was following the usual music policy of American soul and blues, and at the moment they sat down they had playing 'Every Little Bit Hurts' by Brenda Holloway, a record that Jacobs didn't know although the message in the title resonated with him.

However, the volume was too much for the kind of quiet, detailed conversation he needed to have, and so Jacobs suggested that they leave and go for a drink somewhere. Fenton agreed, quietly amused to see the normally cool and calm Jacobs visibly flustered. They disappeared out into the night and Fenton guided Jacobs into a small pub around the corner in Wardour Street. Jacobs purchased the drinks while Fenton grabbed a table in the corner, away from prying ears and eyes. He couldn't help noticing and smiling at the number of customers in the unashamedly gay establishment who nodded and smiled at Jacobs.

He seemed not to notice, or maybe that was years of practice. He sat down opposite John Fenton who, knowing he had the upper hand, waited for the lawyer to open the talking. It wasn't a long conversation. Jacobs clearly thought he could charm Fenton into a position of weakness, but Fenton was too shrewd for that. Even worse was when Jacobs changed tack and tried to browbeat Fenton about the contract signed by Seltaeb and Brian Epstein.

Fenton was sure of his ground, and refused to concede anything. Jacobs knew that Fenton and the Seltaeb group were in the right in terms of how the contract had been assembled, but he was neither willing nor able to concede that point at that juncture. But his attitude and his superciliousness made raising the matter of the photographs even harder.

Fenton was sure of his position and quietly enjoyed the spectacle of watching the oily Jacobs squirm. He confirmed that there were photographs, that the photographs involved Brian Epstein, and that the photographs were so explosive that they would have meant the ruination of Epstein and the whole tour.

He further confirmed that the existence of the photographs had become known to Nicky Byrne who, in an act of impetuosity, told one of his contacts in the garment trade in New York, someone supplying Beatles t-shirts to Seltaeb, about the problem. The man had promised to handle it and reported back to Byrne within hours that the situation had been negotiated.

Jacobs demanded details. Fenton couldn't supply them. He hadn't even been in New York on the night in question, but he freely agreed that it wasn't a good move to allow crime figures to have a link with the Beatles or Brian Epstein.

Crime figures. Organised crime. The mob in New York. They were the people Nicky Byrne had involved in the problem, and both Fenton and Jacobs had real and justified fears that the problem would not end there.

But the conversation and the drink did end at that point. Jacobs could tell that he would get nothing more from Fenton, and John Fenton knew very well that he and his colleagues in Seltaeb held all the cards, and indeed 90% of the money.

Jacobs slithered away, determined not to give all the details to Epstein, and indeed it was quite some time later that Epstein learned the true horror of the New York photographs and their extended ownership.

David Jacobs returned to New York two weeks later to try to retrieve something from the mess, and particularly to meet with Nicky Byrne, but that again was not a happy meeting. He was received by Byrne initially in his suite, and then in the lobby of the Drake Hotel, which was situated on Park Avenue and 56th Street. The Drake became legendary in the late sixties and seventies as the desired destination hotel for British bands like the Who, Led Zeppelin and Slade, and many tales of rock 'n roll excess flowed from the Drake. Nicky Byrne wasn't ever in a band, but arguably some of the wildness of the rock era was first visited on the Drake by Nicky Byrne.

The hotel had always enjoyed strong show biz connections. The major star of the silent film era, Lillian Gish, lived at the hotel for several years, while the famous restaurant owner, Toots Shor spent his final years there, and one of the great names from the golden era of American song writing, Jerome Kern, collapsed in front of the Drake on November 5th, 1945 and died later that day from a cerebral haemorrhage.

It emerged that both Lord Eliot and Malcolm Evans had stayed at the Drake with Byrne during their first nights in New York but they had quickly departed for a quieter, more normal environment. Jacobs had discovered that the pair were sharing an apartment in the Village, enjoying a sybaritic, young man lifestyle and making the most of all the opportunities - social and sexual - that Seltaeb and a loose association with the Beatles could provide.

Jacobs tried to get to meet with Eliot and Evans, without success. He suspected, correctly, that the word had come back from Fenton in London that they should avoid contact and certainly confrontation with Jacobs. But such strictures didn't apply to Byrne in his ivory tower at the Drake.

Jacobs was appalled by some of the stories he heard about the lifestyle being enjoyed by Byrne, the easy way he had taken to it. Limousines on permanent standby, helicopters, charge accounts all over Manhattan, the wildest of lifestyles paid for by Seltaeb, and indirectly by the Beatles.

Jacobs managed that one conversation at the Drake with Nicky Byrne, a session studded with quaffing champagne from fine crystal and a shared greeting with virtually everybody wandering through the lobby of the distinguished old hotel. As a serious discussion, it was a waste of time. Whether it was drink or drugs, the substances, added to Byrne's dismissive attitude, made any kind of serious discussion hopeless, at least as far as the basic Seltaeb business contract was concerned.

Byrne was more helpful though with regard to Epstein's indiscretions. He clearly found the very concept of gay sex very amusing, and clearly enjoyed the discomfort shown by Jacobs at the tone of the conversation. Byrne described in lurid detail what the photographs showed, and was cheerfully explicit about how much of himself Epstein showed in the photos. The only note of seriousness came when Byrne described what steps he took when he heard about the existence of the photographs.

He didn't, and was explicit that he wouldn't, give full details, but the key point of his tale was that he had been contacted by someone in the media in New York warning him that some alarming photos were being offered around. From that point Byrne contacted someone he had met in New York through Seltaeb - he wouldn't give a name or any details - and that person handled, or rather, negotiated, the problem. Byrne would not, or perhaps could not, explain the word "negotiated". Jacobs tried, desperately hard, to discover if this meant money, or violence, or sexual favours but Byrne refused to comment further.

All he would say was that the problem had been negotiated. He said it with an infuriating smirk on his face and Jacobs was hard pressed not to slap him. But that would have achieved absolutely nothing. Jacobs told Epstein as much when he met him ten days later on his return to London.

Epstein was relieved by what Jacobs told him about the photographs, but less than sanguine about the Seltaeb contract. After all, as he sharply pointed out to the lawyer, he, Epstein, had merely signed what Jacobs had put in front of him. The situation wasn't helped when Jacobs tartly responded that the same situation applied with the Beatles. They just signed what Epstein put in front of them.

Epstein and Jacobs had discussed in a very general sense the future for Epstein and the Beatles, particularly in terms of Epstein's desire to re-negotiate the EMI contract to provide the Beatles with a much better royalty rate on sales, a rate more commensurate with their undoubted and growing status. And although he hadn't articulated the problem to the Beatles manager, Jacobs was very aware that there were a number of questions and issues around Epstein - both social and financial - that threatened his apparently perfect life. And the Seltaeb situation could only add massively to those problems.

Jacobs didn't dwell on the difficulties with the Seltaeb contract. It was clear that Epstein blamed him, but neither of them knew, or could imagine, just how bad it was going to get. At that moment though Epstein was consumed with the planning for the forthcoming world tour, and particularly the long summer tour to America which he was discussing in detail with people like Sid Bernstein and Nat Weiss.

Before that, he entered into a flurry of activity which consolidated his business interests around the Beatles and other NEMS acts. He had already increased the share capital of NEMS Enterprises Limited, but during April he joined the Pilgrim Theatre Limited as a director, and took up a similar role in May with the new company, Gerry and the Pacemakers (Films) Limited. He then further expanded his film interests by joining Long Distance Films Limited alongside Karel Reisz and Tony Richardson, and other major film industry figures.

But the most significant development in terms of the problems which lay ahead of him came on May 12th when another new company was formed. This was Lenmac Enterprises Limited, a music publishing company, and, as the name would suggest the company's activities revolved around the songs of Lennon and McCartney.

Lenmac was a development from Northern Songs, which was led by Dick James, and was set up to collect the monies gathered by Northern Songs from the UK. Crucially all overseas royalties, particularly the fortunes building up from sales in America, were kept outside Lenmac, and the ownership was very different from that imposed on Northern Songs. At Companies House the ownership of Lenmac was very simple: 40% John Lennon, 40% Paul McCartney, and 20% NEMS, but one of the aspects that didn't occur to either of the songwriters until much, much later was that Brian Epstein claimed director's fees in addition to his overall 25 per cent.

The work of setting up Lenmac had been charged by Epstein to chartered accountant James Trevor Isherwood of the London firm, Bryce, Hanmer and Isherwood.

As part of the process, Epstein visited the company's office in Albemarle Street to discuss and explain the thinking behind Lenmac which was effectively to collect the Performing Rights Society fees, monies collected on behalf of Lennon and McCartney in return for their copyrighted songs being played in concert, or on radio or television.

The details weren't unusual and the requirements weren't difficult for someone as practiced as Isherwood. He was even acquainted with Epstein from the past as he had lived in Liverpool, where he had done some accountancy work for Harry Epstein's furniture store.

The unusual aspect came out in the conversation between the two men. Epstein explained the history and the details of his existing management contract with the Beatles. It came as some surprise to the highly experienced Isherwood that Epstein was actually taking 25% of the gross income rather than the 10% or even 12.5%, which Isherwood believed to be the norm.

Even more painfully for Epstein's artists all his expenses were taken from the artists' gross income, and these expenses were quite comprehensive, including office rental, staff salaries, travel, telephone costs, and expenses for general entertaining purposes.

And, as one of the many long-term worries in Epstein's mind, he knew that in three years time his management contract would be up for renewal, and reduction of the set fee would be inevitable. In his darkest moments he worried about the implications of the Beatles, particularly Lennon, coming to the conclusion that he had ripped them off. Whether such a charge could be justified or not, conversations like the one with Isherwood showed that there was at least a case to answer. And any financial disasters, like Seltaeb was threatening to become, would only add more fuel to that particular fire.

There were other distractions though and on May 30th 1964 Derek Taylor, the Beatles new press guru, took charge of a press conference at the NEMS offices by the Palladium to announce details for their forthcoming world tour. The schedule was to include concerts in Denmark, the Netherlands, Hong Kong, Australia and New Zealand, and inevitably, the schedule required and expected four Beatles to be performing at the various concerts.

Fate was to intervene and Ringo Starr, who was at Prospect Studios in Barnes with photographer John Launois in a session for the famous American magazine "Saturday Evening Post", collapsed part way through. A local doctor was called in and, after examining the stricken Beatle, sent him to the private patient's wing of University College Hospital. The diagnosis was acute tonsillitis and pharyngitis, and Starr was ordered to stay in the hospital under blanket conditions of total rest and quiet. But this presented a crisis for the group, and particularly for their manager. A Beatles appearance without one of the group? It was a ludicrous proposition and the obvious and immediate reaction was to cancel, but commercial considerations would have made that extremely difficult, not least because of the imminence of the American tour later in the summer.

Had American promoters started to worry about their dates then the American tour, on which so much was riding for the future, might be in jeopardy. On an immediate basis, cancelling the dates in Denmark, Holland, Australia and New Zealand would have left many thousands of fans extremely disappointed and frustrated; in addition, the costs of cancelling concerts at such short notice would have been prohibitive.

Consultations took place over that evening with the remaining three Beatles plus Neil Aspinall and Mal Evans, and the general opinion moved slowly in favour of bringing in a replacement for Ringo, especially as his illness was not expected to be protracted and there was every expectation that he might rejoin the group before the end of the tour.

George Harrison was particularly averse to using a replacement, but even he was persuaded, not least by the argument from Mal Evans that if the group had to bring in a temporary replacement then the logical candidate was Ringo. Trying to replace John or Paul or George would have been another calamitous matter, dangerous to try and probably impossible to achieve. Although, as Mal Evans noted with chilling foresight, that only applied while and because they were performing on stage. If and when they ever stopped performing on stage as the Beatles then theoretically it might be possible to replace one of the other three.

But they were never going to stop performing on stage so the hypothetical situation would....could never arise.

The decision was taken to bring in a substitute drummer with the main requirement being somebody with adequate skills and technique but little or no public profile. That ruled out immediately any approach to prominent pop drummers of the time so names like Mick Fleetwood, John Weathers, BJ Wilson, Jim Gordon, and Nick Mason were very briefly considered and then discarded. Some because of various other playing commitments; all because their existing profile was too great. For the same reason, even despite the nice touch of irony it might have created, the name of Alan White didn't receive serious consideration.

In the end, it was George Martin who came up with the solution, a drummer who could meet the twin requirements of competence and anonymity. This was a journeyman drummer named Jimmy Nicol. He was then 24 years old and had played in a number of bands and on several sessions, which was how he had come to the attention of George Martin. Although he had recently formed a new group called the Shubdubs it was obvious that he wouldn't pass up the opportunity to join the Beatles, even if just for a few dates. Nicol had been on the recording scene for several years by then. He had started off as a drum repairer working for Boosey and Hawkes, but then developed into playing with groups like Georgie Fame's Blue Flames. More pertinently for the Beatles connection, he had recently backed the latest Epstein-protégé Tommy Quickly, and Nicol had also featured on an anonymous cover version album called "Beatlemania".

This low-cost album was released on the budget label Top Six through Pye, and featured the unaccredited group, Ghost Squad, which included Jimmy Nicol on drums. Totally coincidentally he had also, at that time, adopted a Beatle-style mop-top, and so he even looked the part. Of course a similar situation today would find a dozen likely candidates already featured in Cover groups, but 1964 was decades ahead of such tributes being paid to the group.

George Martin called Jimmy Nicol, explained the situation, and invited him down to Abbey Road to meet the Beatles and move the project forward.

The remaining Beatles had cancelled a recording session scheduled for that night to allow time to rehearse with their new drummer. Fortunately the set list wasn't huge and Nicol only had to learn ten songs which, given the extreme popularity of the Beatles at that time, were hardly new to him anyway. The eleventh song which would normally have featured in the set was dropped as that song, 'I Wanna Be Your Man', was Ringo's solo. One unexpected benefit of Nicol's earlier session work was that of the ten tracks to be played on the tour in Europe, Australia and New Zealand exactly half had been featured on the Beatlemania budget album on which he had played, the album which achieved the distinction for such a budget album of going into the official UK album chart and climbing just into the top twenty.

Within twenty-four hours of the call from George Martin to invite him over, Jimmy Nicol was on his way to Copenhagen for his first date as a temporary Beatle, having secured a temporary leave of absence from a co-operative and understanding Georgie Fame. Nicol's status as a temporary Beatle continued through a tv show and a second concert in Amsterdam before the group and their extended party took the long flight from Schiphol

Airport to Hong Kong. In those days long haul flights were less plentiful and so their BEA flight stopped several times, at Zurich, Beirut, Karachi, Calcutta and Bangkok, to re-fuel. The journey, if not the earlier concerts gave Nicol plenty of time to appreciate what being a Beatle entailed. At the airport in Beirut, police reacted to what they saw as a riot by turning fire-fighting foam on the hundreds of fans who invaded the runway. In Karachi, even at 2am, hordes of shrieking fans appeared, ruling out any attempt to wander round the terminal. In Bangkok, over a thousand schoolchildren rampaged through the airport demanding that the Beatles come out to greet them.

For the three Beatles, and Epstein, Aspinall and Evans, this was fairly commonplace but for newcomers like Derek Taylor and particularly Jimmy Nicol it was an exciting, and occasionally frightening revelation.

Especially as the reception in Australia was, if anything, more chaotic and riotous than their welcome in America several months earlier. Massive crowds assembled to greet them with an estimated 300,000 people gathering in Adelaide, and not many less turning out in Melbourne. The continual craziness, allied to the constant need to perform at press conferences and to behave for civic dignitaries and minor politicians, was starting to impact on the group, and Nicol was in a unique position to see what impact that pressure could have.

And that tour would see the first manifestation of a trend which became much, much worse in America later in the year. Desperately ill people were wheeled out in front of the group, not just for the fillip of seeing the Beatles, but also for the near-messianic impact of being in their presence. The pressure of such situations could have driven many people crazy, but sadly for the Beatles such scenes were becoming almost mundane.

The show at the Festival Hall on Dudley St in Melbourne on June 17th saw the return of Ringo Starr. He had been discharged from hospital on Thursday, June 11th after spending the minimum allowed time of one week in bed. Heavily dosed with legal drugs he made the long flight to Australia, via San Francisco, Honolulu and Fiji, accompanied by Brian Epstein, with the minor hurdle of a press conference in San Francisco before he made the transfer from Pan-Am to Qantas.

During his stay in the hospital Ringo had not had his tonsils removed. That delight would wait until early December. Instead, the hospital, mindful of Epstein's needs, cured the tonsillitis, patched the drummer up, and sent him back to the Beatles.

He came in, and the unfortunate Jimmy Nicol flew out, into obscurity. He didn't even get the chance to say goodbye to the Beatles. His flight took off while they were sleeping. Brian Epstein took him to the airport from the hotel on Bourke Street at 8am, at the airport presented him with the agreed fee of £500, and also gave him an engraved gold watch.

And the Beatles, with Ringo back behind the drums, carried on breaking attendance records in Australia, and the fervour of their welcome in that part of the world convinced many in the party, including tour manager, Lloyd Ravenscroft, that the group were bound to return, but it would never happen.

Among the many conversations on the long journey back to England, one particularly sparky version happened as Mal Evans and Derek Taylor discussed the high and low points of the tour, and particularly how well Jimmy Nicol had stood in for Ringo Starr. And Mal Evans was quick to raise the topic once again, in a purely hypothetical sense of course, that the experience with Jimmy Nicol had convinced him that it would be possible to replace a more prominent group member. If, of course, the group were no longer performing on stage.

But that was a non-event. It simply couldn't happen. No group would be able to survive without performing on stage so the topic was moribund. Instead, the pair abandoned the wild chat and turned back to the serious matter of uppers and whisky and coke.

Before the group left New Zealand the soundtrack to the film, "A Hard Day's Night (Original Soundtrack Album)" was released in the States as United Artists UAS 6366. This was the prize that United Artists had been seeking, the first of three albums from films, which United Artists had been convinced would lose money, although given what had already happened in 1964 they were rapidly changing their minds.

The album featured the tracks performed by the Beatles in the film, with the rest of the album fleshed out by the instrumental pieces from the film. Unusually these weren't just fillers and some, like the whimsical 'Ringo's Theme (This Boy)' played by George Martin & his Orchestra, were charming and attractive in their own right.

United Artists were only interested in the American market and so, yet again, the equivalent British album was significantly different. No instrumentals, just Beatles tracks, and the first Beatles album not to include any covers.

At the time, "A Hard Day's Night" became the fastest-selling album in UK chart history, with 1.5 million copies sold during the first two weeks after its release. It also made the Beatles the first act ever to have simultaneous Number One singles and albums on both sides of the Atlantic.

All of the Beatles songs on the United Artists soundtrack album were also subsequently released on Capitol as well, either on the "Something New" album or as various 45-rpm singles. But it can't be denied that the UA strategy worked, as their soundtrack album went straight to number one. And several years later, United Artists decided to get out of the record business, and disposed of their catalogue to Capitol, and that company promptly reissued the "missing" album on their label.

The Beatles record producer, George Martin, received an Academy Award nomination for his score in the film, but neither the Beatles nor Lennon and McCartney were nominated for their music.

The launch of the soundtrack album in the States came some three weeks before the scheduled opening of the film in America. On July 1st United Artists released the astonishing news that the soundtrack album had sold one million copies in just four days. Billboard reported that the album had become one of the fastest selling LPs in the history of the record business. It reached the top of the American charts on July 25th and then spent fourteen consecutive weeks in that position.

The release of the album in the States ensured that the return to London for the group was tinged with great excitement because they were coming back to yet another first, the British Film Premiere for "A Hard Day's Night".

The Royal World Premiere had been scheduled at the London Pavilion on Monday, July 6th in front of Princess Margaret and Lord Snowdon, with proceeds from the prestige event going to benefit two charities, the Variety Club Heart Fund and also The Docklands Settlements. Naturally the performance was a sell-out, with VIP seats available for 15 guineas, approximately £275 today.

The crowds around the theatre were enormous. Piccadilly Circus, and parts of Shaftesbury Avenue and Coventry Street were closed to traffic, and police estimated a crowd of some 20,000 were crammed in the streets trying to see the Beatles, with police leave cancelled and more than two hundred police on hand to try to keep order.

Although the glamorous World Premiere in London was a big deal it cannot be doubted that for the Beatles and, to a lesser extent, for people like Neil Aspinall and Mal Evans, the second Premiere four days later was even more significant. On Friday July 10th there was planned to be a second premiere in Liverpool and there was a definite sense of apprehension about what the reception would be.

All of them knew that there had been unhappiness when they grew too big for the Cavern, and then the move to London, by the individuals and then NEMS, had seemed to confirm a divorce between Liverpool and its most famous if not most favourite sons.

But the reception in Liverpool calmed all such fears. From climbing off their plane at the airport, still called in those pre-tragedy days Liverpool Airport, it was a constant spread of people desperate and happy to welcome back their returning heroes. It was a triumphant parade all the way back into the centre of Liverpool, with police estimating that up to 200,000 Liverpudlians were lining the route along the roadside. A civic reception had been arranged at the Town Hall, a scene of some symbolism. The balcony at the Town Hall was where famous sons and daughters of the city, generally football players, came out to receive the adulation of their adoring fans.

And that is exactly what happened with the Beatles. At the Town Hall they were greeted by a phalanx of civic dignitaries, all desperate for a sliver of reflected glory from the Beatles. Most prominent in the party was local Member of Parliament, Bessie Braddock, who represented Liverpool's Exchange Division, who hugged each Beatle in turn, and each of them couldn't help to notice her prominent Cavern Club membership badge.

A rather bland meal came next and then the four Beatles were guided out onto the balcony which overlooked Castle Street. More screaming crowds, and the Liverpool City Police Band serenading them with 'Can't Buy Me Love'. The Lord Mayor, who was then Alderman Louis Caplan made a speech in the large ballroom of the Town Hall in which he formally and warmly welcomed the Beatles back to their city and told them how proud Liverpool was of them and what they had achieved. The ceremony concluded with all four Beatles being presented with the keys to the city.

It was a beautiful, moving ceremony made all the more intense because the Beatles were clearly taken by surprise by the intensity and warmth and emotion of the welcome back to Liverpool.

The only slightly uncomfortable note was that all the tributes, all the praise for the honour that had been brought to Liverpool, were directed at the Beatles. Nothing was said of Brian Epstein, another prominent Liverpudlian, who was there, as ever, standing off to one side, smiling broadly at the latest triumph achieved by his boys.

But without Epstein?

Liverpool police had assembled the biggest security operation in their history, and it performed perfectly. The atmosphere in the streets was one of celebration and pride, and hardly any trouble was reported in central Liverpool.

The ceremonial part of the evening finished around 8.30pm and then the Beatles party had to leave the Town Hall to fulfil the reason for their visit.

A customised Austin Princess limousine ferried them the short distance to the Odeon Cinema for the second charity premiere of "A Hard Day's Night".

It was a struggle to get through the crowds and even someone as important as Mal Evans was temporarily left behind in the confusion. They were greeted at the cinema by the Liverpool City Police Band playing the 'Theme from Z-Cars', at that time the opening music to a major television police drama set in Liverpool, but now better known as the music which greets the Everton team as they take to the field at Goodison Park. After the energetic rendition of 'Z-Cars' the Police Band treated the crowd to a medley of Beatles hits.

The reaction to the film inside the cinema was almost ecstatic, but, given that it was a home crowd, it was hardly any wonder. People like Epstein were more inclined to wait and see what the attitude would be among the public, in Britain and America, before deciding if the venture had been an unqualified success. All the signs were good, and the early indications from United Artists were extremely positive. It was strange to see how quickly and completely the picture had changed.

The initial approach about the film had come just a few months earlier to Epstein, in the autumn of 1963. At that time, apart from farsighted people like Sid Bernstein, the fame of the Beatles was strictly a British phenomenon. That was the reason for United Artists taking the decision to limit the film to a derisory budget, and a very restricted shooting schedule, and even to produce the film in black and white.

Had the United Artists management known what was going to happen to the Beatles in America in 1964 it is inconceivable that the film would have been made in black and white, but it is more than possible that a more lavish production would have lost some of the simple charm of "A Hard Day's Night".

On the same day as the premiere in Liverpool came the release of both the single 'A Hard Day's Night' and the album which omitted the orchestral pieces which adorned the soundtrack album in the States, substituting them with a number of extra Beatles songs. Both single and album raced to the top of the British charts demonstrating the continuation of the group's unrivalled position at the top of the entertainment world in the UK.

During those summer months Epstein was not worried about Britain. He was wholly engaged in planning for the upcoming tour of America, which was to be the most intensive series of dates undertaken by the Beatles since their earliest package tour days on shows with Helen Shapiro and Roy Orbison. He was also increasingly disturbed by what Seltaeb were doing in America, but he privately hoped and believed that a face-to-face meeting with Nicky Byrne and possibly other more rational Seltaeb people might resolve the situation satisfactorily. In this respect, he was going against all that David Jacobs had told him. The information from Jacobs about Seltaeb had become increasingly gloomy and pessimistic but, as with so many other warnings from Jacobs, Brian Epstein was instinctively inclined to tread his own path.

In the frantic few weeks between the UK film premieres and the departure for the American tour Epstein packed in a lot of activity. He made two trips to America within ten days ostensibly to arrange touring arrangements in America for other NEMS artists than the Beatles. He had scheduled American tours in early 1965 for each of Cilla Black, Billy J. Kramer and the Dakotas, and Gerry and the Pacemakers and Epstein's first visit was to confirm all the necessary arrangements.

There was also talk of a major tour of America involving Gerry and the Pacemakers, Billy J. Kramer and the Dakotas, and Tommy Quickly, and Epstein's second trip to the States was officially intended to enable him to finalise the various details. In fact, it was a cover story. Although he did clearly have conversations about touring while he was in New York, the point of the trip was much more personal. Because of the Seltaeb activity he was conscious that a forest fire was starting and he wanted and needed to douse the flames before they threatened to damage the imminent Beatles tour.

He used the Delmonico as a base, intending to check out the security arrangements before the Beatles party arrived there for their stay during the New York dates at the end of August. He had toyed with the idea of staying at the Drake to observe Nicky Byrne's excesses at first hand but Jacobs had advised against it. Instead Epstein returned to the Delmonico for two nights, had a couple of brief meetings about Gerry Marsden and Cilla Black, another long meeting about security arrangements for the Beatles, but nothing with Nicky Byrne. It wasn't apparent to Epstein but by that point Nicky Byrne had his eyes set on other targets and he was actively trying to court Chris Blackwell, famous for the creation of Island Records, to join with him in a new venture. Blackwell was in the States in the summer of 1964 looking after the young Millie Small, whose record, 'My Boy Lollipop' was climbing the Billboard charts, reaching Number 2 in early July. By that point, the obsessive Byrne had decided that Blackwell was his ideal contact, and he may even have concluded, based on the warnings from Eliot and Evans and Fenton, that the glory days with Seltaeb couldn't last.

By that point, after seven months in New York, the Chelsea socialite was virtually out of control. Epstein was forced to appeal to third parties and intermediaries to persuade Byrne to meet him but the efforts proved futile. Instead Epstein had to slink back to London, no further forward with Seltaeb and crucially not having been able to learn any more about the mysterious photographs taken during the visit to New York in February.

The one bright point in the gloomy trip was the announcement in Billboard that sales of the soundtrack album for "A Hard Day's Night" were already so large that all the costs of making the film had been met. The gamble taken by the United Artists Film Division had been repaid massively, and they still had another two films to come to fulfil the terms of the agreement with Epstein. Discussions were already underway with Bud Ornstein from United Artists about future activities, but they were to take an unexpected turn with Epstein before the end of the year.

And, in the latest in a chain of disastrous decisions, Epstein was to make another calamitous decision relating to that United Artists agreement, but before that there were other mountains to climb and windmills at which he and the Beatles could tilt.

In mid-August on consecutive days there were major events. On August 11th the Beatles began work on what would eventually become their fourth album, "Beatles for Sale", and on the following day the US premiere of "A Hard Day's Night" was held at the Beacon Theatre in New York, just twenty-four hours before five hundred US cinemas started showing the film.

There was one final inconvenience for Dick Lester before the premiere. An executive for United Artists in Hollywood tried to persuade him to dub the Beatles with mid-Atlantic accents. Unsurprisingly, and pleasingly, he refused!

More than one hundred cities in the States had asked United Artists for an early print of the film, and a series of preview showings produced takings in excess of half a million dollars. Indeed United Artists were able to make the amazing announcement that the first film by the Beatles had become the first production in the history of movies to be able to declare a net profit while filming was still underway.

Demand for "A Hard Day's Night" in the States was intense. Over one thousand prints of the film were requested in America, while the equivalent demand in the UK was for one hundred and ten prints, contributing to a worldwide demand which was approaching two thousand. During the frantic post-production period, with Dick Lester working twenty-hour days in the edit, United Artists stated that the film would be shown on a saturation basis in every available market around the world.

On that basis the version shown in the States and Canada and Australia, as English-speaking countries, was identical to the British version. On mainland Europe the situation was slightly different. Sub-titles covered the dialogue while the title in various European languages reflected the difficulties of directly translating the idiom inherent in the title.

Consequently the Netherlands called the film "Yeah Yeah Yeah Daar de Beatles", France went with "Quatre Garcons dans le Vent", and Germany, which had a closer association with the Beatles, through Hamburg, than anywhere else in Europe chose "Yeah Yeah Yeah die Beatles".

Most strangely, Italy used a title, "Tutti Per Uno", which echoed the title of a song from the Cliff Richard film, "The Young Ones", which was ironic given that John Lennon and the others despised that type of formulaic pop film and Lennon frequently expressed his worries that "A Hard Day's Night" might turn out that way.

One of the anomalies about the release schedule for "A Hard Day's Night" came in Sweden which enjoyed its premiere of the film during a brief visit to that country by the group at the end of July. The sub-titled film achieved similar acclaim there as elsewhere in Europe although curiously the four performances by the group at the Johanneshovs Isstadion, a leading ice hockey arena in Sandstuvagen, were not totally sold out.

Strangely, the single 'A Hard day's Night', was issued in Sweden two full weeks before the release in the UK or America.

A brief package of home dates including Blackpool, Bournemouth and Scarborough were arranged around the short Swedish trip but everything in that period in the first half of August was merely the preparation for the monumental event in late August and September, the first full tour of the United States.

The final significant event in England, before the departure for America, was a lavish party at Brian's apartment at 15 Whaddon House in Knightsbridge, the apartment he would use as his London base until early 1965 when he would move to 24 Chapel Street. The guest list at the party was truly star-studded with many of the leading figures in British and international show business present. There were the Beatles and their supposed rivals, Mick Jagger and Keith Richard, and Lionel Bart and Judy Garland, Tito Burns and George Martin, Alan "Fluff" Freeman and Brian Matthew, Alma Cogan and Tommy Steele, plus a host of pop stars on the actual or desired NEMS roster including the Searchers, the Fourmost and Peter and Gordon.

It was a glittering, triumphant evening and Brian Epstein was, as ever, the perfect host, and, as toasts were offered to future successes, it was perfectly natural that his thoughts were already dwelling on the triumphs, and perhaps problems, that America might bring.

Whispers were already reaching the Beatles circle about Seltaeb and the ridiculous amounts of money being made in America from these absurd trinkets. Epstein had largely been successful up to that point in keeping the details, and the true horror, from the group, and he fondly imagined that he could keep a similar level of control in America, but that moment had passed.

The genie was out of the bottle and a host of people, led in his uncoordinated, selfish way by Nicky Byrne, were in action all over America grimly unaware that they were about to ensure that Epstein's control of the situation would never be total again.

The flight to America on August 18th was a long haul to San Francisco where their first concert, at the Cow Palace, was scheduled for Wednesday, August 19th. Because of the length of the flight a couple of temporary re-fuelling stops had been arranged, but these turned into fan gatherings as well. The first stop was at Winnipeg in Canada where the group stepped off the plane to conduct a series of radio interviews in front of 500 fans screaming from the airport roof.

Several hours later, the plane made a second stop at Los Angeles where the group endured even more interviews, while up to three thousand fans created bedlam in and around the airport.

The short hop to San Francisco meant that the plane touched down at 6.24pm, but, by that time, American media, with a little help from the Seltaeb connections, had ensured that very few people in California and beyond were unaware that the Beatles were on their way. Police reckoned that the airport was swamped by some ten thousand fans desperate to see and greet the Beatles. One of the people eagerly awaiting the arrival of the group was Bess Coleman. She had been flown out to the West Coast the previous day to prepare for the tour and to ensure that she was on hand to join the party as they climbed off the plane.

The authorities, in a laudable attempt to manage the situation, had erected a structure about a mile from the airport concourse. They had labelled this structure "Beatlesville", and the intention was that a gentle, whimsical meet and greet, with suitable photo opportunities, would be presented by the Lovable Mop-Tops and the crowd would cheer and applaud and go home, happy and satisfied. But in an eerie foretaste of what was to come all over America during the next month the mood would not tolerate such innocent gentleness.

Crucially, ideas like "Beatlesville" came from PR and marketing people in the venues or the host cities, people who had no experience of just how elemental and raw a Beatles appearance, of any kind, would be at that period. Nobody asked the advice of people who knew what would happen, people like Epstein or Derek Taylor or Mal Evans or even those like Bess Coleman who would become terrifyingly aware in the next month of the savage implications of being in the Beatles bubble.

No matter what fond plans the organisers had for "Beatlesville" they had to be rapidly abandoned. The Beatles dragged themselves off the plane and were driven from the plane to a point alongside the platform from which, according to the schedule drawn up by the civic dignitaries, they were meant to ascend the platform and greet their adoring fans.

However, the atmosphere and the noise were so intense when the limousine slowed to a halt the Beatles stayed in the car trying to decide what to do. Mal Evans was all for leaving immediately. Derek Taylor and Bess Coleman were part terrified and part enthralled by the passion flooding down towards the platform and the car.

But the Beatles had seen scenes like this before and so they wearily, warily decided to climb out and greet the fans.

Having decided it was worth the risk they left a considerable delay before entering the compound to wave to the crowd. Ringo happened to be the first out of the car but his appearance merely raised the crowd to a new peak of hysteria. Thousands of the kids charged forward, putting the fence under severe pressure and inflicting serious damage on a row of parked cars which had been left as an impromptu barrier.

His fellow Beatles joined him on the platform but this merely created more fierce screaming and a low guttural roar which clearly concerned the Sheriffs. Their response was one of panic, and they quickly forced the Beatles off the stage and into the cars. There had only been time for a few token waves to the crowd before security considerations meant that they were hurried into their limousines and driven rapidly away from the airport.

There had been talk of some kind of triumphant cavalcade from the airport through San Francisco to their hotel but the Beatles, led by a strident George Harrison, vetoed the idea. He was insistent that just a few months after John F Kennedy's tragic assassination, it would be stupid to give a madman with a rifle a chance for obscene immortality.

The premature departure from the airport wildly enraged the crowd. Not content with merely waving in the direction of the Beatles, or screaming their joy, the crowd had become animalistic, charging and climbing and collapsing the fences, and the limited security force, just 185 County Sheriffs from San Mateo, had come under great and increasing pressure.

Most of the Sheriffs had never seen anything like it; to many in the Beatles party the shocking scenes came as a real surprise and a genuine worry, but in classic Groundhog Day style, those scenes were to be repeated, and even outdone in brutality and savagery, as the Beatles criss-crossed the continent over the next month.

The party containing the Beatles was driven to the Hilton Hotel where they occupied the luxury suite on the 15th floor, but there started a pattern which they would see and suffer all over America. Everybody it seemed wanted to see and meet the Beatles. Police, security, politicians, local celebrities - the list was endless, and the opportunities for the group to rest from the constant pressure were severely limited.

At least in San Francisco it was still a novelty. Before long it would become painfully gruelling. The noise, from the screaming fans, even though the vast majority were kept far away, far below in the streets, was piercing and constant, and there were constant shrill interruptions that were markedly closer as fan after fan try to find a way to get through the security. On the sixth floor of the Hilton a 44 year-old woman was attacked and knocked unconscious. Her screams for help were ignored. People, including security staff, assumed she was just another distraught Beatles fan.

While they were in the Hilton preparing for the first concert Brian Epstein received a visit from Charles O. Finley, the multi-millionaire, and owner and president of the Kansas City Athletics baseball team. Finley professed to be disappointed that Kansas City hadn't been included in the Beatles tour itinerary and he had made a promise to the city that he would get the Beatles to appear in Kansas City. He went through an increasing series of bids with Epstein before he, and the Beatles, agreed to arrange an extra show. The result was that for that single night in Kansas City near the end of the tour the Beatles would earn $4838 per minute.

In the wake of such events, the concert twenty-four hours later at the Cow Palace on Geneva Avenue came as something of a relief. The Cow Palace lies in Daly City just south of San Francisco and is one of those sprawling multi-purpose arenas that are a feature of major American cities. The main tenant in 1964 was the San Francisco Warriors but there was no competition when the Beatles opened that 1964 tour there.

Satisfaction with the venue was such that the group were to finish their 1965 American tour at the Cow Palace. For pop concerts the attendance was usually limited to 17,130 seats and all of them had been sold some time earlier. The fans were presented with a bill, topped obviously by the Beatles, but including stellar names like the Bill Black Combo whose leader had been a hero of the Beatles since his early days in a trio with Scotty Moore and a young Elvis Presley. Also on the bill were the Exciters, the Righteous Brothers and the great songwriter, Jackie DeShannon.

In truth, it was a losing battle for all of them, and even for the Beatles. The noise from the crowd was so loud and so sustained that the acts simply couldn't hear anything, and the Beatles days of cynically going through the motions, not caring if the songs were performed properly or not, were born in the bedlam of that North American tour.

The set list for the tour rarely varied. At most concerts they featured 'Twist And Shout', 'You Can't Do That', 'All My Loving', 'She Loves You', 'Things We Said Today', 'Roll Over Beethoven', 'Can't Buy Me Love', 'If I Fell', 'I Want To Hold Your Hand', 'Boys', 'A Hard Day's Night' and 'Long Tall Sally'.

The only occasional variations came when they omitted 'She Loves You', started the concert with 'I Saw Her Standing There' and finished with the anthem, 'Twist and Shout'.

Epstein had arranged a charter plane for the tour, and the pattern was set where they would invariably finish a concert and depart immediately for the airport where their plane would be waiting to take them to the next city.

Often they would be in the air before many of the fans attending the concert had returned to their parents' cars.

From San Francisco the party flew immediately after the Cow Palace show, across the state border to Las Vegas, Nevada. Two shows had been organised there, to take place in the yawning emptiness of the Convention Center on Paradise Road in Las Vegas.

Because they arrived after 1am, the party were spared the chaos which greeted them at San Francisco, and the stay at Las Vegas passed comparatively peacefully after worrying trouble on their arrival when some 2000 fans indulged in a mini-riot, despite the early hour in the morning. Police in Las Vegas had perhaps learned from the struggles of the Sheriffs in San Francisco because they didn't hesitate or hold back. They turned the dogs on the crowd which got rid of the fans, but didn't dissipate the tension in the air. That carried over to the concert hall later that day when the police tactics caused many people to question if it was worth it for a mere pop concert.

The Las Vegas concerts even threw up a real danger to life when police received a credible bomb warning between the afternoon and evening shows. Conversations with Brian Epstein quickly reached the conclusion that the second performance should be cancelled. However, the police reluctantly concluded that riots and violence would ensue from the 8,000 frustrated fans and the certainty of that violence outweighed the possibility of a bombing.

Perhaps unbelievably, commercial pragmatism won the day and the evening performance went ahead, blessedly without a bomb. But the police were extremely severe with the fans once the second show finished, and many in the Beatles party; particularly Derek Taylor; were greatly disturbed by what they saw as the unpleasant atmosphere which was starting to corrode the innocent joy which the Beatles delivered. The disillusionment suffered by Taylor would bring him to hand in his resignation on the last night of the tour. Disputes with the increasingly skittish Epstein were definitely a factor but overwhelmingly the gentle Taylor despaired of the way the authorities chose to deal with kids whose only crime was liking the Beatles.

And Taylor wouldn't be the only casualty of the 1964 tour. Bess Coleman would abandon the Beatles after the tour, while she nursed the wounds inflicted at various concerts. Diana Vero was less physically damaged but she too refused any possibility of revisiting the frightening experiences of August and September 1964. Her introduction to the Beatles was very quiet. She had helped Taylor with the transcribing and typing of the manuscript for Epstein's autobiography, "A Cellarful of Noise", but that type of withdrawn work couldn't prepare her for the vicious, mindless behaviour she saw on the tour, and sadly it would get worse after Las Vegas.

Seattle was next and unfortunately, once again, the most notable aspect of the visit to that city was the violence and damage and mayhem. The police had insisted on a process of getting the group offstage and away, often before the final note had stopped ringing through the hall. The exit was invariably through a human corridor of burly police or security guards when the main consideration was not the value of the performance just concluded but a simple, fundamental concern for life and limb.

But those dangers also applied to the fans. A number of kids had been badly hurt in Las Vegas, and in Seattle a young girl fell some twenty feet from a balcony onto the stage. Getting them away after the Seattle show proved even more difficult than usual and the Cadillac meant to be taking them back to the Edgewater Inn was ripped apart by the fans and so badly damaged that the escape from the hall had to be abandoned. The group had to skulk inside the dressing rooms for almost ninety minutes before police concluded that the crowds had cleared sufficiently to attempt another escape via an ambulance.

Vancouver came next and if members of the Beatles party hoped that the Canadian personality would indicate a more orderly bunch of fans and a less injury-strewn concert they were disappointed.

The crowd made concerted attempts to smash down the stadium gates at the Empire Stadium which were almost twelve feet high. The Beatles had started their performance when the gates finally gave way, but police and security staff managed to block it with their bodies. Dozens were hurt and crush injuries, particularly broken ribs, were plentiful, and as at every concert on that tour there were scores of cases of shock.

And Derek Taylor looked at the sorry scenes in Vancouver and called it "War. Not music. Not a concert. It's a war zone!" Disbelieving colleagues like Bess Coleman ruefully agreed with him, but the same comment could have been made about virtually every venue in 1964.

Nobody was more unhappy about the extreme situation than Brian Epstein. He had always taken a paternal delight at seeing the success achieved by the Beatles. While he relished the various other manifestations of success - the gold records, the film, the glitzy television shows - the greatest level of success for the Beatles in Epstein's estimation came on stage, with the peculiar, unique alchemy that those four individuals realised when combined together.

America in August and September 1964 ought to have been the apogee of all Epstein's dreams for the Beatles. Adored by virtually a whole continent, feted by the most active entertainment industry in the world, the Beatles ought to have been in a very special place, and he should have been alongside them. Instead they were crawling around like frightened animals, restricted to giving limited stage shows devoid of genuine emotion and their peerless stagecraft, and desperate to get off the stage within seconds of the final note of the last number. The party had settled into an unpleasant, uncomfortable pattern. Get the group off the stage and into the transport, hopefully in one piece, and then race to the airport where they would all board the plane.

It was not coincidence that Epstein invariably booked hotel suites on the top floor. In that way they were the furthest distance possible from the constant din in the streets below. Physically the top floor location meant that the intruders, and there were always hordes of them, had to fight their way over the maximum distance to get within touching distance of a Beatle.

It was in Seattle that a journalist warned Derek Taylor of a new danger, one that they genuinely hadn't anticipated. The claim was that there were women, mothers, encouraging their daughters to try to bed a Beatle. Most of the daughters didn't need any encouragement but the warning from the journalist to Taylor concerned the danger of one of those girls then crying "Rape"! Epstein through NEMS had already paid off various girls in England on behalf of various Beatles; they didn't want to start similar payments in America.

The plane journey taking them away from one show and towards the unknown terrors of the new city was the only few minutes of peace the Beatles party could enjoy. But it became a remarkable piece of the tapestry of that tour that the atmosphere on those midnight flights was rarely one of exultation or joy. Instead there was invariably a sullen, disbelieving silence as each of the individuals thought back over the horrors of the previous few hours, of the violence, of the frightening intensity of the fans, of the unremitting rigour of the police and security.

Mal Evans was frequently wide-eyed in disbelief. He, in many ways, was closer to the physical aspects of the crowd scenes than the others, given his early days as a bouncer at the Cavern. He couldn't comprehend the fanaticism being shown over and over again by the crowds, but he was even more startled by the way the police behaved. The scenes he saw in 1964 created in Mal Evans a lifelong distrust of the police and the way many of them chose to react to situations, and that suspicion was never to leave him.

The next stop after Vancouver was Los Angeles with possibly the most important date of the tour at the Hollywood Bowl. The prominent local DJ, Bob Eubanks, from station KRLA had made a personal booking for the Bowl by taking out a $25,000 loan secured against his home.

The security payment was necessary because the management of the Bowl needed to be persuaded into giving permission for the Beatles to perform at the venue. Apparently, there was some doubt as to whether or not a mere pop group was capable of filling their famous amphitheatre. But Eubanks' faith and foresight was rewarded when all the 18,700 tickets were sold in less than four hours in early April. Again, the era, and the available technology had a real impact. No online booking of tickets, no tablet or mobile involvement. Instead Highland Avenue was swamped with hundreds of teenage girls camping out overnight waiting for the ticket office to open at the Bowl, and, by the time the facility opened the following morning, the queue stretched virtually all the way down to Hollywood Heights.

The reward for Bob Eubanks, besides the finances, was to present the press conference before the show at his nightclub, the Cinnamon Cinder, which was then a teen-focussed nightclub located in Studio City on Ventura Boulevard.

To cement his part in the story Bob Eubanks then provided the announcements from the stage, and the introductions to the Beatles, at the actual concert at the Bowl.

Before the show, there was the obligatory press conference during which the group received five gold records and the key to California. Of course, at the Hollywood Bowl they were less than a couple of miles from the iconic Capitol Tower, the historic home of Capitol Records. Given the incredible success that Beatles records had achieved during 1964 it was a heaven-sent opportunity for the record company to laud the group and trumpet their role in that success. Not surprisingly there was little mention of the cold-shoulder shown by Capitol to the Beatles through virtually the whole of 1963.

For Epstein, and the group, the concert at the Hollywood Bowl would prove to be the highlight of the tour. The Hollywood Bowl was obviously one of the world's great venues. For four young men from Liverpool, no matter what success the previous two years had brought, Hollywood had a mystique and allure that couldn't be denied. And as Epstein stood at the back of the seating staring down at the stage with its beautiful white shell-structure covering, and the hills in the background with the Hollywood sign seeming to glow at the summit of the hills, it was hard to imagine that life could get better.

There was still some trouble surrounding the concert but it was small-scale stuff compared to San Francisco and Vancouver, closer to minor vandalism than rioting. Indeed the major complaint about the event came from the traffic congestion. Local press went to town on the massive traffic jam which afflicted Hollywood for hours after the concert, as thousands of cars headed for the Bowl to enable parents to pick up their kids after the show. Police and firemen had set up roadblocks and closed off the whole Bowl area and further out into Hollywood, and an elaborate system of passes was set up to enable residents to get back to their homes.

More than five hundred youngsters who had not obtained tickets demonstrated their frustration at being unable to get into the concert, but the violence was mainly verbal. A number of arrests were made but for largely trivial, public order or disturbing the peace offences. One photographer's car was climbed on by a number of kids anxious to see the Beatles leave the Bowl. Not surprisingly, the bonnet and roof of the car were significantly damaged, but that was the most visible example of mayhem.

There was also a mini, but relatively well-behaved riot backstage as the kids tried to get near to the group but, as usual, a well-practiced routine got them away from the stage before most of the crowd realised they had gone. A limousine had been stationed next to the stage for the duration of the show, and the impression was clearly given to the kids that the limo would be the means by which the Beatles departed. Instead they raced off-stage and were thrown into a dishevelled Dodge Dart compact by Mal Evans and driven rapidly away into the Californian night.

Although the show was generally seen as a triumph, it was clearly the single show which had caused the group most anxiety, not least because Capitol had decided to record the show. The taping was done by people sent to the Bowl by Capitol but it would be many years before the tracks performed by the Beatles at the Hollywood Bowl would see the light of day.

After the concert the group were invited to accept some more Capitol hospitality and attended a party at the lavish Bel Air residence of Mr.& Mrs. Alan Livingstone, the president of Capitol Records. In typical Hollywood fashion they decided to make the evening a charity fundraiser, with the theme of the party being "Buy a ticket and meet the Beatles". Guests were charged $25 per head and more than five hundred people stood and stared at the Beatles. More than $10,000 was raised for the Haemophilia Foundation of Southern California, and Epstein made a sizeable but unpublicised donation of his own.

The Beatles manager had rented a private, gated property for the touring party, and so that night, after leaving Alan Livingstone's house, they travelled to the house at 356 St. Pierre Road in Brown Canyon, Bel Air. As the night moved on, the local West Los Angeles police detained more than fifty teenagers in technical custody for violating a curfew which had been set unreasonably early at 10pm. Around five hundred fans gathered on Sunset Boulevard near the junction with Bel Air Road hoping to see their heroes, and the police hurriedly blockaded St.Pierre Road.

It wasn't Vancouver or Las Vegas or Seattle or even San Francisco, but the wild scenes in Los Angeles were on a different level of villainy. More than $5000 worth of damage was inflicted on garden shrubs and flowers by the rampaging mobs, and terrified locals had to resort to turning on their garden sprinkler systems to drive away the gangs of excited children.

Inside their compound in the rented house there was a peaceful, normal atmosphere, the first time the party had been able to feel that way since their arrival at San Francisco Airport on August 19th. During a leisurely evening in the house a couple of them managed to watch the re-run of the original Ed Sullivan show on which the Beatles made their American bow, just six months earlier but already a lifetime ago.

Two more days rest and recreation followed in Los Angeles as the group and Evans and Aspinall were able to let some of the bruises of the previous week subside. During the same period Epstein and Derek Taylor were busy, attending meetings with Capitol and also other major media figures, including United Artists. Unnoticed by everyone, including himself, Derek Taylor was building up a roster of contacts in Southern California which would see him representing the Beach Boys and the Byrds and helping organise the Monterey Pop Festival within three years.

Everywhere Epstein saw displays of how widespread and insidious had been the Seltaeb effect. David Jacobs had given him some disturbing figures before he flew out to San Francisco. Tons of Beatle wigs were sent to the States during 1964, with the clear suspicion that there were many, many more being produced locally. More than 50,000 rolls of Beatle wallpaper had been shipped over to the States, with half that total being delivered before they left America in February. Inside the Capitol tower he was given an even more painful demonstration of just how successful Seltaeb had been. The Capitol Marketing Department had taken it on themselves to acquire a copy of every single piece of Beatles merchandise or memorabilia that became available during 1964, and there were hundreds of such items.

Inside one room inside the Tower, a room bearing the scrawled title "Chamber of Horrors", was a cavalcade of plastic and cheap linen tat. For years afterwards Epstein would shudder at the memory of those hideous items, all bearing the image or the name of one of the Beatles, and often all four.

As well as the inevitable toy guitars and drums, there was a variety of different Beatles dolls, myriad wigs, trays, coat hangers, wallets, toothbrushes, towels, clocks, Beatles stationary, sweets and chewing gum, plates and key rings "straight from Liverpool, England". There were Beatles clothes, John Lennon caps and Ringo Starr socks, and a crazy range of Beatles furniture, from sofa beds to tables to metal filing cabinets to chairs with the image of the group or an individual Beatle embroidered on the back

Epstein counted thirty-four different t-shirt designs before giving up counting. It looked like there were hundreds more.

Jewellery seemed to be a particular favourite. Bracelets, rings, watches, pendants - all carrying the image or the badly copied signature of an individual Beatle or, for the more expensive items, all four. There were scarves, and mugs, plastic vials of "authentic" bath water, bubble gum, liquorice and dozens of other types of sweets, unopened cans of "Beatle Breath", badges of every conceivable size and design, and hundreds of black and white and colour picture magazines devoted to the group.

Colour and black and white photographs of the Beatles covered every wall, often framed, generally badly, but always with a retail price which didn't reflect the value of the goods.

In the end, Epstein had to leave the room. Nausea was overcoming him, not just because of the inevitably shoddy standard of the goods. He had fought against the merchandising of cheap material in Britain a year earlier, but one despairing look around the Aladdin's cave at Capitol made him realise that the battle, and indeed the war was lost.

More worrying though was what this signified in terms of the Seltaeb situation. One of the Capitol people had helpfully, and cheerfully, given him a sales sheet which totted up some of the relevant figures.

The Reliant Shirt Corporation - more than a million Beatle Shirts sold in three days; Remco - Beatles dolls selling 100,000 a day, now meeting 500,000 order; Lowell Corporation - Beatle wigs selling out, now selling over 35,000 per day.

The scale of it was overwhelming, and it made him feel sick. Not just because he was offended by the fact that the vast, vast majority of the stuff was cheap crap. No, the real, inescapable fact was that 90% of the revenue, the king's ransom in revenue, that the crap represented would not go to the Beatles. It would go elsewhere.

They didn't know about it, but inevitably the day would come when he couldn't keep it hidden any longer, and he truly feared what would happen on that day.

But as ever he was able to pull himself together, and push his personal troubles to one side, and focus on the matter in hand. At that time in his life and career, Epstein was empire building, both for the Beatles and his various other NEMS acts, but also actively pursuing his more private activities, this despite the unusually stern warnings from David Jacobs before Epstein flew out of London.

A hurried meeting with a fitness instructor from Long Beach, a sweaty encounter in a shabby motel off Ventura, before Epstein crept back to the house on St.Pierre still looking round frantically for the hidden cameras about which Jacobs had warned him. On that occasion he was in the clear but the chances he was accustomed to taking were growing bigger and more frequent. A desperate dilemma and one for which there was no solution, no matter how huge the Beatles or NEMS became.

There was one more concert on the west coast, in Colorado, before the schedule took the Beatles party east. There was one single concert in Ohio, in Cincinnati in front of 14,000 fans before they followed the usual pattern of flying out directly after the show. They headed straight to New York to prepare for the two scheduled concerts there, but the plane was one passenger light.

Brian Epstein hadn't been at the concert at the Cincinnati Gardens on Seymour Avenue, and he failed to turn up at the airport for the New York flight. He had confided in Derek Taylor about a developing problem which involved the fitness instructor who had followed him from Los Angeles and was exerting an unhealthy hold over the depressed Beatles manager.

Taylor, who had been growing increasingly fond of and close to, Brian Epstein was concerned about his friend but he was helpless to divert him. As such he passed on the message to the party on the plane from Epstein that if he didn't make it back for the flight to New York they should go on without him. He would meet them at the Delmonico the following day

And that's what happened.

In my detailed research into the Beatles, I came to realise that from the vast cast of characters there were a lot of villains, horrible venal people, and a very restricted number of heroes, decent people who just tried to do the right thing even if it didn't particularly benefit them. Of course the vast majority of people were at neither extreme, neither good nor bad, just ordinary, but sheer normality made me appreciate the heroes even more, simply because they stood out in such strong relief against the rest.

And very, very high on that list of heroes was Derek Taylor, whose writing ability, temperament and sheer goodness marked him out as a rare human being. Of all the people in the Beatles tale that I regret that I didn't have the chance to meet the most grievous loss was, for me, Derek Taylor. He died of cancer in 1997, well before I was pointed in the direction of the absurd Paul McCartney story by Jeff's brother, Tony.

I never met Derek Taylor, but everything I read and heard about him in the course of the research made me wish I had. And made me wish that Brian Epstein had been fortunate enough to have more colleagues or friends like him, most importantly more people who would have had the strength of character to be honest with him.

If so, how much might have turned out differently.

Epstein turned up at the Delmonico Hotel in New York in the early evening of Friday August 28th. He had been missing the whole day, indeed a day and a night, and though many in the party had suspicions about where he had been nobody voiced an opinion. At the time they had more urgent matters to handle. There was a helicopter flight booked to take them out to the gig in the unlikely setting of the Forest Hills Tennis Stadium.

Enterprising promotion had brought a music festival to the tennis stadium that summer, bringing in names like Barbra Streisand, Harry Belafonte, Woody Allen, Johnny Mathis and finally the Beatles. The helicopter was scheduled to take them from Manhattan over the East River and then south East into Queens to the famous tennis venue. The helicopter was late taking off, and that was because the Beatles party was late getting to the heliport in Manhattan. The simple reason for the delay was the absence of Epstein. A cover story was put out that the delay was caused because the pilot hadn't received clearance for the flight but that was subterfuge. It was Brian Epstein's sad, unexplained absence. Nothing more.

But then he turned up and calmly took charge as though his prolonged absence was the most natural thing in the world.

The helicopter dropped them close to the security entrance for the artists and within twenty minutes they were on stage. It was the usual 29-minute set, no concessions to the eastern audience or to the triumphs of six months earlier with Ed Sullivan on Broadway.

The unusually shaped venue held 15,983 people, and was a complete sell-out. Extra seats had been added very late at a slightly exorbitant price of $6.50, but to preserve the increasing sense of War Zone the audience were kept back from the stage by an eight-foot high fence which had naturally been topped with barbed wire.

It isn't difficult to imagine what the group thought. Playing music that nobody, least of all the men on the stage could hear, playing for people, generally kids, who were risking physical injury just by being there, and playing in an environment that stank of aggression. It was an unpleasant cocktail, for the four men on the stage but also for those in the party like Mal Evans and Derek Taylor, and those like Bess Coleman, Diana Vero and Wendy Hanson weren't immune to the negative feelings that were coming over the whole party.

Because there was a second concert at the same venue the following evening there wasn't the usual need to race away from the venue to get on a plane and escape from the madness into the clouds. A catering company had been engaged to lay on drinks and some snack food for those who stayed on after the concert and a number of people joined the group and their extended party in the backstage area.

There was no intention to stay there for long. The hotel was a strong lure, and the Beatles had heard a strong rumour that Al Aronowitz, last seen aboard the train to Washington in mid February, would be coming to the Delmonico to see them again, and he would be bringing somebody with him.

One Bob Dylan.

For that reason alone, nobody was disposed to hang around at the tennis stadium making small talk to a crowd which was mercifully thin on journalists or media. The one source of mystery and slight entertainment was a small group of people who nobody but Brian Epstein seemed to know, or at least he appeared to know one of them.

And he was arguing, gesticulating at this man, in a most unBrian-like way. But amazingly the man wasn't shrinking away. He stood speaking to Epstein, arguing back at him, and then laughing at him.

Laughing at Brian Epstein? It was unheard-of, but there wasn't time to dwell on the mystery. Derek Taylor ushered Epstein away, and Bess Coleman shepherded the four Beatles out of the secure area and into the transport.

Fifty minutes later they were safely back in the Delmonico, safe from the yelling hordes in the streets below. And then Mr. Dylan arrived.

It became a matter of record, of myth and legend, that this was the evening that Dylan introduced the Beatles and Brian Epstein to the joys of marijuana. However, there seems plenty of evidence to suggest, if not prove, that the Beatles had at least a passing knowledge of weed prior to that. Still, there are plenty of stories from the likes of Mal Evans to describe the effect that the evening had on the Beatles, and above all, if the influence of the drug helped them forget some of the horrors and tribulations of the tour then it served a useful purpose.

One more night at Forest Hills in front of 16,000 fans and then, after a night staying locally in New Jersey they were back on the same treadmill on Sunday August 30th with a concert at the Convention Hall in Atlantic City with an attendance of 19,000 fans screaming throughout the full twenty-nine minute performance. The transport arrangements seemed grimly arranged to suit the general mood and the cynical feelings the Beatles were sharing with each other and Evans and Aspinall and Taylor about the tour. They left the hotel on the afternoon of the concert crouched in the back of a local fish truck, which stopped a short distance from the location of the concert, the Convention Hall, where they switched to their waiting tour bus which was better equipped to withstand attacks from the marauding hordes masquerading as fans.

Conversely, they departed from the Convention Hall in a battered laundry van, where the smell was rather better but still weirdly inappropriate for the biggest pop act in the world.

Serious thought, and an element of military planning, was going into the question of how to get the group into and out of the venues. Dummy vehicles were increasingly brought into the picture but, safety considerations aside, it is easy to see why the group were growing acerbically unhappy with their predicament. Mal Evans was a constant target for their ire. He and Derek Taylor shared a world-weariness and gentle cynicism which fitted the mood perfectly, but both of them felt, as the tour moved into September that it would be a bitter struggle to the last date. It had already been confirmed that the last show would take place in New York, in a charity concert on behalf of the United Cerebral Palsy Fund.

For the first, and only time, on the American adventure the touring group broke up on the night of the Atlantic City concert, and while some stayed locally at the Lafayette Hotel on North Carolina Avenue the rest made the journey out to the coast.

The show in Atlantic City was the prelude to a couple of days off, spent in the beautiful surroundings of Cape May, at the beachside Marquis de Lafayette Hotel, and the complete touring party reassembled there on the last day in August. The two days spent relaxing on Beach Avenue by the waters of Delamere Bay were completely therapeutic and allowed some of the scars and bruises of the concerts to ease. In many cases the scars weren't just mental. Bess Coleman had already been knocked unconscious in one of the frantic scrums as the Beatles rushed urgently to escape a stadium and the crowds trying desperately to stop them. She had also been knocked off her feet on a different occasion as people saw that she was carrying an armful of Beatle photographs, and tried to grab them from her. The unassuming Bess took the bumps and scrapes as badges of honour, proof of her loyalty and dedication to the cause, though she, like Derek Taylor and Diana Vero had been too sickened by what they had seen on the tour to want to continue once the American tour concluded. The unhappiness was not with the Beatles or even with Epstein. Instead it was a weary dislike of the lifestyle, of the restrictions, of the painful security, of the constant wailing attention from thousands of hormonal teenagers.

It was too much, far too much, to bear, and Taylor, Vero and Coleman would, very reluctantly cease their daily involvement with the Beatles soon after the American venture was over.

It was quite intolerable. They all agreed that. But then, they all wondered, what the hell must it be like for the Beatles themselves?

The first date in September came at the Convention Hall in Philadelphia, the first of seven consecutive shows in cities like Indianapolis, Milwaukee, Chicago, Detroit, Toronto, and Montreal. There were thousands of screaming fans, dozens of injuries, a couple of mini-riots, and what to the British eyes was massive over-reaction by the police and security.

Invariably the Beatles would be refused permission to even wave at the fans, generally numbered in thousands, who would wait to greet them at airports, often well after midnight. The Beatles would be ordered into their protective car or wagon and raced away from the airport, away to the protective sanctuary of the hotel room, from which they could only escape for the few minutes on stage.

And this group of dates threw a fresh concern into the mix. Death threats were made against the group, primarily Ringo Starr, at the time of their show at the Forum in Montreal. Those responsible were French-Canadian separatists who singled out Ringo Starr because of his Jewishness, which was doubly unfortunate because the Starr family has no Jewish members or associations. The result was that inside the Forum the police stationed a number of riflemen and sharpshooters watching the crowd. During the concert Ringo's raised platform had a plain-clothes policeman positioned permanently alongside and the thoughtful Ringo had raised his cymbal array up to hide him a little more from the audience, but for the entire show the Beatles, and their party watching in the wings, were desperately anxious, hoping that nothing untoward would happen.

Derek Taylor remarked to Mal Evans that in any normal universe the idea of someone shooting a Beatle was absurd and pathetic, but it was a grim possibility. And yet again the touring party were forced to wonder if it was all worth it.

Of course, on strictly commercial levels the answer was an overwhelming 'Yes'.

During that week over 150,000 fans attended the various concerts with the takings approaching a million dollars. Even with the impact of taxes the Beatles were making a very good return for their labours and in addition, Brian Epstein had revived an old practice which proved very lucrative over the years. The promoter, or where appropriate, the arena manager was required to hand Epstein a brown paper bag containing a slice of the takings which somehow would not appear in the official receipt figures. It wasn't always a bag, it wasn't necessarily brown, but it was always cash, and invariably a large amount.

He had been doing this very successfully since the very early days with the Beatles, and he was certainly not the only manager at it. However, as manager of the biggest group in the world, he was quite possibly doing it more often and for larger amounts than other people. Local promoters in England were desperate to book the Beatles and so the brown paper bag system became commonplace, and on the final Beatles trip to Hamburg a payment of 1000 marks was made by Horst Fascher to Epstein under the table to ensure the appearance of the group at his club. It was widely believed that Epstein split the cash up among the Beatles after he had deducted his 25% for NEMS, but, as the money was never declared and very rarely even seen, it is difficult to be absolute about it.

In any event, the amounts of money available from the American gigs made the European brown bag returns seem quite insignificant, but in a strange way the easy availability of that money seemed to make the Seltaeb nightmare even worse.

Wherever he went he was assailed by mountains of Beatles memorabilia and souvenirs. It stood to reason that not all of it could be licensed by Seltaeb but he had seen the name on products too often, in places across America, not to know that the Seltaeb group were absolutely swamping America with merchandise.

And the Beatles were only getting 10%.

Just 10%.

It was scandalous. Frightening, and he had already instructed Jacobs in long-distance calls and a couple of testy telegrams to find a loophole or a way to renegotiate the contract, ideally before he returned to New York at the end of the tour.

Until then he was forced to endure the growing misery of the security and the paranoia and the thoroughly unpleasant conditions, conscious of the growing unhappiness of many of those in the party. Mal Evans and Neil Aspinall he didn't really worry about; they had suffered far worse with the Beatles in terrible conditions in the UK, but he was increasingly worried about how Derek Taylor and particularly the three women in the party - Bess Coleman, Wendy Hanson and Diana Vero - were feeling. They didn't complain, but, standing in the wings at the side of the stage during the Beatles performances, he could look into their eyes and see a mixture of apprehension and disgust. Not at the Beatles or the music, but at the conditions and the atmosphere and the circumstances.

At the start of the tour, and certainly back in the high promise of February, that look would have been excitement and expectation, but that had gone, and, given the circumstances, Epstein wasn't sure that it would ever return.

Following the second show in Montreal, the group were hurried out of the Forum with the usual lack of style or finesse but for once, nobody was in a mood to complain. The fear of guns and bombs was in all their minds and so there was greater urgency than ever to get out of the host city.

The plan was to fly back over the border and south to Jacksonville, Florida, but once again the fates, or whatever it was cursing that tour, took a hand. Hurricane Dora had swung inland, becoming the first recorded tropical cyclone to make landfall over the northeast coast of Florida, and Dora was also the first storm to inflict hurricane force winds on Jacksonville since records began. In its passage, Hurricane Dora caused the deaths of five people and created more than $200 million of damage.

But, as Jacksonville was directly in its path as the Beatles plane flew south, the air traffic control ordered the plane to divert south to Key West, on the southernmost tip of Florida. The journey was bumpy, but not especially so, but as they approached the airport over the Everglades it emerged that the runway at Key West wasn't long enough for their plane, which meant that the pilot would have to try to land with full reverse thrust. This was not the easiest manoeuvre or the most comfortable process for the passengers, but despite a number of concerns they got down safely. But yet again shared glances among the Beatles party spoke the silent question, "Is this really worth all this?"

Two days later, they took a flight back to Jacksonville. As the plane circled above the city it was buffeted heavily by winds which were the tail end of the hurricane. Much of the city had been heavily damaged and the devastation was evident from the air. Electricity was unavailable in parts of the city, and public transport was restricted. A large number of the 32,000 seats were left empty because the holders of the tickets just couldn't get there.

The wind was frighteningly strong even at ground level and Ringo Starr and Mal Evans decided that it would be prudent to secure his drum platform and so Evans spent an hour lashing the platform to the stage with ropes purchased hastily from a nearby shipping merchants. Evans wasn't convinced that this would be a perfect solution, especially seeing the way the wind was blowing Ringo Starr's hair as the concert started. As extra security, Mal Evans dropped his not inconsiderable bulk onto the back of the platform behind Ringo's seat as the group continued their set. Evans later remarked that all he could think of was The Wizard of Oz and being blown away by the hurricane, though he took comfort in the fact that he was in Florida, not Kansas.

For once, the worse trouble at the concert was political rather than violent. For most of the American tour the Beatles had been stalked by a group of television and newsreel cameramen who had consistently taken unauthorised footage, which later appeared on television or even in cinemas with no payment or royalties paid to the group. Epstein had complained about this, had argued with some of the cameramen, but made no progress. But at Jacksonville the group made a stand and declared that they wouldn't start the concert until the cameramen left.

They refused, and it was a stand-off, with the huge crowd getting increasingly angry about the delay. Finally, the enterprising Derek Taylor took the stage, explained the impasse in pithy language, and caused a near riot. The police took the hint, and ordered the cameramen to clear out, and the concert went ahead.

Directly after the concert they scrambled into the cars which took them to Imeson Airport for a late flight to Boston, but there were few in the party sorry to leave Florida.

The end was now in sight. There were to be concerts on consecutive nights in Boston, Baltimore, Pittsburgh, Cleveland, New Orleans, Kansas City and Dallas before a short break in New York and then that final concert in the city before the flight home.

By the time the party embarked on that last group of concerts it is fair to describe the people on the tour as like an army unit that has been in major combat, under severe pressure and looking forward to relief and release.

Boston, Baltimore and Pittsburgh passed largely without incident but the situation had deteriorated so much that dozens of injuries, attacks by police on the crowds, and desperate dashes by the Beatles to avoid or escape the very people who were supposed to adore them - all this was considered "largely without incident". The only people who saw the situation in its true technicolour horror were those at the eye of the storm, and for once that wasn't really the Beatles. To a large extent they were isolated and insulated from much of the mayhem, and it was inflicted on, and endured by, the others in the party.

Much of the pain and disillusionment wasn't being felt by Epstein. He had flown back to London to deal with various on-going NEMS matters and crucially to discuss the Seltaeb crisis with David Jacobs. The lawyer had told him by telephone and telegram that he thought he had devised a solution to the

Seltaeb mess but, given the sensitivity of the subject, Epstein had ordered Jacobs not to commit any sensitive information, particularly figures, to paper.

Instead, it was worth making the long flight home to meet with Jacobs and discuss the situation in detail. Once again they resorted to the beach at Brighton on a beautiful early September morning, a day so perfect that it was hard to imagine there were any problems in the world.

Jacobs' initial strategy for the resolving of the Seltaeb crisis was simple. A re-negotiation of the contract. He wearily batted away Epstein's demand just to scrap the contract and start again. He was shocked to hear his friend speak that way. It was totally uncharacteristic of the Beatles manager, and the bitter demand made Jacobs realise yet again just how deeply the Seltaeb problems had affected Epstein.

Slowly, patiently, he explained that legally it just wouldn't be possible to scrap the contract, but, to his enormous credit, Epstein then waved away the legal argument and concentrated on the moral and ethical viewpoint that, however attractive it might be, it would be simply wrong to abandon the contract. They, as NEMS, had made an agreement with Seltaeb and it would be kept. He just wanted to try to change the terms of the contract to reduce the painful impact it was having on finances, and potentially on his relationship with the Beatles once they learned what had happened.

Jacobs told him of the conversations which he had conducted with John Fenton, and even an abrasive meeting in New York with Nicky Byrne. The result of the discussions was the basis for a revision to the contract between NEMS and Seltaeb, and they spent an energetic hour discussing options for the contract and for future relations with NEMS. Not for the first time Jacob expressed the bitter wish that all the Seltaeb negotiations could take place with John Fenton, or Lord Eliot or Malcolm Evans.

But that was a forlorn hope, and Nicky Byrne would stay as an element, and an expensive thorn in NEMS side, for the foreseeable future.

Jacobs and Epstein concluded their discussion with the agreement that Jacobs would take matters as far as he could with Fenton in London and then fly back to the States to meet Epstein and Seltaeb people in New York at the end of the tour. Despite Epstein's prompting Jacobs was at pains not to quote, or even suggest, the revised numbers he had discussed with Fenton. He didn't want to stoke the fires under Epstein, because he knew that even if the revised figures made the situation better for NEMS - and how could it not be improved - he would still be angry.

Very angry.

So Jacobs carried on speaking to Fenton, and Epstein flew back to the maelstrom which was the 1964 tour. By the time he was back on the ground the tour had reached Ohio and so Epstein made his way to the Public Auditorium in Cleveland. The few days away had helped him forget the more squalid and painful aspects of the tour but just an hour in Cleveland brought back the nasty recollections of San Francisco and Vancouver and the rest.

In Cleveland, besides the inevitable mini-riots outside the hotel and the venue, there was a demoralising new low reached during the Beatles performance. Halfway through the anodyne delivery of 'All My Loving', with the four Beatles looking on in disbelief, the local police Inspector, Michael Blackwell, strode confidently onto the stage, microphone in hand, and stopped the concert.

Blackwell and his deputy, Carl Bare, gestured to the bewildered Beatles to stop playing but, not understanding what was happening, they continued. Blackwell pompously took George Harrison's arm and started to guide him towards the tour party at the side of the stage, seemingly unaware of the lead which secured Harrison and his guitar to the amp at the back of the stage. Harrison angrily threw off the policeman's hand. Given the obvious impasse, the group complied with the police instructions and 'All My Loving' ground to an uncomfortable end.

The four Beatles gathered in the centre of the stage uncertain whether to bow or not, glancing nervously off to the side of the stage. Epstein was trying to work out what was happening and to decide on a course of action when Mal Evans pre-empted his deliberations. Conscious of the recent death threats to the group Mal dashed onto the stage and ushered them off, and only the other members of the touring party appreciated the significance and the instinctive bravery that made him put his body between the Beatles and the crowd.

Having got rid of his support attraction, the police inspector stood waiting for the booing and whistling from the crowd to end. That took several minutes. Not surprisingly, the large crowd were incensed at the development and only went quiet when they realised that the self-important Blackwell was waiting to make an announcement. The steel safety curtain descended while he was milking the moment and making the most of his instant of fame.

He portentously informed the crowd that he would allow the show to continue if the crowd would remain in their seats. Given that most of them, though loud and excited, were still in their seats it seemed an unnecessary demand but it was supplemented by an impromptu appearance from the morning programme hosts from local station KWY, Harry Martin and Specs Howard, who repeated the instruction and gave the message more impetus. Order was only completely resumed when Derek Taylor, not well known to the crowd but identifiable as part of the Beatles entourage and equipped with a distinctive English accent, asked the crowd to remain in their seats.

Once the police were happy that the crowd behaviour was back within acceptable limits the concert resumed and ended without further incident.

There were more problems getting the group clear from the venue with the police running a decoy vehicle to lure away the fans, but once they and the support party were away they raced to Cleveland Hopkins Airport, and their Lockheed Electra took them directly to New Orleans. They left behind hundreds of fans rioting around the stage door, a series of nightstick charges from the police, and sundry broken and damaged limbs. All in all, another quiet night out at a Beatles concert. It was no wonder that everybody on the flight to Louisiana were looking increasingly longingly to the end of the tour and release from the misery it had become.

And then New Orleans became another chamber of horrors. The planned delivery to the Congress Inn by helicopter had to be cancelled when the helicopter blew a front tyre. To cover for the transport shortage several limousines were ordered but they went to Moisant Field, New Orleans International Airport instead of New Orleans Lakefront Airport where the Beatles plane was supposed to land.

Until just after the Second World War Lakefront Airport had been the main air facility for the city but was then replaced by Moisant Field, better known today as Louis Armstrong International Airport. Lakefront was badly damaged by Katrina and now, and indeed in the sixties, was more used by charter and private flights, and occasional military traffic.

The Beatles' party jumped hurriedly into the limousines and set off, initially flanked by police cars and outriders. Then, almost unbelievably, the car containing the four Beatles became separated from all the other cars and found itself travelling a different route. Given the security problems that had afflicted the tour it was incredible that such an elementary mistake should have been allowed to happen.

The Beatles car reached the hotel where, given the early hour, there were just a few hundred fans but, seeing the Beatles without the usual heavy protection, they charged the car. Police quickly and roughly forced the fans away and waved the Beatles car into the appropriate space but in the panic and confusion the Beatles car reversed into a local Kenner police patrol car, though only minor damage was caused.

But the chaos was far more serious at the venue, City Park Stadium. A series of temporary barriers had been erected to keep the fans away from the stage but a huge group of several hundred fans broke out from the seats and tried to scale the barriers to get to the stage. New Orleans Police Department had cancelled all leave and more than two hundred officers plus a number of stewards were involved in a pitched battle with the fans for almost half an hour before they were forced back to the stand.

Mounted police were hurriedly brought in to patrol the area in front of the stage, and more temporary barriers were introduced while the concert was underway, as police tried to control the fans. Over two hundred fans collapsed, and there were a large number of crush and trampling injuries.

Sadly that situation had become commonplace and unremarkable, so much so that the mad scenes on the field didn't even merit comment as the Beatles flew off to Kansas.

The show in Kansas City wasn't on the original tour schedule. The day in question was meant to be a rest day this was the extra show purchased at such lavish expense by Charles O Finley when he met Epstein in San Francisco before the first concert.

Epstein had left the decision up to the Beatles at that time, aware that playing Kansas City would mean them sacrificing a rare rest day. When the decision was made, the importance of a rest day had no significance though by the time they flew to Kansas City the mood had definitely changed.

Finley had offered a record fee of $150,000, a figure which was almost guaranteed to show a loss, even if the stadium was full. In the event there were just over 20,000 fans inside the 41,000-seater stadium, although local reasons and a clear antipathy to Finlay, caused many fans to boycott the show. In addition, ticket prices were high, particularly for the best seats. At $8.50, those seats were more expensive than anywhere else on the tour.

It was estimated that Finley, owner of Kansas City Athletics, lost between $50,000 and $100,000 through sponsoring the show, but even so, he then donated a further $25,000 to Mercy Hospital.

As a unique concession to this extraordinary event the Beatles added an additional song to their normal programme. The old Wilbert Harrison number, 'Kansas City'/'Hey, Hey, Hey, Hey', appeared later in the year on "Beatles For Sale" but was not a number they were used to playing in concerts in 1964. However, given their location, it was a political and popular choice, and the crowd showed their appreciation towards the Beatles.

But, as happened so ever on the tour, the excitement and the passion in the crowd bubbled over and the concert had to be stopped, with a heavy threat of likely cancellation of the show, if the atmosphere didn't become calmer. It eventually did and the concert carried on to its natural end.

As one strange postscript to the concert the Muehlebach Towers, where the Beatles had stayed, sold the bed linen used on the beds used by the four Beatles, 6 sheets and eight pillowcases, to a man from Illinois for reputedly $750. A similar thing happened after the Detroit concert some days earlier and, as there, the pieces of linen later emerged cut into small squares, mounted, and sold as souvenirs.

From Kansas City, the party headed south-west to Dallas, and into more bedlam and controversy. The party had been booked into the Cabana, a hotel part owned by Doris Day and her son, record producer Terry Melcher, and the Texan fans had the hotel under siege when the Beatles party arrived. The limousines were swamped by fans especially because the security staff were thin on the ground.

As the group tried to make their customary dash into the sanctuary of the hotel they were intercepted by hundreds of fans. Ringo Starr and George Harrison were cut off from the others and the eager fans leapt on them. Both men lost their shoes, and Harrison was knocked over but quickly dragged to safety by the amazing Mal Evans.

The struggle went over for several minutes during which several cars were severely damaged, and a young fan was pushed through a glass door leaving her with significant loss of blood and major lacerations to her head and face.

Following the concert they were driven directly to Dallas Love Field where their chartered plane took off just after 11pm taking the party to Missouri for their final rest day in America. During the short flight, the whole party on the plane joined in an impassioned chorus of 'Happy Birthday' directed at Brian Epstein, who was then presented with a number of gifts, some attractive and some severely impractical.

It was a rare moment of levity and pleasure on a painful trip, partly induced by a definite out of school/end of term feeling. All of the people on the plane could see the imminent end of the tour, and the return home, and for several there was a real sense of closure as they knew that their days with the Beatles were nearly over.

Dallas was the penultimate date on the tour, the last date before a day off on, of all things, a ranch in the Ozarks. Reed Pigman, the owner of the ranch was also a Texas airline magnate owning American Flyers Airlines, and he had secured the contract to fly the Beatles across America on the tour. The travelling dates concluded with Dallas on September 18th, and with the last date in New York not taking place until the 20th Pigman invited Epstein and the party to avail themselves of his hospitality on his ranch before heading on to New York and their last performance prior to the return to England. By that point the tour had already covered twenty-five cities and performances of thirty-four concerts in just thirty days. On the Friday evening, the Beatles performed before 15,000 fans in Dallas and then they flew to Walnut Ridge, Arkansas. At that destination Pigman picked them up in his twin-engine seven passenger Cessna and flew them across to Oregon County in Missouri. Before travelling to Alton, the Beatles made a brief stop in Walnut Ridge.

The Walnut Ridge airport provided the ideal spot for the group to change planes before heading to Missouri. The runway was built as a training facility during World War II and was equipped to handle large aircraft. Also, the Beatles could avoid the crush of screaming fans by landing at a secluded airport at the edge of a small town.

From Walnut Ridge, the party were flown on to Alton, arriving at 3a.m. on Saturday morning at the ranch where they sat up drinking and playing poker until dawn broke over the Ozarks. The pleasures on that Saturday were simple, including even more poker, horse riding, fishing and driving around the barn and the grounds. A picture spread on these innocent few hours was carried in Life magazine later in the year in October.

That quiet seclusion couldn't last and Pigman had to take them back to what the newspapers called civilisation. They went back via the Walnut Ridge Regional Airport in Arkansas, where a plaque remains in place to this day commemorating the historic visit of the Beatles to their small town in 1964.

The party boarded Reed Pigman's plane for the flight to New York, where they caught a helicopter to shuttle them into Manhattan.

The concert was a grand charity event at the Paramount Theatre on Broadway, labelled "An Evening With The Beatles" with Steve Lawrence and Eydie Gorme.

The streets around Broadway were swarming with excited Beatles fans and police estimated that some 100,000 fans were present, with just two hundred policemen on hand to control the crowds. The Beatles were due onstage at 10.45pm but each set for the other acts on the bill were curtailed so that the Beatles could take the stage 45 minutes earlier.

The tickets for the concert had been on sale for $100 to a combination of young fans and the society elite from New York, and the Paramount was bursting with 3,682 people. Backstage was crowded with the great and the good, with Ed Sullivan and members of his staff from the February show joining him for a nostalgic encounter with Epstein and the Beatles. Sid Bernstein and Nat Weiss also made it backstage, and there was clearly a sense that something life-changing had ended.

For it was truly, finally over. That 1964 tour of America which, by any standards, was quite extraordinary. The Beatles provided 32 shows at 26 concerts in 24 cities in 34 days, and had spent 63 hours travelling 22,621 miles since 18 August with 22,441 flying and 180 on the road. Never again would the group undertake, or endure, such a tour, but the painful memories would linger. That sort of gruelling itinerary, though quite commonplace in Britain, was absurd in a country the size of America, and a schedule which was the subject of disbelief and laughter when first announced

The last night in America was spent at the Riviera Motel close to John F Kennedy International Airport, from which the party was flying back to London the following day. After the concert, the Beatles and a few members of the tour party went to the Motel accompanied by Bob Dylan and his manager Albert Grossman, who spent a couple of hours discussing the tour with the Beatles.

Epstein wasn't with them. He stayed in Manhattan after the concert and travelled with Mal Evans back to the Delmonico to meet David Jacobs. He had flown in two days earlier as arranged with Epstein, prepared to meet Nicky Byrne, Lord Eliot, Malcolm Evans and any other Seltaeb people that he could track down.

Epstein had given him a brief but Jacobs was adamant that it would make perfect sense for Epstein to be absent from the pivotal Seltaeb conversations, not least because Epstein had also been absent from the meetings with John Fenton. Jacobs hadn't been explicit with Epstein about how the conversations had gone, and how he had skirted round the brief given by Epstein. The main reason for Jacob's slippery conduct was that he wanted a free hand to negotiate with Seltaeb, but the secondary reason was that he really didn't expect it to go well, and he didn't want to be constrained by Epstein's paranoia, either in words or in person.

They met in the suite which Jacobs had reserved on the 5th floor at the Delmonico. Mal Evans sat slightly uncomfortably as Epstein and Jacobs made small talk while the waiter delivered drinks. Then Epstein asked Evans to recount to Jacobs the story about the disturbing phone talk he had taken back at the Plaza in February. It wasn't strange that this was the first time that Evans and Jacobs had met to discuss the plaza call.

They very rarely met, were hardly ever in the same place, and, prior to the short meeting at the Delmonico, Mal Evans had only ever exchanged one brief sentence with the lawyer.

He told the story quickly. There wasn't much to tell, but Epstein was relieved to hear Mal tell the tale virtually identically to the way he had recounted it to him twice previously. Jacobs made notes, didn't ask questions, and nodded once in Epstein's direction when he had finished writing.

Evans took that as a signal that his participation was over and he was correct. Epstein asked him to wait in the foyer of the hotel for him, adding helpfully that Mal should get a drink.

He dutifully left the room but Epstein waited until he heard the door firmly close before he was certain that Evans had departed. Even then he delayed a few moments longer by silently pouring two drinks and placing one on the table next to Jacobs. Only at that point did he feel safe or confident to open the conversation on the painful and possibly disastrous subject of Seltaeb.

Jacobs quickly gave an overview of his various meetings, investigations and discussions over the previous few weeks, particularly those involving Fenton and Byrne. In response Epstein demanded to know if NEMS were going to have their money returned, but Jacobs patiently, gently had to point out, yet again, that the money hadn't been stolen by Seltaeb. Like it or loath it there was a legally binding contract and Seltaeb were merely taking what they were legally entitled to under that contract.

Epstein's thunderous expression gave his reaction. There was a pregnant silence which lasted for half a minute before Epstein asked the killer question about the renegotiation of the contract. Jacobs was able to pass on the welcome news that he had negotiated a renewed contract, and Epstein brightened, until he returned to the question of replacement of revenues.

Jacobs firmly had to inform him that such return of revenues would not happen because, as he reasonably asked, why should Seltaeb bother?

Epstein then asked the vital question. What would be the new percentage to be taken by NEMS?

Jacobs bit his lip. This was the moment he had been dreading. When he replied "49%", it seemed as though Epstein aged twenty years in a minute.

Epstein tried a couple of different routes to see why it was 49% rather than 90% or even 99%, but Jacobs had to keep gently batting back his obstinate outrage. Finally the Beatles manager asked Jacobs to give him the figures he had been collating on Seltaeb sales in 1964, and projected turnover in the next year.

Sales in 1964 to date: approximately $58 million (worth some $560 million today).

When he heard that figure Epstein lost interest in projections for the following year. The only thing that mattered was the awful, dreadful news that the grey-pallored Jacobs had just delivered.

$58 million. In less than one year. And the Beatles, his Beatles, would get just $5.8 million.

And Seltaeb, four or five very lucky young men, were going to pocket almost $53 million.

And Brian Epstein's world began to fall apart.

The Beatles caught the flight back to London after the colossal American tour and returned, not as conquering heroes, but as a group of people battered into submission by everything they had seen and experienced over the previous month.

And this applied to nobody more than Brian Epstein. He could feel his control over the Beatles starting to unravel. Not rapidly, for the ramifications of the Seltaeb disaster would take time to leak out, but both he and David Jacobs agreed that the contract problems with Seltaeb could, and probably would, cost the Beatles tens of millions of dollars.

He could only hope that Jacobs could work some legal magic to claw back some of the fortunes which Seltaeb had already cleverly diverted away from the Beatles. It was likely to be a forlorn hope, but all he could do was clutch at straws.

He had charged Jacobs with creating a plausible lawsuit against Seltaeb, and the lawyer was still in America speaking to possible witnesses.

Neither man held out great hopes for success. Even worse, Jacobs had considered the possibility that a lawsuit filed in American courts might drag on for years with untold consequences for Brian Epstein, and the Beatles.

On any level, it was not a pleasant prospect.

Epstein, despite the glory of the homecoming, had other problems. Derek Taylor had provided his resignation on the last night in America. A silly spat over a limousine outside the Paramount was the ostensible cause but both men knew it was coming. Taylor's nerves were ragged after what he had seen and experienced on the tour, and he had a desperate need to get away from the mayhem which permanently surrounded the Beatles.

In truth Epstein needed Taylor far more than Derek Taylor needed the job, but the silly row escalated to the point where the men were exchanging insults. Of course the situation, and the heightened emotions of the tour, were at the root of it, but Taylor had decided weeks earlier that he would leave.

The silly row with Brian Epstein was simply the final straw. Epstein tried hard to pull things back and get Taylor to withdraw his resignation but it was too late. But, to his immense credit, Taylor agreed to work a three-month notice period to show his successor the ropes, and possibly instruct him or her in techniques to handle the increasingly volatile Epstein.

It was a grievous loss. Taylor had only been working with them for a few months but his calm implacability and dry sense of humour made him a popular member of the NEMS family. He had been working as both press officer for the Beatles and also as Brian's personal assistant, and they were big shoes to fill.

There was one nagging cause of disagreement between the pair. Taylor had frequently voiced his displeasure with the police behaviour shown towards the fans on the tour. Epstein, perhaps for distinctly personal reasons, was far more circumspect and controlled in his remarks.

At that time Derek Taylor had no reason, apart from an occasional injudicious joint, to worry about, let alone fear, the police in America. Brian Epstein was in a different position entirely. He knew that his liaisons with unnamed young men in New York and Los Angeles were severely unwise, and potentially fatal to his career and that of the Beatles, but he found it almost impossible to stop taking chances. The only concession he would make to the assorted warnings was to restrict his secret liaisons to the two coasts. Middle America wasn't ready, perhaps never would be ready for the way Brian Epstein lived his private life.

But it wasn't just the violence of the police that had distressed Derek Taylor. He criticised their venal corruption and that the fact that they were often the most avaricious in terms of demanding autographs and pocketing souvenirs. On one occasion Epstein's brown bag receipts was knocked from his hand in the melee after one of the concerts. He was lifted to his feet by a burly cop - he was surrounded by cops - but the bag and its contents had vanished. For various reasons Epstein shared Taylor's distaste, but for his own private reasons he tried to be more guarded in his criticism, particularly in public.

The fact that Taylor would speak openly and forthrightly to his colleagues in the press about his feelings about police behaviour did not go down well with Epstein and created a friction between them which was exacerbated almost daily on the American tour.

It didn't become clear to Epstein until the plane was high above the Atlantic that it wasn't only Taylor he would be losing. Both Diana Vero and Bess Coleman had decided that life with the Beatles, though incredibly exciting, was simply sucking away too much of life. Both women, for different reasons, walked away, and Epstein would feel their loss keenly.

Wendy Hanson did return to NEMS with Epstein. After a brief holiday to restore some equilibrium after the American tour, she was back at work at Sutherland House in mid-October. This meant that she slipped back into the NEMS operation shortly after what would prove to be a crucial meeting for Brian Epstein.

On October 7th he met with the four Beatles and producer of "A Hard Day's Night", Walter Shenson, to discuss the second Beatles film. This was scheduled to start filming in February or March of the following year.

Plans were already underway for different filming locations around the world and, given the unexpected success of the first film, the pressure from United Artists was already starting.

It was no wonder. They had embarked on the venture with the Beatles almost a year earlier in the expectation that the film would be at best a modest success in Britain, but that United Artists would recoup any losses via the soundtrack album which was always their main interest.

But then, to nobody's surprise except perhaps United Artists, the film was a roaring commercial and critical success, and of course the soundtrack album proved to be one of the biggest sellers of the whole year. This changed the thinking of United Artists about the next stage in the three-film deal they had struck with Brian Epstein in 1963.

Once the first film and soundtrack was released, and the sales proved to be so enormous, United Artists directed Walter Shenson to get moving with the follow-up.

The meeting on October 7th at the Dorchester was the first tentative and gentle step on the road which would lead to the film "Help!" in 1965. Even though the Beatles, particularly Lennon, were unhappy with various aspects of "A Hard Day's Night" it was generally conceded that many elements of the film were worth persevering with, and so producer Shenson and director, Richard Lester, remained, and personalities from "A Hard Day's Night", names like Victor Spinetti, carried on into other roles in "Help!"

The first point on which agreement was going to be reached was that not under any circumstances would this film be created or regarded as "A Hard Day's Night 2". A general distrust of the film industry demonstrated that the group and Epstein would not endure a simple cash-in job, trying to replicate the success of the first film by just copying the elements of that first film.

But the conversation with Shenson, who was in ebullient mood, quickly calmed those fears. The huge returns from "A Hard Day's Night" meant that United Artists were happy to open the purse-strings with the immediate impact that the budget for "Help!" was more than three times the meagre budget allowed to the first film. And, crucially, as there was no need for the economy measure of filming in black and white, Dick Lester was free to film the new one in colour.

Although the meeting on October 7th was only an initial get-together about the proposed new film, all those present were aware that the very success of "A

Hard Day's Night" put pressure on the group and the film-makers to match the excellence of that first film. "A Hard Day's Night" was a massive success for many reasons. One was surely, particularly in America, because most people simply didn't expect it. Fed a diet from Hollywood of teen movies featuring the likes of Frankie Avalon and even Elvis, the average cinemagoer clearly could not have expected "A Hard Day's Night" to be as good as it was.

But such success raised expectations massively for the second film and there were a few worries voiced in the conversation with Walter Shenson about the capacity to the second film to match, let alone surpass, "A Hard Day's Night".

For his part, Shenson wouldn't countenance any negativity about the future prospects. His stock was soaring with United Artists, and politically he was in an incredibly strong position with the company, a situation he would exploit in the future by persuading United Artists to revert the rights in the film to him after a number of years. That turned out to be a brilliant move, and a goldmine, but would not become even a firm idea until well after the second film had been made and become a success.

Shenson prepared for the meeting with a very shrewd move, guaranteed to strengthen his position with Epstein. In the very first meeting about a potential Beatles film Brian Epstein had astonished the United Artists people by stating at the outset that he could not consider going forward in the negotiations for less than 7.5% for the Beatles. The United Artists people had disguised their reaction well. They had been expecting a demand for up to 25% and were prepared for that, but "A Hard Day's Night" got underway on the basis of the Beatles receiving 7.5% of the proceeds.

Now though, in the wake of the huge success of the film and the unprecedented sales of the soundtrack album, United Artists were able to be generous. Walter Shenson was authorised to inform Epstein that, as a gesture of the company's thanks and appreciation, United Artists would, without prejudice, increase the Beatles share of the proceeds to 20% and this surprising deal was fully sanctioned by Bud Ornstein.

Naturally Epstein was surprised and grateful. Any small triumph in commercial terms was welcome, especially given the daily news of the lingering disasters caused by the Seltaeb deal. Epstein's gratitude towards Shenson and United Artists was genuine and profound, and clearly influenced his level of co-operation on the second film and indeed further proposals to emerge in the coming weeks and months.

But he would not find out for even longer that even in their seeming generosity United Artists were still making an extra margin on the Beatles.

The Seltaeb issues caused Epstein to question, and even doubt, the instinctive faith he put in people. This led to a number of interesting developments, not least the clear fact that new people opening negotiations with him after he came back from America in September 1964 encountered a rather different individual than earlier in his career. Sharper, more brittle, less inclined to trust to his judgement of people, and instinctively more suspicious of people and their motives. Of course, it could be argued that Epstein would have changed that way in any case, but the simple fact was that he was soured and wounded by the Seltaeb fiasco and he was never the same afterwards.

One of the earliest people to suffer from the new, less trusting Epstein was a hard-nosed television executive from New York named Al Brodax. He had developed a sizeable reputation in television in the States and in the early sixties had been responsible for the success of the Popeye cartoon series through the company for which he worked, King Features Syndicate.

The Popeye series established a successful process for Brodax. He raised investment of $25,000 which allowed production to get underway, with the result that 220 Popeye cartoons were produced. In their first year Brodax and his associates realised a return of $3 million.

Brodax had a chance meeting with a man who was trying to interest King Features, responsible for syndicated print material, comic strips like Blondie and Barney Google, in a similar strip cartoon on the Beatles.

Those efforts came to nothing but the idea interested Brodax and he began to explore the possibilities for an animation about the Beatles, especially given the sudden quantum increase in interest in the Beatles. With interest from the Lionel Train Inc., which then led to an interim deal from ABC, Brodax had the collateral to move forward. A series of drawings were commissioned as illustrations which would form the basis for any proposed animated tv series, and with that ammunition, he travelled to London to meet Epstein.

The session took place at Sutherland House and, if Brodax thought he was in for an easy ride with the effete Beatles manager, he was quickly disavowed of that impression. Epstein eventually agreed to the proposal to create a Beatles cartoon series to feature a Beatles song in every episode but the price was prohibitive. Al Brodax was shocked by the cold remorselessness of Epstein especially as various contacts in New York, particularly various Sullivan people, had described Brian Epstein as "a pussycat".

The conversation at Sutherland House was followed by two more sessions before agreement was reached, and only then did Epstein turn the details, and the proposed deal over to David Jacobs to draw up as a formal contract. That alone was a demonstration of how things had changed in the wake of Seltaeb. The days when Epstein would casually pass projects over to David Jacobs and trust him to deliver were over; Seltaeb meant that Epstein and the Beatles would inevitably carry some major costs, but, whatever haqppened, Jacobs would not be paying.

Brodax wasn't the only person to suffer the new, rigorous Epstein. He was just the first. The tv programme which was released as The Beatles would not appear on American television until September 1965 but throughout that period Brodax would grow increasingly exasperated with Brian Epstein. At his best Brodax would describe the Beatles' manager as "difficult", but Brodax was very rarely seen as anything better by the many people unfortunate enough to work for or with him.

During those first few weeks after returning from America Epstein was primarily occupied in dealing with the inevitable feeling of anti-climax after such a massive, life-changing event. Fortunately, the day-to-day requirements of keeping up with NEMS business meant that he had very little time for self-pity or introspection. His autobiography, "A Cellarful of Noise", was published at the beginning of October, and he was dragged into the usual round of promotional activities to support the book.

One activity which would have been used to publicize the book was announced, but later quietly dropped. Brian Epstein and his friend, Lionel Bart, announced grand plans for a gala concert to star their mutual friend, Judy Garland. Like so many of the grandiose schemes thought up by Bart and Epstein this gala concert for Judy Garland never happened.

On the level of more conventional activity he had quickly dropped the Beatles back into their touring schedule. A fresh British tour started in Bradford on October 10th featuring Mary Wells, Tommy Quickly, The Remo Four, Sounds Incorporated, Michael Haslam and the Rustiks. This was another tour based predominantly on cinemas or major theatres. The Beatles, even without the American success that year, had outgrown the more intimate venues they were playing only eighteen months earlier.

But Epstein was still trying to maximise time by fitting in recording sessions and interviews and press and tv appearances around the touring schedule. They were still recording material for the new album planned for release before the end of the year to take advantage of the critical Christmas market, and of course there was the need to record a fresh single. Once again, with commendable refusal to follow American patterns, the single and its b-side would be stand-alone tracks, not part of the album, and both single and album were planned for release one week apart at the end of November.

It was a desperately gruelling schedule but it was all the four Beatles had known for almost two years. However draining it became, it was still manifestly better than the circuit they had been playing, prior to the arrival of Epstein.

October brought a couple of significant developments in America with the Beatles record releases. On October 15th, Capitol legally took control of the material that Vee-Jay had milked so successfully throughout 1964. The agreement between Capitol and Vee-Jay was legally implemented that day and Vee-Jay dropped out of the picture, at least so far as new releases were concerned.

Before that though they had one last dash at the sunlight. Two albums were released in October, 'The Beatles Versus the Four Seasons' and then 'Songs, Pictures And Stories Of The Fabulous Beatles'. Both of these were shameless exploitation devices, a last attempt to squeeze some revenue from this unexpected cash cow before it all ended in the middle of the month.

Epstein was aware of these shenanigans but also conscious that Capitol was rapidly bringing the situation under control and ensuring that pirates like Vee-Jay would not be allowed to threaten his operation. After all, one set of pirates like Seltaeb were more than enough as a headache, though, as 1964 approached its end the Seltaeb situation was changing from headache to open wound.

At least Wendy Hanson returned to the fold in October and he was able to sense some stability and normality returning to the operation, and Wendy's return was a counter-balance to the imminent departure of Derek Taylor. On several occasions since the return from America, Epstein had tried to persuade him to stay, making very generous offers of improved terms and conditions, greater responsibilities and the like, but Taylor would not be moved.

He did go with Brian Epstein to the ceremony where the Beatles were awarded four prestigious Ivor Novello Awards, for 'She Loves You" (most played and biggest seller); 'I Want To Hold Your Hand' (second highest plays); 'All My Loving' (second song of the year), but that was the last formal event Derek Taylor would attend before ending his brief tenure as Epstein's assistant.

Shortly afterwards Brian Epstein recorded his only appearance on the famous British radio programme, Desert Island Discs. This quaint programme is part of the fabric of British life, having been a staple on BBC Radio 4 for several decades. The premise is simple. The guest has to choose eight pieces of music they would like to have if stranded on a desert island. They can also choose one book and one luxury item. The programme is a gentle overview of the life of the guest and some surprising revelations can be made by the guests, even in the choice of musical pieces which often seem designed to improve the social standing of the guest rather than truthfully reflect music that they love.

Brian Epstein's list of choices and indeed his demeanour on the programme was very different. As ever he was beautifully and softly-spoken, sounding more like a diplomat in the higher civil service than a mere pop manager.

More than one commentator remarked on a wistful air of melancholy or sadness underpinning his remarks, even though his pride in the NEMS stable, particularly of course the Beatles, shone through. His choice of music was telling. Only two pieces reflected his interest in pop. One was an orchestral piece by the George Martin Orchestra performing 'All My Loving' whilst the other, almost inevitably, was from his beloved Beatles, with 'She's A Woman'.

All the other pieces were essentially classical, reflected the sophistication of his upbringing and his life away from NEMS. There was Johann Sebastian Bach, Quartette Trés Bien, Sibelius, Michael Olatunji, Max Bruch, Carmen Amaya and Fiesta de Jerez.

For the two extra choices he chose Elected Science by Thomas Merton as his book, and for his luxury item he elected to take on the island with him Painting materials.

As I conducted my research into the book I found my admiration for Brian Epstein growing almost daily, and that feeling became even greater when one of my contacts at the BBC managed to let me have a copy of the Desert Island Discs programme featuring Epstein. This was broadcast on November 30th 1964, at a point when he was undoubtedly the most important pop manager in the world, at the top of his profession and yet, and I swear I'm not imagining or inventing this, there was an unmistakable air of sadness about him and the things he said. Of course, I was listening to it on a tiny reel-to-reel spool so the quality left a lot to be desired. It hadn't been copied onto cassette, let alone any digital format.

I only heard it once. Even the excellent Desert Island Discs archive doesn't have a copy of it so I never heard it again, but I never forgot it and that beautifully modulated voice bursting with pride about what his boys - not him - had achieved. And I remember switching the silly little tape machine off at the end of the show and thinking of that famous, probably apocryphal, quotation "And Alexander wept because there were no more worlds to conquer". Brian Epstein didn't weep that night on Desert Island Discs but I thought I could hear it in his voice. A silent sadness that spoke volumes.

But I freely admit if anyone delivered a script for one of my tv epics containing emotional slush like that I'd kick his backside down the stairs. But in this single case - Brian Epstein - it was true. One of the saddest things I've ever heard. But my respect and admiration for him as a man was locked in aspic when I was fortunate enough to listen to that programme more than forty years after it was first broadcast.

The frantic recording pace since the return from America produced the usual sparkling results, and so the new single, 'I Feel Fine' was released in the

UK on November 27th, with the new Beatles album, 'Beatles For Sale' hitting the shops early in the month on December 4th 1964.

Inevitably, both discs were massive sellers, but the album betrayed the incredible pressure that the group had been under that year. Unlike the previous album, "A Hard Day's Night", which featured exclusively tracks by Lennon and McCartney, the new album, for purely expedient reasons, included five songs which had been staples in their performances in Hamburg and Liverpool. Songs like Chuck Berry's 'Rock and Roll Music', and 'Everybody's Trying to be My Baby' by Carl Perkins, 'Mr. Moonlight' by Roy Lee Johnson, and the timeless 'Words of Love' from Buddy Holly were a fitting testament to the group's roots.

In addition they added the song which they had brought into the set at Kansas City in September, and 'Kansas City/Hey-Hey-Hey-Hey' completed the collection of classics and standards which would never again be used to adorn, or flesh out a Beatles album.

There was one other old song appearing on the album, albeit one which most people hadn't heard previously. This was 'I'll Follow The Sun' which had been a song written by Paul McCartney several years earlier, part of the vast anthology of songs, both finished and in fragment form, that he had sitting around in his room at the top of Jane Asher's house in Wimpole Street.

The album had an advance order of more than 750,000 which had never been achieved by a British album previously. It had the distinction of knocking "A Hard Day's Night" off the top of the album charts, and giving the Beatles the single and album at the top of the charts at Christmas 1964. The album even had the rare distinction of entering the singles chart in its own right, and managed to climb to number 22.

That was exciting for the group, their manager, and their legions of fans, but Epstein's temporary reverie was cut cruelly short by a notice that appeared in The Times on December 9th. The report stated that Lord Eliot was suing Nicky Byrne for damages of $1million, and alleged that Byrne had spent $150,000 of Seltaeb funds for "comfort and personal gain". Further allegations in the lawsuit related to Byrne spending substantial amounts, as much as $19,000 a week. There were other details concerning charge accounts at Fifth Avenue stores, chauffeurs and helicopters, and the withholding of royalties due to NEMS.

Although Jacobs had warned Epstein that trouble was building up internally among the Seltaeb group, the piece in the Times was a body blow. If the parties in Seltaeb were warring against each other then it was, on the face of it, a good thing for NEMS, but Jacobs had already warned Epstein against the likelihood of cross-suits. He had made another visit to New York in mid-

October, a fact-finding trip to establish what had happened in the wake of the contract alteration during the summer.

The news was part good, part bad. Seltaeb seemed to be adhering to the new contract, and the level of activity certainly hadn't diminished. Indeed Jacobs took the arbitrary decision not to give Epstein all the information about what he had seen, and learned, in the States. The Beatles manager was going through one of his periods of acute depression, when only larger handfuls of pills or the threatening company of one of his anonymous male friends could temporarily drive away the demons.

The Seltaeb situation was peculiar. On any normal basis, it ought to have been a relatively simple problem. A deal that had gone wrong. Re-calculate, re-negotiate, and move forward. In his relatively brief period with the Beatles as manager, Epstein had suffered several setbacks that would have demoralised a lesser man. In earlier periods Jacobs had been able to bring his friend to raucous laughter by reminding him of the time he had rung Capitol in 1963 to get an update on progress, if any, with Beatles records. The receptionist quite correctly asked his name and which act he was representing but then quite innocently had asked "The Beatles? Are they affiliated with this label?"

That kind of simple joy seemed to have deserted him, and the Seltaeb debacle was to blame. Nothing Jacobs tried seemed to help, not least because he knew that Epstein blamed him.

And Jacobs knew that Epstein was right.

Nevertheless giving him full chapter and verse on what was happening with Seltaeb would, in the short term, prove counter-productive, and in November 1964 Jacobs sensed that he was about to find a new ally who might have been able to extricate Jacobs, and Epstein, and NEMS from the Seltaeb mess.

Geoffrey Ellis was a friend of Brian Epstein's and had been so for years before the record shops and the Beatles entered his life. Ellis and Epstein had shared interests, of a non-sexual variety, in Liverpool as young men before Ellis went to America to work. A number of friends came to Liverpool docks to wave him on his way, and Brian Epstein was among them.

While in America, during a period in Chicago, Ellis had acted as host to Epstein's parents who were in America sourcing furniture contacts. He showed them a few of the sights in Chicago and shared a meal at their hotel where their son back in England featured prominently in the conversation.

By this time, Brian was making a success of managing the record department at the shop and Ellis was pleased, though slightly surprised, that his old friend had gone down this path.

And then, just before the end of October 1963, Epstein sent Ellis a letter informing him that he would be coming to America shortly to investigate the chances of bringing the Beatles to the States. This was Epstein's first visit and so it was entirely natural that he contacted his one friend in the city about it, and it was on the recommendation of Geoffrey Ellis that Epstein booked into the Regency Hotel, on Park Avenue, by East 62nd Street, within a decent roar of Central Park Zoo.

Because Geoffrey had to work on the days that Brian was in New York on that initial visit, he didn't go to the Delmonico, or meet Ed Sullivan or even Bess Coleman.

But he did get invited up to the Plaza three months later when they made their triumphant initial visit to America, and while Epstein was clearly enjoying the company of an old friend, he was also clearly weighing up whether to ask Ellis to join in the NEMS adventure.

Ellis was working in insurance, of all things. But he did have an accountancy background, and a welcome work ethic, and was totally trustworthy. Given the rapid expansion of NEMS interests and activities during the first half of 1964 it would have been remiss of Epstein not to scout talent that could help build NEMS.

Geoffrey Ellis ticked all the boxes and so, during another American trip later in the year, Epstein asked him to leave his work in America and come and join NEMS. It was an intriguing, frightening prospect but it was potentially extremely exciting.

And Epstein went out of his way to explain why he needed Ellis and his particular skills to help with the expansion of NEMS, and Ellis bought into the vision.

He came back to London in November 1964 arriving on Saturday, November 14th, only to find that his welcoming party was Alistair Taylor, not Brian Epstein. This surprise and unexpected absence was just the first of many. To try to make up for the unexplained failure to appear at the airport Epstein took Geoffrey out on the Sunday evening to a special show at the Palladium featuring Judy Garland and her young daughter, Liza Minelli.

A private supper later with the extravagant star of "Wizard of Oz" was a suitably starry introduction to NEMS and London for Geoffrey Ellis, and as big a change from the rigorous world of insurance as can be imagined.

He started work the following morning just a few yards away from that same London Palladium. At that point, most of the staff were still survivors of the traumatic move from Liverpool to London, and, as an exiled Scouser, Ellis was made very welcome. The main focus of activity at that time was the preparation for the next Beatles Christmas extravaganza, "Another Beatles Christmas Show", which was opening on Christmas Eve at the Hammersmith Odeon. Once again, there was a stellar bill which included the Yardbirds, Elkie Brooks, Freddie and the Dreamers, Mike Haslam, and the Mike Cotton Sound. The show was compered by Jimmy Savile in the days before his extra-curricular activities became such a subject of disgust.

Ellis was able to acclimatise himself to the NEMS way of operating by observing and assisting with preparations for the Christmas shows. On a related but slightly more flippant level, he was involved in the preparations for the posting out of the 1964 Christmas record to the thousands of members of the Beatles Fan Club, and that activity alone suggested the scale of what he was now part of, even if what he had seen in New York earlier in the year hadn't convinced him.

But his quiet, understated competence and confidence was sufficient to persuade the other NEMS people that he was a valuable acquisition. More importantly, David Jacobs was also impressed and began to hope that Geoffrey Ellis might prove a valuable ally in the struggle with Seltaeb, particularly if that included becoming one of the few people who could move Epstein to act.

In this aspect, as I learned later in spectacular style, Ellis proved as helpless and largely impotent as most other people around Brian Epstein. Unlike many of the other leeches and vermin and cockroaches that were starting to sniff around NEMS, the unprepossessing Ellis never seemed to be operating on a private agenda. His devotion seemed total. His commitment was to Epstein and to helping him develop the NEMS business. To that end he was to prove invaluable in the messy, tawdry struggle to bring the Seltaeb problem first under control and then towards a form of resolution.

As part of his work on the Seltaeb issue, and of course his faltering attempts to redeem himself with Brian Epstein, David Jacobs spent time in New York speaking to people who might help with what he increasingly feared would become proceedings in the American courts. He received significant help from Walter Hofer and also the indefatigable Sid Bernstein, both of whom were able to provide copious details, through their army of contacts in New York, about Nicky Byrne's lifestyle. It seemed a reasonable assumption that this was being funded from the Seltaeb revenues. The piece in the Times raised the question of how much of that lifestyle had been sanctioned by the other people in Seltaeb.

More worryingly, NEMS, through Hofer and Bernstein, began to hear stories about disputes affecting Seltaeb, disputes relating to licenses and what companies were allowed to produce under the licence which Seltaeb had granted.

The simple inexperience of the Seltaeb people was starting to prove costly. Licenses handed out in cavalier fashion for first an advance check and then the agreed percentage of royalties were starting to hit problems and conflicts.

Company A obtained a licence to produce Beatle Watches; Company B obtained a licence to produce Beatles jewellery. Company B clearly and reasonably believed that the category "jewellery" included the sub-category "watches" and were not best pleased to see Company A advertising and selling those watches, goods that Company B clearly and reasonably believed were their exclusive preserve.

The sudden increase in publicity about these disputes in the second half of 1964 was worrying enough. More distressing for Epstein and the NEMS office was that many licence-holders, in the situation of Company A or B, simply despaired of trying to extract a sensible resolution from Nicky Byrne. Quite often such companies, knowing that the Beatles were at the centre of it all, totally ignored Byrne and went directly to Epstein or NEMS.

The unacceptable result was that the NEMS offices at Sutherland House began to attract letters and phone calls and even an occasional visit from irate people, upset by the mismanagement of the Seltaeb contracts and licenses. This unexpected development drove Epstein to near despair. He and the Beatles had been shafted, legally admittedly but still very painfully, by Seltaeb and yet were now being harangued by people who felt they had been wronged by the way the licenses had been allocated.

And while there was no violence, and at that stage not even a threat of it, there was still an unpleasant undertone to the situation that made people around Epstein, people like Ellis and Jacobs and Alistair Taylor worry. Some of the characters around Epstein had always been dubious. Now there was a new source of concern for those trying to protect him and his best interests.

Epstein had flown to America in the last week of November to try to accelerate the career of Tommy Quickly via his new single 'The Wild Side of Life'. The party included Derek Taylor, who was rapidly approaching the end of his period working for and with Brian.

As ever the frenetic Epstein packed a series of meetings into the several days in America, on both coasts. He had a number of meetings in Los Angeles with people relating to the next American tour, which was already being discussed back at NEMS on a protected timeline of late summer 1965.

Before leaving Los Angeles, Brian took part in a couple of business meetings with Lew Grade relating to potential television projects both Beatle-related and non-Beatle, but, as ever, many of these projects never saw the light of day.

He also took the opportunity to pursue his more private pursuits, having been given contact details for someone in the Los Feliz district of Los Angeles, and he spent two consecutive nights at a house not far from the famous garage where Walt Disney did the first ever sketches of Mickey Mouse. The nights spent by Epstein in the house on Hyperion Avenue were passionate and brutal, and led him to beat a hasty retreat over to the east coast, although he retained a sweet memory of a good-looking actor named John he had met at a party on Hyperion before the fun began.

Back in New York, he was able to identify his bruises and the cut on his face as the result of a mugging in central L.A. and most people bought the patently false story. Those who knew more about his dangerous lifestyle nodded sympathetically and wondered if there was not some way that this gifted man could find happiness without risking so much in the process.

The object of the trip to New York, which lasted into the early days of December, was to arrange various details for 1965 appearances in the States by acts from the NEMS stable. More importantly, he was meeting Walter Hofer and Sid Bernstein about Seltaeb. The meetings were separate. Although the Americans obviously knew each other very well, Epstein was eager to speak to each man and use their expertise on different aspects of the Seltaeb dilemma.

So Bernstein was used to get information about Nicky Byrne and his lifestyle and the spending of the Seltaeb money. Hofer was brought into detailed discussions on how and when NEMS could take out the lawsuit against Seltaeb and on what grounds. The complaints already reaching NEMS in London seemed to indicate significant and substantial grounds but Epstein needed to examine the situation with someone like Hofer who understood the American legal system far more than he did. Significantly, he went into the discussions with Walter Hofer without David Jacobs by his side, a situation which would have seemed unthinkable just a few months earlier.

Walter Hofer had already played a part in the Beatles story. He had been introduced to Brian Epstein by Dick James, back in the days when Epstein could bear to be in the same room as James. Coincidentally Hofer had been the attorney that Capitol engaged in December 1963 to write to the radio stations on the east coast that were having the gall to play the new Beatles single ahead of release. Hofer, on behalf of Capitol, issued the Desist notice to people like Carroll James. It didn't work, but that was not Hofer's fault and his involvement, plus the earlier introduction from Dick James, made Epstein think of Hofer when looking for a commercial attorney in New York.

Again, in earlier days it would have been entirely natural for Epstein to ask Jacobs to source a qualified American attorney, but the question simply didn't arise, and Jacobs only found out about the launch of proceedings in America after the decision had been taken.

An early report providing information about Seltaeb was handed to Epstein when he arrived in New York, but it didn't make comfortable reading.

Besides the unhealthy number of potential license conflict claims, there were details provided which indicated that the interim accounts provided by Stramsact/Seltaeb to NEMS were perhaps economical with the truth. The document listed a number of companies that appeared to be on the verge of launching proceedings against Seltaeb.

It was grim, deeply disturbing reading.

It settled the topic in Brian's mind and so his instruction to Walter Hofer at the end of their meeting was simple and, for Epstein, surprisingly blunt.

"Sue the bastards!"

The launch of the proceedings by Lord Eliot against Nicky Byrne at least released one of the bastards from the proceedings. The report which had been prepared for Epstein detailed the fact that, beside Eliot's clear and justified complaints against Nicky Byrne, there was also the wider consideration that as a participant in legal proceedings there was a possibility that, should Lord Eliot lose, then the family estates in Cornwall could conceivably have been at risk.

On any reckoning, this was an absolutely minute risk but, as a member of such a weighty family and heir to the title, it was demonstrably a possibility that Lord Eliot could not countenance.

It later transpired that the advice given to Lord Eliot was that by opening proceedings against Nicky Byrne before the inevitable suit from NEMS then Lord Eliot could justifiably argue in the NEMS suit that he should be excepted because of the prior suit.

It was unrealistic to launch proceedings against Seltaeb without launching equivalent proceedings against Stramsact, and so two separate but connected lawsuits were approved by Epstein.

Because he was three thousand miles away he was isolated from a surprise story that arose while he was in New York. A report in the British press detailed the news that Brian Epstein had been approached about selling his management of the Beatles: not NEMS, just the Beatles, but that he had rejected the possibility of interest in any such offer at any price.

It was a typical newspaper puff-piece. Unaccredited, with just a vague mention of "according to a source" which, for most readers is another way of saying "made up nonsense".

However, there was some substance to the story and that might have accounted for the vehemence and speed with which the denials were released. The problem with the story was that it was nine months out of date. Brian Epstein had received a serious offer to fund future activities for the Beatles via an injection of $2million with a transfer to RCA records. A number of other possibilities were mentioned to Epstein but these never made it as far as a contract, and Epstein in his usual polite manner gently rejected the takeover.

However, the man making the offer, a hard-talking accountant from New York, promised Epstein that he would be back.

It would not be an exaggeration to state that Epstein hoped it would not happen. He was no snob but there were some people, crude, overbearing, foul-mouthed with whom he was forced to associate for business reasons, but fortunately the success of the Beatles insulated Epstein from the need to be involved with such people. Having rejected the offer in March 1964, and having no wish or intention of selling his contract for the Beatles, Epstein had every reason to hope and indeed expect that neither he nor the Beatles would ever have to deal with people like Allen Klein.

When he returned to London on December 3rd, he was relatively content that he had taken steps via Walter Hofer to lance the Seltaeb wound. This brief release gave him a few days to indulge in slightly lighter activities and so he was able to visit Ringo Starr in hospital at University College Hospital, London. This was Starr's return visit to have his tonsils removed after the treatment in July which, because of the demands of the Beatles tour of Australia, could not go as far as the full operation.

That had been arranged for December and so Starr went into to University College Hospital on December 2nd and was released fourteen days later. Fortunately, on this occasion, there was no need for Jimmy Nicol to be involved in any way.

Epstein was also able to attend the premiere of the first Gerry and the Pacemakers film, "Ferry Cross The Mersey", which was held at the New Victoria Cinema in London, with, it must be admitted, rather less glamour and flourish than met the premiere of "A Hard Day's Night" four months earlier.

The success of the Beatles continued unabated and before the middle of December there came news that 'I Feel Fine' had sold in excess of one million copies and provided the group with yet another gold record.

The continuing success of the Beatles records, and especially the priceless Lennon and McCartney songs, had created another subject for discussion at the top of NEMS. Now that Epstein had Geoffrey Ellis on hand to bounce ideas off they moved to an intensive investigation of how to save the Beatles some of the fortunes they were losing.

This didn't mean Seltaeb. That word was forbidden and unspoken in front of any one of the individual Beatles for quite some time. As 1964 ended, Epstein was still fondly, but foolishly, hoping that he could manage the Seltaeb disaster and claw back significant monies for the Beatles.

The discussions which started in late 1964 concerned that most tedious of topics, tax, and plans were laid to start a full project aimed at improving the Beatles financial position in 1965, probably using the new film as a vehicle. But prior to that there was a short period of almost pure enjoyment for Epstein. The last two weeks of the year were possibly the best weeks of his life. At the summit of professional achievement, with a year of incredible achievements behind him and the glittering promise of further triumphs to come. He had even made a deal with Bud Ornstein, the head of production in Britain for United Artists, who had given the green light for the three-film contract for the Beatles. He was also the man who had authorised Walter Shenson to increase the Beatles share of the film proceeds from 7.5% to 20%, as he pointed out to Epstein on more than one occasion.

Having overseen the glorious success of the first Beatles film, Epstein and Ornstein saw the opportunity for future success and greater personal returns, and so Ornstein left his job with United Artists and joined Epstein in a new venture, a film production company, to be called Pickfair Films Limited.

The second Beatles Christmas record was dispatched to the huge and still-expanding Fan Club, many of whom had booked for tickets at the Christmas Show which opened on Christmas Eve at the Hammersmith Odeon. Epstein would be there most nights of course, not gloating about his success but visibly enjoying the love being shown to his boys by so, so many people.

That rare happiness was also extended to his private life. In December, he purchased and moved into a new house at 24 Chapel Street in Belgravia. With Belgrave Square close by and Buckingham Palace Gardens just a stone's throw away this was the height of social attainment, and a true indication of just how far he had come.

And he was in love.

Other people described it as just another infatuation but Epstein was adamant that his feelings for Dizz Gillespie were different. He made that obvious to the world by making Gillespie the first actor to be signed to NEMS, and the announcement on December 20th 1964 was accompanied by a series of press photographs of John "Dizz" Gillespie resplendent in a new wardrobe funded and chosen by Epstein.

He claimed to be an actor, a fact slightly borne out by the conversation he had enjoyed with Epstein at the house on Hyperion as they were ripping the clothes off each other. At Epstein's suggestion, and funding, Gillespie followed him to New York where they spent a couple of illicit nights together before Epstein had to return to London.

But that was on the firm promise of an imminent reunion and a career breakthrough for Gillespie. Plane tickets were provided and Gillespie appeared in London in the middle of December, ready for his unveiling as the new artist on the books of NEMS.

To virtually everybody observing the situation, NEMS employees, Epstein's friends, business colleagues it was a nonsense and an embarrassment. It was hard then, and even harder later, to find anybody with a good word for Gillespie.

I met one person in London who claimed to have met him in the sixties and this contact of mine, who has no reason to lie, described Gillespie as an evil, brutal parasite taking advantage of Epstein's gentle nature and generosity to bully him into providing drugs and large amounts of money.

He was clearly a good-looking young man, but they weren't exactly thin on the ground for Brian Epstein. As such it is genuinely hard to understand the attraction, but there is a chance that the timing played a big part in it.

Epstein felt he had been badly let down in the Seltaeb matter by people he trusted, particularly David Jacobs, so when people like Jacobs, and many others, were so virulently critical of Dizz Gillespie there was an almost petulant response from Epstein. He embraced and supported and lauded the American, particularly praising his acting abilities which had led to him being the first actor ever signed to NEMS. Indeed the unfortunate Geoffrey Ellis was put in the invidious position of being required to draw up a NEMS management contract for Gillespie. That contract provided an advance against future earnings, with a weekly payment of £50 being made to him, though he seemingly never showed thanks or appreciation for his extreme good fortune.

He was clearly disliked and in some cases despised by most of the NEMS staff, and those of Brian's associates who met him. The distaste was not because he was homosexual. On the contrary, for all the people concerned liked and or loved Brian Epstein, and the homosexuality of the Beatles manager was an open secret to virtually all those concerned. The dislike of Dizz Gillespie was simply because he was a thoroughly unpleasant character. While it seemed clear to virtually everybody that he was simply using Epstein, it was continually galling to the NEMS circle and to people like David Jacobs that Epstein simply couldn't, or perhaps wouldn't, see through the shallow cruelty of Dizz Gillespie. Perhaps the most strident comments on the character of Gillespie came from Nat Weiss who, with his American background and contacts, knew a bit more about the unsavoury Gillespie than most people in England did.

It was a particularly difficult situation because Gillespie came onto the NEMS books as an actor, the first member of that profession to join NEMS. Claiming that Gillespie was, or even would become, a major actor would have been a difficult stance to maintain even in Liverpool or Manchester. In the heart of London's theatre land, with acting greats on virtually every corner, Epstein's claims for Gillespie were treated with derision.

The relationship was clearly based on nothing more than sex, although Epstein sadly seemed to have convinced himself that there was something more substantial in their relationship. But, given the brutal weeks that followed, it is difficult to see Gillespie as anything more than a violent gigolo who saw Brian Epstein as a soft touch and a valuable mark. Epstein's fabled generosity seemed capable of inflaming Gillespie into savage rages. He hated it on the rare occasions when Epstein refused one of his wilder, more expensive ideas, but he also bitterly resented his position of absolute weakness when Epstein's wallet opened, as it frequently did for Gillespie.

In such situations, in almost every situation, Gillespie's instinctive response was via his fists or his boots or even whatever implement could be grabbed and used as a weapon. Gillespie hung around in London, causing unpleasant scenes at the NEMS offices and often at Chapel Street, and then he regularly disappeared, leaving London with a bag full of Epstein's cash and several possessions from the house.

And possibly, probably Brian Epstein was the only one to feel any sorrow about his departure.

But by then, he was sinking ever deeper in the troughs caused by depression and the pills, disappearing from NEMS for unexplained, erratic periods. Such absences were not a major problem in early 1965 but they would deepen and worsen over the next two years. He was lucky, as was the business, that NEMS was populated by such loyal, dedicated and capable staff. Those people were increasingly called upon to compensate for the deficiencies in Epstein's performance, attendance and, on occasions, his sheer reliability.

Finally, even Epstein had endured enough from the erratic Gillespie. He paid for him to fly back to America, despite being aware of large amounts of money that had been stolen from the elegant new house on Chapel Street. It took some strong words of persuasion from various of Brian's associates to convince Gillespie that leaving the country might be a sensible option, and the fact that the physically imposing Mal Evans was one of the people having the proverbial "quiet word" couldn't have been coincidence.

He left England early in 1965 on a winter day piercingly cold for those who had followed him to Heathrow to be certain that he did catch the plane. The general feeling was one of "Good Riddance" but he vowed that he would see Epstein again in America and, most regrettably, he would prove to be correct.

With the chance of casual violence inherent in Gillespie now departed Epstein had another period where throwing himself into work provided the perfect distraction from his personal miseries. At the start of 1965, he had four major projects for the coming year: resolving the Beatles tax problems, getting the new film concluded, resolving Seltaeb, and arranging another American tour for the summer period.

Of course, there were a myriad of other events and commitments but those four situations were the major matters he felt that he had to deal with, whilst keeping the other situations ticking over via the various people at NEMS, particularly Geoffrey Ellis. Many of those commitments were outlined in a Press Conference at the Dorchester in which Epstein outlined the plans for the Beatles for 1965. These were to include a European tour in July, which, according to Epstein would feature a live television broadcast from Paris, to be viewed across Europe, though not in Britain. He also provided very general details about an American tour in August, which this time was likely to include Mexico but not Canada.

The final major announcement within the Press Conference concerned the new film, which then had the working title "Eight Arms To Hold You". Epstein provided some confusing information on the likely date for work starting on the film, confusing because while he was vague on the likely starting date tickets were already sitting in the NEMS office for the Beatles party to fly out to the Bahamas on February 22nd.

It passed most people's attention but on the same day another music publishing company, Maclen Limited, was formed with just three directors, Lennon, McCartney and Epstein. The significance of Maclen would become clearer as the Northern songs situation progressed, and there were major steps being taken in January 1965.

The first of the tasks before the NEMS group concerned the resolution of the tax situation and in this Brian Epstein was greatly fortunate in that Geoffrey Ellis was now part of the team. At arms length from NEMS, but definitely part of the trusted advisers group, was the accountancy firm of Bryce Hanmer Isherwood. The last named partner was James Trevor Isherwood who had known Brian for several years given that, while working out of the company's Liverpool offices, he had been responsible for some work for Brian's family which led him into contact with Brian and eventually some work for the Beatles.

It was that work which had led Isherwood in 1964 to get involved in the setting up of Maclen, the operation to collect royalties paid to Northern Songs, the publishing company Epstein had set up under the stewardship of Dick James. That initial conversation was just two years earlier but Northern Songs was already massively profitable and Dick James drove round in his chocolate coloured Bentley with the look of a man who buys a winning lottery ticket every day.

Now though, the very success of the Beatles was threatening to cause a major financial problem. At that time the taxation levels in Britain for major earners like the individual Beatles were prohibitive and crippling. The top rate in 1965 was 70% and it would leap to 83% within two years, complemented by an additional 15% surcharge on investments, sometimes termed "unearned income", meaning a potential tax rate of 98% for the super rich, a bracket into which the Beatles were climbing.

Responsible management of their individual affairs meant that Epstein insisted that his staff and advisors continually monitored the circumstances of his charges, particularly the Beatles, to try to lessen the impact of things like tax on them. Because of their unusual situation, such problems often impacted on the Beatles more early, and more grievously, than other acts. The NEMS advisers, particularly James Isherwood, had been mentioning for several months the inevitable arrival during 1965 of something called Capital Gains Tax which would be a device to stop people saving or avoiding Income Tax by diverting their income into capital.

The arrival of Capital Gains Tax sometime in 1965 was inevitable, given the enthusiasm and zeal with which the Labour Chancellor, James Callaghan, had been promoting the egalitarian benefits of the new system.

However the situation developed it was inevitable that the Beatles would be required to make significantly higher payments to the exchequer, and the duty of the NEMS advisers was to find ways to mitigate those extra payments. One way that presented itself very quickly involved Northern Songs, the song-writing company set up to publish the material written by John Lennon and Paul McCartney.

The first meeting to explore the position was defined several times by Epstein as Exploratory; part of his normal job to manage the Beatles and find methods and systems to make their personal and professional lives easier and, wherever possible, better.

Over the months leading up to September 1966 this would be a regular mantra at the meetings where Epstein hosted the Beatles to discuss a particular issue or the overall position. He was constantly at pains to demonstrate to them that he had their best interests at heart, and that work was constantly taking place, even if they didn't see it, to enhance their personal and professional circumstances.

This strange incantation had two purposes. Mainly he was intent on impressing upon the group just how valuable, if not indispensible, he was, particularly in a scenario when his management contract had now passed the halfway point. The renewal date in 1967 had seemed aeons away. Now Epstein had the sense that it was racing towards him like a train in a tunnel. Ahead of that date, he was convinced that he must use every opportunity to reinforce his position and reputation in their minds so that the renewal date would pass without question.

But there were two major problems. The first, inevitably, was Seltaeb, and the fortunes which were bleeding away from the Beatles on a daily basis.

He had done, and was doing all he could to correct the situation but it was inevitable that the members of the group, particularly John, would go into melt-down if and when they learned the true extent of the Seltaeb disaster. He couldn't prevent that. All he could do was try to limit the damage and pray that they never got to hear about it.

The other, related problem also concerned money. Despite the perception among the public that the four Beatles were incredibly rich, the facts were rather different. They were still on the derisory royalty rate afforded to them on their first EMI contract, and they were still paying 25% of every pound earned to NEMS, the arrangement which had so surprised James Isherwood a year earlier during the Maclen discussions. For both reasons Brian Epstein feared the future, feared the realisation among the Beatles that, though they had done very well financially from their career, the real winner was their manager.

The initial proposal in that initial meeting related only to the main songwriters, John Lennon and Paul McCartney. By this point, everybody in the room understood the value of copyright, and the fact that the copyright in the songs written by Lennon and McCartney constituted a very valuable asset.

Paul McCartney had attended a luncheon at the Café Royal on January 4th which was held to honour Dick James and his role in the music industry. Epstein didn't attend, partly because of his growing friction with Dick James, but mainly because he was so emotionally distraught about the Gillespie affair.

McCartney was there, representing the songwriting partnership, and it was during the convivial event that Dick James made the astonishing revelation that Lennon and McCartney had earned in excess of £1million just as songwriters in 1964 alone!

Of course, as with every number relating to music publishing, it isn't as simple as the statement that they received more than £1million. There was a long line of people, starting with Dick James himself, who would take a slice of that income, meaning that they would be left with substantially less than the mystical £1million.

But, to be fair to Dick James, the point he was making was that John Lennon and Paul McCartney were doing very well. And they were.

However, the NEMS advisers were concerned to ensure that the pair were not penalised by future tax legislation and so the suggestion from James Isherwood was that they should take advantage of the very narrow window still open before the introduction of Capital Gains Tax to realise some of the existing value in Northern Songs in a tangible form.

Isherwood, following consultation with lawyers and tax experts, proposed that the existing structure of Northern Songs, which had remained undisturbed since the creation of the company, should be changed by means of 25% of the shares in the company being sold to the public with the company thereafter being quoted on the London Stock Exchange. The suggested date was February 1965, and the topic was then open for discussion, though neither Lennon nor McCartney were sufficiently informed to play a significant role in the increasingly complex discussions. It didn't matter - they trusted Epstein.

In the existing structure, DJM (Dick James Music) held 50%, with half of that owned by Dick James himself and the other half held by his colleague and accountant friend, Charles Silver. Of the 50% of Northern Songs remaining John Lennon took 20%, Paul McCartney a further 20% with the remaining 10% held by NEMS Enterprises.

There was a standing arrangement whereby NEMS did not take its normal management commission from the songwriting earnings. The justification was that the percentage of 10% held in the company made up for the deficiency.

Under the terms of their agreement with Northern Songs, Lennon and McCartney agreed to an exclusive songwriting contract with the company under which all future compositions from the date of the agreement would be automatically assigned to Northern Songs. In return, the company would pay the two songwriters royalties after the deduction of a 10% commission by DJM from the gross income of Northern Songs.

This deduction was justified, and justifiable, on the basis that it was neither proposed nor envisaged that Northern Songs would be required to carry any normal overheads like office space or staff or office services, all of which would come from DJM. And all the critical financial management for Northern Songs - royalty payments, accountancy, and exploitation of assets - would also be performed by DJM, freeing up Lennon and McCartney to do what they did best - write songs.

At the inception of the company, there were four directors, Dick James who was Managing Director, Charles Silver who was Chairman, plus James Isherwood and Brian Epstein.

Crucially for future developments neither Lennon nor McCartney were suggested as, or asked to be, directors, the belief in 1963 being that their collective interests would be adequately and properly represented by Epstein and Isherwood.

Despite the comforting smug glow that hindsight provides, it is indisputable that neither of the two Beatles would have been interested in being directors even had it been offered. Equally it was inconceivable to any of the parties involved in setting up Northern Songs that the day could dawn when John Lennon and Paul McCartney would not want to act in tandem.

Under the terms of the Isherwood proposal the sale of 25% of Northern Songs would mean that each of the four original shareholders - Lennon, McCartney, NEMS and DJM - would sell a quarter of their original shareholdings. The price received from that sale would then be distributed to those original shareholders in the company.

Isherwood estimated that if the sale were to prove successful then both Lennon and McCartney could expect to receive just under £100,000 each. This would be a net amount, completely free of tax, because the process would take place before Capital Gains Tax appeared in the spring. This was more money than any of the Beatles had received in a lump sum up to that point, and would be worth just over one and a half million pounds in modern currency!

One small problem was that company flotation was normally subject to a five-year trading limit, but Northern Songs had only been in existence for just two years. In normal circumstances that would have ruled out any prospect of a flotation for Northern Songs for at least three years but, as ever, normal rules didn't seem to apply to the Beatles. Discreet enquiries had been made by various people including David Jacobs, and it was made plain that an application properly and formally presented would receive approval.

Two factors came into play. The first was the undeniable attraction at that time of any involvement, however vicarious, with a Beatle, and of course all four was far, far better. And the other point which was possibly more important to the Stock Exchange was that, by any of the standards of the time, Northern Songs was a very unusual and very successful company; hardly any overheads or Costs of Sale, extremely profitable, and with no apparent impediments to future success.

Given the complexity of the scenario and the fact that large sums of money were in play, the accountants and lawyers gathered to rip the flesh from the bones. Because the flotation involved legal skills outside the normal competence of David Jacobs, the legal work was not assigned by Epstein to Jacobs. Instead it went to a prestigious firm named Goodman Derrick and Co., who were based in Bouverie Street just off Fleet Street.

The grunt work was performed by one of the firm's younger partners, Alan Leighton Davies, but occasionally meetings would be taken over by the senior partner, Arnold Goodman, who would go on to achieve fame and notoriety in later years as Lord Goodman.

This absurdly Dickensian character had achieved fame standing at the right hand of Prime Minister, Harold Wilson, and in later years was accused of misappropriating large sums of money from a client's account.

Strangely, he didn't use that money for his own personal benefit. He seems to have spent most of the alleged £1 million to fund various Labour Party activities including campaigns on behalf of Harold Wilson, though Wilson clearly knew nothing about the origins of the funds.

The client from whom the money systematically disappeared was the Portman family who owned a large batch of real estate in central London. Arnold Goodman was sole trustee of the family trust, and, because of the claim that Goodman misused the family's money, Lord Portman issued a writ in 1993 demanding a full accounting of how Goodman had managed his family's money since the 1950s. The Portman family had regularly questioned Goodman about the handling of their funds, but like so many of his political friends, he proved effortlessly skilled at answering anything but the question that had been asked.

The most relevant reorganisation of the family estate had taken place late in 1954 when Lord Portman was just twenty years of age. He took advice from his father and the imposing Goodman, and just signed everything handed to him. Such trust must have made Goodman feel very comfortable when he heard about the complete trust the Beatles showed when signing, without question or even reading, everything that Epstein gave to them.

Goodman was a perfect man for Epstein to have on side and indeed, with his social and political connections, and his Jewish origins, Goodman was clearly somebody whose friendship Epstein was anxious to cultivate. Goodman was devoted to opera, a taste in which Epstein shared. He also greatly enjoyed dining in grand settings and maintained a corner table at the Savoy Grill, where he displayed a schoolboy's love of its English school-dinner menu and huge jugs of lemonade.

On every level, he was an exceptional man and an extremely able lawyer and perhaps, in the social circumstances of Britain in the mid-sixties, the ideal man for Brian Epstein to have on his side.

The process leading to the eventual flotation required constant meetings, which alternated between Argyll Street and Bouverie Street. As always in these situations, they became infested with people with skin in the game, and an interest to defend. A constant absence from the meetings was Brian Epstein. He had no real interest in the subject under discussion and, more importantly, his physical and mental state at the time wasn't wonderful. The scars, visible and emotional, from the brief, explosive affair with Dizz Gillespie would take some time to heal, and there are people who think that they never really did.

Epstein had delegated Geoffrey Ellis to stand in for him at the meetings, another demonstration of his foresight in asking Ellis to join NEMS.

Alongside Ellis at the interminable meetings were usually Dick James and Charles Silver from DJM, James Isherwood and a gentleman called Ivor Lewisohn who was there representing the stockbrokers who would actually conduct the sale of the shares.

Given that there was significant money involved, the statutory requirement is that every document must be subjected to the utmost scrutiny. This necessitated every detail in major documents like the Offer For Sale being checked and double-checked, with every number subjected to examination and every word considered for accuracy and nuance.

Unfortunately for Brian Epstein, such meetings contained far too much accountancy and far too little creativity, and he very sensibly gave Geoffrey Ellis his head. One extra benefit of that arrangement was that it minimised the occasions when Epstein had to be involved and interact with Dick James. Although he always would respect the part that James played in getting the Beatles their start, Epstein had grown to slightly dislike the way James always tried to bombast his way into discussions, and particularly the way he cavalierly assumed credit for the widespread success the Beatles had achieved.

Perhaps because he hadn't known him for long, or perhaps because the demands he made of people weren't so extreme, Ellis wasn't as riled by Dick James as Brian Epstein visibly was. For that reason alone, it made for a more harmonious business meeting when Epstein was absent from the discussions about the flotation. But it was entirely proper that Dick James, as one of the largest shareholders should wish to be present. He tended to alternate with Charles Silver until the latter stages of the process but if he thought there was anything odd or sinister about Epstein's continued absence Dick James made no comment.

Although Ellis was still comparatively ignorant about the NEMS methods, he clearly acquitted himself well and dragged the process through to its conclusion. Given the imminence of the legislation on Capital Gains Tax, all parties realised the urgency of the situation and a number of late night sessions were required to get the issue document complete to everybody's satisfaction. That stage was reached at the end of January 1965, an incredibly speedy turnaround for a flotation, even one with the particularly favourable circumstances surrounding Northern Songs.

There remained just the difficult formalities of signing the copious documents to formalise the process. Neither Lennon nor McCartney had played any role in process through January but now, at the final stage, their participation was both necessary and indeed essential. It might seem strange that they had not been involved, even as observers, in any of the meetings which were likely to deliver the equivalent of more than a million pounds to each of them, but this is testament to the total, unwavering trust that they invested in Brian Epstein.

The trust that he was determined would not be ripped away by revelations about Seltaeb.

The basic requirement was for John Lennon and Paul McCartney to sign a bunch of the prepared papers, which also included a new exclusive songwriting contract with Northern Songs. This document was key, and absolutely vital, to the flotation. The only asset for the company was the songs written by Lennon and McCartney and though the material written over the previous two years was a treasure trove and had made several people, including Dick James, very rich, those songs were an asset which had already been realised.

The flotation of the company, if successful, would be based on the continued value of songs like 'Please Please Me' and 'She Loves You' but far, far more attractive and important was the future riches that Lennon and McCartney might deliver.

For that reason their signatures on that new, exclusive contract were crucial. The new contract was scheduled to commence on the actual day of the stock market flotation, nominated as February 5th. As an extra fillip the terms for Lennon and McCartney had been improved. They were afforded an increased percentage of royalties, rising up to 55%, for all songs delivered after the flotation.

To finalise the weary process the last meeting was set up at Bouverie Street. Epstein made a rare appearance, accompanied, somewhat grudgingly by both Lennon and McCartney. The august figure of Arnold Goodman took charge, buoyed up no doubt by the very considerable fees his firm would be obtaining from the work.

It was essential for both Lennon and McCartney to be present to sign the many papers which included their legal agreement to sell a proportion of their existing shareholding.

One of Goodman's juniors took charge of the boring part of the proceedings, guiding various participants around the separate sheaves of legal papers spread around the beautiful oak table in the boardroom at Goodman Derrick. There was a peculiar system in play which clearly made perfect sense to the junior but was bewildering to everyone else present except the lawyers. The whole thing was greatly amusing to John Lennon.

Virtually all the papers were encased in one or more coloured elastic bands, and the colours were there to designate and identify who had to sign which specific papers.

Thus the black bands around documents showed that all parties had to sign. A green band meant that the document in question only required the signature of John Lennon and Paul McCartney, while a red band meant that the signatures of the two Beatles were required along with that of Brian Epstein.

It was a strange, but gently amusing situation, especially as it came at the end of such an intense period of discussion and negotiation. It was all going well until that same junior noticed a tiny error in one of the documents. It was trivial, perhaps unimportant, but it was a legal document and possibly millions of pounds might be at stake in the future, so nobody was willing to take any chance.

Yet again, technology, or the lack of it, played a key role. This meeting was obviously before the advent of computers and word processing and instant printing. Given that a hand-written correction to the document was legally impossible, a fresh copy of the twelve-page document had to be typed. A star typist in the pool at Goodman Derrick was summoned and set to work but the work, and the necessary checking was likely to take around thirty minutes.

With classic and characteristic impatience, both John Lennon and Paul McCartney claimed prior appointments and an urgent need to leave. In truth, they simply didn't want to be there, despite the minor inducement of a million pounds for signing the documents. Epstein tried to persuade them to stay, but failed, and even the considerable arguing skills of Arnold Goodman met a brick wall.

The two Beatles departed and caused a good deal of anger and embarrassment in the room.

The provision of the signatures of the other relevant parties, primarily James and Silver, took place and was completed when the replacement document appeared and had been checked.

But the signatures of both Lennon and McCartney simply had to appear on the documents. Given the imminence of the flotation there was no time to be wasted and so the only alternative, given that the two Beatles wouldn't or couldn't return to Bouverie Street, was to send the documents to them in the hands of someone competent to observe that the process was conducted properly and then provide a signature as witness.

One of the Goodman Derrick people went out to John Lennon's house to conclude his part in the proceedings, and that was accomplished without misadventure. However, securing McCartney's signature was more awkward.

Within hours of the Bouverie Street meeting he had left the country on a previously arranged, but unpublicised, holiday with his girlfriend, Jane Asher. Maintaining the essential level of secrecy to ensure that McCartney's secret destination wasn't revealed to press or public, Brian Clarke from the Goodman Derrick office took the next flight after McCartney and Asher, and followed them to their secret location in Tunisia.

There he took McCartney through the document, showed him where he was required to sign, and then witnessed in all the appropriate places. One quick drink, and a taxi back to the airport and the return flight brought him back to London with the all-important signed papers. And with that, the final piece in the puzzle, the flotation could go ahead. In the process, 1,170,000 of Northern Songs' five million shares were made available to the public, and, in an echo of the flotation of football clubs many years later, it wasn't just the institutions that were purchasing shares.

The flotation was an immediate financial success and many small investors, better recognised as fans, purchased shares, not with a view to any financial killing but just for a chance of owning a part, however small, of the Beatles. There were a particularly heavy number of smaller applications from America, proof that despite the trouble and violence which bedevilled the summer tour in 1964, the love for the Beatles ran deep in the American psyche.

After the flotation, the majority of Northern Songs' shares were still held by the Beatles or Brian Epstein. Both John Lennon and Paul McCartney held onto 750,000 each, while NEMS Enterprises held 375,000. In addition, George Harrison and Ringo Starr both had a shareholding of 40,000. Finally, Dick James and his friend and business partner Charles Silver both kept hold of 937,500 shares.

Each Individual share in Northern Songs started with an initial price of 7s/9d (now approximately 39p). There was a requirement on investors that they subscribe to purchase a minimum of two hundred shares at a collective value of £39. This price took the package and the offer beyond the pockets of most fans, although a number in America still participated.

On the opening of trading on February 18th the price dropped sharply by more than 25% to under six shillings, but within a couple of days the shares had recovered and were trading at double the opening amount before the end of the month.

When the flotation took place, Northern Songs held a valuation of £2.7 million. The company's previous owners had each disposed of one quarter of their original holdings, which produced for John Lennon and Paul McCartney a tax-free bonus of £94,270 each.

But despite this significant financial triumph, nobody bothered to explain to the two Beatles that allowing a level of public ownership in their company effectively left the door open to predators with the company now potentially vulnerable to future takeover attempts.

Nobody explained it but, as demonstrated by their arrogant refusal to wait to sign the essential documents, there is no guarantee that they would have listened anyway.

And all the mayhem and heartache to come years later started arguably because nobody thought to explain one of the inevitable possibilities inherent in a flotation process. Nobody told Lennon and McCartney. They never thought to ask. It was a constant theme throughout Epstein's management of the Beatles, and that way lay madness and a great deal of grief.

When the Northern Songs flotation took place in 1965, Michael Joseph Jackson was just six years old, although he would start performing that year in the Jackson Brothers, the precursor to the Jackson 5, which would not appear in the form we remember them until 1966.

But as a small boy it was unimaginable that a document being signed thousands of miles away in London would eventually put him on a collision course with......

With who?

But inside NEMS and Bryce Hamner the flotation was a cause for celebration. The manoeuvre had made both John Lennon and Paul McCartney very rich men, and there was clearly much more to come.

And over at the offices of DJM the joy was virtually unconfined. By the fact of simply meeting Brian Epstein that day and, of course, being reasonably successful in his job, Dick James was suddenly even richer than either Lennon or McCartney, thanks to his slightly larger ownership of Northern Songs shares.

It was hard to begrudge the jovial James his good fortune but, not for the last time in the Northern Songs saga, the casual observer was left wondering why and how the people actually producing the creativity which delivered the songs could end up as less than total winners.

And as one slightly ironic postscript to the whole Northern Songs flotation drama, there came an announcement in early February that Dick James had taken out an insurance policy, on a key man insurance basis, which provided £500,000 worth of life insurance cover on his two most lucrative clients, John Lennon and Paul McCartney.

But at NEMS there wasn't time for indulging in the euphoria produced by the flotation. The immediate concern was meetings which had been arranged with EMI which would, Epstein hoped and believed, deliver a much better royalty rate for the group, and a rate more commensurate with their reputation and status as quite simply the most important group in the history of pop music.

At the same time, Epstein was busy planning the year's activities for the group. He could take out substantial blocks of time for major projects - the new film which was provisionally entitled "Eight Arms To Hold You", touring appearances in Britain and Europe and, most importantly, the second tour of America. In relation to America he was in regular contact with his trusted contacts in the States, Sid Bernstein, Nat Weiss, and Walter Hofer, and it was a call from Bernstein on January 10th that produced the most surprising and audacious suggestion for the next American tour.

Bernstein had been promised that any future Beatles appearances in New York would be promoted by him, and since the meeting with Epstein prior to the Carnegie Hall show in February, Bernstein had been thinking and planning for that next New York appearance. Epstein had smilingly turned down Bernstein's proposal for a hastily-arranged Madison Square Garden show, but Bernstein had neither forgotten the conversation nor reduced the scale of his ambition or planning.

Consequently, when he rang Epstein in January it was with a proposal that took even Epstein's breath away. Bernstein wanted to stage the Beatles during the tour of America in August at Shea Stadium.

Epstein had heard the name but knew little of the stadium or what it represented. In those days there was very little media coverage in Britain of American sport, and so even the New York Mets were unknown to Epstein.

He began to pay serious attention when he started to quiz Bernstein on details, and particularly when he was told that Shea Stadium, more properly titled The William A Shea Municipal Stadium, held some 55,000 people!

The number took Epstein's breath away. Developments in the seventies and since have made the world used to the spectacle of huge outdoor concerts in front of tens of thousands. In 1965 it simply didn't happen, and so it was a revolutionary and slightly scary prospect.

Epstein didn't turn Bernstein down. If nothing else, he was always open to the prospect of his Beatles breaking records and becoming the first act ever to achieve something. But even by the astonishing standards of the Beatles, a concert outdoors in front of more than 50,000 people would indeed be epoch-making. Epstein asked Bernstein to put together a firm proposal with details relating to the venue, and they pencilled in a date of Sunday August 15th.

Epstein knew that he didn't need to chase Bernstein about the project. It could safely be left in his capable hands, and so Epstein was able to concentrate on the offers for dates in other American and Canadian cities.

At that time, quite understandably, he and NEMS were fielding proposals from virtually every major city in the States. However, despite the clamour and the incredible offers that were arriving almost daily, Epstein had, after discussion with the Beatles, decided to severely curtail the number of concerts and the number of cities visited in America.

The experience of the 1964 tour was thrilling, and would never be forgotten by any of those who experienced it, but with the thrills came horrors and they would never be forgotten either.

So he was routinely dismissing offers which totalled millions of dollars confident that he would be arranging a tour that would be shorter, safer and more enjoyable for all concerned. But, ever the showman, he had thought over the possibilities offered by Bernstein's suggestion of Shea Stadium, and he had discussed it with Geoffrey Ellis who knew the location far better than him.

The result was that he told Bernstein to go ahead and create the booking, and with that call, the era of Stadium Rock was born.

Press releases were coming increasingly under the control of Tony Barrow although by that point he didn't need to search for coverage. There was so much activity around the Beatles camp that media always knew there would be solid, juicy stories coming out of NEMS, and editors knew very well that a cover photograph of a Beatle, or two, three or four, would definitely increase sales of that newspaper or magazine.

The release came through to the press on February 12th that for that third film, this before the second one had even started pre-production work, the Beatles would star in a film adaptation of the Richard Condon novel, "A Talent For Loving". This western novel was based on a genuine story and concerned a gruelling 1,500-mile horse race that took place between the Rio Grande and Mexico City in 1871.

The story hung on which of the participants in the race would win the love of the glamorous and wealthy girl.

The story at the time was that Richard Condon was already hard at work adapting the script from his own novel. Even more intriguingly the press release, picked up to great effect in the music press by papers like Melody Maker and New Musical Express, gave some ideas about how the Beatles would appear in the film, specifically as a group of brave, pioneering Liverpudlians who had travelled west.

Inevitably, the release gave full vein to cartoonists and artists to show one or more Beatles, although it was almost always Ringo, dressed as a cowboy!

The film sat on the back burner for many months and then, without fanfare, was quietly dropped from Beatles consideration. It appeared in cinemas in 1969 as "A Talent For Loving" starring Richard Widmark, Caesar Romero, Genevieve Page and Topol.

One of the interesting political points in the press release was that it stressed that "A Talent For Loving" would be the initial film to be made by the Beatles exclusively for Pickfair Films, this being the new company set up in December 1964 by Epstein with former United Artists executive Bud Ornstein. The press release also divulged that the Pickfair management group had been expanded to include James Isherwood.

Isherwood was also to play a part in the next strand of Epstein's quest to improve the financial status of the Beatles, and thereby reduce or hopefully hide the effects of Seltaeb. Epstein organised a meeting at Manchester Square with the senior people at EMI. He explained to Ellis, who went with him to the meeting, that the purpose of the meeting was part PR but mainly the opening gambit in his move to improve the Beatles recording contract.

Despite everything that had happened since 'Love Me Do' the Beatles were still on the original contract offered to them by George Martin in 1962, and that had offered the lowest possible royalty rate to an EMI artist. Quite reasonably, Epstein believed that the group had now earned a bigger slice of the cake. In this respect he had asked James Isherwood to obtain and furnish him with relevant information which Epstein had digested and learned but had in his briefcase on beautiful vellum sheets typed by Wendy Hanson.

That information divulged that EMI profits in 1964 were expected to be up 80% on the comparable figures for 1963, and that year's figures had shown an almost unbelievable increase in profits by 220%!

And the vast majority of this torrent of extra income was being generated by the Beatles. On a matter of simple justice, it might have been expected that a major increase for the Beatles, and perhaps also for producer George Martin, would have been recommended and provided by EMI without being asked. A tiny increase had been forced through by George Martin in 1963 but that was absolutely minute when put alongside the gargantuan profits being made by EMI.

So EMI had not bothered offering the group more money, though they were happy to award prizes and trinkets such as those provided at Manchester Square on February 16th by Sir Joseph Lockwood who took great pleasure in handing to the various Beatles assorted silver and gold discs and a collection of Japanese dolls. This extreme generosity was extended three days later when Lockwood hosted a lavish function at the Connaught Hotel in Mayfair where the major figures of EMI and Capitol and the recording industry gathered to pay justified tribute to the Beatles and their incredible accomplishments over the previous year.

The group and Epstein took the accolades with good grace, but the glitz of the occasion didn't blind Epstein to his main objective, to wrest more money from EMI. And he knew that the Beatles achievements in 1963 and 1964 had given him, acting as their manager, almost total control over the situation. Of course, Epstein approached the situation with EMI with his customary courtesy and charm. Not for him the foul-mouthed, bullying tactics which had recently been used to very immediate effect in New York by Allen Klein who had browbeaten RCA into a whole series of unwanted concessions to their artist, Sam Cooke.

The same Sam Cooke that Allen Klein had tried to use as a ploy to get hold of the management of the Beatles a year earlier. Epstein had laughed his clumsy approach away on that occasion, and he would have been horrified if anybody in EMI were to regard Brian Epstein's name with the same repugnance as so many record executives were starting to regard Klein.

Although like Klein the realisation had come to Epstein that in the delicate matter of negotiations with record companies there was simply no question. The power, all the power, lay with the artist - as long as that artist was successful.

And there was no artist that was as successful, by every measurable standard, as the Beatles. There was no hint of triumphalism in Epstein's nature, but he would not have been human if he hadn't remembered all those trips to London desperately hoping that a record company - any record company - would listen to the Beatles and hear what he could hear.

The group that were going to be Bigger than Elvis! The Biggest Act on the planet, and now it had all come true, and he was being driven to Manchester Square with Geoffrey Ellis ready to get for the Beatles their just reward.

Even the short journey was a type of vindication. Arriving outside the EMI offices in Manchester in his luxurious Bentley was a quiet way of saying, "See? Look what I told you!" to all those inside who had doubted the Beatles. This was especially the case when he could climb out of the Bentley and look up respectfully at the stairwell which had formed the backdrop to the picture of his boys which had adorned the cover of their first album, "Please Please Me".

He didn't expect EMI to capitulate immediately and offer a massive increase in royalties and improved conditions. It was going to be a process conducted over a series of meetings, and that was one reason that he had been insistent that Geoffrey Ellis accompanied him. Epstein had no intention of being present for every meeting with EMI about a revised contract. He had no interest in the detail and had concluded, correctly, that Ellis would be far better equipped to deal with the grunt work and get the negotiations to the point where a deal was ready to be signed. At that point Epstein could re-appear, do the PR bit, and sign the agreement.

Essentially this was the function Arnold Goodman had fulfilled in the Northern Song Flotation negotiations and Epstein had been impressed by the way Goodman conducted things.

That first meeting started off badly, because Epstein had been blindsided by the number of people EMI brought into the meeting.

Beside Sir Joseph Lockwood who was chairing the meeting there were six other EMI personnel: Len Wood and Ron White representing the record company, senior people from accountancy and legal departments. Also present was Sir Joseph's personal assistant, William Cavendish.

This presented an imposing display on the other side of the boardroom table from Epstein and Ellis, and Brian Epstein, quietly annoyed, determined that it wouldn't happen again.

And so, for the next meeting a few weeks later Epstein insisted on returning with Geoffrey Ellis, but this time they were accompanied by James Isherwood, representing NEMS accountancy interests, and David Jacobs who was there to counterbalance the EMI legal presence. The numbers still weren't equal but there were four shadows on the NEMS side of the table, the Beatles, and their invisible presence tilted everything in favour of NEMS.

Epstein took great pains and pleasure in re-defining the injurious financial terms under which the Beatles were working. They were receiving one old penny per single sold. The NEMS management contract took 25% off the top leaving the remainder to be split equally four ways. The result was that, for example, in the case of 'She Loves You', then well on the way to being the best-selling single in British history, each of the Beatles received the magnificent sum of 18.75% of a penny! Of course, there were caveats - their small holding in NEMS, songwriting royalties and so on - but by any standard it was a pitiful return.

Fortunately, the people sitting on both sides of the table knew that and agreed that an improvement had to be hastily found.

The fact that the planned improvement took several months to be agreed and implemented should not detract from the way the various parties applied themselves in the resulting negotiations. But for NEMS those discussions were far more in the hands of Geoffrey Ellis or James Isherwood. Brian Epstein was willing, desperately interested, but all too often absent.

It wasn't always debauchery or pills that kept him away from NEMS. The large blocks of time devoted to major Beatles projects, often out of the country, meant that Brian Epstein would be with the group overseeing things, ensuring that nothing could be allowed to disturb the equilibrium of his Beatles. Increasingly though he wasn't needed to stay with the group for the entire periods. The growth in assurance and reliability of trusted sidemen like Neil Aspinall and Mal Evans, plus the newer people like Tony Barrow, meant that he felt confident in their ability to handle any situation that might affect the Beatles.

It was understood now that even in high-pressure situations like the American tours he would not be present and on hand every minute of every day. He had resorted to topping and tailing such projects and dropping in for major events like Hollywood Bowl.

And the other inescapable fact was that the Beatles themselves were growing out of and away from a need to be constantly managed by Epstein. They had endured it during the very early days when he was knocking off the rough edges and taking them up the ladder of stardom a rung at a time. Now though, by the time of their second film, there was a definite change in attitude. Rather like teenagers growing resentful of their parents' constant attention, and wishing to fly the nest, the Beatles were increasingly eager, and able, to demonstrate their independence from Epstein.

Whether it was petulant displays like Lennon and McCartney walking out of the Flotation signing meeting, or the individual Beatles registering disapproval of Epstein's even commenting on new recordings, there were walls being erected between Beatles and manager, walls which hadn't existed before 1965.

In a way, projects like the filming of the second film fitted that profile. Once contracts had been signed Epstein had very little part to play in the mechanics of the film until the day some months hence when he would need to don his expensive tuxedo and go to the World Premiere.

Because of the timing of that second film there was no possibility of Epstein being able to launch his new film production company, Pickfair, with a Beatles film. Although United Artists had been dismissive about the prospects for any Beatles film when Epstein signed the agreement with Walter Shenson the American company had their minds and attitudes changed completely by the avalanche of money coming in from both film and soundtrack sales.

Had "A Hard Day's Night" been a flop or even just a modest success then it is conceivable that Epstein would have made an offer to buy out the United Artists interest, and had the Beatles not taken over America and the World in 1964, then quite possibly the second and third Beatles films might have been produced by Pickfair.

But in the case of the second film there was absolutely no possibility that United Artists would relinquish any aspect of their total control. NEMS had liaised with the London office of United Artists and the arrangements for the shooting of the film had been influenced by some specific financial considerations put forward by NEMS.

The script had been quite cynically constructed to include filming in places that the Beatles wished to visit, and so the location shooting was to take place in the Bahamas and also in the Austrian Alps before returning to England. However, the Bahamas also provided another benefit and Epstein and Ellis had been working with James Isherwood on tax-break incentives, and the Bahamas afforded special advantages. As a result yet another company, Cavalcade Productions, was set up as the vehicle through which those tax advantages might flow.

The Bahamas had long been fabled as a suitable location for offshore investments and by happy coincidence, one of the former partners in Bryce Hanmer Isherwood, Dr Walter Strach, had recently moved to Nassau, the capital of the Bahamas, with a brief to monitor and promote a variety of schemes involving offshore earnings. His main remit was to help create such structures to assist the firm's clients, and though the Beatles were not their highest-earning or highest fee-paying clients they were comprehensively the most glamorous clients for Bryce Hanmer Isherwood.

In conjunction with Isherwood and others in the London office Walter Strach devised a process which involved substantial amounts of the large fees paid to the Beatles for their work on the film being paid into an account which was effectively a trust. None of the Beatles had access to that money, or indeed any control over the distribution of the funds.

Some time after the release of the film, and the involvement of the four Beatles taking part in a high-profile ceremony at Buckingham Palace, a story started making the rounds that Epstein had been involved in some illegal activity in the creation of the Bahamas shelter. The story then had Epstein panicking and, desperate to avoid investigation and possible disgrace, offered to drop the scheme and pay all the required British taxes on the monies involved. In return for providing the British exchequer with so much extra income Epstein demanded, or was offered, MBEs for the four Beatles.

Obviously, these honours were awarded in June, although, curiously and poignantly and tellingly, no similar honour was offered to Brian Epstein. On the face of it the story sounds like specious nonsense, and perhaps some gentle racism against the proudly Jewish Brian Epstein. And yet it has always seemed strange and perhaps a little cruel, that Epstein, the mastermind behind the Beatles success and everything which came out of NEMS, should have been singled out to be ignored by the establishment. Although, it must be admitted that other people asserted that the failure to award an honour to Epstein was the result of his increasingly frantic personal life rather than any sharp practice in the use of overseas tax legislation.

That sounds quite convincing until you think about all the crooks, idiots and downright monsters who have been honoured by the British Honours System. Whatever the reason for Brian Epstein being ignored it seemed shabby treatment of a man responsible for so much good, and so many benefits for the UK.

The Beatles were sent out by NEMS on a flight, accompanied by actress Eleanor Bron, on February 22nd, ready to commence location shooting the following day. It was a largely enjoyable period in the Bahamas with one highlight being an appearance from former press officer Derek Taylor, on assignment from Station KRLA in Los Angeles. Apart from the enjoyably social duty of catching up with the Beatles and old colleagues like Neil and Mal, there was a more uncomfortable side to Taylor's presence. The radio station was paying him a hefty fee to try to get exclusive material and some scoops thanks to his relationship with the group. Epstein wasn't happy with such a plan, and though he got some interviews, it was never as simple or as close as he had hoped. And Brian Epstein was polite and charming, but there was a reserve, a distance, that Taylor hadn't detected while he was working for Epstein in London.

A line had been crossed, and Taylor would never get the same open access while Epstein was alive.

There was better news for others in the Beatles circle. George Martin's contribution to the amazing success of the Beatles, and his role in massively improving the profits of EMI, was finally recognised by his bosses at the record company. In 1964, his salary as Head of Production at Parlophone was £7,800. In 1965, the generous management upped his salary to a magnificent £8000: this for a man who had produced the records which occupied the number one position in the British charts for 37 out of the 52 weeks in 1963. Given that the first of those number ones, 'Please Please Me' didn't reach that position until mid-February the true picture of Martin's dominance is even more remarkable. Of the remaining 45 weeks in 1963 after 'Please Please Me' hit number one, George Martin's productions were at the top of the chart for 37 of those weeks - a remarkable performance in any era.

Many of those discs then became massive sellers in America and round the world in 1964, and George Martin truly delivered countless millions in profit for his employers, who showed their immense gratitude by awarding him a salary increase of £200. By any standards, absolutely incredible!

To comply with United Artists stiff schedule the film songs were expected to be completed before the start of location shooting. The first session at Abbey Road to prepare material for the film took place several days before the flight, but by the time the group arrived in the Bahamas a substantial batch of songs were in the can, though two of those tracks - 'That Means A Lot' and 'If You've Got Trouble' would remain unreleased for thirty years.

The working title was "Eight Arms To Hold You", although that name was widely unpopular among cast and crew, and when Capitol Records released the first single, 'Ticket To Ride' /'Yes It Is', the A-side of the single was actually credited as being from the film, "Eight Arms To Hold You".

The name of the film was not changed to "Help!" until much later in the process, indeed, after the Beatles returned to Britain at the end of March. In an attempt to replicate the success of the process of creating the theme song for the first film Walter Shenson asked Lennon and McCartney to create a song called 'Help!' which was delivered within forty-eight hours.

The full soundtrack album had to be completed piecemeal, during various breaks in filming, though this was hardly an unusual process for the group. The group had been forced to record the three albums since "Please Please Me" in this intermittent fashion mainly because of the demands of live appearances in Britain and further afield. The soundtrack album was not completed until just six weeks before its release date.

As a diversion from the pattern used so successfully on "A Hard Day's Night", George Martin was not asked to provide the instrumental soundtrack for the new film. It appeared that some minor friction had occurred between Martin and Dick Lester, the film director, and this led to Martin being cast aside. His place on the new film was taken by Ken Thorne leaving George Martin to deliver the timeless quote, "I was included out!"

Brian Epstein flew out for two days in the Bahamas to check on progress and to spend an evening with Walter Strach discussing tax strategy, an aspect of his work becoming ever more important. Then he flew back to London to attend to other matters including his attendance at another prestigious awards ceremony. The Carl-Alan awards were presented on March 8th at the Empire Ballroom in Leicester Square. He was there to accept an award on behalf of the Beatles, and so he took back to the NEMS office the award of Best Group of the Year, handed to him by Princess Margaret.

Twenty-four hours later he was in planning mode as he chaired a meeting designed to finalise the dates which would feature on the forthcoming American tour. A number of promoters were contacted with the bad news that they had missed out on the 1965 tour but for most of them Epstein held out the possibility that circumstances might change for the tour in 1966.

The main, hugely exciting news to be revealed from the meeting, was the surprise announcement that Epstein intended to have the concert at Shea Stadium in August filmed! News of that concert had already leaked out. It was too lavish and outlandish a proposal to be kept quiet, and developments in the States ensured that the news about Shea Stadium would leak out sooner rather than later.

Epstein had asked Bernstein not to advertise the concert until the fees had been paid, but then told his American friend, "I can't stop you from talking about the concert, now can I?"

Bernstein got the message and so he started a process of passing on news about Shea Stadium by word of mouth, initially just in his local area in New York. Because he was so well known in New York as the man who had brought the Beatles to Carnegie Hall he was constantly being asked when the Beatles were coming back. Epstein's tacit permission was all the enterprising Bernstein needed.

He got a PO Box at the local post office and started to tell kids where to apply for tickets, just by sending letters and the required money. And in just three weeks in the spring of 1965, Bernstein sold out Shea Stadium, 55,600 tickets, and every one sold without a single advertisement. He even received a letter applying for tickets from behind the Iron Curtain but as a marketing enterprise, it must have been the first example of successful social media activity ever.

Up to 1965 a rock or pop act hadn't even attempted a concert in a stadium before. It was truly groundbreaking, and much of the success in the advance planning was down to Sid Bernstein and his unique relationship of trust with Brian Epstein.

Unfortunately for Epstein he not could spend time delighting in the unique glory of the prospect of Shea Stadium. The plans were set for a tour to start with the historic Shea Stadium performance, given that the date in question had been agreed with Epstein some time earlier.

There would be two other cities approximately on the eastern side of the continent, Atlanta and Toronto. One appearance in the south in Houston, Texas. Two dates in the mid-west in Chicago and Minneapolis, and then four dates on the west coast, Portland, San Diego, Los Angeles, and finally San Francisco. Inevitably, the LA show would be a return to the Hollywood Bowl given the absurd level of critical attention their show in September 1964 had attracted.

But the severely limited dates meant major disappointments for a lot of halls and cities, particularly those that thought they had served the Beatles well the previous year. But the memories for the Beatles and Brian Epstein and people like Mal Evans and Wendy Hanson were still vivid with the blood and the broken bones and the wailing children.

No member of the Beatles had asked Epstein to spare them from further horrors of that kind again on the road in America. They didn't need to. Epstein had been there as well, not for all the shows, but enough to know just how bad it was at times. The sight of Bess Coleman prone and unconscious, a thin trickle of blood down her forehead, being loaded hurriedly into an ambulance backstage at one of the shows was seared into his memory.

There was no need to request or demand a more humane schedule for the American tour, and that schedule had been fully decided before the end of winter.

10 cities, 16 shows, 20 days, but the kick-off, the absolute show-stopper would be Shea Stadium on August 15th, and even with all the amazing things Epstein had seen and experienced in the past two years he couldn't help but be excited at the thought of it.

Shea Stadium! 55,000 people! The Beatles! Amazing.

But before that, he had to oversee the completion of the film, and to make some serious moves on the Seltaeb disaster.

After returning from the Bahamas, the extended Beatles party then flew to Austria to film the alpine sections of the new film. They stayed at the strangely named Hotel Edelweiss in Obertauern. Brian Epstein came with them for the first few days and occupied a two bedroom suite at the hotel with Geoffrey Ellis, and there, free of the constant distractions of London, Epstein was able to read up on the copious papers about Seltaeb prepared by David Jacobs, Geoffrey Ellis, and Walter Hofer, and that process, greatly aided by the beautiful Austrian air, focussed his mind on what needed to be done.

Although he had given Walter Hofer the sharp and, for Epstein, crude instruction to "Sue the Bastards!" he was aware that it wasn't as simple as that. The last few weeks had seen Hofer amassing information and preparing the ground for the American proceedings which Epstein wanted to launch as quickly as possible. Ideally, he wanted the whole Seltaeb mess settled and buried before the Beatles went back to America in the summer. That way he could hopefully keep a lid on it and prevent the details of the sordid mess leaking out to anybody else, particularly the four Beatles.

Hofer had faxed over various suggestions and proposals and now, stimulated by the sharp mountain air, his mind was clear on the next step.

Unfortunately, it became clear that Epstein had grievously underestimated the obduracy of the Seltaeb operation which, by early 1965, was being increasingly concentrated in and personified by Nicky Byrne. His erstwhile partner Lord Eliot had filed suit in New York against Byrne and had escaped from the madness by departing for England. Others in the original group had either left the organisation or gone to ground and while it may have looked to Epstein that Seltaeb in the shape of Nicky Byrne would be an easy nut to crack he would be proved seriously, and expensively, wrong.

Based on Hofer's summation and advice, Epstein authorised him to launch full proceedings in the American courts against Seltaeb, with the rider to enact parallel proceedings against Stramsact in England as and when appropriate.

As a prelude to full litigation, Hofer was instructed to demand full and accurate accounts, plus a current trading activity record and a full book inventory of amounts owing and amounts due. Hofer had delicately warned him that it wouldn't make easy or pleasant reading, and, though Epstein agreed, the embattled Beatles manager genuinely felt that he had no option but to proceed through the courts. The amounts of money being lost were horrific. Far, far worse was the potential fall-out if the Beatles ever found out about Seltaeb.

But he genuinely and confidently expected that it would all be over by the time of the concert at Shea. After all Seltaeb was increasingly concentrated in the form of one man, Nicky Byrne, and who was he to stand against the might of NEMS and EMI and Capitol and, most powerfully, the Beatles?

At the start of World War 1, there was a popular belief that "it will all be over by Christmas". Sadly, tragically, all the people saying that were desperately mistaken. In February 1965, Brian Epstein believed that the Seltaeb mess would be over by August.

He was wrong. Equally desperately mistaken, and completely wrong.

The production of the second film ground forward but, despite the glamorous locations and the enhanced budgets and the involvement of stellar talents like Eleanor Bron, Leo McKern, Victor Spinetti, Patrick Cargill, Roy

Kinnear and John Bluthal, there was a clear sense that it wasn't the same, wasn't as joyfully innocent as "A Hard Day's Night".

That was a view which would be endorsed by the critics after the film's release although commercially it was yet another tremendous success. The soundtrack album also managed to shore up United Artists' profits considerably that year.

Judged on its own merits the film was an enjoyable romp, making good use of the extra facilities provided by the greatly inflated budget, and the many benefits provided by colour. The settings in the Bahamas contrasted with the icy beauty of the Austrian Alps although perversely the temperatures in the Bahamas were extremely low, forcing the cast to wear warm clothes instead of the thin costumes they had expected.

A vastly increased budget, colour stock, exotic overseas locations, and a lavish publicity campaign - and this time there was expectation and anticipation for what the group might deliver. There were lots of funny moments, some good jokes, and, inevitably, some glorious moments but the parts seemed greater than the whole.

And in many instances, the film represented a real moment of change in the lives and careers of the Beatles. The last album to appear before "Help!" was "Beatles For Sale" and the cover artwork showed the four Beatles staring sullenly at the camera, and the smiling, laughing, joking Moptops have clearly left the stage. In their place are four young men worn down by what they'd seen and done and endured over the past couple of years. Their grim expressions on the front of "Beatles For Sale" spoke volumes, but primarily told the world that the four of them would not play the game any more.

That was a hard lesson for the world and Britain to learn, but they would all have to learn it. And so would Brian Epstein.

They came back to London on March 22nd, ready for some final days shooting at Twickenham to finish off the film. That period took them through almost a month to the middle of May and besides Twickenham took in memorable sessions on Salisbury Plain and, most poignantly, at Cliveden House in Berkshire on May 10th and 11th. In the film Cliveden doubles for Buckingham Palace, and Cliveden was also the location where four years earlier John Profumo had enjoyed the naked swim with Christine Keeler, starting their affair which ultimately brought down the MacMillan government.

In 1963, it was arguably the advent of the young, lively, irreverent Beatles which put into starkest contrast the dour, tired, old men who formed the Conservative government at the time. It was a gross simplification, a cliché, but like most clichés, it had more than a grain of truth.

The setting at Cliveden had a personal significance for Paul McCartney who had just taken ownership of his first home, an imposing Regency townhouse close by the Abbey Road Studios. Because of the many conversions that he and Jane Asher wanted to make to the structure it would be almost a year before he finally moved in to the imposing house.

Besides the extensive building works the long delay was forced on McCartney by the various tours and filming commitments and holidays out of the UK. During the months leading up to the final move into the house in March 1966 McCartney was able to move a lot of personal possessions into storage rooms at the house, stuff that had been held for him back in Liverpool or even in the top floor room he occupied at Jane Asher's house. Those possessions included lots of vinyl albums, many, many clothes and a wealth of songs, often existing as mere fragments of lyric or melody, with some of them dating back to the mid-fifties.

And standing on the sweeping lawns at Cliveden the significance of the setting was possibly lost on the four Beatles but not on the more cultured and worldly-wise Epstein, who was particularly conscious of changing times. At the end of March, he had shepherded the group through what would turn out to be their final recording for Thank Your Lucky Stars, the show which had given Epstein his introduction to Dick James and had been a major factor in the creation of Northern Songs.

At the end of March he flew back to New York for further discussions about strategy with Walter Hofer. Whilst there he had other meetings, other dinners to attend, and there was also the slight hope in the back of his mind that Dizz might reappear, though everybody who wished him "Good Trip" was thinking exactly the opposite.

The main objective of the trip was to launch Cilla Black in the States via the Ed Sullivan Show. This wasn't her first trip but he had decided that she was now ready for the big step forward, and what better vehicle than the Sullivan Show, especially after what happened in February 1964? He was also negotiating for her first major cabaret engagement which, by beautiful coincidence, would take place in one of the venues at the Plaza later in the year.

While they were in America things continued to develop at NEMS. At the end of the month, Epstein formally took over the Saville Theatre in London which he clearly hoped to develop into a theatrical oasis, and perhaps even provide an outlet for his own thwarted theatrical ambitions. Although that aim would never be realised, he did manage to make the Saville the temporary location for some of the most exciting concerts ever staged in London. But as a conventional theatre, it wouldn't work, and it never had. That was the reason that the previous owners, Bernard Delfont and Tom Arnold, were so eager to open a partnership with Epstein. It would suck money and resources from Epstein and became another source of difficulty and problems for him.

While he was away the group performed yet another final event signifying the massive change that would come into their lives over the next year. The BBC programme, Top of the Pops, had only been in existence for fifteen months but was comfortably established as the most important pop programme in Britain. It was still being broadcast from a converted chapel in Manchester and would stay there for a further two years before the inevitable move to London.

But while Epstein was trying to sort out his many problems in New York the Beatles made their final mimed appearance on a live Top of the Pops programme, wearing the same fawn-coloured jackets that they would wear shortly afterwards at Shea Stadium. Although the Beatles performance on that edition of Top of the Pops was wiped as was customary for BBC programmes at that period, most unusually a fragment of that performance appeared a few weeks later in an episode of Doctor Who, and that performance fragment, with the Beatles miming to 'Ticket to Ride', survives in that episode of Doctor Who.

Epstein and Cilla Black finished their business in New York and flew back to London in time for Epstein to attend an event which was always a highlight of the year, the NME Poll Winners concert at Wembley.

But before he left New York, on the last night in his favourite city, Epstein received a surprise call while he was in his hotel room at the Waldorf Towers packing for the journey back home. The desk receptionist told him that a friend was in the reception area and passed the phone over to the newcomer. It was Sid Bernstein. The shock, and surprise for Epstein was palpable. His first thought was that there was a problem, but Bernstein was quick to assure him that there was nothing to concern him. He asked if he could come up to Epstein's room, but promised he would only detain him a couple of minutes.

Epstein was bemused. It was always a pleasure to see Sid, but they had met for lunch at the Plaza just two days earlier, and Bernstein had given no indication that he would want or need to meet up again before Epstein flew out. Apart from a general overview of preparations for Shea and a quick run-through of arrangements made for the concert, most of the conversation revolved around Bernstein's constant fund of gossip - sometimes scurrilous, always entertaining - about figures in the American entertainment world.

There were two topics that Bernstein avoided. One was Seltaeb, because he knew how much pain and anxiety the subject was causing his friend, and, in any case, it was more properly dealt with by Walter Hofer.

The other topic was Dizz Gillespie who, reports had it, had flown back to New York after being bribed to get out of London. Prior to Epstein's departure from London with Cilla Black some days earlier, friends of NEMS in New York were contacted by David Jacobs and Geoffrey Ellis to ask them to keep an eye out for Gillespie and to try, by whatever means possible, to keep him away from Brian Epstein.

Sid Bernstein naturally was one of those friends and he had diligently kept a brotherly eye on Epstein's activities in New York that week. Inevitably, given Epstein's lifestyle and proclivities, there were periods and activities which Bernstein couldn't track, and genuinely didn't want to attempt it.

Though his surprise visit to the Waldorf was not to enable him to check that Gillespie had re-appeared, Bernstein was certainly relieved to find Epstein alone in the hotel suite and clearly not intending or expecting visitors during his last few hours in New York.

Bernstein didn't take up too much of his friend's time. As they stood looking out of the large window towards Madison Avenue and the elegant spires of St. Patrick's, Epstein offered his friend a drink, but he smiled and refused. Instead, he pulled a white envelope out of his jacket pocket.

Epstein took it and delicately ripped it open. Inside was a money order made out to NEMS.

It was for $100,000. An advance payment for ticket sales for Shea Stadium, and possibly one of the most amazing moments in Brian Epstein's remarkable life.

He was back in London just in time to catch the Beatles performing at the New Musical Express Poll Winner's Concert being held, as usual, at the Empire Pool Wembley. An indication of the power and importance of pop music at that time was that other acts on the bill included the Rolling Stones, the Moody Blues, The Animals and the Kinks.

The Beatles were allowed just five songs and performed 'I Feel Fine', 'She's A Woman', 'Baby's In Black', 'Ticket To Ride' and 'Long Tall Sally'. It was a sample of the music they would take out on the road in Europe and America in the coming months, and the hysterical crowd of some 11,200 gave them a taste of what was awaiting them in the States. If they thought that America's version of Beatlemania had dissipated since September 1964 they were to get a rude awakening.

Three days after Wembley the group received their first-ever Grammy Awards. They were nominated for 'I Want To Hold Your Hand' in the Record of the Year category, and in the Best Contemporary Song category for 'A Hard Day's Night'. Perhaps surprisingly, given its important role in the Beatles' breakthrough, 'I Want To Hold Your Hand' wasn't considered the Record of the Year. Any Beatles disappointment was tempered by the receipt of two other Grammy Awards for Best New Artist Of 1964 and also for Best Performance by a Vocal Group, this for 'A Hard Day's Night'.

A short European Tour had been arranged for late June starting in Paris and including fifteen concerts spread over nine dates around Europe. The reception for the Beatles wasn't as universally joyful as in Britain and the US, and attendances were sometimes not a sell-out, particularly in Rome.

The tour was also notable for the level of violence inflicted on the fans, and both the group and people like Mal Evans raised their voice against what they saw as unwarranted brutality. There was an especially unpleasant scene in Madrid, in the outdoor venue, the Plaza de Toros de Las Ventas, which was also the bullring in the city. Brian Epstein had spent time there the day before the Beatles concert watching a bullfight. This was part of his long-term love of bullfighting which would later be manifested in his sponsorship of the English bullfighter, Henry Higgins.

The European tour, their final such concert visit to the continent, was not a happy event for the group or their management. The group's displeasure with the venues, the security arrangements, and, yet again, the playing facilities was tangible and communicated itself not to the fans but certainly to those like Barrow and Evans and Aspinall who were with them on the road every day.

But on one absurd level, it didn't really matter because by the end of May 1965 the Beatles, the lovable Moptops from Liverpool, had been elevated to the ranks of the British Establishment. On June 9th came the formal announcement that "The Beatles are named to the Order of the British Empire on the Queen Elizabeth II's birthday honours list published this day".

Whatever the reasons and justifications for the award it was certainly unprecedented for a pop group, a mere pop group, to be honoured in this way. At the time, few eyebrows were raised at the seeming failure to acknowledge the part played in the Beatles success by Brian Epstein, although, quite reasonably, the surprise at Epstein's snub did increase as time moved forward.

But the surprise at Epstein's exclusion was nothing compared to the widespread fury expressed across the Commonwealth at the very fact of the Beatles being awarded the MBE. Newspapers received a flood of complaints. If it happened today, allowing for the fact that it is most unlikely that the same rancour would be caused, the complaints would be far more widespread, but even so the torrent of complaints took many by surprise. The upset caused by the awards reached its peak when reports appeared in the press about people returning their awards in protest about the Beatles accepting their MBEs.

An august group of people including Jack Berg, Former Member of Canada's Parliament, RAF Squadron Leader Paul Pearson, David Evan Rees, World War Veteran Col. George Wagg, Hector Dupuis, Douglas Moffit, Richard Pape, Stanley Ellis and Cyril Hearns returned their MBE's in protest at the Beatles receiving theirs. They were not the only ones.

As ever Epstein stage-managed the announcement of the awards perfectly. Normal procedure is that no information about things like the Queen's Honours List is to be released to the public, and embargoed until midnight on the day of the announcement. To ensure smooth management of the day Epstein had arranged a press conference at which media could ask relevant questions of the Beatles on the day that the news was released to the world.

McCartney was away on holiday in Portugal but returned early at Epstein's request to sit alongside the other Beatles. Epstein himself had been in Blackpool the night before the MBE announcement watching a concert starring Billy J. Kramer and the Dakotas.

He conducted a blizzard of interviews in his hotel room in Blackpool before flying back to London to pick up John Lennon and escort him to the press conference. On the morning of the announcement all the parents of the Beatles received a huge bouquet of flowers, the kind of small but sensitive and kind gesture for which Epstein was justly famous.

The group were nominated for the award by the current Prime Minister, Harold Wilson, who coincidentally was also the Member of Parliament for Huyton on Merseyside. It was Wilson who had shamelessly tried to get the maximum number of photographs with the Beatles when presenting them with a Variety Club award at the Dorchester. The nomination of the Beatles for an award was viewed quite cynically at the time, as a blatant attempt by the shrewd Wilson to present an image of a Prime Minister in touch with the younger generation. The legendary White-hot heat of the Technological Revolution had cooled a little by this point but Wilson and his advisors totally understood the value of appearing to be in touch with popular culture. Indeed, it was during the following year, 1966, that England won the World Cup giving Wilson the chance to utter the fatuous boast, "England only ever wins the World Cup under Labour!"

The press conference had to held at lunchtime at Twickenham Film Studios because the filming schedule for the new film, called "Help!" since April 13th, was still so tight. It was a cheerful, exuberant affair made memorable by Paul McCartney's throwaway quip that "MBE must stand for `Mister Brian Epstein'."

June and July were pregnant with announcements as the final preparations were made for the World Premiere of the new Beatles film, and also for the imminent American tour. The premiere had been set for Thursday, July 29th and was held, just like the previous film, at the London Pavilion.

The area around Piccadilly was packed with fans although the numbers were allegedly fewer than for "A Hard Day's Night" a year earlier. Police estimated that some ten thousand fans watched excitedly as the group arrived in a large black Rolls-Royce. The Royal guests were Princess Margaret and Lord Snowdon, who had supposedly delayed their summer holiday to be present at the premiere. The filming was followed by a lavish party in the Orchid Room at the Dorchester Hotel.

United Artists tried something new to capitalise on interest in the Beatles and so they allowed the film to go out on general release in several English seaside towns, including Weymouth, Barnstaple, Clacton, Lowestoft, Brighton, and Ramsgate.

The American version of the 'Help!' single appeared on July 19th with the British copy hitting the shops a week later, while the same-name albums, with the inevitable differences between the two versions, appeared in August - the 4th for the British version and the American version a week later.

Once again the American version was very strictly a soundtrack album with the seven songs from the Beatles fleshed out by the assorted instrumental pieces performed by the Ken Thorne Orchestra, and generally written by the man himself. Short pieces like 'The Chase' and 'In the Tyrol' occupied the same level of prominence in terms of sales as 'Ticket to Ride' and 'You're Gonna Lose That Girl', meaning that in terms of revenue, particularly the precious publishing revenue, Mr. Thorne did very well indeed from the very strange falling out between Dick Lester and George Martin after "A Hard Day's Night".

The release schedule for product in the States was still bewildering to British eyes. The removal from the releasing schedule of Vee-Jay, Tollie and Swan had cleared up a large amount of the confusion, but the insistence on maintaining a twelve tracks per album maximum continued the crazy process. American albums were always a mishmash of tracks on the current British album, whichever tracks were left off the previous album, plus any b-sides which hadn't yet made it to an American album.

The most current British album in the early months of 1965 was "Beatles for Sale" but when the American album most current in scheduling to that one, "Beatles VI", was released in the middle of June it took the bewildering situation to fresh levels of silliness.

"Beatles VI" was the seventh Beatles release on the Capitol label, but even so it was the ninth album to be released in America in less than eighteen months, with the other two coming from United Artists, "A Hard Day's Night", and Vee-Jay, "Introducing The Beatles".

On the "Beatles Vl" album were the six tracks from "Beatles For Sale" which hadn't appeared on the previous Capitol release, "Beatles '65", plus the b-side to the single 'Ticket To Ride' which was 'Yes It Is'. Then two tracks which would shortly appear on the British "Help!" album, 'Tell Me What You See' and 'You Like Me Too Much', and finally two tracks included solely because of their American links. Both songs were covers of old Larry Williams numbers, material which had been an essential part of their act in Hamburg and the Cavern.

'Bad Boy' would not even appear in Britain until late in 1966 when the first Beatles compilation album, "A Collection of Beatles Oldies" was released for the Christmas market in the UK.

The other track cynically inserted to meet the needs of the American fans was 'Dizzie Miss Lizzie' which would finish side two of the British release of "Help!".

'Beatles Vl' opened with another old classic from the far-off days at the Cavern and Hamburg. 'Kansas City'/'Hey, Hey, Hey, Hey' was the number they had included in their set when they performed in Kansas City the previous September. Just as when it had been released on "Beatles for Sale" in Britain the track was incorrectly listed just as 'Kansas City' and it took a gentle correction from lawyers from Venice Music to get the label to see a correction, though the cover remained the same.

The marketing people at Capitol saw very good reasons to include a famous reference to a famous American city on an album released just weeks before the group returned to America. The fact that the group would not be playing Kansas City this time on tour played no part in the decision.

More important by far was to get "Beatles Vl" released promptly and to leave as much time as possible between the release of that album and the soundtrack to "Help!"

"Beatles Vl" was released in America on June 14th, and "Help!" came out in the States on August 13th. A gap of sixty-one days. Incredible.

But, there was some excuse because, as Capitol's marketing people, and indeed most of America knew, the Beatles were coming, again! Their flights to the States were booked and they were leaving from Heathrow on August 13th which meant that everybody in America and Canada with any kind of marketing angle on the Beatles, including Capitol and Seltaeb, were primed and ready for an onslaught from the time their plane took off from London.

Before that, the group and Epstein endured a blizzard of activity either to clear the decks for a month's absence, or to physically prepare for the strains of another American tour.

Epstein took on another directorship, this time of Harrisongs Limited, the music publishing activity for George Harrison. He had started his own publishing company in September 1964 by purchasing an off-the-shelf company called Mornyork Ltd. and changing the name in December of the same year to Harrisongs. Although Harrison was originally committed to Dick James Music, in tandem with Lennon and McCartney in Northern Songs, he was increasingly dissatisfied with the situation and the relationship with Dick James. His unhappiness would see its greatest expression in the acerbic song 'Only A Northern Song' which Harrison would later submit for the film "Yellow Submarine".

But when he took Brian Epstein as a director of Harrisongs such disputes were years in the future, and quite unimaginable.

The Beatles manager, in the spirit of clearing the decks, slipped out the news that plans to film "A Talent For Loving" as a Beatles cowboy film to appear after "Help!" as their third film had been quietly dropped. No reason was given, although the presence by that stage of Pickfair as a major element in any deliberations was clearly a factor.

The booking which Epstein had been negotiating earlier in the year for Cilla Black was realised when he flew to New York with her to help her prepare for a three-week engagement at the Persian Room in the Plaza Hotel, New York. This was a prestigious gig by any standards. In its relatively short history the Persian room had played host to many jazz and vocal greats, names like Duke Ellington, Eartha Kitt, Miles Davis, Liza Minnelli, Billie Holliday, Andy Williams, Peggy Lee and John Coltrane. Booking Cilla Black in to play that room, knowing the great names that had preceded her, was an amazing testimony to the faith he had in the young girl and her talent.

Accompanying her on such a nerve-wracking trip was typical of Epstein the man, and Epstein the manager. During the period in New York, he caught up with Bernstein and Hofer, acquainted himself with the latest Seltaeb disasters, and met with various unsavoury characters who knew perfectly well who he was. The days when he could slip under the radar in New York or Los Angeles had long gone. His face was possibly better known in New York than it was in London. That should have alerted him to the dangers both real and possible, but the danger was always part of the thrill.

And being in New York meant that he missed one of the most illustrious moments in the Beatles television history. The instant when, on Blackpool

Night Out, George Harrison stepped to the front of the stage and announced "And so, for Paul McCartney of Liverpool - Opportunity Knocks!"

Lennon leaves to the right, Harrison dances off to the left; Ringo Starr stays rooted to his drum kit. McCartney strides to centre stage, acoustic guitar in hand, the set darkens and two follow-spots pick him out as he sings, for the first time in a live setting, 'Yesterday'.

It was remarkable not so much for the awesome properties of the song but for the first sight of the Beatles split up into individual units. It took the huge viewing audience by surprise. Lots of artists and recording managers heard McCartney sing this plaintive ballad and realised that this was an exceptional song. Probably nobody realised just how special 'Yesterday' was, or is, but it's more than possible that of all the millions watching McCartney singing alone on that blackened stage Dick James was the only person with every hair on his body standing on end.

At the start of August Epstein had informal conversations with several trusted members of the press and informed them there would be no further Beatles UK tours that year. Although that would turn out to be less than accurate, it was indicative of a mind-set in Epstein, and the realisation that things were changing. There had already been a familiar exchange, but much nastier, earlier in the year when Harrison and Lennon and McCartney had bitterly informed the press that there would be no Christmas show in 1965, no more Christmas shows.

Whether that was after discussions with Epstein or not wasn't made clear; the simple fact was that they were leaving him, first and slowly, mentally but he knew that the full divorce was only a matter of time.

And in a weird demonstration of the direction in which things were going Epstein made announcements that Cilla Black would make her debut in pantomime in "Little Red Riding Hood", while Billy J. Kramer with the Dakotas would star in "Mother Goose", and Gerry and the Pacemakers would take leading roles in "Cinderella".

In the last couple of days before heading off to America Epstein had an enjoyable meeting with an old friend from Granada Television in Manchester. Johnny Hamp had been Head of Light Entertainment for that wonderful commercial television station for several years and during that period had been responsible for every Beatles performance on Granada.

Now he had come up for an idea showcasing the music of Lennon and McCartney, a programme in which the Beatles would play some numbers, but crucially the show would feature other artists performing Lennon and McCartney songs.

They met for lunch in London and as always with two such educated and personable men, the conversation was rich with memories and anecdotes and laughter, lots of laughter. They ran quickly through the commercial questions which, as usual with Epstein, were handled quickly, without playing games, and concluded with a handshake. The final part of the conversation was the part they both enjoyed, talking about possible artists and likely songs, and Hamp was left with the brief to come back for a meeting on Epstein's return from America with a full proposed running order, budget outline and the minutiae of detail that would go into an hour long television spectacular.

That was Epstein's last formal engagement before leaving for the summer American tour. The night before they left London the film "Help!" received its premiere in New York, but tellingly none of the Beatles were present and of course Epstein was also absent.

He was back in London, at Chapel Street, preparing for the anxieties and unparalleled joys of seeing America going wild, yet again, about the Beatles. It was an early start the following morning and he met with the rest of the travelling party at Heathrow at 9am on August 13th. When it came time to board their TWA flight they waved farewell to approximately one thousand fans gathered on top of the terminal building. There was something controlled and respectful about the arrivals and departures in London. The fans, despite the excited frenzy, just seemed happy to be there, to see the Beatles, and to get a wave from one or more Beatles. The police were invariably good-natured about the pushing and shoving and screaming. In England, it rarely got worse than that.

But just the arrival in New York at 2.30pm demonstrated the difference. The plane was greeted by a massive group of reporters and cameramen from press, radio and TV, but, acting on police orders, the plane parked up almost two miles from the main terminal at JFK, meaning that the estimated six thousand fans were denied the chance to greet the Beatles.

Instead, the party was ferried directly to the Warwick Hotel where Epstein had asked the NEMS people to reserve the whole of the 33rd floor for the Beatles party. The hotel had engaged extra security and so there were guards posted on every entrance and exit to that floor to keep out uninvited visitors.

The first inevitable duty was the obligatory press conference. This time it was under the direction of press officer Tony Barrow, who provided a light touch in controlling the enquiries for the 274 media personnel. For some observers who had witnessed the press conferences in February and then August 1964 there was a discernable change in 1965. There was an edge, a reserve that hadn't been there before. For some Americans watching the Warwick Hotel press conference, plus others later on the tour, it marked the first demonstration of the Beatles growing tired with the charade, with the games they were continually required to play, and with the price they were forced to pay.

So, once their press duties were over, the Beatles were escorted back to their luxurious prison on the 33rd floor. Luxurious undoubtedly, but still incarcerated by fame and the demands of thousands of fans shrieking their devotion far below on 6th Avenue and 54th Street. In the script of "A Hard Day's Night", scriptwriter Alun Owen gave Wilfred Brambell, mischievously playing Paul's grandfather, the line "So far, I've been in a train and a room, and a car and a room, and a room and a room!"

It was an amusing line, and delivered with waspish intent by Brambell, but the same line could have been delivered, with more bitterness, by any of the Beatles. Superb comfort, and every need provided for, but for the simplest, basic need - to be left alone and to live a quiet life, something that most of us take for granted but totally denied to them - and this even before the cesspit of social media and celebrity obsession became commonplace..

That was denied them, although as many people and particularly the press reminded them, there was the continual reassurance of their individual and shared millions to console them. Epstein was worried throughout the American tour that the Seltaeb dam might burst in front of the Beatles exposing the extent of the mess to the group.

There was one especially fraught moment in that first press conference when a reporter shouted a question about problems with licensing merchandise. Epstein froze, but fortunately, more exciting questions about Shea Stadium drowned out the boring financial question and the moment passed.

Barrow got the signal to wind things up and so the danger of the intemperate question was averted, but Epstein knew it could not be avoided forever.

The Beatles went back to their detention on the 33rd floor, prepared for a relatively quiet evening as they readied themselves for several hours rehearsing and then recording another edition of the Ed Sullivan show on the following day. Once again, although it would not be admitted in any public forum at the time, this was to be the Beatles final appearance on the show that broke them in America.

Given that it would be their fourth and final appearance, it fitted into the sad sequence of final appearances which had dominated their media work over the past few months. BBC Radio, Top of the Pops, Thank Your Lucky Stars and now the Ed Sullivan Show - they had all played major roles in the creation of the Beatles legend but that period was slipping into sepia.

Over their four days at the Warwick, the group entertained a series of high-profile visitors like the Ronettes, the Supremes, the Exciters, and, of course, Bob Dylan, but such visits merely emphasized their virtual incarceration.

That didn't affect the rest of the party and people like Epstein, Barrow, Aspinall and Evans were able to come and go in New York with some ease. On the first night in New York Epstein went to dinner with Sid Bernstein to discuss final arrangements for Shea Stadium which was only forty-eight hours away.

Barrow and Aspinall stayed in the suite, busying themselves with the various needs of the Beatles and delighting, yet again, with the astounding number of radio stations and tv channels.

For his part, Mal Evans escaped from the hotel for the evening. He hadn't enjoyed the flight, and didn't like the overt nature of the security that had descended yet again when they touched down in New York. He had arranged to meet somebody for a drink, a girl he had met the previous summer in New York backstage at the Forest Hills show. They had met again on a couple of his trips to New York earlier in 1965, and they had a standing arrangement to meet up for a drink when he came back in August.

She was an English girl who had been living and working in America for more than two years so she knew the city, knew the transport system, and knew the places to go and the places to avoid.

Her name was Chrissie, short for Christine, and though she knew about his connection to the Beatles, it had never seemed to him that she was seeing him just as a way to get to the Beatles. And that was a pleasant change for Mal Evans. Although people like him in the Beatles circle had done very well over the years from the Beatles cast-offs or rejects, it was still galling to meet a girl and know that the moment would arrive, generally sooner than later, when THE question would come, "What's Paul really like?" or "Tell me about John?" or "Is Ringo as cute as he seems?".

It used to drive him mad, and yet that was one of the attractive things about Chrissie. She knew about the Beatles - it had been George Harrison spilling a drink on her that caused them to meet - but she barely mentioned them. She obviously loved the music but demonstrably wasn't using Mal as a way to get access to the Beatles.

And it didn't hurt that she was very funny, and very pretty, and had an English detachment which he found beguiling, and, above all, she could spell irony and understand it and that was rare in New York in those days.

He had arranged to meet her in a bar near Café Wha? on MacDougal Street in the Village, but quite by chance he saw her as he was walking towards the meeting spot. They hugged, and he planted a chaste kiss on her cheek. Things hadn't moved any further than that between them at that stage, and she excitedly told him about a change of plan. She was going to take him to a surprise event, something that he would enjoy, something to do with the Beatles. He groaned at the mention of the name. It sounded like yet another come-on, although he knew she wasn't like that.

She was insistent that it would be good fun, and she was, at that stage in her life, very hard to resist, so he went along with her and accompanied her to a place somewhere near Bleeker Street. Still in the Village, but it was dark, and he was so busy talking to her that he didn't notice where they were going.

But the impact of what he saw that evening was to change his life, and that of the Beatles, and of Brian Epstein in a fundamental way.

Although that wasn't what Mal Evans was talking about when he got back to the suite at the Warwick. He was just captivated by the silliness and the splendour of what he had witnessed on Bleeker Street. It was a new phenomenon in America, Beatles Look-Alike competitions, and though New York and Los Angeles and San Francisco were the hotbeds for this absurd level of fan devotion, they could be found in many other US cities, certainly until 1966.

Mal Evans went into great detail about the competition he had just witnessed, the enthusiastic crowd, the sponsorship by radio stations though he couldn't recall if it was WINS or WABC and WMCA, and there seemed to be some kind of involvement with American Bandstand.

But the most memorable aspect of the event was the contestants, and Mal Evans enjoyed the audience reaction as he described the many shortcomings of the various entrants, and just how far they differed physically and facially from their chosen Beatle. Apart from one contestant. A man nominating himself as a look-alike Paul McCartney, and from the reaction of Mal Evans it was clear that this man must have been very convincing.

The mood was broken, or maybe enhanced, by a throwaway comment from John Lennon who announced, "Must have been a really ugly bastard", bringing out laughter from everybody listening.

But the Paul look-alike that night wasn't a really ugly bastard.

Anything but!

It was a young man who looked so much like Paul McCartney that he not only won the look-alike contest on Bleeker Street but he temporarily fooled Mal Evans who clumsily brushed shoulders with the chap when he was leaving the bar with Chrissie.

Temporarily disorientated by Budweiser, Mal wasn't looking where he was going and turned back towards the stranger as he headed towards the door after the minor collision. Instinctively he grinned and muttered "Sorry Paul."

The stranger smiled. It was obviously a regular mistake people made with him. "I'm sorry. You've got the wrong guy" he explained.

"Hey, you just won that competition! I'm Mal Evans, I work with Paul. You really do look like him!"

"Oh, thanks. Thanks a lot" said the stranger. "Quite a few people tell me that!"

He held out his right hand and shook Mal Evans' hand.

"My name's William. William Campbell."

In any book on the great events in rock and pop history there are a few events that must be included. Live Aid inevitably is one as is, on a much sadder basis, the plane crashes that took away from us Buddy Holly and then Otis Redding.

But any such list has to include the concert on August 15th 1965 at Shea Stadium in New York. It was such an astounding evening that a mere recitation of statistics fail to do it justice. It is especially significant that stadium rock, with fifty pantechnicons delivering massive equipment and stage sets, has become commonplace, and gatherings of tens, and occasionally hundreds, of thousands, at a rock concert doesn't raise an eyebrow.

But in 1965, things were very different. Major concerts were held at prestige venues like the Royal Albert Hall or Carnegie Hall. Conventional touring venues were the halls or even cinemas in the centre of every major town, and this was the circuit which the Beatles had built up to under Epstein's management in the two tumultuous years from 1963 to 1965.

In the States they had played at a series of arenas during the 1964 summer tour and the summer tour a year later would feature a number of similar venues with some repeats like Hollywood Bowl and Cow Palace in San Francisco

But on every level, Shea Stadium was different. The scale of it, the audacity of putting a mere pop group on at a venue like that in front of 50,000 fans - it took the breath away. The media in America, knowing full well what such a concert at Shea Stadium entailed, had made more of the event than their British equivalents, and of course Sid Bernstein, with his gift for publicity and promotion, maximised every opportunity to promote the event.

Not in an attempt to sell tickets. That goal had been achieved several months before the Beatles even returned to the States in August 1965. Before the rigours of the Shea Stadium show, the group had to venture from their base high in the Warwick Hotel to make a return appearance at the Ed Sullivan Theatre. This was not to be another live appearance like the epoch-making show on February 9th 1964. Instead, in the style which was becoming the pattern, they were recording a programme for later transmission, but this would be the last time the group would physically appear inside the famous theatre on Broadway. After the 1965 tour, they would resort to providing Sullivan with video clips for the new singles. Sullivan and his staff were grateful for the material but it was never the same as having the Beatles in the theatre itself.

A convoy of black limousines had been held outside the Warwick for the Beatles party. They left the hotel at 10.15am and made the short trip to

Broadway, and started rehearsals at 11am. The work went on all afternoon and into the early evening, with the group skittish and argumentative about problems in the studio, particularly with the sound balance.

It was 8pm that night before they were happy with the way it was sounding. The studio manager went for a recording at 8.30pm during which they featured 'I Feel Fine' and 'I'm Down'. Ringo contributed 'Act Naturally', which was followed by 'Ticket to Ride'. Then came the showstopper. Paul McCartney was introduced by George Harrison who told the watching millions that this was a new song called 'Yesterday'. McCartney sang it solo, accompanied by a string quarter from the Ed Sullivan orchestra. The short set ended with 'Help!' made notable because John Lennon managed to forget some of the lyrics, but in the midst of the bedlam hardly anybody noticed.

The recording was put on one side for transmission later in the year and would be shown long after the Beatles had left the country.

The party returned to the Warwick after the Sullivan taping and prepared for the rigours of the following day. None of them had visited Shea Stadium previously. It wasn't like footballers who traditionally visit the site of that day's game a couple of hours prior to the match. In their day the Beatles had a number of venues to which they would return, with the Cavern being the most obvious example, but as their fame increased the number of shows decreased. One of the results was that there were few surprises for the four Beatles as they walked, or more often ran, into their playing positions on the stage.

America was different. As Epstein would quite naturally take the highest bid from an area and locate the Beatles performance there, it meant that they would often find themselves on a stage and in circumstances they hadn't encountered before.

The show at Washington Coliseum in February 1964 was perhaps the best example, until Shea.

Problems at and around the stadium had started long before the Beatles got there. At every venue on the tour, there were long, earnest discussions among the police and the security people about how to handle the huge crowds and the inevitable trouble. For the Shea concert there was a concern that the crowds might jam the tunnels under the East River and so police instructions compelled the group to travel by limousine to the East River Heliport. From that point they went by helicopter over the East River and Queens until they arrived at the World Fair site. The journey had been arranged to provide them with a spectacular sightseeing trip over the skyscrapers of Manhattan. There had already been arrangements made months earlier to film the concert and the build-up, and Epstein had refused offers from other operations to ensure that his own in-house film company, Subafilms Limited was recording everything in conjunction with Ed Sullivan Productions Inc. And so cameramen from Subafilms were on the helicopter with the Beatles capturing images of that timeless panorama and also of the boyish wonder on the faces of the Beatles as they contemplated the majesty before them and the incredible few hours awaiting them.

The World Fair site is now better known as Flushing Meadows Corona Park, and in 1978 became the home of the United States Tennis Association, and, not surprisingly, the US Open tennis tournament is played there every August.

At the time the Beatles went there in the helicopter they were landing on the site of the World Fair which was in the second year of its run. It had proved a financial disaster and from its inception had run into problems with the international body that licensed such World Fairs. Because of those problems, most major countries boycotted the event, which caused major organisational problems. Some of those difficulties were partially solved by smaller countries taking space, and this produced some unexpected benefits like a massive increase in popularity for Belgian waffles and the chance for visitors to view something wondrous and unique. In the Vatican Pavilion, those attending the Fair could see Michelangelo's Pietà, this being the only time that the Vatican has allowed it to leave the St. Peter's Basilica.

Among the smaller countries that took up the chance to display at the New York World Fair was Indonesia, but various political problems between the United Nations and Indonesia led to the country withdrawing from the United Nations early in 1965, and the country also withdrew from the Fair in March 1965. In retaliation, the Fair Corporation then confiscated and closed the Indonesian pavilion, and it remained closed and barricaded for the whole of the 1965 World Fair season.

Although in terms of world politics the impact on the Beatles was unimportant, the anti-western feeling engendered by this situation took several years to abate. In the summer of 1966 the Beatles were to fly into a firestorm in Manila, the roots of which had nothing to do with the group but some of the immediate causes could have been spotted as the helicopter hovered over the Fair site before landing. The Hong Kong pavilion was brilliantly illuminated as was the Polynesia pavilion around one hundred metres away. The dark space between them was occupied by the locked and barricaded Indonesian pavilion, the darkness thrown into deep relief by the pavilions on either side and the magnificent Unisphere to the rear.

Quite naturally, the Beatles were oblivious to the site. To them it was nothing more than a place to land the helicopter close to the looming mass that was their destination, Shea Stadium.

The police transferred the Beatles party from the helicopter to a Wells Fargo armoured van which would take them into the stadium. As a nice touch, each of the four Beatles was handed a Wells Fargo agent badge which for any English boy of their age looked like the silver star that sheriffs wore in the Wild West.

Prior to the appearance of the Beatles the fans were treated to a full bill, and so the 55,600 fans sat through introductions from Cousin Bruce Morrow and Murray the K, and performances from The Discotheque Dancers, Brenda Holloway and the King Curtis Band, Cannibal & The Headhunters, Sounds Incorporated, and Sid Bernstein's favourites, the Young Rascals.

Finally, the waiting ended. Ed Sullivan was introduced on stage, "The Number One Showman of the World and, most important of all, a Great American!", with the incongruous sight of the white-shirted Mal Evans toiling behind him connecting leads to amps on the pitifully small equipment that the group were using.

Rather helplessly, Sullivan held both arms in the air as though that would hold back the noise bellowing down towards him, and announced, "Now, ladies and gentlemen, honoured by their country, decorated by their Queen, loved here in America, here are The Beatles!"

Looking at the footage now it is remarkable how many people, kids, in the audience were carrying binoculars. They really were that far away!

The four of them walked briskly and ran across to the stage area, turning and waving as they moved forward, all of their faces telling of their disbelief at what they were seeing around them. The Beatles ran onto the field and climbed onto the stage at 9.16pm, to a barrage of noise, which took the screaming to new levels. Not just because of the number of people creating the incessant din. There seemed to be a fresh, visceral intensity at Shea that took even the seasoned observers like Epstein, Aspinall and Evans by surprise. Sullivan shook hands with each of them in turn, looking even more the proud uncle at a wedding or bar mitzvah, but the sight of the grey-suited Beatles sprinting across the playing field to reach the temporary sanctuary of the stage is a timeless image.

The group lined up in front of brand new 100-watt amplifiers specifically designed for the group by Vox, but they were totally inadequate to combat the noise levels cascading down from the stands.

In desperation, the group debated the problem with Mal Evans who switched over to the in-house PA system. That had slightly more reach in the upper, more distant areas of the stadium but the sound produced was feeble and insipid set against the sharp, unrelenting screaming.

The rehearsals back in London had settled on a tight, twelve song set for the tour which invariably ran 'Twist And Shout', 'She's A Woman', 'I Feel Fine', 'Dizzy Miss Lizzy', 'Ticket To Ride', 'Everybody's Trying To Be My Baby', 'Can't Buy Me Love', 'Baby's In Black', 'Act Naturally', 'A Hard Day's Night', 'Help!' and 'I'm Down'. At some dates on the tour Ringo's solo featured 'I Wanna Be Your Man' when that song replaced 'Act Naturally'.

For the spectacular final song at Shea, John Lennon delighted the crowd, and his fellow Beatles, by playing the organ run on 'I'm Down' using his elbows. This was a rare flash of exuberance and pleasure, and a brief throwback to the boyish delight they showed in every encounter on their first visit to America in February 1964.

The documentary was filmed using a dozen camera operators in the helicopter and in the stadium, and the resulting film, shown on BBC at 8pm on March 1st 1966, and then on ABC on American television in January 1967, is replete with priceless images. There is a very telling vignette as the group start to emerge from the underground area in response to Sullivan's words "Loved here in America, here are The Beatles!" The pathway onto the field was guarded by a number of policemen who moved aside to allow the group to run between them. One anonymous policeman is facing the crowd, watching for signs of trouble. As the first Beatle, McCartney, appeared, the noise level improbably, impossibly shot up by several decibels. In response, the policeman's face was etched in pain and he clapped his hands to his ears as if trying to protect himself from the wall of sound.

During the intro to 'Baby's in Black', Lennon stops as he notices a lone girl desperately trying to run across the vast space between the seats and the stage. Inevitably she was apprehended before she could get anywhere near them. But it was a constant surge of people, invariably girls, leaping over the fences and trying desperately to cross the preposterously wide spaces to the stage before capture. None of them made it. The footage shows dozens being lifted bodily and carried away to some secure area, while other police are more active in consoling sobbing fans, occasionally reviving a girl who had fainted to the floor.

The crowd scenes are impressive and yet intimidating. Dozens of young girls imprisoned behind chain fencing. Mothers solicitously handing out handkerchiefs and tissues to their distraught daughters. Middle-aged couples in loafers and sneakers looking as though they are on their way back from a yard sale. Cops sitting two metres apart behind white, temporary fences staring nervously at the unprecedented scenes in the stadium seats.

In the middle of 'A Hard Day's Night' the camera swings back to take in Brian Epstein standing solicitously at the side of the stage, head bobbing gently in time to the music, looking for all the world like a deputy sales manager at a wedding. His eyes leave the group as he stares round at the amazing panorama of people - all there to see his boys.

The final number of the concert, McCartney's raucous 'I'm Down', crashes to a halt. The group bow and say Goodbye before hurrying off the field, causing another mad stampede out of the seats to get onto the field. The police are suddenly over-run.

Having completed their standard 30-minute set of a dozen numbers, minus a fair number of the standard lyrics, they climbed back into the white Wells Fargo van, $160,000 richer, which amounts to just under $100 per second of their performance.

When they had discussed the arrangements for the show Epstein asked Sid Bernstein what he was going to charge for admission. Bernstein replied, "$5.50, $5.75." The cautious Epstein then asked what would happen if Bernstein couldn't fill Shea Stadium, and, laughing, Bernstein told him that he would pay Epstein $10 for every unsold seat.

Sid Bernstein didn't have to pay an extra cent to Brian Epstein. The concert at Shea Stadium was epoch-making, one of the great events in rock and pop history and represents one of the pinnacles of achievement for the Beatles, for Brian Epstein, and principally for the remarkable Sid Bernstein.

If my research into the McCartney and Epstein story exposed me to the host of sharks and con-men and racketeers who infested the Beatles story I was also fortunate enough to learn something about some very fine human beings. By any estimation Sid Bernstein would be near the top, if not at the summit, of that list.

The Beatles returned to their isolated glory at the Warwick and held court there for twenty-four hours. The day after the Shea Stadium concert had been held in reserve in case the weather proved so bad that a day's postponement was required. The balmy weather on the 15th meant that the concert went ahead without problems, and in the process gave the Beatles a full day off to recover from the bewildering wonder that was Shea Stadium.

The Warwick became a musical retreat for a day with the Beatles being visited by American musical royalty including the Exciters, The Supremes, the Ronettes and, of course, Bob Dylan. It wasn't an occasion for jamming, for trying out new songs. Instead it was an occasion for story and anecdote, mainly circling around the amazing events in Queens the previous evening.

WABC again managed to stage a remote broadcast from the Beatles' hotel. As a lasting commemoration of the Shea Stadium appearance, radio station WABC initiated a contest to allow a listener to design a medal to honour the group. This most unlikely tribute was named "The Order of the All American" medal, and was awarded to each of the four Beatles by Bruce Morrow.

As with the previous New York appearance the remote microphones placed by WABC technicians were invaluable in providing WABC with easy and guaranteed access to the Beatles in their hotel suite for the medal awarding ceremony.

Inevitably it was given maximum exposure on-air with the repeated declaration, "Yet another Beatles exclusive from WABC".

Only Aspinall and Barrow remained almost permanently in the suite. Both Brian Epstein and Mal Evans went out for the evening. Epstein was, yet again, treading a very dangerous path in some of the less fashionable clubs around Times Square. Evans only went six floors away from the 33rd floor where the Beatles were taking audience with Dylan and the rest.

Mal Evans went, by prior arrangement, to the suite on the 27th floor at the Warwick where, he learned over drinks, one of Chrissie's colleagues, somebody called Byrne, had a suite permanently reserved.

Chrissie explained that for various reasons Byrne had been called out of town for the week, leaving the suite free. Chrissie commandeered it, and she and the very willing Mal Evans put it to very good use that night.

Epstein had ensured that a plane was permanently on hire for the Beatles party for the duration of the tour and the plane, a Lockheed Electra from American Flyers, was on standby to transport them north to Toronto, ready for the concerts at the Maple Leaf Gardens on August 17th. Two concerts had been arranged, each attended by 35,000 people, and these passed off relatively incident free. More serious problems occurred earlier that morning when, having flown into Toronto, the group and their party were ferried to their hotel, the King Edward Sheraton. This was the same hotel used in their trip to Toronto the previous year, which in itself was unusual.

The disruption, the upset caused to other guests, even the occasional severe damage, invariably meant that hotel management were reluctant to accept repeat bookings from the Beatles.

And of course their overwhelming fame meant that it was no longer possible to register for rooms under the anonymous label of messrs. Lennon, McCartney, Harrison and Starr. It worked once with the Plaza; that ploy would never work at that august establishment again.

By the summer of 1965, the worldwide fame of the Beatles meant that any approach to a hotel would bring instant recognition, followed invariably by the turning down of the proposed booking.

However, the situation at the King Edward Sheraton was rather different. They had welcomed the Beatles back to the hotel and been relieved to find that the scenes in King Street outside the hotel were less frenzied and chaotic than the previous year.

Then there were thousands of kids besieging the hotel and keeping up a nonstop curtain of noise outside in the street. The more laid-back atmosphere in 1965 meant that disruption at the King Edward was mostly confined to a number of enterprising fans who had booked rooms in the hotel for the likely nights of the Beatles visit.

Such people, being guests who had paid in full for rooms, could not be ejected just because they were clearly there to hunt for the Beatles. This presented new problems for security at the hotel, and also for occasional Beatles security like Neil Aspinall and Mal Evans, and this pattern would be repeated at other cities across America. The problems in the streets had largely disappeared but had been concentrated far more inside the hotel buildings.

Epstein had decreed that the Beatles party would follow the travelling pattern established so successfully during the previous American tour. As soon as a concert finished, unless there was a second one scheduled at the same venue, the group would race off-stage, into the waiting secure transport, and then speed to the local airport where the Lockheed Electra would be fuelled and ready to take off. Invariably the Beatles party were in the air in less than an hour from the end of the concert. They would fly to the next city on the schedule, land, and be ferried to the hotel where they would be locked in, partly by the security and partly by the fans, before the race to the venue during the afternoon or evening.

It was a bruising, claustrophobic life, and not difficult to understand why it had begun to pall. Even luxury can get boring when there is nothing else, 24 hours a day.

From Toronto, the plane took them south to Atlanta where they were scheduled to play just one show at the local baseball stadium on August 18th, albeit to another huge crowd of 35,000. Most unusually for venues on that tour, the Atlanta Stadium was equipped with a superlative sound system which meant that the group could, to their amazement, hear what they were playing. It was noticeable that in a succession of press conferences after Atlanta one or more Beatles would make a point of praising the quality of the sound produced at what became known as the Atlanta–Fulton County Stadium. They didn't say that its quality showed up the inadequacies of the equivalent systems at other venues. They didn't need to!

After Atlanta it was on to Houston, arriving at the airport known locally as Hobby just after 2am. This was the first instance of real trouble from the crowds, mainly because police and security was totally inadequate for the task before them. Even as the Beatles plane touched down there were people racing across the runway towards it, from a crowd estimated at some four thousand - even at that hour in the morning.

As the plane slowed to a halt in front of the terminal people began climbing onto the wings and the fuselage. Most were merely excited to be so close to their heroes but there were others, stoked on drink or substances, who were oblivious to the trouble they were causing and the dangers they were creating.

There was a group of a couple of dozen dancing on one of the wings, cigarettes in virtually every hand, and this within feet of the fuel tanks on the plane.

Even though it was approaching 3am it was a very warm, sultry night in Houston and the kids on and around the plane were in a party mood, and there were hardly any police or security on hand to restore order.

The Beatles party was marooned on the plane for almost thirty minutes before a forklift truck, accompanied by three policemen came to give them an ungainly, but welcome, escape from the plane. The forklift was a vehicle normally used for loading food onto planes, and clearly unsuitable for offloading any passengers let alone very important people like the Beatles and their colleagues.

In the circumstances they didn't have the luxury of debating the issue. The party clambered out of a rear door onto the forklift which started to back away from the plane to lower the party to ground level to get into the Brinks armoured truck which was hovering near the tail of the plane.

Unfortunately some of the excited crown jumping and dancing on the wings caught sight of the Beatles making their escape. Shrieks of joy and feverish pointing at the forklift alerted the rest of the crowd who immediately started advancing on the truck. In the melee, even though it seemed like a madcap scene from "A Hard Day's Night", one of the party suffered a serious injury.

Brian Epstein, one of the last to leave the plane, was left with one foot on the plane and one on the forklift as it began to retreat from the plane to escape the feverish crowd. Epstein lost his balance and dropped some five metres onto the tarmac, landing on and severely damaging his back.

He was carefully picked up and taken to the hospital by taxi while the group went via the Brinks truck to their base at the downtown Sheraton-Lincoln Hotel. Another undistinguished scamper from the truck to a dirty and smelly freight elevator led them finally to their suite of rooms on the 10th floor.

Epstein returned an hour later, clearly in pain, and even more highly dosed than was often the case. He claimed that it was only bruising but the damage caused by the Houston fall would affect and afflict him for the rest of his life.

There were two concerts in Houston at the Sam Houston Coliseum in front of just over 25,000 fans. If anything, the conditions backstage were the worst that the Beatles party had experienced in America, with the only fortunate note being that the backstage chaos wasn't replicated in the security. The oppressive high summer heat seemed to calm people down although there were still isolated instances of heavy-handed policing which caused Mal Evans regular concern.

There was a vicious circle precedent being set where the police and security in a particular city were anticipating trouble and so dealt with the young crowd in ways that were often quite physical but were not always required or necessary.

But inevitably in such situations, violence, from whatever direction, prompted more violence or trouble as a response, and so the spiral begin. And the unfortunate repercussion was that police and security in the next city on the tour, or further down the schedule, heard about the trouble - often seeing the scenes on the evening news - and made their preparations accordingly. Those preparations never involved a reduction in forces or force.

As usual the party left immediately after the Houston concert and flew during the night to the next venue, Chicago. Police preparations were already well advanced but the trouble in Houston caused a speedy re-evaluation. The police immediately refused permission for the Beatles plane to land at O'Hare Airport because of the disruption they feared it would cause. Instead it was diverted as it approached Chicago and landed with little fanfare at Midway Airport early on the morning of the concert. Only some four hundred fans had guessed they'd be there, but there were still more than two thousand distraught and disappointed fans out at O'Hare who took some persuading that the Beatles would not be coming to the airport.

The usual limousine cavalcade ferried them across Chicago to their appointed hotel which was the Sahara Hotel in Schiller Park. The hotel management, in a gesture of magnificent stupidity, had made an announcement that the Beatles would be staying there. The same management were then surprised and outraged when their establishment was swamped by noisy, enthusiastic fans desperate to meet a Beatle. So much din was created by the fans racing around the building, which was woefully underprepared for such scenes, that most guests, including the Beatles party, got little if any sleep.

The doubleheader at Comiskey Park later that day took in shows at 3pm and 8pm in front of more than 50,000 fans. The police inside the Stadium had drawn up a robust plan with a firm line of policemen standing shoulder to shoulder guarding the plywood bandstand which had been erected on second base on the field. The scenes at Chicago mirrored those a few nights earlier at Shea although on a smaller scale and without the overwhelming sense of history being made.

All of the grandstands in the bleachers surrounding second base were overflowing with excited fans, and there seemed to be a real empathy between the group and the fans that day. John Lennon appeared on stage wearing the black leather cap which would become a major fashion item in the following months, and he was still wearing the cap an hour later when the Beatles were able to enjoy one of those rare and all too infrequent moments of normality.

On the way back to the hotel, the party, augmented by a bunch of girls accompanying the Beatles, called in to Margie's Candies, a part sweet shop and part sit-down ice-cream parlour, in Bucktown on the north side of Chicago. They ordered several six scoop Atomic Sundaes which the four Beatles shared with the girls, while Mal kept guard at the front door like an American secret serviceman guarding the President.

It was a brief passage away from the madness, which was demonstrated by the fact that receipts at Comiskey exceeded $150,000 compared with a year earlier when at the Chicago Amphitheatre the show made less than 20% of that figure, albeit from just one performance.

But even in the midst of the back pain caused in Houston, Brian Epstein was viciously aware that he needed to ensure that the takings were as high as possible to compensate for the Seltaeb losses. The legal situation, as mournfully described by Nat Weiss, was starting to turn ugly and yet everywhere Epstein looked, there seemed to be thousands of the infernal Seltaeb promoted merchandise items.

In a rare break from the established pattern the Beatles made a flight in daylight on the afternoon of August 21st and were greeted by approximately 3000 fans at the airport. The afternoon flight was a matter of convenience owing to the relatively short distance between Chicago and the location for their next concert, Minneapolis in Minnesota. This was just one show at the Twin Cities Metropolitan Stadium, with a crowd of approximately 22,000 people, disappointing in the 40,000 seater stadium. It became a matter of local myth that the promoter of the concert, Reggie Colihan who was known locally as "Big Reggie", was the only promoter who managed to lose money on promotions for the Beatles and the Rolling Stones.

Scenes of that Minneapolis concert show wide open spaces in the stands, criminal gaps given the huge demand for tickets. The story in the area was that the promoter had come under pressure not to actively promote the concert because of fear of riots, but despite the trouble at the airport, Minnesota seemed no more prone to massive violence than any other city on the tour. The intercession of the local police chief may have had an effect though, as the Beatles were to discover when they finally got back to their hotel.

Once again the stage had been erected near second base, some forty yards from the nearest fan. The enjoyment of the fans, and even that of the group, was spoiled by the pitifully inadequate sound system, and this was yet another example of the recurring nightmare where the group lost interest in their performance because the screaming was so loud and constant that nothing could be heard. And even on the very rare occasions when the crowd din subsided, the PA system was almost always woefully inadequate to carry the group's sound with any true power to the audience.

There was another sound problem at Minneapolis. The audience and the performers were constantly assailed by the constant circling of a press helicopter above the crowd. The noise and the downdraft was an irritation throughout virtually the entire Beatles performance but the authorities seemed powerless to intervene. In addition the helicopter was fitted with a sign from which flashed the message "Welcome Beatles".

Fortunately the security and the police were well-equipped to deal with any trouble. A contingent of three hundred police officers, all furnished with 42-inch-long sticks, were on duty, complemented by the Metropolitan Stadium security crew of 150 ushers, and both ushers and police had been supplied with smelling salts to use in case fans fainted.

There was a small-scale press conference held before the concert in the Minnesota Room inside the stadium. Five policemen nervously shunted the group into the room which eventually held over 150 people in a sweaty, bad-tempered encounter. It was made lighter by one of the few charming moments of the whole tour when a local disc jockey, Bill Diehl from WDGY, brought on two young representatives of a local music shop, B-Sharp Music. They presented George Harrison with a brand new Rickenbacker 360-12 guitar on behalf of the musicians of Minnesota.

Harrison was delighted and genuinely touched, especially when he heard later that the idea of providing it came several weeks earlier when another Liverpool group, the Remo Four, had visited the shop and bought a Rickenbacker and told the staff that their friends the Beatles would love one.

Another Liverpool link in the press conference came to light years later when it emerged that participating in the event as a representative of station KOMA in Oklahoma City was a young Liverpudlian called John Ravenscroft. He would go on to permanent fame in Britain as DJ, John Peel.

As part of the regular routine of subterfuge to try to get the group out safely, the fans were allowed to surround a limousine parked conspicuously outside the stadium. No announcements were made but the fans made the obvious inference that the Beatles would be leaving the stadium in that vehicle.

Instead Mal and Neil furtively sneaked the four Beatles into a Falconers' laundry vehicle which gave them a bumpy and uncomfortable ride to their hotel, the Leamington Motor Lodge on 4th Ave. The laundry truck wasn't fitted with seats and so the Beatles were forced to use folding chairs which had been left in the back of the truck for them.

Efforts had been made to fool the fans into thinking that the group were staying elsewhere in the area, but the fans were getting wise to the regular subterfuge. It was an unusual night on that 1965 tour, a throwback to earlier, simpler times. Do the show, stay overnight at a local hotel, and then leave sometime the following day for the next venue.

There was a certain amount of crazy self-publicity from the hotel about the possibility of the Beatles staying there, and that problem was then aggravated by a shocking inadequacy in the security provision at the Lodge. Once again the advice offered by the people who knew the situation best of all, Epstein and Evans and Aspinall, wasn't ignored. It wasn't even requested.

So the bedlam at the airport had resulted in a mob of more than 3000 fans charging the plane and then the Beatles cars, leaving the 55 Bloomington policemen surprisingly incapable of dealing with the large crowd.

And then the hotel was pathetically understaffed by security staff. The group and their party were unable to rest, assailed by constant raucous noise from the crowd in the street and even hordes of fans who had gained entrance and were roaming the corridors. Most unusually, the hotel employees proved less than perfect hosts and seemed as intent on securing a Beatles souvenir as any of the fans. And into this chaos stepped an overbearing superstar, Minneapolis Police Inspector Donald Dwyer. This representative of the Minneapolis force had clearly taken early exception to what he perceived as the wanton behaviour of the Beatles. Matters came to a head when he threatened to arrest Paul McCartney for having a young woman in his room.

The young blonde woman in question came out of the room to prove that she was not a local resident and was, contrary to Dewer's suspicions, over 21, but Dewer, guardian of local morality, was accusing the Beatles party of luring young girls into their rooms on the fifth floor of the hotel. The situation was proving tempestuous and Epstein, because of pills and the pain from the back condition, was in no state to exert his normal charming, and occasionally lucrative, control over the situation.

Instead Evans and Aspinall and Barrow had to suggest caution and prudence, and that sensible advice was taken but that just meant that the party were even more delighted than usual to get out of that city the following morning.

Inspector Dewer never had the misfortune of coming across the Beatles again. On the tour of the country that took place a year later there was no return to Minneapolis. It is quite likely that the bids from other cities in that part of the country were higher, but it is also quite likely that counsel from voices like Aspinall, Evans and Barrow let alone the four Beatles themselves would have argued against any return.

Instead the redoubtable Inspector Dewer was able to concentrate his considerable energies on playing a major role in the race troubles in the city in the following two years. His delicate leadership of the riot squad during disturbances in 1966 and 1967 was particularly inspired. During the Aquatennial Torchlight Parade there was an altercation caused, Dewer stated, by two black girls fighting over a wig that one was wearing. Police intervention led to a stand-off with a crowd around two hundred strong. There were claims that police used a club or a stick on one of the women, but whatever the background, Dewer used his riot squad to restore and enforce order.

And the Beatles, quite coincidentally, never would return to Minneapolis. But if they thought that flying out of the city would end their problems they were to be shockingly proved wrong.

Take-off was routine. Relatively few fans had struggled out to the airport and the journey, virtually due west to Oregon, was going very smoothly until, around three hours into the flight, one of the four engines on the Lockheed Electra caught fire. At that time the plane was flying through a deep gorge which had the effect of adding to the drama of the smoke pouring out of the stricken engine.

The pilot got the plane to land safely but the situation was sufficiently serious for several people on the plane to fear the worst, and more than one Beatle had cause to remember the premonitions about Buddy Holly that had caused them to take the train to Washington in February 1964. Indeed John Lennon was moved to scribble a quick self-obituary on a small piece of paper which he hastily folded inside a film canister, believing that it might survive any crash. The plane managed to make it into Portland but the damage to the engine was too severe to be quickly repaired and so arrangements had to be made for a replacement plane to be flown into Portland for the use of the Beatles party for the remainder of the tour. The replacement was a Constellation which they used for the remaining week of the tour, but ironically and sadly the repaired Electra crashed the following year into a hill on approach to Ardmore Municipal Airport in Oklahoma, killing all 5 crew members and 78 of the 93 passengers on board the plane.

Fortunately no disaster happened approaching Portland, but it was yet another grim day on a tour which had precious little joy for those in the Beatles party.

And yet Oregon signalled the weary arrival on the west coast, the leaving behind of many of the more pressing problems, and finally, thankfully, the last phase of the tour.

There were two shows at the Memorial Coliseum in Portland, made most notable because of a visit backstage after the first show from two of the Beach Boys, Carl Wilson and Mike Love, who managed to get backstage access through the intervention of local radio DJ, Steve Brown of KISN. The meeting between the pop superstars was largely uneventful apart from a question from Paul McCartney asking Carl where his brother Brian, the leader of the Beach Boys, was. On being told that Brian Wilson had abandoned touring, in favour of staying at home, and concentrating on producing and recording, McCartney and Lennon exchanged a telling glance. It was another silence that spoke volumes although McCartney's brief comment to the effect that it sounded like a good idea was to have greater import in the months ahead. Another notable visitor to the concert was poet, Allen Ginsberg, who sat in the audience and later wrote a poem about the concert which he called "Portland Coliseum".

To compensate for the time spent waiting in Portland before the two shows the Beatles contract provided for them to be supplied with various luxuries. Anybody with any knowledge of modern rock star contract riders, and even myself with my more limited exposure to the demands of various television divas, would be shocked at the paucity and simplicity of the demands made by the Beatles who were, at the time of the Portland concerts, undeniably the most successful and famous show business act in the world.

The Portland promoter was asked to supply a portable dressing room, preferably a house trailer which should include four cots, mirrors, an ice cooler, portable TV set, and clean towels. On a wider front, the group requested adequate police protection, plus a hi-fidelity sound system with an adequate number of speakers, and finally a platform for Ringo Starr and his drums. In terms of transportation, the demands were equally simple, being Two (2) seven-passenger Cadillac limousines (air-conditioned if possible), with chauffeurs.

That was it. No white Arabian ponies bearing ice sculptures of the act, or bowls of exotic fruits flown in from Europe, or entirely white rooms, or vats of chewy sweets with all the brown ones removed.

Minimal, and very simple, requirements with perhaps the most notable being item number 5 on the rider which reminded the promoter that "Artists will not be required to perform before a segregated audience." That was an unusual and a brave stance for an act to take in America at that time, and Epstein and the Beatles deserve to be commended for their stand.

There was a definite easing of tension in Portland, and the closeness to the west coast was clearly a major factor. And, like any group of schoolchildren counting down the days to the start of the school holidays, arrival on the west coast meant that the number of days left to endure the misery of the tour could be counted in single figures.

They left Portland late on the night of August 23rd directly after the concert. The damage to the Electra had ruled it out of consideration and so there was a Constellation waiting on the runway for them. Given the fact that the Constellation could not make the journey as fast as the Electra there was some discussion on the plane about whether or not they should stay the night in Portland. Unfortunately Epstein's state of mind, largely because of the back problems, was such that he was less organised, less decisive than usual. The debate ran on for many minutes with the limousine and driver waiting on the tarmac before Mal Evans sprinted down to tell the driver that he could leave.

Five minutes later the plane was airborne with more than one of the passengers glancing nervously out at the wings, totally conscious that the flight on the previous day could have turned out tragically.

In this case, fortunately, the seven hundred mile flight south to Los Angeles passed without incident and the Beatles and Epstein plus figures like Aspinall and Evans were able to doze fitfully until the plane landed well before dawn.

Once again NEMS had taken advantage of the few days rest in Los Angeles and so a house, owned by Zsa Zsa Gabor, had been reserved and rented in Benedict Canyon in Beverly Hills. The house rental was made supposedly under strict security, but yet again local radio stations and the press were passing out the "secret" address within hours of the group landing in the city. The imposing house had four bedrooms, six baths, hardwood floors, two wet bars, five fireplaces, a wine cellar, pool, and six-car garage. With the security in constant attendance on the far side of the gates it was an ideal retreat for the group, and the perfect place to spend their last few days on the tour.

But the security could never keep the fans out entirely and there were constant attempts to climb the exterior walls to gain admission to the property. Once again the general area was flooded by fans desperate to find and see the Beatles, but the frenzy was less extreme and widespread than in the previous tour and even the police were able to be rather more relaxed than had been expected. There were twenty police on duty on the start but that was reduced to just a dozen police officers by the second day, and they were backed up by several security men provided by the Burns Agency.

That air of relaxation permeated through to the group who were able to enjoy several days rest and relaxation in that beautiful setting, and at least some of the anxieties created on the American tour started to ease. The routine at Benedict Canyon consisted of breakfast at around 2pm, sunbathing and swimming during the afternoon, then dinner followed by a private screening of the latest films. The house had a magnificent view across the canyon and was the perfect place for them to unwind.

While the group and the road managers relaxed by the pool Epstein and Barrow were out in Los Angeles holding meetings about matters relating to the Beatles and the rest of the NEMS stable.

One highly significant meeting took place in a room at Capitol on the second day in the city. Epstein had already endured a fairly abrasive meeting with some of the Capitol marketing people who had presented him with a complete overview of sales activity for the Beatles since the start of the year.

Obviously the numbers were impressive, stunningly so, but Epstein, more irascible than usual because of the back pain, was bewildered and annoyed by the way the American release schedule differed so glaringly from the tried and trusted British schedule.

Because the situation was so stressful he was not in the best of moods when he moved gingerly into the next room for the next meeting. His temper was not improved by the realisation that in moving into the next room he was passing within a few feet of the Aladdin's Cave which had affected him so badly the previous year. The Aladdin's Cave of Seltaeb merchandise.

Seltaeb. That name again.

Fortunately the second meeting was to prove a major distraction from the Seltaeb nightmare. Epstein sat down with representatives of King Enterprises, the company with whom he had agreed a contract late in 1964 to produce a Beatles cartoon series for television. The main purpose of the meeting was to show Epstein examples of the artwork which would feature in the show and on the wide table were laid cells showing the illustrations of Lennon, McCartney, Harrison and Starr plus a few backgrounds.

Epstein readily admitted that he was no expert on animation styles and processes but he promised to take the cells back for the Beatles to view. Then the meeting turned to the harsh commercial aspects of the deal. Epstein was shown tables of figures displaying the various agreements that had already been reached for overseas sales of the programme. He was also told that American transmission of the first programme was only weeks away, with that initial show scheduled to appear on ABC on the morning of Saturday, September 25th - just three weeks after the Beatles party was due to fly home from America.

In another time Epstein would have been intrigued, fascinated by the material relating to the cartoon series, but he was too tired and too battered by the happenings of the past three weeks to be able to concentrate on matters of detail. And even if he had been in the mood, his attention was completely diverted by the revelation as the meeting ground to a conclusion.

The representative from King, after regaling Epstein with projected figures and visuals, enthusiastically told the Beatles manager about the plans and possibilities for merchandising prompted by the programme.

Merchandising was already being discussed and planned in conjunction with the approved merchandising company, Seltaeb.

Seltaeb. That name again.

For the Beatles, the stay in Benedict Canyon was idyllic. Long, leisurely days by the pool, eating, drinking and indulging themselves with their new favourite substance, LSD. On August 24th they entertained a number of friends who braved the security outside the house and came in to meet the Beatles. At various times over the day they were visited by Eleanor Bron, their friend from the "Help" filming, and also Peter Fonda. The latter encounter was highly fuelled by Lennon's consumption of acid and he also claimed later that his song 'She Said She Said' came directly as a result of his conversation with Fonda that day.

On the same evening the group and Epstein were invited back to the palatial home of Alan Livingstone, still riding high as head of Capitol Records. It was a glittering social occasion during which the group were presented with a number of gold records and other awards signifying their incredible commercial success during the previous year. It was a high visibility Hollywood event studded with Los Angeles royalty, names like Jane Fonda, Rock Hudson, Groucho Marx, Dean Martin, Hayley and Juliet Mills, James Stewart, Edward G. Robinson, Jack Benny, Vince Edwards, Gene Barry, and Richard Chamberlain. To fit in with the setting and the background of many of the guests, the evening concluded with a screening of Clive Donner's film, "What's New Pussycat" which had only been on release for a few weeks.

McCartney and Harrison slipped away while the film was still in progress. They had been contacted by Derek Taylor to inform them about and invite them to a Byrds recording session where they were working on a track which would appear later that year on their next album 'Turn Turn Turn'. The track they were recording that night in front of the two Beatles was the Dylan classic, 'The Times They Are A Changin''.

The following day meant more relaxation and lazing by the pool, enlivened during the afternoon when two girls leaped from a helicopter and landed in the pool in front of the startled Beatles. The security outside the gates had raced into the area around the pool when they saw how low the helicopter was hovering, and they were able to grab the two girls and get them off the premises very quickly. The Beatles and Evans thought the incident was very funny and showed admirable enterprise on the part of the two girls, but Epstein, mindful of earlier threats of shots at the Beatles, complained bitterly to the police who ensured that an exclusion area was imposed above the house.

Epstein was suffering severe pain from the back injury and this was bringing him to increased consumption of uppers and downers. He was managing his time in the house carefully, preparing for the final few concerts and also for the summit meeting which had been arranged for the 27th. That night, the Beatles were due to meet their greatest hero, Elvis.

The meeting had been arranged by Epstein and the manager of Elvis Presley, the legendary Colonel Tom Parker. The negotiations leading up to the eventual meeting were delicate and prolonged, paying due attention to the needs of security and also the essential need to ensure that no offence, intentional or accidental, would be given to any of those attending the session.

With a concern for detail more suitable for a major political summit, the negotiations were concluded and so, just before 10 p.m. on the 27th, Colonel Parker and one of the Memphis Mafia, Joe Esposito, went in a couple of limousines to the Benedict Canyon house. They picked up McCartney, Lennon, Harrison and Starr, plus Brian Epstein and Mal Evans, and returned quickly to 565 Perugia Way where Elvis had been staying since his return from location filming on "Paradise, Hawaiian Style".

Perhaps surprisingly there was a large crowd by the gate. Epstein was concerned that Elvis or the Colonel might suspect that the Beatles camp had released details of the meeting, but the culprit was much closer to home. Although the Colonel did not have any press involved in the meeting he had carefully leaked a hint about the meeting to a few fan clubs, and the result was bedlam on Perugia Way.

The Beatles walked up to the front door just before 11pm to find their host waiting on the doorstep to greet them. He escorted the four Beatles into a massive living room where the men stood awkwardly at first until Elvis broke the ice, and from that point it was a convivial and revealing evening, with the two most powerful managers in history, Parker and Epstein, smiling good-naturedly at the antics of their boys.

There was some music, much discussion - not least because on both sides, Beatles and Elvis, they were meeting and speaking to one of the very, very few people on the planet who understood just what it was like at that exalted level of stardom.

Eventually it all broke up just after 2am, and the Beatles party left bearing gifts of a complete set of Elvis albums, gun holsters and attached gold leather belts, and, curiously, a table lamp shaped like a wagon.

Lennon, in particular, was disappointed by the visit, feeling that it reinforced his long-held view that Elvis died in the army. Perhaps the most vivid impression was made on people like Mal Evans who learned that Elvis permanently carried ten road managers and all of them, with their wives and families, lived in the house with him either in Memphis or LA. During the evening, in conversation with people like Joe Esposito and Alan Fortas, Mal Evans began to see just what demands the Beatles organisation made of him and for what comparatively meagre rewards.

Men like Mal Evans didn't join the Beatles to get rich, but it seemed extremely unfair that huge amounts of money were being made and very, very little of it percolated down to people like Evans and Aspinall.

There wasn't time for the usual leisurely start to the day on August 28th. Epstein, Evans and Aspinall ushered the group out onto a customised luxury touring couch to make the road trip down to San Diego. Normally they would have flown, but an airline strike was having a real effect, and causing problems for air traffic. As a result it was decided that politically it would make sense to make the relatively short journey, at least in American terms, by road. The promoters initially offered to put a very ostentatious tour bus at the disposal of the group, but Epstein decided to make his own arrangements.

Down the exotic beauty of the coast highway, through Long Beach, San Juan Capistrano and San Clemente, down to San Diego for the usual set in front of 21,000 fans at Balboa Stadium.

Yet again this was a concert which was not a complete sell-out, with more than 10,000 seats remaining unoccupied. Clearly there were concerns that the fabulous interest in the Beatles, as displayed so vividly in 1964, had dimmed, although there were suspicions that the late date confirming the show meant that advertising and selling tickets was compromised. In addition a well-publicised rivalry between two local radio stations, KCBQ and KGB, may have contributed to confusion about the concert which then had an impact on ticket sales.

The show opened at 8pm. with 17,013 fans inside the Balboa Stadium on a warm Californian evening. After the same backing ensemble which had been with them since Shea Stadium - Brenda Holloway et al - the Beatles were introduced at 9pm by Les Turpin, the programme director at KGB. They dashed on, delivered their usual breathless thirty-one minute set, and then it was over.

There had been talk that a local British eccentric named Lord Tim, who purported to know the Beatles personally, would play a major part in the proceedings, but local power politics ruled him out. Instead he disappeared into the background and spent twenty years building up stories of his exploits and planning how he could wreck the life of England cricket legend, Ian Botham.

As the concert pounded through the final number, the group were watching as ever for the transport out of the stadium. The tour bus had pulled in to stand behind the stage and at the final bow the four Beatles ran for the safety of the bus as the fans broke through the chain link fence and stormed towards the stage.

They made the bus safely but then - nothing. The engine refused to start, and the Beatles party watched, increasingly nervously, as the driver tried to start the engine as the crowd turned away from the stage and headed for the vehicle.

Finally, the engine turned over and the bus pulled slowly away then raced out of Balboa Stadium to leave the fans behind on the field. But thoughts that the problems were over were dispelled shortly afterwards when more mechanical problems forced the bus to grind to a halt in the parking area of a San Diego mortuary, Abbott & Hast. The Beatles were left in the ignominious position of being forced to move all their equipment and possessions into a fleet of rented limousines to get them back to Los Angeles. Because of the delay, a large number of fans caught up with the Beatles party and there were frequent incidents on the journey back to Beverly Hills. On one occasion, at a halt on the road, gangs of fans leapt from their cars and started jumping on the cars containing the Beatles.

It took all the efforts of people like Mal Evans to get the kids off the cars without harming them - kids and cars - but it was a messy, unpleasant, frightening end to the concert and a reminder of unsettling scenes earlier in the tour.

But it was nearly over. There were only two nights in the warm luxury of the Hollywood Bowl before the final date in San Francisco, and then home. The first Hollywood Bowl concert was preceded by yet another PR event at Capitol Tower where Alan Livingstone presented them with a gold disc for sales of the "Help!" soundtrack plus other awards. Then they were led into the security of a Brinks truck which took them out to the Bowl.

It was noticeable that security had been stepped up and policemen were clearly visible on the hills surrounding the Bowl, in an obvious attempt to deter kids without tickets from making trouble. Once again it was a capacity 18,000 crowd although that number was swelled by one when a fan gave birth to a baby boy in the car park before the show.

Apart from unexpected births the concert went ahead largely without trouble, although Capitol's latest attempt to deliver a professional recording of the Beatles Live in Concert were thwarted, yet again. Problems with McCartney's microphone meant that announcements and vocals on the first few songs were distorted or inaudible.

In the event the two shows at the Hollywood Bowl in 1965 were recorded, although despite the misleading sleeve information, the album "Beatles Live at the Hollywood Bowl" which was released in 1977, is a combination of performances from 1964 and 1965, a triumph of George Martin's ability to concoct a masterpiece from not entirely wonderful material.

During the concert a helicopter flew around the area bearing an illuminated sign that said "Boss radio KHJ welcomes the Beatles to Boss Angeles", but really Boss radio KHJ should have been saying goodbye. There was nothing like the trouble seen there the previous year, with the worst incident concerning one or two over-enthusiastic fans who suffered a soaking from diving into the pool. Nothing more violent than that. It was all very sedate after the wildness and brutality of Minneapolis and other stops on the tour, but it was almost done.

They went back to the house in Benedict Canyon after the final Hollywood Bowl concert and had a leisurely, dreamy party for the whole Beatles entourage plus the reporters who had stayed with them on the wearying jaunt around America. The pool-side party was a last chance to exchange good wishes before the trip north the following morning to San Francisco for the final shows of the 1965 tour, back again at the Cow Palace.

They had been scheduled to stay in the Cabana Hotel, a rather gaudy hotel on El Camino in the Californian town of Palo Alto, more famous now for Silicon Valley and Steve Jobs. In those days it was a much quieter and sedate place, but the peace was disrupted when the Beatles arrived on August 31st. The remote location, deemed sufficiently distant from the Cow Palace crowds, still managed to attract a screaming crowd of some three thousand fans who based themselves in and around the hotel's parking area and spilled out across El Camino Real. Some of the more impassioned fans even evaded the guards and tried to climb up the grating on the outside of the hotel, trying to reach the Beatles on the 8th floor, but fortunately police and hotel staff were able to get the crazed fans down before any major injury was suffered.

The police overtime bill for Palo Alto was huge. The local council reckoned that it cost almost $12,000 to organise a special detail of eighty men and thirty-two patrol cars to cover the hours that the Beatles were in the town. The hotel paid an additional $4300 for temporary security guards, many of whom were American football players from the University of Santa Clara team.

Despite the lavish security presence the greatest problems came at the traditional point of maximum weakness - arriving at or leaving a venue. At the hotel there were chaotic, farcical scenes, again reminiscent of out-takes from "A Hard Day's Night" where gangs of young girls, plus a few boys, surrounded the Beatles cars, blocking off any point of escape either forward or back, and then climbed all over the cars and jumped and danced on the top.

In the comparable scene in "A Hard Day's Night" the director, Dick Lester, had told the Beatles to act scared. In Palo Alto they weren't acting.

Things were different the next morning, with the police learning from the frightening mistakes made during the Beatles arrival. The hotel and the security let it be announced that the group would be leaving their Room 810 Suite, taking the north side elevator down to ground level, heading past the Cabana kitchen and exiting the building through the service entrance.

To maintain the deception, two decoy limousines and a Brinks truck were positioned by the service entrance, but in fact the Beatles were directed by the police out of the hotel's south side entrance. There was a momentary confusion with the Beatles expecting, and looking around for, the usual limousine, but then the blue and white 1.5 ton delivery truck pulled in front of them. Desperate to avoid the fans who would only take moments to realise that they had been deceived, the driver raced away towards the exit only to be alerted by Beatle voices, in another unwitting echo of "A Hard Day's Night", that Ringo Starr had been left behind.

Brakes had to be hastily applied, and Mal Evans reacted quickest by dragging the solitary Beatle into the sanctuary of the back of the truck.

There was an afternoon and then an evening performance in front of first 11,700 people, and then 17,000 fans. The second and final Cow Palace show was even rowdier than many shows on the tour as many of the near-18,000 crowd went berserk during the 31-minute performance.

Before the group even reached the stage, a brunette teenage girl dashed through security and hurled herself at the group before being carried away by security. And that image, of young girls writhing in a mix of agony and ecstasy while being manhandled out of harm's way, was just one of the many vivid images from that concert. Dozens of girls threw themselves bodily at the stage and more than a few actually made it as far as being able to touch a Beatle. At that point even the successful ones were dragged away and the looks of resigned bewilderment which pass across the Beatles faces in the grainy YouTube footage are very telling.

During the evening performance there was a succession of major problems. The performance was actually halted because the security staff made the group aware that there was a serious medical problem in the audience. It fell to McCartney to appeal to the audience to move aside to allow the police and security to remove a pregnant woman who had fainted in the crush near the front. Dozens of fans collapsed and passed out when rows of seating, not secured as firmly as required, worked loose and allowed fans to push forward on those in front and rush the stage.

The fans were in many cases out of control, and fought with the police and security. The scenes were so bad that the Beatles had to leave the stage until order was restored.

They did come back. They did finish the show, but the mini-riot was symptomatic of the atmosphere which had pervaded and afflicted the whole tour.

The final amazing image from the concert and indeed the tour was when a line of newsmen, realising the danger of the situation, took up position facing the audience, standing side by side with arms linked to provide a barrier between the group and the audience who were threatening to go completely out of control.

Just as happened in Minneapolis, Mal Evans later remarked on the vivid similarity between that scene and some of the images in the film "Zulu" which he'd seen earlier in the year. A thin line of men nervously staring out at imminent attack, fearful of what would, could happen next.

And it was no wonder if one or more Beatles wondered, as they were smuggled away yet again in an armoured vehicle, if it was really worth it!

That battling chaos at Cow Palace neatly bookmarked the Beatles touring days in America, matching up with similar riots in San Francisco a year earlier at the very start of their first tour.

And though the Beatles would return to America for the third and final time in 1966, that was after "Bigger than Jesus", and after that nothing would or could be the same again.

By 1966, the band decided that individually and collectively they were finished with the complete craziness that accompanied their live performances. After a final Candlestick Park performance on August 29th 1966, the Beatles would never tour again, but San Francisco, and the incessant violence, played a major part in the evolution of that decision.

The Beatles party limped back to England, with Epstein suffering most of all from the effects of the long overnight journey. He had already asked the

NEMS office to book an appointment with his doctor for the day after the flight, fully aware that the strains of the flight would almost certainly have exacerbated the damage caused on the airport tarmac at Houston.

Before that he had to throw himself back into the NEMS routine immediately as, in his absence, there were a number of outstanding issues that needed handling. Chief on the list was meeting with David Jacobs to discuss the festering crisis with Seltaeb. He had news, bad news from America. Nat Weiss and Walter Hofer had met with Epstein three times during the duration of the tour to examine the situation and in particular the progress of the litigation. The information they passed on hadn't improved Epstein's mood in America. Thinking over the situation on the journey back across the Atlantic had made him both angry and pessimistic about the future. It was hard to ignore the nagging worry that Seltaeb was threatening to explode, and there was no telling where the fall-out might end.

But at least there was some good news to compensate for the gloom, and the sharpening pain in his back. There was news that Northern Songs had delivered a profit of £621,000 in the past year, and there was a congratulatory bottle of champagne and an invitation to dinner from Dick James. In response Epstein gave the champagne to one of the girls in the NEMS office and ignored the invitation. His days of socialising with Dick James were past, and they would never again enjoy the friendship so obvious in the early days of their relationship.

George Martin, hard on the announcement of his resignation as head of Parlophone, had let the music world know that he would be forming a new company, which would be known as AIR Productions. He would lead the company alongside two EMI other producers who were similarly tired of the constraints imposed by the major companies. Both the other producers had solid reputations in the industry and the likelihood that their years in the business would attract artists to their new production centre. But George Martin had the Beatles!

The group, and Brian Epstein, had encouraged Martin's ambitions, with the group particularly critical of the way he had been treated by EMI. The colossal success in 1963, 1964 and 1965 in Britain and around the world for NEMS artists wasn't down to George Martin, but he had played a significant role in that incredible story and the parsimonious response of EMI to Martin's modest and reasonable expectations of reward had rebounded on the company.

George Martin had left EMI after 15 years to offer himself as a producer for hire via Associated Independent Recording with the guarantee from his most famous clients that they would insist that he was the only producer they would use. EMI were left in the painful position of being forced to use the producer they had just shabbily allowed to leave their service and, to use him, be forced to pay much more than their norm.

EMI couldn't refuse. It was the Beatles making the demand and by 1965 nobody was in a position to say no to the Beatles.

Epstein could even look forward with some sense of anticipation to the launch of the cartoon series in America. He wasn't thrilled with the quality of all the artwork, although he was pleased to see that some instances seemed more impressive than others. This perturbed him until he learned that the scale of the work required for the cartoon series meant that King Enterprises, the company at the heart of the project had, through Al Brodax, put the animation work out to studios all over the world, including studios less than a mile from the NEMS offices in Argyll Street.

The genesis of the programme would have interested Epstein, had he not taken such a dislike to Al Brodax, the pugnacious New Yorker who had negotiated with him for the rights. After reaching agreement with Epstein in London, Brodax had sorted out investment for the planned programme with Anson Isaacson, President of A. C. Gilbert Company, which was a leading American toy manufacturer, responsible for the very successful Erector Set and also The Chemistry Set.

Brodax went to meet Isaacson at his Chicago office but was kept waiting for more than ninety minutes in the lobby. Eventually Isaacson bustled out, apologised profusely for keeping him waiting, and asked him what he was pitching. Brodax showed the initial artwork, some of the same pieces he had shown to Epstein, and Isaacson leafed through them and bought the programme, and commissioned a 26-part series - and all this without Brodax even getting through the door.

Of course, in 1964 just the name "The Beatles" was virtually a guarantee of success and Brodax's pitch, which was based on a plan of a short cartoon each week created around a story based on a single Beatles song, was almost irresistible.

And for Isaacson the huge attraction, apart from the investment potential of a share in the concern which made and sold the programmes, was the toy potential. Selling dolls and toys via a primetime Saturday morning kids cartoon based around the Beatles was, many reckoned, the most certain children's success since Mickey Mouse.

And it didn't take Isaacson long to get working on the merchandising possibilities running like a rich seam of gold through the planned programme, and that research led his marketing people to realise that there was one organisation they needed to speak to and deal with before the chance was lost.

Not the Beatles. Not NEMS. A company called Seltaeb.

By the end of 1964 Variety was able to announce the agreement between NEMS and King Partners, and the plans for airing in the fall of the following year. Following conversations with Anson Isaacson it emerged that James E.Duffy, VP of Sales at ABC had told Brodax that ABC would screen the twenty-six six-minute episodes as the completed series.

During the frantic months between the Variety announcement and the launch of the programme in September 1965 there was a fantastic amount of activity to complete the stories and the animation and to ensure that ABC didn't reject any of the work. The process was established where the storylines had to go to Brodax for approval, and then out to ABC for their sanction, and, once those vital two steps had been realised, the scriptwriters got involved.

To provide the all-important voices, given that there was no possibility whatsoever that the Beatles would contribute to the programme with any voiceovers, Brodax turned to an American star, Paul Frees, and an English stalwart, Lance Percival. In the final mix Lance Percival was asked to provide voices for McCartney and Starr, while Frees was responsible for Lennon and Harrison, plus any other voices that might crop up in the programme.

Even the voices and vocal styles had to be approved by ABC and on one memorable occasion in the early summer of 1965, Al Brodax travelled to London with Paul Frees and Ed Vane of ABC to meet Lance Percival and to decide what to do about the voices in the planned cartoon. Frees and Percival went through their paces in what was virtually an audition before both Vane, on behalf of ABC, and Brodax pronounced themselves satisfied. The strange thing about the process was that neither Frees nor Percival were trying to imitate the voices of the actual Beatles. Indeed Lance Percival freely admitted that he had deliberately made Ringo's voice slower than it actually was, and slightly more Birmingham than Liverpool. This was a deliberate, contrived attempt to make the cartoon more accessible to American ears, and worked superbly, even if the vocal characterisations were invariably hated by English people including the Beatles themselves.

But the massive success of the cartoon series was still in the future in the middle of September 1965. Epstein had given the Beatles several weeks off to recuperate from the strains of the American tour. They had split up after landing at Heathrow and he was slightly uneasy at the grimness with which they took their leave of him. Only Ringo Starr was anything like normal but collectively they gave the impression that the wounds caused by the American tour would take a considerable time to heal. With the other lingering problems, particularly Seltaeb, Epstein couldn't help wondering just how the future would develop for him and his boys.

At least, he could console himself, he had been able to leave them with something of a smile, something like the raucous self-deprecating humour which, from the earliest days, he had always thought was one of the Beatles' most attractive aspects.

He had deliberately delayed showing them the initial artwork for the cartoon series, thinking at first he would show them the illustrations on the night of the meeting in Hollywood. Then he thought better of it and decided to show them the artwork in San Francisco, but the blood and the violence at the hotel and the Cow Palace made mention of a cartoon series seem inappropriate.

But on the plane, on the way back to England, he knew he couldn't delay it any longer. The group would disperse as soon as they got off the plane and it was quite possible that he wouldn't see some of them until after the programme aired in America.

Of course those days were light years away from modern technology where a tv show in America can be viewed within hours over here, and even a mobile phone can take a very acceptable image which can be transmitted to another continent within seconds.

There was no chance of that happening with the cartoon series but it was quite inconceivable that at least one of the Beatles wouldn't hear about it and, even worse, see their individual depiction before Epstein had broken the news.

He was left with no choice. He waited until the flight was well underway, which meant that the Beatles had enjoyed a glass or two or three, and were slightly more relaxed than earlier. He took the artwork out of his briefcase and, with a few words of introduction and explanation, handed the sheaf of cell illustrations round, The first set went to John Lennon who was sitting closest to Epstein, and the second set was handed to George Harrison. Both Beatles leafed through the sheets without comment or visible expression. Lennon passed his copy on to Starr while McCartney took the sheets from Harrison.

It was McCartney who gave the first comment, and it wasn't complimentary. With a whoop of laughter and derision he disappeared out of First Class to take the illustrations to show to Aspinall and Evans who were sitting, as usual, in economy. It was a regular bone of contention, the conditions of work, but Aspinall and Evans were too loyal and too devoted to the Beatles to make an issue of things like travel arrangements. The short-lived hilarity about the illustrations provided a rare opportunity for the kind of communal travel that some might have thought the norm.

McCartney invited them forward to join in the general ridiculing of the cartoon and though people from economy coming into First would normally be frowned upon, they were being invited by a Beatle, and that made all the difference.

And the laughter and general mickey-taking about the way the boys had been captured by the cartoonists made for a pleasant and less strained end to the flight, and one less worry for Epstein.

While the Beatles were taking their well-earned holiday, the edition of the Ed Sullivan Show, filmed in New York at the time of the Shea Stadium visit, was screened on September 12th at 8pm EST. The other acts on the bill included Soupy Sales, Allen and Rossi, Fantasio the Magician, and Cilla Black. Once again the broadcast was a major success and secured a 60% share of the total audience.

The next time Epstein was together with all four Beatles was over a month later when all five of them attended a party thrown by Brian's friend, Lionel Bart, at his home, The Priory, at Seymour Walk, to celebrate the launch of his new musical, "Twang". The party, which was well up to Lionel Bart's usual standards of lavish hospitality, was being held shortly before the Manchester tryout of the new musical which, Bart thought, would be another huge success to build on the worldwide hit that was "Oliver". There was every indication that Bart's hopes would be realised. He was the golden child of British musical theatre, he had written a show around a British folk hero, Robin Hood, and the show featured some stellar talents like James Booth, Ronnie Corbett and Barbra Windsor. Unfortunately the show was a complete and overwhelming flop, both in Manchester and, much more painfully in the West End. It opened at the Shaftesbury Theatre on December 20th and closed just after a month later, losing Bart his reputation in the industry and virtually all of his fortune.

The party in October 1965 would be one of the last demonstrations of Lionel Bart at the head of British show business. Within months he had toppled from his pinnacle and would never climb back, and with the fickle brutality of people, most of his fair-weather friends turned their backs on him. One of the few who didn't was Brian Epstein.

The party was held on October 9th which also happened to be John Lennon's birthday, and quite naturally the four Beatles wanted to celebrate the event, and so they left Lionel Bart's party and went elsewhere to celebrate Lennon's birthday privately. Epstein would have been torn between wanting to support his friend Lionel and wanting to join his boys in celebrating John's birthday. In the event he did not need to worry about the decision. It was taken out of his hands. He wasn't invited to join in the celebrations with the Beatles, and that was another sign of a change in the air. He had not always attended celebrations with the Beatles in the past, but he had never been denied an invitation previously.

Never.

In the middle of October Epstein returned to America. The nominal purpose was to view the edited film of the Shea Stadium concert in August, and Sid Bernstein who sat next to him at the viewing told Brian Epstein that he had an urgent matter to discuss with him. They arranged to meet for dinner at the Waldorf before Epstein flew home, and Epstein turned his attention back to the wonders of the Shea Stadium concert on the screen before them.

In addition to the Shea Stadium viewing there were a couple of other critical reasons drawing him back to the States, and they both involved Seltaeb.

In the first place he had been alarmed by the responses given to him on the night the Beatles had driven to meet Elvis. The two managers had swopped notes and found various areas where their view converged, despite the obvious differences in personality. Parker was a huckster, a simple, crude individual who struck very, very lucky with Elvis but lacked any ability to see beyond the simple demands of the job as it had always been for the carnival caller.

Epstein was completely different. A far more eloquent and sophisticated man, he was much more capable of seeing his artists as real people and as something beyond a revenue-generating opportunity.

But Epstein was astounded to hear the stories Parker told him that night. Even allowing for Parker's innate flair for exaggeration, it was clear that on the merchandising front alone Epstein was in second or third division in terms of thinking, compared to Parker. The revised deal with Seltaeb, dating from August 1964, raised the NEMS share to 46% or 49% - there was even confusion about that – but that single conversation with Colonel Parker made Epstein realise that even at 49% he and NEMS and, crucially, the Beatles were severely missing out.

One of the purposes of the trip in October was to follow up on the information gleaned from Colonel Parker, but the more immediate and painful requirement was to deal with the legal minefield which Seltaeb had become.

The original group that had formed Stramsact and Seltaeb was in disarray thanks in no small part to Nicky Byrne's wildness and recklessness. Lord Eliot and Malcolm Evans had abandoned New York in favour of a less lavish but equally less legally-imperilled lifestyle back in England. The lawsuit by Lord Eliot against Byrne, alleging all manner of reckless housekeeping with the Seltaeb funds was still meandering through the courts, dragging other legal proceedings into its mass like the proverbial snowball rolling down a hill. However, the simple fact of creating that suit against Byrne ensured that Lord Eliot had placed a solid legal wall between his family's ancient Cornwall estates and the Seltaeb mess.

But it seemed that nothing could deter or deflect Byrne from his single-minded pursuit of merchandising dollars and anything that might benefit Nicky Byrne. Consequently, Walter Hofer was forced to explain to Epstein in a brutally combative meeting at Waldorf Towers in New York that the battle lines had been completely drawn with Seltaeb. It was already a messy battle, but it was likely to become bloody, very bloody.

Hofer showed Epstein details of major retailers cancelling orders as a direct result of the on-going legal battle between Seltaeb and NEMS, with such companies clearly nervous of being dragged into that legal saga. Hofer also had to suffer the wrath of Epstein by showing him the contractual papers which revealed that NEMS were being fined substantial amounts for failure to meet various signed merchandising agreements.

Most difficult of all was the revelation, via the kind of sterile legal papers that Epstein completely hated, that Byrne had launched a counter-suit against NEMS, accusing Epstein and the company of selling licenses direct to clients behind the back of Seltaeb. The counter-suit from Byrne was seeking to claim $5 million from NEMS.

The strategy meeting about Seltaeb ran into three long sessions spread over two days, but the result was that Epstein allowed himself to be advised or persuaded to launch a counter-suit based on the alleged withholding of due royalties by Seltaeb.

Law suits, and counter suits, and a claim for five million dollars, and millions and millions of dollars already missing, and still the Beatles didn't know. But how long would it be possible to keep that secret?

Hofer was delegated to build up the countersuit based very strongly on the specific factual allegations made in Lord Eliot's proceedings against Byrne, given that Eliot and Malcolm Evans had seen examples of Byrne's wanton excesses at first hand, and much of that licentiousness would have carried over into his dealings with NEMS. He had taken great pleasure in handing over the initial $9,700 cheque to Epstein in February 1964, but since then payments, though they had certainly happened, had failed to follow the pattern or regularity and certainty that Epstein expected, and usually demanded. And there was also the small matter of Nicky Byrne's less than total attention to detail. Stories about charge accounts for a coven of girlfriends at a host of 5th Avenue stores had left Epstein and David Jacobs and Walter Hofer wondering whose money was being frittered away on expensive clothes.

Epstein lived in almost daily dread of Lennon or McCartney or Harrison confronting him with examples of the Seltaeb largesse, luxuries which, however the matter was judged, had come from the Beatles garden. Nowhere else.

It was not a happy return to England, made worse because Sid Bernstein, over dinner on Epstein's last night in New York, was forced to pass on some more bad news. His contacts in entertainment in New York had let him know that there was, as the urbane Bernstein phrased it, deep unhappiness in the manufacturing and garment industries in the city about money being lost because of the Seltaeb-NEMS dispute. Unusually for discussions between Bernstein and Epstein there was an edge of anger which crept into the discussion. Epstein was clearly in Bernstein's view not appreciating the gravity of the position, and Bernstein was struggling to make his friend understand the potential risks in the route he was following. Bernstein concluded by telling Epstein that these were not the kind of people to mess around, but Epstein only made matters worse by telling Bernstein that he did a very poor Marlon Brando impersonation.

His return to London brought a flurry of activity. There was a Joan Baez concert the same night at the Royal Albert Hall which he attended with David Jacobs, giving them both a chance to catch up on and develop thoughts around the Seltaeb situation.

Epstein gave Jacobs various instructions and it didn't escape the attention of David Jacobs that all those instructions involved actions in Britain. He was excluded from the legal activity in the States which was a blow both personally and professionally. He couldn't quibble with the competence of Walter Hofer to handle the litigation process in the States. But he couldn't shake off the suspicion that he was being excluded from further involvement in the Seltaeb litigation because he was being blamed by Epstein because the whole thing had gone so wrong. And he was correct.

There was a busy week after the Joan Baez concert leading up to the momentous event at Buckingham Palace on October 26th. There was the annual, and delightful, recording of the annual Christmas record for members of the Beatles Fan Club with a planned delivery date just before Christmas. Capitol sent news that a recent Beatles single, 'Yesterday'/'Act Naturally', had achieved gold status in America, just a month after release.

This achievement, hard on the heels of the gold record for 'Eight Days A Week'/'I Don't Want To Spoil The Party' added further fuel to the argument about why those songs, particularly 'Yesterday', had never been released as a single by Parlophone in the UK.

Early reaction to the ABC cartoon series about the Beatles was highly complimentary, with praise being lavished on Al Brodax's production by critics and public alike. The unexpected success caused a surge in sales of Beatles singles and albums and, to everyone's surprise, induced another spike in sales and orders for merchandise, particularly merchandise produced under the

Seltaeb banner. The sales weren't immediately a problem for the goods were already on the shelves. Orders for fresh supplies or even new items were a different matter and ran immediately into the nightmare of the Seltaeb-NEMS litigation. The wholly undesirable result was that, for many months, orders, and monies, were accepted but nothing was delivered because the legal processes effectively froze all activity except for, rather strangely, the accepting and banking of monies. And those monies, in increasingly large quantities, began to be frozen, locked into the litigation process until the dispute between Seltaeb and NEMS reached resolution.

But, as Sid Bernstein tried to warn Epstein in New York, there were a large number of manufacturers, both small and large, who risked losing a fortune over the Seltaeb fiasco. Those people were already angry but, as Bernstein struggled to explain, that anger could easily develop into something worse. And, Bernstein had stated very forcibly, those people and companies, would not vent their anger against an inconsequential merchandising operation like Seltaeb; they wouldn't even waste their time on an amorphous organisation like NEMS. Instead the focus for the anger and the retribution would be Brian Epstein and, more painfully, the four Beatles.

And the central agony of Brian Epstein's incredible life was encapsulated in that most difficult situation. He risked humiliation – not disgrace, not exposure, for neither of those would have mattered – but humiliation if and when the Beatles found out the full extent of the Seltaeb disaster.

The date was still almost two years away but in Epstein's mind the coming renewal of his management contract with the Beatles was looming ever larger. He had seen the four Beatles sign the original contract at the start of 1962, and Epstein and the four Beatles, now including Ringo Starr, had signed the revised contract in October 1962. That meant that the contract would expire on the last day in September 1967, and a new contract would need to be agreed and negotiated and signed by then.

And Epstein was painfully aware that there were increasing signs of tension between him and his beloved Beatles. A growing distance, an increasing reluctance to do something that he suggested or recommended or demanded. Touring was becoming a constant source of tension, particularly in America, and he was very conscious that he would need to manage the personal relationships with the Beatles as individuals and the group as a collective if their increasing independence from him was not to result in disaster when the contract came up for renewal.

He still had some big cards to play. The continuing worldwide success of the group meant that he was in a position, as Beatles manager, to cleverly re-negotiate the royalty rates on record contracts for the Beatles. It was an absurdity that the biggest and most successful group in the world should be receiving royalties lower, albeit proportionately, than other groups who had followed the Beatles through the door that his group had so successfully and triumphantly kicked open.

He was determined that over the next eighteen months he would secure new deals for the Beatles so that the renegotiated contracts would greatly increase their net earnings from record sales. With astute management of offshore accounts he would be able to show the group greater earnings under his management, with a much higher retention of that money, and he believed....hoped that this would be a proposition that the Beatles couldn't reject.

But there were two nagging worries about this amicable projection. The first was the visible success of some of the newcomers in the industry at getting money out of record companies. Sid Bernstein and Nat Weiss had told him about someone called Allen Klein who was achieving great fame in New York by his bombastic tactics in record company offices, tactics which were abhorrent to Epstein but had obviously secured unexpected millions for Klein's clients like Sam Cooke and Bobby Darin. It didn't escape Epstein's attention that this was the same Allen Klein who had tried to buy the Beatles management contract from him a year earlier. He hadn't liked Klein then and the more he heard about him the less he liked the sound of things, but, he tried hard to persuade himself, the Beatles, his Beatles, would never be taken in by an East Side hustler like Allen Klein.

At the heart of all his thinking, his deliberations, lay Seltaeb. Even if there were no great disturbances between group and manager, the disclosure that millions of pounds had been thrown away would inevitably sour that relationship and severely damage, if not kill the chances of a renewed management contract in 1967. As 1965 moved into autumn his thoughts were firmly on a speedy resolution to the Seltaeb crisis - ideally without the Beatles hearing anything about it, plus successful renegotiations with EMI, Capitol and the others, all to prove just how astute and irreplaceable he was as a manager. And with that goal in mind he was determined to organise the two major tours lined up for 1966, America and Japan and the Philippines, to be the most comfortable, as performances, and financially successful of the group's career.

It was a great plan, but even without the pain of his personal life, and the on-going agony in his back, and the violent mood swings caused by the pills, it would have been difficult to achieve. And so much would go wrong over the following ten months that all the careful planning was to crash around him.

The greatest cruelty of the situation was that he could not discuss this greatest fear with anyone. Not with the NEMS staff, even Ellis, who understood the financial aspects of the Seltaeb mess but never comprehended the dangers it presented for Epstein. Not with Walter Hofer and Sid Bernstein who understood the commercial havoc being wrought by Seltaeb but never realised, because he never mentioned it, how massively dangerous the situation was for him. Not with David Jacobs who was made painfully aware of how much the Seltaeb disaster was causing Epstein commercially, but not about the emotional damage the Beatles manager was suffering.

And not, most obviously, with the Beatles who had been kept like children in a state of benign ignorance about their true situation, not just in terms of Seltaeb but a host of other contractual issues. The terror which afflicted Epstein was the certain knowledge that like children the Beatles had grown up and realised that they didn't have to just accept information or instructions without challenge any longer.

Brian Epstein, the man who the tabloids painted as "The Man with Everything", was in that most painful of situations – wracked by doubts and concerns about a crisis but without anybody, not a single soul, with whom he could discuss the agony.

In a perverse way, these anxieties came to a head for him on October 26th when the Beatles, his boys, went to Buckingham Palace to be invested with their MBEs. This major event came just two days after Epstein, on behalf of the Beatles, turned down another invitation to star at the forthcoming Royal Variety Performance. Epstein was keen for the Beatles to feature in the show, but they, in another demonstration of independence, refused.

But they couldn't refuse the Palace. The four Beatles drove to Buckingham Palace in Lennon's black Rolls Royce, although when the party assembled at the Palace their numbers had swelled. John Lennon was accompanied by his wife Cynthia and his aunt Mimi; Paul McCartney was with his father James and also Jane Asher; George Harrison was accompanied by his wife Pattie, and his mother and father, Louise and Harry. Finally Ringo Starr was with his mother, Elsie, and stepfather, Harry. The only other member of the party was Brian Epstein.

The Beatles were conducted to the Great Throne Room in time for the 11am ceremony. Lord Cobbold, the Lord Chamberlain, read out the four names individually; they stepped forward and bowed to the Queen who shook their hands, spoke a few words to them, before pinning the medals to their jacket lapels.

The gates outside the Palace and the space back to the Victoria Memorial were busy with thousands of fans who were desperately keen to show their devotion to the group on what was becoming an increasingly rare public appearance in Britain.

They left the Palace and went to provide a Press Conference at the Saville Theatre, where they answered with the usual unfailing good humour the same questions over and over again. Hovering in the background, inevitably, was Brian Epstein, his wide smile displaying the pride he evidently felt in this latest incredible achievement by his most famous charges. Although he never voiced any unhappiness about his isolation from the award there were many who were surprised if not mystified by the fact that the man behind NEMS, the man who had taken the Beatles from local obscurity to a position of total domination of the pop world, had been cold-shouldered. Suspicions about anti-semitism were raised, as were similar concerns about his homosexuality, but whatever the causes it seemed a particularly vicious rebuff to the most successful pop manager that Britain or the world had ever produced.

In the wake of the MBE delights, Epstein took the group into another rare pleasure which was the recording of The Music of Lennon and McCartney, the programme he had discussed with Johnny Hamp of Granada Television before the American tour.

Two days had been set aside for the filming by the Beatles, but the filming of other artists went on much longer. One of the most notable additions was the famous clip of Peter Sellers narrating 'A Hard Day's Night' while acting the part of Laurence Olivier playing Richard lll. It is a precious and priceless addition to the programme complementing the mimed appearances by the Beatles perfectly. There are other gems in the programme, including a segue from Paul McCartney singing 'Yesterday' into Marianne Faithful performing the same song. But it is Peter Sellers for which the programme is remembered.

Allegedly he wore the same wig and part of the costume worn originally by Olivier when he played Richard lll, and there are claims that he spent more time trying to get the false nose right for the part than he did rehearsing or filming.

He had to finish his part of the filming very promptly partly because of union restrictions but more particularly because there was a car waiting to take him to Heathrow for a flight to America to promote "What's New Pussycat". The short clip featuring Sellers is still a huge success on YouTube, almost fifty years after the programme was filmed.

Hamp conducted proceedings with his customary shimmering brilliance, and the two days on set at Granada in Manchester gave the Beatles a nostalgic look back at their past. Hamp even had the chance for a moment of huge embarrassment caused inadvertently by Lennon and McCartney.

The night before filming started, they travelled over to Manchester ready for an early start in the studio. Looking for some entertainment for the evening and not knowing Manchester very well, they invited Johnny Hamp to join them for a drink. He was reluctant to go out for the evening having preparatory work to finish for the filming on the following day but the meticulous Hamp would never have knowingly been discourteous to anybody, particularly artists. He met Lennon and McCartney in the centre of Manchester and suggested they go to the Phonograph, a club near Granada studios, where he knew they would not be hassled by people. But in case they were worried about possibly being refused admission he reassured the pair with the comforting news that as he was well-known at the club there would be no problems at the door!

It was only as they walked into the club that Johnny Hamp realised that he was with probably the best known pair of men on the planet, and he was promising them that there would be no problem getting into a club in Manchester - because they were accompanied by him.

That tone of familiarity and warm friendship was conveyed in the programme which was a highlight of the Beatles work on television. But it was to be the final appearance in person at the Granada Quay Street Studios, forming the pattern of final appearances which had already included Thank Your Lucky Stars and various BBC outlets, and now took in perhaps the most fondly-regarded tv studio. It was Granada who, albeit fortuitously, had filmed the only live footage in the Cavern by the Beatles, that grainy black and white performance of 'Some Other Guy'. And Granada had provided a number of other precious television pieces featuring the group during their rapid claim to fame including the famous appearance in late November 1963, which was repeated during Christmas week on Scene at 6-30.

This was the appearance which featured the long, impromptu interview with the Beatles and Ken Dodd managed, with some difficulty, by Gay Byrne. The interview even featured a name check for Bill Grundy, a Granada stalwart who would achieve lasting fame more than a decade later by hosting an infamous interview with later pop idols, the Sex Pistols.

But the Granada appearance was notable for the performances, albeit mimed quite badly, of 'This Boy' and 'I Want to Hold Your Hand', played in front of a huge billboard of the Daily Echo.

On YouTube there is a very funny clip of George Harrison, circa 1976, watching an old clip of the 'This Boy' performance from that Granada appearance in 1963, where he watches his much younger self and his three friends at the moment just before they went to America and conquered the world. He laughs fondly at the antics, and joins amusingly with the harmonies, but there is a sadness and a wonder in his eyes.

A discernable sadness that so much had gone forever, but also a wondrous delight at how young they were in that clip, and how much they achieved.

During November there were two very tangible signs of how things had changed for the group and how they intended to interact with the record industry. On November 7th it was announced that Capitol Records were withdrawing all promotional support for the new American single release by the Beatles, which was 'Boys'. The group had decided, and informed the record company, that they considered the record unrepresentative of their current sound, and Capitol simply capitulated and withdrew support for the single.

Two weeks later the Beatles spent a day at Twickenham effectively anticipating MTV and the route to be taken by pop tv programmes for the next fifty years. During that day they filmed promotional film clips of the songs 'We Can Work It Out', 'Day Tripper', 'Help!', 'Ticket To Ride' and 'I Feel Fine', and these clips would appear on television in America, Japan and the rest of the world, not just the handful of British TV shows. Given the imminence of the Christmas buying season this was a particularly well-calculated effort to maximise the Beatles exposure in markets all round the world, and more than one observer noted that with such a strategy the need for the group to make the brutally gruelling tours which had been the norm were disappearing, if they hadn't already gone.

But what if the group didn't want to make tours any longer? If they had decided that they, like Brian Wilson, didn't need to subject themselves to the pain and anxiety of touring, then what of the manager whose role was to organise and oversees the tours? Without the tours, whither the manager? And Epstein asked that question more than anybody.

It was clear to everyone around him, particularly those at NEMS, that his mood swings were becoming more extreme, more volatile. He had always been mercurial but by late 1965 those flashes of temper were becoming more marked, and often, more frightening. Epstein's temper had always been a feature of his temperament, as witnessed by the regular resignations by people like Derek Taylor and Brian Sommerville and Wendy Hanson.

Whether it was the gradually increasing drug intake, or the sheer pressure of work, or the secret terror of a Seltaeb-induced rejection by the Beatles, the simple fact is that in modern parlance Brian Epstein would have been considered bi-polar. While that is almost certainly medically correct the inescapable truth is that he was a very, very sad individual. And for a man who, in material terms, had everything, it is a telling commentary on his tragic life.

The pressures of business meant that he could only escape when on holiday or on the frequent occasions that he would vanish into London's seedy underworld, or the equivalent locations in New York or LA or Amsterdam, in search of sexual release and a brief respite from the demons assailing him. He was fortunate in one respect that he was active in an era before mobile or cell phones meant that for most people, particularly executives, there is no escape if people want to find you.

The period immediately prior to the next British tour in December saw another small significant change in the way things had always been for the Beatles. The balance engineer at Abbey Road, who had been involved with them since their first visit to the studios in June 1962, Norman "Hurricane" Smith, was being promoted. EMI were making him a producer, and his base would be the A&R Department at Manchester Square.

The promotion of Smith was a partial attempt by EMI management to plug the gap caused by the departures led by George Martin just three months earlier. Joining Martin in the forthcoming Associated Independent Recordings (London) Limited would be fellow EMI men, John Burgess and Ron Richards, plus Peter Sullivan from Decca.

For George Martin this would prove an especially sweet situation. Not only would his new company benefit enormously from the on-going relationship with the Beatles but he would also be able to claim, and receive, a royalty from all future Beatles' productions.

But if life for George Martin was looking sweeter, by December 1965 the demands on Epstein were almost intolerable. For good and bad reasons there were a host of people seeking him, claiming his time, forcing him into corners. People like Bill Harry have claimed that Epstein was very bad at delegating and, as things crowded in on him, there is plenty of evidence to support that contention. He often tried to make creative moves that would have led to such sensible delegation but all too often he regretted any move that might later lead to a loss of power or influence, especially if one of the results might be a potentially disastrous leaking of information about things like Seltaeb.

During November 1965 a new company had been started in America called Nemperor Artists Limited, although it would not be incorporated until the following June. Nemperor was a name which came from the slightly sarcastic title that Derek Taylor labelled Brian Epstein with - the Emperor of NEMS - and the company was set up with American attorney, Nat Weiss, to arrange and manage tours in the States, primarily for American and NEMS artists. The first group to come under that banner would be the Cyrkle, who had a major hit with the Paul Simon/Bruce Woodley song, 'Red Rubber Ball'.

After a day spent in a leisurely rehearsal at the flat shared by Mal and Neil at Montagu Mews, the Beatles were ready for their next and what would prove to be their final British tour. There is a photograph taken on that day which shows the four Beatles sitting on chairs holding acoustic guitars and strumming through a number, presumably from the set-list for the forthcoming tour.

Aspinall and Evans hover behind McCartney and Starr, looking for all the world like nervous supply teachers invigilating over exams.

The 1965 British tour comprised just eleven shows spread over just nine days, and took the group to Glasgow, Newcastle, Liverpool, Manchester, Sheffield, Birmingham, London and Cardiff. Following the trend of that year these shows featured the final appearances by the Beatles in those major British cities including, most poignantly, the December 5th concert at the Liverpool Empire. After 292 Cavern shows, plus a handful of appearances at other Liverpool venues, the Empire concert brought an end to an era.

It was never admitted, or stated publicly, but there were those in the Beatles camp, like Mal Evans, who wondered if they would ever come back. It wasn't just because of the growing weariness with the nonsense that dominated and distorted every concert. All those involved with the Beatles were aware that the growing complexity of their recordings was increasing the difficulties of reproducing those sounds on the stage and throwing real technical problems on the group and their management.

And, as if to concentrate attention on the issue, the tour was being staged to coincide with the release of a new album, "Rubber Soul", and a new double-A sided single, 'Day Tripper'/'We Can Work It Out'. The tracks on the album, or at least the British version, were 'Drive My Car', 'Norwegian Wood', 'You Won't See Me', 'Nowhere Man', 'Think For Yourself', 'The Word', 'Michelle', 'What Goes On', 'Girl', 'I'm Looking Through You', 'In My Life', 'Wait', 'If I Needed Someone', and 'Run For Your Life'.

The tour featured an unaltered set list of 'Dizzy Miss Lizzy', 'I Feel Fine', 'She's A Woman', 'If I Needed Someone', 'Ticket To Ride', 'Act Naturally', 'Nowhere Man', 'Baby's In Black', 'Help!', 'We Can Work It Out', 'Day Tripper' and 'I'm Down'.

Leaving aside regular crowd pleasers like 'Dizzy Miss Lizzy', and new single material like 'We Can Work It Out' there were just two numbers included from the new album, 'Nowhere Man' and 'If I Needed Someone'.

No room for timeless classics like 'Girl' or 'Michelle' or 'In My Life', especially as the constant bedlam at the shows meant that playing or even hearing the more delicate numbers was a growing problem. If the audience and the Beatles couldn't hear 'Dizzy Miss Lizzy' or 'I'm Down' then it made it virtually impossible to consider playing 'Michelle' or 'In My Life', let alone 'Yesterday'.

But it is a tribute to the incredible professionalism of the Beatles that they were able to deliver an artistic triumph like "Rubber Soul" in such a short time. Recording of the album had started as recently as October 12th, making it almost miraculous that the group could produce such an intricate, elaborate and progressive album so quickly. The second day of recording saw the group move into a working pattern which would become their norm as, for the first time ever, with the recording of 'Drive My Car' on October 13th the Beatles carried on recording past midnight.

The final concert took place in Cardiff and apart, from signalling the end of that brief tour, was not greeted with any fanfare. Lennon, McCartney and Harrison stayed overnight in the area while Ringo Starr drove back to London to attend the Christmas party at the Scotch of St.James club in Westminster.

The group met the following afternoon at the NEMS offices in Argyll Street in an inconclusive, and often tetchy, meeting also attended by Walter Shenson and Brian Epstein. Given the involvement of Shenson the subject matter was obviously the next Beatles film, and in particular the conclusion of the contractual obligation on the Beatles to deliver three feature films for United Artists.

The first film, "A Hard Day's Night" had been a tremendous commercial success for the film company: "Help!" was also successful, albeit less so.

Although there was no longer the imperative to crash out the film product to ensure that the product didn't emerge after the group lost popularity, United Artists were still keen to continue the successful momentum.

Shenson had come armed with various suggestions but he, like everybody, was conscious that the Beatles invariably got their own way. And in this respect it seems certain that even Shenson was surprised by the change in the dynamic behind the relationship between group and manager. They did "A Hard Day's Night" because Epstein told them to make the film: a similar democracy applied with regard to "Help!" but by late 1965 things had changed completely.

The argument went on for several hours but, like petulant children, it seemed that the only thing on which the four Beatles could agree was that they couldn't and wouldn't, agree with anything proposed by Shenson or, more tellingly, Brian Epstein.

He even dragged out again the concept of filming Richard Condon's "A Talent for Loving" but there was no interest whatsoever in the project. It had been announced early in the year that this would be the third Beatles film. Then, during the summer, came the quiet announcement that filming of this novel had been shelved, but Epstein, having bought the rights to the book, was always hopeful, if not confident, that he would be able to persuade the group to fall into line.

The meeting with Shenson was yet another painful revelation to Epstein that the dynamic in his relationship with his boys had changed dramatically, and perhaps terminally. In other circumstances, given his tendency to flare-up it might have been possible for Epstein to rant and rage and get his own way, and there had been a number of instances over the previous three years when Epstein's temper had shocked the Beatles, even Lennon, into following his dictates. Now though, the four Beatles were older, somewhat wiser, and much less willing to simply follow instructions.

It was strange for Shenson to see this seismic shift in action. It was exhilarating for the Beatles, admittedly to markedly different extents, to experience it. It was galling and chastening and deeply troubling for Epstein to endure it.

And the other factor preventing Epstein from losing his temper at this rare instance of independence or defiance was Seltaeb. The fear of provoking the Beatles into any action that might mean them stumbling onto the raw details of what Seltaeb meant, and what it was costing.

There would be other flashes of real or fabricated interest in another film project. A futile attempt at coaxing an acceptable script from Joe Orton brought little but pain, and there was even a suggestion of the Beatles taking four leading roles in a film of Tolkien's "Lord of the Rings" but even that lavish scheme fizzled into nothing. There seemed very little interest among the Beatles in another film project.

But the Beatles failed to appreciate the gravity of the situation. They were committed contractually to a third film with United Artists and it was a legal obligation that was of scant concern to any of them. Yet again it was a matter that would come back to occupy, and even haunt them, in years to come.

It wasn't all dark. There were a few flashes of good cheer on occasions, particularly when NEMS persuaded Harrods to open after hours to allow the Beatles to shop at their leisure without being bothered by fans. This rare pleasure was normally only afforded to members of the Royal Family and demonstrated, yet again, just how important they were as individuals and to the general sense of well-being in the country.

A much happier event was the showing of the Johnny Hamp programme, The Music of Lennon and McCartney, which was greeted with critical and public acclaim. The only dissenting note came from the scheduling of the initial broadcast. Unusually, and perhaps unforgivably, for a broadcaster based in the north of England Granada allowed the London area to see the programme twenty-four hours before the rest of the country.

London saw the programme on Thursday, December 16th with the rest of Britain given access the following evening, and though the Beatles performances of their new single were received well, it was to Peter Sellers that the greatest reaction came, so much so that in the Christmas chart of 1965 his unique version of 'A Hard Day's Night' climbed to number 14.

Christmas loomed and to recognise the season NEMS issued a Season's Greeting from NEMS Enterprises notice in the music and entertainment press. Every NEMS artist was mentioned: the Beatles, Gerry and the Pacemakers, Cilla Black, Billy J. Kramer and the Dakotas, the Fourmost, Sounds Incorporated, the Moody Blues, Tommy Quickly, the Remo Four, Cliff Bennett and the Rebel Rousers, the Silkie, the Rustiks, Paddy, Klaus & Gibson, Michael Haslam and the Paramounts. The notice was signed by Brian Epstein, and there were many comments from observers that it smacked a little of the official Christmas Greetings from the Royal Family or the Prime Minister.

The more important point was what the notice, and indeed the activity that Christmas represented. Although the latest Beatles Christmas record, the third, was distributed to the 67,000 members of the Fan Club a week before Christmas there would be no Christmas show at a London venue for the usual two weeks over the Christmas season.

The equivalent shows in 1963 and 1964 had been fantastically successful, both financially and in terms of raising the profile of the group. Perhaps the triumphs of the previous eighteen months meant that by the end of 1965 there was no need for Epstein to worry about elevating the profile of the group. More probably, the scornful derision shown by Lennon, McCartney and Harrison earlier in the year to the very prospect of another Christmas show pointed the way forward. Whether Epstein wanted it or not there would be no Christmas show, and another part of the glittering but short-lived Beatles legend was finished for good.

"The Beatles Third Christmas Record" was little more than a marketing exercise conducted by the organisation behind the group. The love that the Beatles had for what they were doing, what had made them famous, was fading fast. They still loved music; increasingly they hated being the Beatles.

And the stark absence of yet another "Beatles Christmas Show" was highlighted by the appearance of Epstein's next three main stars in that British Christmas variety standard - pantomime. Cilla Black made her pantomime debut in "Little Red Riding Hood", at the Wimbledon Theatre in London, while Gerry and the Pacemakers starred in "Cinderella" at the Gaumont in Southampton. At the other end of the country stablemates Billy J. Kramer and the Dakotas appeared at the Globe Theatre in Stockton in "Mother Goose".

The steady pruning of the NEMS roster to remove promising but non-performing artists like the Rustiks, Mike Haslam and, most painfully of all, Tommy Quickly, showed NEMS adjusting to realities that Epstein had seemed oblivious to, and, for a long period, able to keep at bay.

1966 would be the year was Swinging London sprang to life, but it would be the start of the end for NEMS. People like Vic Lewis and Robert Stigwood were hovering, eager for a slice of the NEMS pie, making overtures to the embattled Epstein. The weary Epstein would not prove able to keep them at bay for long. Of course there were sound business reasons for commercial involvements with the likes of Lewis and Stigwood, but the organisation after they became involved ceased to be NEMS in all but name.

Discussions with Vic Lewis had taken place during the second half of 1965 and met their inevitable conclusion late in January 1966 when NEMS Enterprises and the Vic Lewis Organisation formally announced the merger. The new organisation started trading on February 1st when Vic Lewis became a director of NEMS Enterprises.

In popular mythology Vic Lewis is denigrated as a nobody, another suit who leached off NEMS and Epstein. Nothing could be further from the truth. Vic Lewis had a stellar history in music, first as performer with names like Stan Kenton and Tubby Hayes, and then as an agent representing artists like Dudley Moore and Matt Monro. In addition Lewis was responsible for arranging the gig which was the second most important introduction to America for a British act. It was Vic Lewis who set up Elton John's historic first appearance at the Troubadour in Los Angeles, and this, plus later work with people like Robin Gibb, actually made the merger with the Vic Lewis Organisation a sound move for NEMS.

Epstein was in America in the middle two weeks of January making, and finalising, arrangements for the 1966 summer tour of the States by the Beatles. He was also dealing with the fall-out from a rare administration failure on his part. The Silkie, his new hopes for pop stardom, had flown to America just after Christmas to commence a promotional visit based very much on the template Epstein had set up and exploited so brilliantly with the Beatles and others. A wide programme of tv and radio appearances had been set up for the Silkie and there were strong hopes that, with their resemblance vocally to Peter, Paul and Mary, that they would be accepted and adopted by America. Unfortunately it didn't happen.

Not because of any failings musically or visually in the group. Instead it was an almost criminal lapse in administration on the part of NEMS as there was a culpable failure to obtain the essential visas and work permits.

Without these critical documents the visit couldn't go ahead and the moment for the Silkie was lost. Sadly it would never return.

Within NEMS there were questions being asked about Epstein and the workload he was insisting on imposing on himself. It wasn't his specific fault that the Silkie didn't get their visas or work permits. It was the responsibility of somebody relatively lowly in the NEMS machine, but that wasn't the point. It spoke of a loss of focus, a lack of attention to detail, which simply wouldn't have happened at NEMS a year earlier.

In this instance the victims, sadly, were the Silkie who would never get such a chance again, but the Silkie debacle for the first time created a crack in the façade of the all-powerful, omnipotent Brian Epstein. He would put the group on the bill for the next Beatles tour but it was too little, too late.

The real chance for the Silkie was the promotional visit at the end of December, but, whoever was to blame, it was a tremendous chance lost - or thrown away.

Part of the time in New York involved more pleasant matters - lunches and dinners with trusted friends and confidants like Sid Bernstein and Nat Weiss; less happy sessions were spent with Walter Hofer who had to guide Epstein through the latest unpleasant and painful Seltaeb developments.

There was also a very awkward session in Central Park with a young fitness instructor who clearly felt that the mighty Brian Epstein had discarded him all too casually after a wild night in New York at the time of Shea Stadium.

The instructor displayed his anger in a brutal form inflicting cuts and bruises to Epstein's head and body, with particular damage being done to his back which had never recovered from the injuries suffered when he fell from the plane at Hobby Airport in Houston in the previous August.

Epstein endured a painful, tearful night with the young man before escaping from the city and the country early the following day. His schedule had allowed for him to travel to the Bahamas before the end of the American trip, and the purpose was to check up on the status of the Beatles offshore investments with Walter Strach. Money had been shunted into the Bahamas during 1965 via the location filming of "Help!", and was supplemented by the bringing of suitcases full of bank notes. The result was that that there was a substantial deposit now sitting offshore. Given the desperation being shown by the British government about the state of Sterling it was likely than some kind of aggressive move was going to be made against offshore accounts. Because of the high profile of the Beatles, it seemed very likely that their Bahamas accounts would attract uncomfortable attention.

Epstein only stayed in the Bahamas for thirty-six hours before making the relatively short, leisurely trip to the Virgin Islands where a few days seclusion allowed the physical wounds from his New York adventures to heal, but the mental wounds, his growing worries, continued to build.

In his absence the growing competence of NEMS, despite the Silkie problems, meant that it was largely business as usual. He returned from the

Virgin Islands in the middle of January ready to start making progress in the critical negotiations with EMI.

For several months he had been discussing and debating one major topic with the unflappable Geoffrey Ellis, this being the royalty rate being paid to the Beatles by EMI. They were involved in major discussions with the record company tied to the fact that the Beatles existing deal would expire in June 1966.

There was no intention of moving to another company. That rarely happened in those days, and it would have taken a massive disruption in the relationship between record company on one side and artist and manager on the other for Epstein to contemplate a divorce from EMI. That was not the way Epstein worked.

The coming negotiations would also involve other matters less tied immediately to money. Epstein also had concerns about the number of recordings that the Beatles were contractually bound to supply to EMI every year, and he and Ellis had discussed how they could force a reduction. He had also, in discussions with Ellis, contemplated a number of additional concessions he would try to wrestle out of EMI, not necessarily all at once. He was mindful that a big victory now would do him no harm in demonstrating to the Beatles just how efficient he was, especially with the unrelenting misery being threatened by Seltaeb.

Those additional benefits, he hoped, would include a reduction in the number and type of allowable deductions from valid royalty payments, and, critically, a substantial increase in income from sales abroad. Sales around the world for Beatles product continued to rocket but, thanks to the peculiar structure for royalty payments outside the home territory, the Beatles were earning derisory amounts per sale in many major territories. Epstein hoped to put pressure on those territories via EMI and he was also totally aware that his detailed advance planning, based on regular assessment of record markets round the world, would see him in 1966 taking the Beatles to a number of those areas, particularly Japan, the Philippines and the United States.

It had also been brought to his attention that the new model for negotiation with the likes of Sir Joseph Lockwood, as demonstrated so lucratively by the likes of Allen Klein, was the tub-thumping, cursing, brutal approach. That was not, never would be Epstein's way, but he was conscious that in the short term he had to achieve similar results to the new breed.

1966 would prove to be an absolutely pivotal year in many ways for the group, not least because it would allow them to march confidently into a new way of working. They had one session of work to perform under the control of George Martin and Brian Epstein in early January. After that, apart from minor

PR duties in late March, they did not re-convene as the Beatles until April for the start of the recordings in what would eventually become "Revolver".

The recording session on January 5th was highly significant because it took the Beatles to CTS Studios at 47 Kensington Gardens Square, one of the very few recording sessions conducted by the group outside Abbey Road. The task on that day was very specific and required a deal of secrecy. In essence they were recording various fragments of songs to improve the quality of the proposed television film, The Beatles at Shea Stadium. Effectively they were trying to synch their playing and vocals to the onscreen images, and this was one of the main reasons for using CTS Studios. CTS was an abbreviation for Cine Tele Sound, and the studio had built an enviable reputation in providing audio-visual services to the television and film industries.

There were overdubs laid down for 'I'm Down', 'Can't Buy Me Love', 'Baby's In Black' and 'Dizzy Miss Lizzy', and, in response to George Martin's urgings, they did a complete re-record for 'Help!' and 'I Feel Fine'. The technicians at CTS then used the recorded version of 'Act Naturally' as the version to appear on the Shea Stadium film, which threw up brief bloopers like Ringo Starr singing with his mouth closed!

Other changes, either desired or requested, were abandoned because of a shortage of time. Only one day had been allocated for the work and the new spirit of independence among the Beatles didn't lend itself to extended periods of work without prior notice.

Some of the footage, particularly the audio track of audience responses, from the Hollywood Bowl concert on the same tour was used to flesh out the Shea Stadium film, and the post-production process was much more intricate and involved than had been expected.

The group then came back to Studio Three at Abbey Road on Wednesday April 6th to commence conventional recording and, as a portent of what was to come, the initial session recording music for the new album involved 'Tomorrow Never Knows'. This track would become the final track on the album which when it appeared, five months later, would be hailed as a masterpiece and is still regarded by many as the Beatles' finest achievement.

Whatever the stature of the album it cannot be denied that 'Tomorrow Never Knows' made a profound statement about who the Beatles were and what they had become in the few short years since 'Love Me Do'.

At the start of March, BBC1 in the UK showed the 48-minute film of The Beatles at Shea Stadium in black and white, as television in Britain was not yet fully equipped for colour. The film was generally well-received not least because the sheer scale of a concert in front of 55,000 people was mind-boggling for most viewers. In the States the film was shown in colour in cinemas from January 1967, with a series of press advertisements produced by Klaus Voorman, designer of the cover for "Revolver" and long-time friend and associate of the group.

Two days later, Epstein, rejoicing in the reaction to the film, announced plans for the Beatles touring schedule for the rest of the year. This was to include Germany, Japan, the Philippines and the United States, and was scheduled to last just over two months. Tellingly there were no announcements, nor even any thoughts, about other tours - UK or Europe or elsewhere - and it seems clear that the group's antipathy to touring had already communicated itself irrevocably to their troubled manager.

Following the press conference to make the tour announcements Epstein flew back to America, primarily to deal with arrangements for the upcoming tours, but as ever he had other things on his mind.

While Epstein was in America the NEMS office dealt with press reaction to a sad announcement which was in its own way a commentary on the fleeting nature of fame. One of the old contemporaries of the Beatles from the glory days in Liverpool was Mike Millward of the Fourmost, and previously the Undertakers. He had died in Bromborough Hospital in Cheshire suffering from leukaemia. The Fourmost had been another group to benefit from Lennon-McCartney numbers and George Martin's touch, and another group to benefit from the Epstein stardust, but the magic didn't really work in their case. But the death of Millward was a chastening moment for the NEMS family and even for Epstein, though he was three thousand miles away and deep in even more Seltaeb problems.

In England, the PR assignments for the group during March were relatively minor, and thankfully didn't involve the Beatles in the press conference banality which was becoming another bane of their lives. Unfortunately, as was becoming a fairly constant theme, both PR situations would have dramatic and serious repercussions in the months ahead.

Journalist Maureen Cleave had gone through the usual channels to get approval for a series of articles under the running title “How Does a Beatle Live?” which were scheduled to appear in the Evening Standard in London on a weekly basis during March. As the title implies she intended to interview each of the four Beatles separately, to get a greater sense of the man as an individual rather than just as a member of the group. Maureen Cleave was friendly with the group and had written extensively about them previously and so she was given permission for the short series.

The first subject was John Lennon, and Cleave travelled to his Weybridge home to conduct the interview which was then written and appeared in the Evening Standard on March 4th 1966, as just the first in the four-part series.

The article comprised thirty paragraphs and just over 2100 words, and ranged over a number of topics including Lennon's father, ugly people, toys, books, colonialism, religion, cars, lunch, and money.

From the entire article there were just 417 words relating to Christianity or religion, and indeed Lennon's quoted words on that subject totalled just sixty. The article came out in that evening's Standard and aroused little more than a flicker of interest. Indeed, for the more salacious readers, there was slightly more interest in the wide-spread rumour that Maureen Cleave was the woman with whom Lennon had enjoyed an affair, the liaison which became the subject of the song, 'Norwegian Wood'. There was little or no comment on, or attention paid to, Lennon's remarks or even his thoughts. Not about his estranged father, or Indian music, or Weybridge, or even religion. It simply wasn't that important.

Epstein returned from America to produce one of his most ambitious and successful concerts at Hammersmith Odeon, starring Herb Alpert and the Tijuana Brass. Even though the concert took place on a Sunday, which was traditionally Epstein's night for pop concerts at his theatre, the Saville, it was held at the larger and more established Odeon.

He had intended being back in New York two days later for the 8th Grammy Awards, which were held at the Beverly Hills Hilton in New York. The suspicion was that he had been tipped off that it wouldn't be a profitable trip. In the event he made a wise choice to avoid the ceremony. It was a rare whitewash for the Beatles who were nominated in ten categories but failed to win any of them, and this despite the fact that 'Yesterday' was nominated in six categories! Some of the winners caused an eyebrow to be raised. "Help!" by the Beatles was nominated as Album of the Year but was beaten by "September of My Years" from Frank Sinatra. The rendition of 'It Was a Very Good Year' from that great Sinatra album then defeated 'Yesterday' in the Best Vocal Performance (Male) Category. The Beatles song was also defeated in the category of Song of the Year by 'The Shadow of Your Smile', and also defeated in the category of Best Arrangement by the Gordon Jenkins arrangement of 'It Was A Very Good Year'.

Perhaps most surprising was the defeats for 'Yesterday' in the categories of Best Contemporary (Rock and Roll) Single and Best Contemporary (Rock and Roll) Vocal Performance, Male. The winner in both cases was that eminent rock and roll star, Roger Miller with 'King of the Road'.

To complete the embarrassment for the group they also lost out in four other categories, again with some surprises. They were nominated for Record of the Year with 'Yesterday' and were defeated by the biggest-selling act that year, Herb Alpert and the Tijuana Brass with 'A Taste of Honey'.

In the category of Best Original Score, Motion Picture or TV Show the Beatles were nominated for "Help!" but the winners were the Robert Arnbruster Orchestra with "The Sandpiper". But perhaps the sharpest defeats for the Beatles were in the final two categories. For Best Contemporary (Rock and Roll) Performance by a Group, Vocal or Instrumental the Beatles were nominated for 'Help!' but were defeated by that leading contemporary rock and roll group, the Statler Brothers, with 'Flowers On The Wall'. And then, in the category of Best Performance by a Vocal Group, the Beatles were nominated once again for "Help!" but the winners, perhaps surprisingly, were the Anita Kerr Quartet with "We Dig Mancini".

Ten nominations but not a single success, and this despite the presence of one of the most acclaimed Beatles songs, 'Yesterday', in the list for consideration. The response was instant and harsh. Capitol boss, Alan Livingstone launched an official protest about the results, particularly the failure to select 'Yesterday' as Song of the Year. In a fierce outburst Livingstone claimed that this aberration made a mockery of the whole event.

This complete failure for the Beatles, especially 'Yesterday', made many people question if the period of Beatles dominance over the charts and American show business was over. More sanguine observers suspected that the imminent American tour by the group, plus the release of yet another album, "Yesterday and Today", was bound to restore the group to their position of pre-eminence.

While Epstein remained in England, Walter Hofer was struggling against a torrent of legal activity from Seltaeb. Writs and counter-suits had been flying back and forth and, as ever, the only people gaining from it were the lawyers. To his credit, Hofer was diligent in trying to find a way for Epstein and NEMS to extricate themselves from the mess but Hofer was working under some unusual constraints.

First he had to deal with Epstein's moods and his increasingly brittle temper. Because of his health and drug intake and his dangerous lifestyle, Brian Epstein could often be difficult to deal with, as the frequent sackings and resignations from NEMS would demonstrate. Adding the word "Seltaeb" into that volatile mix was akin to dropping a can of petrol onto a fire. It didn't help Walter Hofer that to a large extent his major responsibility for Epstein and NEMS was dealing with, and hopefully resolving the Seltaeb issue.

And the situation was hugely complicated by communications, and the time difference between London and New York. Even though NEMS and Epstein rarely kept to conventional office hours it was invariably difficult for Hofer to speak to Epstein on the telephone. This was still in the era when direct dialling between London and New York was impossible. Operator involvement was essential and invariably a call had to be booked for a specific time, and this caused Hofer immense frustration when Epstein's erratic lifestyle, and his mercurial temperament meant than even the long-suffering NEMS staff could not find him.

And the final aspect to the nightmare was that only Geoffrey Ellis at the NEMS office was aware of any of the details of the Seltaeb problems, but Epstein was careful, and indeed desperate, to keep the full horrors from his friend. But the situation reached a new low on March 13th when Seltaeb issued a writ for libel in the New York courts against Brian Epstein, NEMS, Geoffrey Ellis and Walter Hofer.

Although Hofer assured Epstein that it was just process, part of the normal backwards and forwards activity of the litigation process, it created a fresh aspect to the nightmare for Epstein, the knowledge that a libel suit meant that it would be even harder to keep Seltaeb out of the hearing of the Beatles.

Fortunately, in one perverse sense, other matters intervened to distract both Epstein and the Beatles. Another PR event took place on March 25th at a photographic studio in Chelsea, arranged for that date to ensure that McCartney had returned from his holiday in Switzerland with Jane Asher.

Two requirements were assigned to the Beatles. The first was an interview and general contrived zaniness as a contribution to a venture prompted by Brian Epstein. As part of his involvement with Disc and Music Echo he had agreed to the Beatles providing material for a free flexi-disc to be given away with the paper on receipt of a number of coupons, unveiled on April 23rd 1966. The Beatles provided material for the disc, "Sound of the Stars", for half an hour in conversation with Tom Lodge, then a DJ on Radio Caroline.

The more important function of the day took place after the "Sound of the Stars" diversion. It had been arranged that several photographs would be taken, some by Nigel Dickson for "The Beatles Book" magazine. More importantly the group then prepared for the second photographic shoot under the stewardship of the photographer, Robert Whitaker who was using space rented by Oluf Nissen for the various events.

This was yet another photo session, just the latest in the hundreds endured by the group since their breakthrough. Now though, as Lennon's bitter remarks afterwards proved, they were no longer willing to subject themselves to the same old routine. Instead they indulged themselves in Whitaker's admiration for Salvador Dali, and worked with him to produce a series of shots, some of which were calculated to derail the "Loveable Mop Tops" image once and for all.

The group appeared in white coats and were surrounded by lumps of meat and broken dolls as part of what Whitaker rather portentously described as a conceptual art piece entitled "A Somnambulant Adventure". Subsequent remarks by Whitaker suggested that he was trying to create a satirical commentary on The Beatles' fame, inspired by the German surrealist Hans Bellmer's images of dismembered doll and mannequin parts.

Any resistance the group might have felt inclined to offer to Whitaker's ideas was swept away in their relief at being offered something different from the usual Beatles PR nonsense.

It was not originally intended as a photographic shoot for an album cover but McCartney seemed to be so pleased with it conceptually, perhaps inspired by his artistic activities in London, that he pushed Capitol to use the shot as the cover for their next American album. He even went so far as to describe the shot as the group's comment on the Vietnam War, although photographer Whitaker would later ridicule this idea.

The same shot was used in Britain in advertisements for 'Paperback Writer' and even appeared as the cover of Disc and Music Echo on June 11th.

But the kind of firm, often censorial control that Epstein had imposed on the group since the early days of 1962 was fading, and arguably fading fast. There was nobody at NEMS to intervene in the matter of the Whitaker photographs, a situation exacerbated by the fact that by the end of March Epstein had returned to New York.

This was for good business reasons relating to the Japanese end of the summer tour. In New York Epstein met with Tatsuji Nagashima to discuss and make arrangements for the forthcoming Tokyo concerts, and once again the constant businessman, Epstein took the opportunity to make a reciprocal arrangement which gave him the British representation for Nagashima's Japanese company, Kyodo Kikaku Inc.

Similar arrangements had been made for the appearances in the Philippines and Epstein's frequent trips to the States had ensured that the various American appearances, albeit even more limited than the previous year, were already set.

While he was away the group had continued the work at Abbey Road on the new album, often sliding well past midnight on a new working schedule created by themselves to suit nobody but themselves. For three of the Beatles, Lennon, Starr and Harrison, Abbey Road was still just a place of work, although it would start to become a place of sanctuary away from a troubled world. For the fourth Beatle, Paul McCartney, Abbey Road became, in late March 1966, a workplace just a short stroll from his new home. After a year's delay, and extensive renovations, the beautiful house on Cavendish Avenue, St.John's Wood was finally ready for him, and Jane Asher, to take occupancy.

The heavy scale of changes to the house, plus the long periods he had spent out of the country with the group during 1964, had meant that moving into the house had been long and frequently delayed. The return from Klosters meant that the moment needed to be delayed no longer and frequently during the recording periods for the new album McCartney would take advantage of occasional breaks to hurry back to the house to work through the daunting prospect of sorting through the massive amount of personal possessions that had been deposited in the house for him.

Included in those possessions was a host of tape fragments of pieces of songs and scribbled lyrics which he fully intended to get round to one day.

Over the coming weeks there would be little public presence for the Beatles, except perversely for McCartney who would be seen far more frequently walking purposefully or driving between Abbey Road and the new house.

Recording was what occupied them, as would be the case for the rest of the lifetime of the group, and during the coming weeks some timeless recordings were created by the group who were increasingly seeing themselves as an entity which existed inside the studios at Abbey Road.

Outside it was an increasingly, and bewilderingly, antagonistic world especially, strangely, for their live appearances, and they were rapidly approaching the point where it was simply too much to endure.

While they continued with the recording of the new album Epstein was starting to come to terms with his new diminished role in their professional lives. With details for the tours all but complete he had little to engage him other than the on-going discussions with Geoffrey Ellis and various EMI people about the new contract.

There were rare moments of lightness when he was able to forget his growing unhappiness. On April 9th he went with Lionel Bart to the Granada in East Ham to view a package tour headlined by the Walker Brothers. It was a show headlined by the magnificent Roy Orbison who, given his gracious behaviour towards the Beatles during the British tour in 1963, was always regarded very fondly by Brian Epstein. Also on the bill was the young Scottish star, Lulu, making a real impression with the success of her first record, 'Shout'.

But it is hard to argue with the view that for both Brian Epstein and Lionel Bart, trapped in individual hells of their own creation, and seeing all they had created starting to crumble around them, it was a rare night free of stress. And while both of them would have argued that they were there to enjoy the artistry of Orbison and to marvel at the fire of Lulu they would also greatly enjoy the superb pop harmonies of the Walker Brothers.

But they would not have been human had those two men, there in the darkness of that East London cinema, not have delighted in the delicious, muscular beauty of Scott Walker, the lead singer of the Walker Brothers.

But such moments of peace were becoming rarer for both of them, particularly Epstein. He was able to enjoy one last flash of triumphant pride in Britain when, on May 1st, the Beatles headlined once again at the New Musical Express Poll Winner's Concert at the Empire Pool, Wembley.

This had been a regular appearance since 1963 and this time on the bill were other stellar pop talents like the Rolling Stones, the Yardbirds, Spencer Davis Group, Roy Orbison, and many others. This would be the final Beatles concert performance in the UK, a brief 15-minute set, but, as a final bitter irony, owing to a contractual dispute the performance wasn't filmed.

The rest of May and much of June saw contact between group and manager quite restricted, not because of animosity but their working lives overlapped less and less. Mid June saw the release in America of the new album, "Yesterday And Today", featuring the cover using Whitaker's photo with the mutilated dolls and sides of meat. Capitol, confident of continued massive sales and with the next US tour imminent, had 750,000 copies readied, and prepared a huge promotional budget to support the release.

No longer did Epstein have to beg or threaten Capitol Records in order to get support for the Beatles. Huge resource was thrown behind "Yesterday And Today" and both Capitol and Epstein were confident of the usual massive sales success.

It was yet another cobbled together package from Capitol who were really starting to upset the Beatles with the way American albums were compiled, showing little if any respect for the work the group put into the sequencing of the British versions. On "Yesterday and Today" the tracks comprised 'Act Naturally' and 'Yesterday' from the British "Help!" album; 'Nowhere Man', 'What Goes On', 'Drive My Car' and 'If I Needed Someone' from "Rubber Soul": both sides of the double A-side single 'Day Tripper'/ 'We Can Work It Out'; and finally 'I'm Only Sleeping', 'Doctor Robert', and 'And Your Bird Can Sing' from the new UK album "Revolver".

Although the album was not going to be released in Britain, the cover art started appearing at the beginning of June, and met a distinctly negative reaction in the press. This was mirrored in America as early promotional copies started reaching radio stations and other media outlets ahead of the planned release date on June 15th. To everybody's surprise the reaction in America was totally hostile, so much so that Capitol were forced into the unprecedented step of recalling the album to change the cover. The various distributers used by Capitol shipped the copies back, and Capitol employed another shot taken by Whitaker to replace what became known as the Butcher's Cover. As Capitol had shipped out 750,000 copies of the album there was clearly an immense cost involved, and later inventories showed that the replacement of the cover cost Capitol some $250,000 which effectively wiped out their expected profit on the release. More costly was the damage to the reputation of the Beatles. For many people the Butcher's cover debacle represented the first slipping of the crown from the heads of the Beatles, but the hope, and expectation, was that the summer tour would restore them to their previous position.

As the furore was building in America the British activity was concentrated on the promotion of the new single, 'Paperback Writer'/'Rain', which was released in Britain on June 9th. On the following Monday the producer of BBC's flagship pop programme, Top of the Pops, tried once again to get the Beatles to appear on the show. It was a regular attempt, and it had always failed. Until this time.

Since the start of the show, on January 1st 1964 the programme staff had tried desperately to get the group to make a live appearance in their studios but they had always been refused. It was puzzling, and quite galling set against the regular Beatles appearances on rival British shows like Thank Your Lucky Stars and Ready Steady Go, and of course The Ed Sullivan Show in America.

But Top of the Pops had never managed to attract the Beatles. When Johnny Stewart wrote to Epstein on Monday June 13th to ask him to persuade the group to appear on the next show three days later it was with no expectation of success. The stars were in his favour. The Beatles were at Abbey Road working on 'Here, There and Everywhere' that day. Epstein made one of his rare visits to the studio that year and mentioned the offer to the group. To his surprise, and the visible delight of the Top of the Pops people, the Beatles agreed. They turned up at TV Centre in White City ready for a 2.30 pm camera rehearsal, yet more publicity photographs and a brief series of press interviews.

The live transmission began on BBC1 at 7.30 and finished at 8.00pm. The Beatles naturally appeared last, miming to first 'Rain' and then 'Paperback Writer', and the unfettered delight of the programme's host, Pete Murray, was a sight in itself.

And this would be the last ever live musical appearance by the group on a genuine pop show. They would appear, famously, on the Our World show in June 1967 to perform 'All You Need Is Love', but that was a one-off and on no grounds could be considered a pop programme.

The Top of the Pops appearance represented yet another departure for the group, made somewhat sadder because nobody, except just possibly the group, realised the significance of what was happening.

The Beatles party flew out of London on the first leg of the summer world tour on June 23rd on a flight which took the group to Munich. The final session of recording for the new album finished as late as 1.30am on Thursday June 22nd showing how tight was the schedule for recording before the departure for the tour. Partly because of the crowded timetable the group left England without having settled on a title for the album. "Revolver" was one possibility as was "Abracadabra", "Magic Circles" and "Beatles On Safari", and the final decision in favour of "Revolver" would not be made until the group were in Japan in July.

The frenzy over the Butcher's cover was gathering pace in America. An instruction had gone out from Capitol to their plant managers to destroy the covers, but only the Jacksonville plant managed to comply, by consigning most of its initial copies to a landfill site.

However, once the scale of the problem became clear, Capitol settled on another solution. They decided to paste another, less provocative, cover over the offending version and this cover, using a badly trimmed version of one of the other Whitaker photographs, became the version which appeared in the stores. It was this version which climbed to the top of the Billboard charts by the end of July, and went gold while the Beatles were in America in August.

Thanks to the on-going communication problems the true scale of the Butcher's cover problems didn't entirely percolate through to the Beatles and Epstein in Germany. They had arrived on the 11am flight from Heathrow, having been waved off by a small number of fans. In Munich the airport welcome was from barely two hundred fans and after a brief interchange with the German press the group and their party were ferried in a fleet of white Mercedes saloons to their base for two nights, the Bayerischer Hof Hotel.

The tone for the disaster-strewn next month was set early. The group were forced to arrive late for a scheduled press conference at the hotel because they became trapped in the lift on the way down from their rooms. They were only locked in the lift for ten minutes but it was an unsettling start to the tour.

The first two shows took place at Circus-Krone-Bau in Marsstrasse but proved a savage commentary on how far their performances standards had slipped. Partly because of the intense recording schedule at Abbey Road over the previous two months they hadn't had time, or simply hadn't bothered, working on a rehearsal of the planned set for the tour. It was a selection of tried-and-trusted material, and there were, very tellingly, no tracks that would appear on "Revolver".

The set list for the tour comprised 'Rock And Roll Music', 'She's a Woman', 'If I Needed Someone', 'Day Tripper', 'Baby's In Black', 'I Feel Fine', 'Yesterday', 'I Wanna Be Your Man', 'Nowhere Man', 'Paperback Writer' and

'I'm Down', and this would remain unchanged throughout the American leg of the tour - despite the possible addition of at least one number from the new album, "Revolver".

But it was the performance of that final song, 'I'm Down', at Munich which epitomised the problems. The group had to have a discussion about the lyrics before starting the song, and even so, McCartney managed to mess up the song. Nobody seemed to notice, and yet, for the Beatles, that wasn't a benefit - it was part of the problem.

After two shows in Essen the group made a nostalgic return to Hamburg. They hadn't been in the city since the stay pre-Christmas in 1962, and it must have been a strange experience for the group coming back as undoubtedly the biggest group in the world.

Old friends and acquaintances gathered backstage at the Ernst Merck Halle including Bert Kaempfert and Astrid Kirchherr, and this was the famous occasion when Lennon apologised to those friends at the concert advising them not to listen to the group because they were playing so badly!

There was a mini-riot inside and outside the hall after the second show, just to remind the group what they had been missing, and then their final trip to Germany was over. They flew back to London on June 27th but after just a few hours the Beatles party was back in the air en-route to Tokyo.

Arrival in Japan was scheduled for June 28th, but, in keeping with the theme of totally unexpected problems besetting them, a typhoon warning caused the plane to make an unplanned stop in Anchorage, Alaska, where they were forced to wait more than nine hours for circumstances to change. The group and their party quickly took over an entire floor of the Westwood Hotel and were taken into the in-hotel club, called Top of the World, by a DJ from the local station WOMC.

Seizing their moment the station began a barrage of updates about the presence of the Beatles in Anchorage which inevitably brought every young girl from miles around to converge on the hotel which was ill-equipped to deal with such crowds. WOMC even parked a caravan outside the Westwood and broadcast live minute-by-minute reports about the status of the Beatles until they departed. They arrived at Haneda airport in Tokyo at 3.40 am on June 30th, but even despite the hour there were some 1500 fans in the airport terminal, excited to see the group.

The heavy-handed and even brutal treatment meted out by a huge contingent of riot police dealt summarily with the fans, but the viciousness of the official actions caused shock even to the battle-hardened Beatles party.

The group then managed to provide five concerts spread over three days at the Nippon Budokan Hall, one on June 30th, two more on July 1st and the final two Japanese shows on July 2nd. On each occasion there were precisely 10,000 fans in the audience. The number is extremely significant given that it testifies to the precision with which the Japanese authorities controlled the concerts.

Following the discussions with Brian Epstein several weeks earlier, local promoter Tatsuji Nagashima had booked the Beatles into the Nippon Budokan Hall, which was considered by many Japanese to be a sacred venue, and could only be used for the presentation of Japanese martial arts. The hall had been chosen as a venue for judo competition during the 1964 Olympic Games, and even such a situation, which obviously brought pride to the country, had caused deep divisions. The decision by Nagashima to allow loud Western pop music into the venue, with the chance or likelihood of frenzied scenes in the crowds, caused deep concern in Japan.

There was widespread opposition to the visit by the Beatles and to the staging of their concerts in such a sacred venue, and the opposition brought forth public demonstrations in the days leading to the arrival of the Beatles. The scale and vehemence of the right-wing opposition even included a number of death threats which had to be communicated to Epstein and the group because of the nature of the danger. Sadly it would not be the last time that they would take to the stage facing death threats on that tour.

The result was that the Japanese police authorities decided to err on the side of caution. Police presence was incredibly prominent and heavy throughout their brief stay in Japan. A total of 36,400 security staff were involved and at each of the Beatles' shows at the Budokan, to control the crowd of 10,000 fans there were 3000 police and security staff. These were placed two abreast at various major junctions or strategic points in every aisle to curtail any unnecessary excitement or move in quickly on any excesses in the crowd, and deal with those excesses in whatever way those forces deemed appropriate.

One unfortunate aspect of the fierce security was that the group were under virtual house-arrest in the Tokyo Hilton for the entire stay. The group would only be allowed to leave the hotel suite to travel, in escorted, heavily-guarded motorcades to the Budokan. When the group attempted, a la "A Hard Day's Night" to escape from their guards they were caught, detained and brought back in disgrace to the hotel rooms.

The Beatles party had been located in plush suites on the 18th floor and the Hilton ensured that all lifts in the complex stopped on the 17th floor. They stationed heavily armed guards outside all lift exits and the various stairwells, and as a final precaution, armed police were based permanently in every alternate bedroom.

The period in Japan ended and the party were collectively and individually delighted to get out of the country and fly to the comparative haven of Hong Kong. Prior to the departure they were able to end one small matter of uncertainty by sending a telegram to EMI in London confirming that the title of the new album would indeed be "Revolver".

There was a ninety-minute stopover in the VIP lounge at Hong Kong during the refuelling process and then the journey continued on to Manila in the Philippines. A huge crowd had gathered at the airport to see and greet the Beatles but the local authorities had assembled a huge security detail to deal with any problems.

Without any discussion or negotiation a group of armed military police invaded the Beatles plane which was waiting on the tarmac. They surrounded the Beatles and forced them off the plane and into what was termed protective custody. Epstein and Mal Evans tried to intervene but were held off by the guns of the police. There were two army battalions in full combat gear in charge of protecting the Beatles, and the group were taken to navy headquarters.

From there the Beatles were transported to Manila Bay onto a private yacht named Marina owned by a wealthy Filipino, Don Manolo Elizalde, who was casually showing the Beatles off to a party of his rich friends like showing a rare specimen in a zoo. The yacht was moored two miles off the coast, and the four Beatles were left to sit in a room with the exits and most points on the deck guarded by even more armed police. This unprecedented arrangement was without discussion or agreement, and completely cut the Beatles from their party for at least two hours. This was most certainly the first time it had ever happened. Epstein wasn't able to reach them immediately and contact wasn't re-established until almost 4am, and it was past dawn before the police finally let them enter the Hotel Manila. Although the excursion lasted less than three hours it was still an extremely frightening and intimidating incident, and represented another new low for the Beatles.

Worse, much worse was to come.

The initial Press Conference in Manila had caused offence. From the Beatles perspective they were being asked the same old questions, in the same old way, with the same old subjects - haircuts, marriage, money.

From the perspective of the Filipino authorities and journalists they were creating simple, respectful questions to be directed at the four Beatles. But the one major difference in the questioning was local sensibility and the instinctive flippancy of the four Beatles. In countries and press conferences around the world, local reporters had invariably asked one or more Beatles what they thought of some aspect or another of the local area. In most instances the replies delivered were noncommital or sarcastic or flippant. No offence was taken, generally because the journalists weren't disposed to take offence and, crucially, the Beatles were not trying to be offensive.

The situation by the time the Beatles reached Manila was very different. They were so sick and tired of press conferences and the mind-numbing repetition that they no longer cared what people thought of their answers.

In addition the situation in Manila was different from things they had experienced previously because of the political sensibilities in the country. Filipinos had strong memories of colonialism and as a people they were not well disposed to being patronised or insulted by white visitors. Memories were still raw about the conditional nature of the independence from the United States after the second world war, and there was a real sense of resentment against white men treating the Philippines with less that total respect.

The fact that the Beatles were obviously not Americans mattered little. It was the visual image of white men from the west treating the Philippines with less than total respect that caused the problems. In many ways Epstein had led the Beatles innocently and ignorantly into a minefield that had been created by cultural and historic factors over which they had no control and precious little knowledge. There is nothing to suggest that Epstein requested or received any advice from the Foreign Office about the trip, and it's hard to escape the belief that the Beatles were going to fall foul of the situation in Manila no matter what happened.

On July 3rd, the day prior to the two scheduled Beatles shows in the city, the Manila Sunday Times ran a story detailing that the President, his wife and their three young children - all Beatles fans - had been invited as guests of honour to the concerts. The article also stated that the Beatles intended to make a courtesy call on the President's wife at Malacanang Palace on the Monday morning at 11am.

In Epstein's mind, let alone those of the Beatles, there was no such plan. They had a schedule drawn up by local promoter Ramon Ramos which included mention of a proposed Palace visit at 3pm. This had already been rejected, as far as Epstein knew and believed, for the very sound reason that their first show was set to start at 4pm, just one hour later. Their preference was to arrive at a stadium at least two hours before the show.

As such, a Palace visit at 3pm was impossible. Crucially, the promoter, Ramon Ramos, didn't want to upset either the Palace or Epstein, and so he did not pursue the matter. This despite the fact that he, far more than Epstein or the Beatles, would have been aware of the danger of offering possible snubs to the Marcos family.

At 10.30 the following morning a Palace official arrived at the hotel to collect the Beatles and deliver them to the Palace. Not surprisingly they were still in bed. Despite requests and demands, Brian Epstein refused to try to wake them.

The repercussions from their apparent snub were considerable. The Manila Times accused the group of snubbing the First Lady and her three children, and keeping a party of 400 people, all friends of the First Family, waiting.

There was little appreciation among the Beatles party just how dangerous the situation was. The ramifications were extremely serious.

On July 4th they played the two concerts that had been arranged at the Rizal Memorial Football Stadium. The afternoon show played to a crowd of 30,000 fans, and the evening performance took place in front of just under 50,000 fans. That second concert was overshadowed by the political troubles suffered by the Beatles but it remains the Beatles' second-biggest concert attendance, surpassed only by the Shea Stadium concert in August 1965.

The promoter, possibly under Palace pressure, refused to pay the Beatles their substantial, and entirely deserved, share of the gate receipts from the two shows on July 4th. A series of death threats and bomb warnings were telephoned through to the British Embassy and even direct to the Beatles' suite at the Hotel Manila.

Epstein realised the delicacy of the situation and was desperate to make amends. He arranged for a locally-based tv camera and sound crew to come to the hotel to record a press statement he had carefully put together with Tony Barrow. Though this was done, there was an unexpected problem when Epstein's recording was played on local television.

Unfortunately, just as the statement started, a surge of static blocked out every tv screen in the Philippines. It totally blanked out every word Epstein said in explanation and contrition, but oddly the static disappeared as soon as the statement ended.

The following day was their scheduled day to depart Manila, but the revenge on the Beatles and Epstein hadn't finished. Overnight all military security had been withdrawn, leaving the Beatles party virtually at the mercy of anybody who wanted to attack them.

A tax commissioner, Misael Vera of the Philippine Tax Authority, was working for the government and insisted that the group could not leave the country until they had paid a large amount in income tax on their concert receipts, even though promoter Ramon Ramos was still withholding those fees from Epstein. A series of escalating rows ensued until Epstein was persuaded that it was a battle he couldn't win and so the simplest remedy, however painful and unfair, was to pay the levy for the tax. Accordingly he filed a bond for 74,450 Pesos (£6840) to settle the matter.

Another problem came to light when Vic Lewis, who was making his first long trip with NEMS, returned to the hotel. It emerged that he had been interrogated by senior military officials through the night and had only been released just after dawn.

On every possible level it was obvious that the imperative was to get to the airport, get on a plane, and get out of the country, but there were still major hurdles to overcome. The hotel had removed all room service and the journey to the airport was very difficult, with abuse and threats in the streets. At the airport the management had given instructions that the Beatles party should be refused any assistance, and this even extended to switching off power to the escalators so that they all had to climb several flights of stairs carrying luggage.

Because of the slow progress up the stairs an angry mob of some 250 Filipinos trapped the Beatles party on the second floor of the airport, and the real nastiness began.

The Beatles and the others were spat at, and jostled and kicked. Although the Manila Times gleefully described the physical damage inflicted on the individual Beatles they came out of the brawl quite well. Others weren't so lucky. Alf Bicknell was knocked to the floor and kicked by military security men, suffering a fractured rib and spinal injuries; Brian Epstein was also kicked and thrown to the floor, suffering a badly-sprained ankle which meant that he had to be helped away; Mal Evans, probably came off worse, after being clubbed to the ground and then kicked several times in the ribs and chest and spine by a number of men.

As the battered party struggled through immigration, another mob appeared, shouting abuse and throwing objects at them. They then had to cross the tarmac to reach the safety of the plane, and many in the Beatles party were thinking only of the likely danger of sniper fire from the terminal as they ran and limped to the plane, and their flight, KLM 862. The plane was due to take off at 4pm but the authorities had one last gruesome surprise for the party. Two of their number, Tony Barrow and Mal Evans, were ordered off the plane and told to return to the terminal. The rest of the party were in a quandary, whether to cut and run, or wait for their friends, albeit not knowing if or when they would return.

Epstein and Vic Lewis were adamant that they should wait, and Epstein persuaded the flight crew to delay departure. Before getting off the plane, Mal Evans had asked the others to take a message back for his wife, clearly fearful that he wouldn't see her again. Fortunately Evans and Barrow returned thirty minutes later, having dealt with nothing more troublesome than a minor administrative error on the entry documents from three days earlier.

The plane took off at 4.45pm to a heartfelt round of applause from many of those on board, especially, of course, the Beatles party. And, as the plane took off, a press statement was issued on behalf of President Marcos stating that "There was no intention or the part of the Beatles to slight the First Lady or the Government of the Republic of the Philippines."

As with so many other places, the Beatles never returned to the Philippines. The difference in that instance is that they had no intention of doing so.

The atmosphere on the plane among the Beatles party was a mixture of relief and wild anger, and that anger was directed at the mess that was the Philippines, and the concerted mess that concerts and touring had become. But the strongest, deepest anger was directed at the man whose fault it all was.

Brian Epstein.

They had tickets booked back to London but Harrison and Aspinall intended stopping off in Delhi on the way back. Unfortunately, even though others in the party had expressed an earlier intention to join George in India, the pain of Japan and especially the Philippines made all of them want to get home as soon as possible. After a short refuelling stop in Bangkok the plane landed in India early on the morning of July 6th.

Totally in keeping with the shambles that the rest of the tour had become, there was a mix-up with the plane tickets. The portion of the flight from Delhi to London had been sold to other passengers and so the Beatles party was faced with the ignominy of being asked to vacate their seats and the plane.

The intention was to spend a quiet three days soaking up India and luxuriating in the fact that in that vast country even a Beatle could enjoy anonymity. The discovery that more than five hundred fans were waiting for them at the airport in New Delhi was a real shock. The fact that their hotel, the Oberjoi, was also under siege, was a really painful blow.

There were opportunities for some sightseeing and some shopping and a little relaxation after the shocks of Japan and Manila, but the most succinct comment on the whole situation was offered by Harrison when they got off the plane in London. The others offered some pithy comments about the behaviour of the officials in Manila but they were careful not to offer any comments which reflected on Epstein.

Harrison was asked what was next on the agenda for the Beatles to which he replied, "We're going to have a couple of weeks to recuperate before we go and get beaten up by the Americans".

At another Press Conference at the airport on the same day Epstein grandly announced that he was cancelling tours to the Philippines by Cilla Black and Sounds Incorporated. In the circumstances there seemed little or no chance of any major British artist risking a visit to that troubled country in the near future so Epstein's statement was perceived as little more than an empty gesture.

The party split up, with all the members returning home to rest and recuperate, and prepare physically and emotionally for the American tour in August. For some of their number, particularly Mal Evans and Alf Bicknell, there were severe physical injuries that needed to be repaired, and even Brian Epstein had suffered at the hands of the mob at the airport in Manilla. The kicks he took had inflamed again the spinal trouble which would impact badly on him in the weeks ahead.

For the Beatles it was a time of quiet and contemplation, and intensive thinking about the role, if any, of touring in their lives. The awful experiences in Japan and Manilla had moved their despair about live performances to a new depth, and there were none of them who were looking forward to the American tour with any sense of anticipation.

Epstein couldn't afford to wallow in his misery. He had lots to do ahead of the American tour and with that in mind he had a pre-tour trip lined up for the last week in July. Although pre-tour organisation was definitely the primary objective, he was also keen to meet Nat Weiss and try to clear any Seltaeb activity out of the way before the Beatles arrived back in America. Although there was always a danger of some mention of Seltaeb slipping into the ears of one of the Beatles while they were in England, that danger was multiplied several times during the period they were in the States. Anything he could do to reduce that danger was well worth it.

In the middle of July he made an important business decision by completely buying out his partners in the Saville Theatre. By purchasing the shares from Bernard Delfont and Tom Arnold he assumed total control of the leasing of the theatre. Those in his circle like Lionel Bart and David Jacobs, who had never been convinced about the Saville theatre proposition, were even more uncertain about this step fearing, yet again, that the calm and controlled Brian Epstein was being driven more and more by impetuous decisions and his erratic drug intake.

He attended the Ivor Novello awards at which the Beatles received the award for Top Selling Single of 1965 for 'We Can Work It Out', plus the award for Most Outstanding Song of the Year for 'Yesterday' and finally for the Second Best Selling Single of 1965 for 'Help!'. Though he was present, and was his usual charming self, more than one friend commented on how tired and strained and indeed ill he looked. He passed it off as the strain of the recent tour, and the injuries suffered at Manilla, and even the long-term back trouble caused at Houston Airport the previous year. But many who saw him that night thought it was more than that.

Over the next week his situation worsened and he was confined to bed at Chapel Street and finally the doctor confirmed a bad case of glandular fever, if not caused then certainly aggravated by the strain of Japan and Manilla. The condition worsened to the extent that, on July 22nd, the NEMS staff were ordered to cancel his forthcoming short trip to America and inform all the scheduled meeting contacts.

In his absence, life proceeded quite normally and quietly at NEMS. Vic Lewis was now well bedded-in, especially after his heroics in Manilla, and Epstein's absence was not suffered as it might have been in previous years. And, in truth, for many NEMS people it was often a relief to be spared the concern about the mood swings shown by the Beatles manager. Whether it was caused by his pill taking, or his love life, or his injuries, it was undeniable that he could often be a very difficult boss. The fact that he was spending more time outside NEMS, either working from home or at one of his many meetings elsewhere, was often a real boon for the NEMS staff.

The absence from the office of Epstein during the last days of July 1966 wasn't a blow to the organisation. They kept things ticking over, particularly the increasingly dependable Geoffrey Ellis, and any last minute questions about arrangements for the American tour could safely be left with him.

He didn't notice the publication on July 29th in America of an obscure teen magazine called Datebook. Epstein wouldn't have noticed it either, even if he had been well. It was a small, unimportant magazine in the American teen market. In its July 29th edition the magazine was running a cover story entitled "The Ten Adults You Dig/Hate The Most." Included in those ten adults was John Lennon, who was effectively skewered by the inclusion of sixty-one words about Christianity and Jesus Christ, the same words which had appeared, quietly and uncontroversially, in the Evening Standard in London earlier in the year.

Datebook simply took the remarks about religion and published them out of context, without any attempt to provide background by using some, if not all, of Maureen Cleave's original article.

For Datebook it became an unprecedented triumph. That edition sold more than a million copies in less than a week and the name of the magazine was used so widely around the world that the publicity value must have been incalculable. But the repercussions around America, and across the Atlantic, in the NEMS office, were scarcely credible.

Almost within hours of the appearance of the article there was an organised reaction against Lennon and the Beatles. American Christian fundamentalists declared themselves to be offended and outraged, and angry gangs, concentrated in the southern states and often with an uncomfortable affinity to the Klan, began to organise bonfires of Beatles records and memorabilia.

The first office burning was announced on radio on August 1st and then it became a rush to demonstrate the scale and depth of the outrage. The media, particularly radio, fed the flames and it became a forest fire of outrage against the anti-Christian Beatles, particularly in the south. Yet again the era, and the technology restrictions, worked against the Beatles.

The trouble had around forty-eight hours to really ferment before the London office was made aware of the issue. Even then there was a natural tendency on the part of most British people, particularly the writer of the original article, Maureen Cleave, to find the whole furore something of an inflated nonsense.

It all seemed a contrived artificial row about remarks which had been taken out of context, but Britain sat forty-eight hours behind the story, and the bonfires of Beatles products were burning higher and hotter all over America.

Disc Jockeys Tommy Charles and Doug Layton from a radio station in Birmingham, Alabama, WAQY, started the process and very quickly that station was joined by more than twenty other radio stations who banned all playing of Beatles music indefinitely from their airwaves. Tommy Charles momentarily increased his fame by organising an event involving a tree-grinding machine into which people were invited to throw Beatles records, turning them to dust.

Perhaps surprisingly, the anti-Beatles fervour wasn't confined to the south. Stations in Boston and New York also jumped on the bandwagon including, most pointedly, the station which had most shamelessly cashed in on the Beatles, station W-A-Beatle-C.

The town of Starke in Florida had the unpleasant distinction of becoming the very first place in the States to physically burn Beatles records. History students would later find the fact somewhat ironic given the public stance on segregation taken by the Beatles two years earlier at the Gator Bowl in nearby Jacksonville.

Investigation later showed that many of those banning the music had never played it anyway, but the anti-Beatles pro-Christianity bandwagon was too attractive to resist. Several stations organised their own local bonfires and went so far as to broadcast live the public burning of Beatles records and assorted memorabilia. People were invited to toss records, books and Beatles merchandise, anything Beatles related, onto a blazing bonfire while smiling at conveniently placed press and television cameramen and holding up the offending items from the Jesus-haters.

There was some delight in NEMS circles when some weeks later they learned that one of the stations most prominent in organising the bonfires, KLUE in Longview, Texas, was knocked off the air the following morning when a bolt of lightning struck their transmission facility. The lightning bolt caused extensive damage to their radio equipment, and left the KLUE news director unconscious.

Other parts of the world joined in. South Africa, safe in its apartheid cocoon, took issue with Lennon's remarks and even the Vatican passed comment on his views. In later times Lennon could have done an interview covered coast-to-coast in America and explained himself. He could have posted a Tweet, or set up a Facebook page or a YouTube channel and explained that he genuinely didn't mean to sound anti-Christian, that he was bemoaning the fact that mere pop groups were more popular than Jesus rather than celebrating it.

But the technology didn't exist and it would a long time, too much time, for the people in England, particularly Epstein, to appreciate the scale and speed of the story in America. This was most unusual, as one of Epstein's greatest gifts had always been his sense of which way the wind was blowing. His glandular fever didn't help the situation either. Without that sudden and unexpected illness, he would have been in America on the day that Datebook was published. He could, and almost certainly would, have dealt with the problem immediately, at source, and it seems fairly certain that it would have remained a short-lived local problem.

Instead it was now an international affair, and Lennon began to look hunted and haunted, even in England where the general reaction was one of amused disbelief at such extreme reactions to remarks that didn't seem so very contentious.

Advice from wiser heads in the States, people like Nat Weiss, Sid Bernstein and Walter Hofer tried to acquaint Epstein and others about the size that the scandal was starting to reach in the States, and it was this kind of counsel that convinced Epstein that something serious would have to be done. He even contemplated cancelling the entire American tour telling Nat Weiss that he would be prepared to pay the likely cost of $1million rather than risk injury to the Beatles, or even worse.

In an accident of unfortunate timing, August 5th saw the release of the new single and album in the UK. 'Yellow Submarine'/'Eleanor Rigby' was another stellar double A-side, while "Revolver" remains, after all these years, perhaps their finest collection of songs in album form. Sadly, the growing firestorm in America threatened to take the gloss off these recorded achievements.

On August 6th Epstein dragged himself off his sick bed at his recuperation spot in Portmeirion in North Wales to take an urgent flight to New York. The purpose was to hold a televised press conference. The objective was to calm things down, and to defend John Lennon against what Epstein clearly felt were unwarranted and unfair attacks.

It didn't really work. Many people had made up their minds despite evidence to the contrary and even Epstein's words did little to stem the bile being aimed at Lennon and the Beatles. Much against his better nature, Epstein, after discussions with Bernstein and Weiss, concluded that the only way to stop the horror from getting worse was for John Lennon to offer a public apology.

Epstein flew back to the UK and entered into a few days fevered debate with the four Beatles about the whole situation, with the two central questions being whether Lennon should offer the apology, and whether the tour should go ahead.

The Beatles creditably stood together, agreeing with John that his remarks were not incendiary and did not warrant an apology. On the wider issue there was more ambivalence, not least because, though there was nothing like a formal agreement or a pact between them, there was clearly an unspoken belief that America would be the end. It wasn't that they wanted to go out in a blaze of glory but after everything - the Cavern, Hamburg, London Palladium, Ed Sullivan, Shea Stadium et al - the performing career of the Beatles deserved a formal ending rather than just an abrupt, enforced stop.

And there was also the realisation among the four of them that the months since April, free from overseas duties and largely free from asinine PR requirements, had enabled them to concentrate their abilities and deliver something quite wondrous in "Revolver". With similar freedom from distractions in the future, what other wonders might be achieved?

So in the end the business arguments prevailed and Lennon agreed to try to make his views clearer, in the hope that his fresh words would constitute an apology. And the agreement and consensus, with a degree of trepidation, was that the tour would go ahead.

On August 11th the Beatles flew into Logan Airport in Boston and then onto O'Hare Airport in Chicago, arriving at 4.55pm. There were two press conferences scheduled, thanks to the severity of the situation. The Beatles party was staying at the Astor and so they progressed there directly from the airport. The first press conference took place shortly after their arrival, and so in Tony Barrow's room at the Astor Towers Hotel, John Lennon sat morose, his fellow Beatles on either side of him. They had longed to free themselves of the monotony of the usual press conference routine, the constantly repeated questions about hairstyles and marriage and earnings. Finally they had got their wish, but not in circumstances they would have desired.

This one found Lennon confronted by what was, in many respects, a baying mob, and many of the press were clearly smelling blood. It was difficult not to feel some sympathy with Lennon, clearly baffled by the vehemence of the questioning and the gleeful reluctance of some of the questioners to understand his comments, or crucially, what he had meant in the original interview.

By this point in the saga, Maureen Cleave had been interviewed about the situation and her candour in defence of Lennon was refreshing, but futile. Normally, press conferences featuring the Beatles were filmed and recorded by local tv and radio, but the event in Chicago had achieved global importance. Extracts from the local footage were carried around the world with the three major US networks, CBS, NBC and ABC, all showing special programmes that evening devoted to the issue. Back in Britain both BBC and ITN covered the press conference, with the time difference between Chicago and London working to their advantage.

It was a cruel, occasionally vicious press conference, and it was clear very early in the proceedings that many of those present weren't at the Astor to get an explanation from Lennon, or to hear an apology and report on the words.

One reporter even asked the group eerily if the whole Datebook thing was an attempt to raise the group's flagging popularity. This was possibly the first occasion that the question of flagging popularity had been raised. Lennon's response was possibly the only moment of humour in a grim session, "I could think of a much easier way".

There was an element of pay-back in play, and the ramifications would be felt by Lennon and the Beatles and Epstein for the rest of the tour and beyond. There were any number of reasons for the desire to see the mighty Beatles squirm, some childish and some quite serious, but the biggest cause of the disillusionment with the Beatles was that they had stopped being the loveable Mop Tops. And in this respect the huge success of the Beatles cartoon series on Saturday mornings on ABC was a prime factor, for the images of the Beatles forever projected in that series were of the Mop Top Beatles - cheeky, funny, irreverent. Not the guarded, world-weary, defensive men sitting in the Astor press conference.

Time, and the world, had moved on for the Beatles and America, and the Datebook incident wasn't the cause of the ending of that stage of the love affair that the country had with the Beatles. Datebook was merely a factor. Nothing more.

The press conference ground to a painful end with Lennon still desperately trying to find words to convince one and all that he had never intended to offend Christians or to disparage Jesus. But there were some, perhaps many, who didn't want to hear any apology, for that was a less sensational story.

Realising the futility of the attempt, the various Beatles minders, with the lead being taken by Tony Barrow, wound up the event. The press left, and Lennon was able to discuss what had happened and to reflect on the whole situation with his friends and colleagues.

At the second press conference held the following day the main topic once again was Jesus Christ, and what Lennon did or did not mean. Curiously there were other questions which related more to the stature of the group in America. One reporter pointedly asked if the group considered they were slipping, and the responses showed that it was a topic which was occupying the thoughts of the four Beatles.

But the purpose of being in Chicago wasn't originally meant to feature such a tempestuous press conference. The real reason was two concerts at the International Amphitheater in Chicago, the same venue used on their first tour in 1964. The bill also included the Remains, Bobby Hebb, the Cyrkle and the Ronettes. The two shows took place in front of 13,000 people at 3pm and 7.30pm, and while there was thankfully little evidence of ill-feeling against the group because of the Jesus furore there was also a distinct and tangible reduction in the excitement levels.

They stayed that night at the Astor before leaving for Detroit early the following morning. They did two shows, 2pm and 7pm, at the Olympia Stadium in Detroit, again a venue used on the 1964 tour. The two shows followed the pattern established at Chicago. Reduced trouble, less police violence, but also a discernable lowering of the volume and excitement levels. A number of tickets remained unused for both shows, as had been the case at Chicago, and there were reports of large numbers of tickets being cancelled at the other concerts on the tour.

During the gap between the two shows, the group watched in pained disbelief as news programmes showed a radio station in Texas, station KLUE, organising and conducting a public bonfire of symbols of the Beatles popularity. To add to the air of menace there was a scene showing a hooded figure described as the Grand Dragon of the South Carolina Ku Klux Klan, Bob Scoggins, ceremoniously nailing a Beatles album to a large wooden cross and setting fire to it.

There were a number of scarcely credible remarks from various other Klansmen justifying their campaign against the Beatles on the grounds that not only were the group, not just Lennon, blasphemous, but that they were not really 'white' either!

Various news reports showed a number of Baptist ministers making the threat to excommunicate any members of their congregation who attended any of the Beatles concerts. Many ignored the instruction, but large numbers of church-goers just stood outside the halls and arenas picketing and voicing their objections to the presence of the Beatles in their city.

The Beatles party left, using the novel transport form of Greyhound bus, immediately after the second show, and headed to Cleveland, Ohio, arriving just before 3am on Sunday August 14th. The mode of travel meant that it was easy to have huddled conversations with different people dropping in and out, and the main topic for discussion was what had become known as the Jesus situation.

But by the time they were driving to Cleveland, it was clear that the attempts to calm the storm, with Epstein's press conference and Lennon's public interrogation, hadn't worked. The frenzy was growing stronger in the south and showed little signs of dying away elsewhere in the country.

The Cleveland date involved just one concert at the Municipal Stadium in front of 20,000 people, but this brought the constant problem of crowd disruption viciously to the fore. Halfway through the fourth song in the set, 'Day Tripper', the baseball field which was the location for the temporary stage was invaded by up to three thousand fans. The four-foot security fence was broken, and then ripped down as the excited crowd burst through. There were too few police and security on duty and they were just helpless in the face of the overwhelming numbers.

The crowd raced for the stage and Mal Evans and Tony Barrow hurried the group off the stage and away to the comparative safety of the temporary trailer parked behind the stage, which they were using as a dressing room. The police brought in reinforcements but it took some thirty-three minutes - more than the length of the actual Beatles performance - to restore order.

During that period, the crowd invaded the stage and the area around it, and there were more unpleasant and violent scenes as the police fought, physically fought the fans, to enable the concert to resume.

When it was finally over and the group had made their usual lightning escape, many of the fans charged the stage and tried to steal Beatles items, including equipment and instruments, as souvenirs. Mal Evans and Neil Aspinall had to repel them until the security forces came to their assistance.

On Monday August 15th they took a plane to Washington DC to play a single concert at the DC Stadium for 32,164 people. Some empty spaces, some rioting, some police over-reaction. The usual, painful routine. What was different at Washington was the appearance before the concert of five members of Prince George's County Ku Klux Klan, dressed in their red, white and green robes, and led by the Imperial Grand Wizard of the Maryland clan. They held a parade and rally outside the venue to protest against Lennon's Jesus comments, and the widespread coverage of their rally, despite being led by just five people, showed that the crisis was far from over.

Immediately after the show the party boarded the tour bus for the journey to Philadelphia. There was just one show there with the most distinctive feature being the size of the crowd. The John F. Kennedy stadium held 60,000 people and if all the seats had been sold it would obviously have broken the Shea Stadium record from 1965. But the total fell far, far short and figures show that only some 21,000 people were in the stadium. Still a huge number but very disappointing, and a definite sign that the Beatles star was dimming.

A new problem affected the smooth running of the show - weather. The concert took place just as a severe electrical storm started, with huge flashes and almost-constant lightning, but the torrential rain thankfully didn't start until shortly after the end of the Beatles set.

Immediately after the show the Beatles party were back on the tour bus which took them to the International Airport in Philadelphia, from where they flew to Toronto for the sixth date on the tour.

Two concerts were scheduled in Toronto at the Maple Leaf Gardens which had been the same venue for the group in 1964 and 1965. The afternoon concert, at 4pm, was watched by 15,000 fans, while the 8pm evening performance was attended by 17,000 fans. The period in Toronto was made notable for Lennon's aggravating the general situation and inflaming the anti-Beatles sentiment even more. In the press conference he was asked, and freely answered, questions about the Vietnam War and draft dodgers escaping to Canada. Despite the urgent signals from the Beatles press representative, Lennon answered the questions as presented and stirred up even more of a hornets' nest back in the States. Above all because, as everybody in the party was painfully aware, there was just one more concert in America, in Boston, before the party would have to travel to the centre of the hatred, to the south. To Memphis.

After the show the Beatles party spent the night in Toronto before a flight south to Boston on August 18th, for a concert at probably their most unusual venue, the Suffolk Downs Racecourse in East Boston, Massachusetts. The concert was held in front of 25,000 fans stationed on the infield at the track.

And then, after a night in Boston, it was a flight into the south. The nadir of the tour, of the whole fetid mess that was the 1966 tour, came in Memphis. This was the Beatles first visit to the city, home of Elvis, and Sun Records and so much music that had been important to them while they were carving out a life as Beatles.

There were two concerts at the Mid-South Coliseum in Memphis, but neither were capacity. The Coliseum at that time was able to hold 13,300 people, but the first show at 4pm had 10,000 people present; the second, at 8.30pm, had the performance taking place in front of 12,500 fans.

Prior to the concert, a remote tv news feed, with the Mid-South Coliseum prominent in the background, showed a Klansman promising "a few surprises" for the Beatles.

The real strength of the anti-Beatles feeling was demonstrated in the Bible Belt, and the Memphis show gave the fanatics a chance to show their reaction to the Beatles and their recent actions. A local preacher, Reverend Jimmy Stroad, staged a loud rally outside the Coliseum, and a number of Klan members also picketed the venue wearing full ceremonial robes.

For the group it ought to have been glorious, a coming together of rock as it was exported by America and then re-imported via the Beatles. But it was anything but triumphant or joyful, and, after 1min 20sec of 'If I Needed Someone', a loud bang on the stage signalled the lowest point, and effectively the precise second when the Beatles ceased to be a touring unit.

Fortunately, the small explosion turned out to be nothing more malicious than a cherry bomb, thrown on the stage by an over-exuberant fan. The days when fans would throw innocent sweets like jelly beans at their favourite Beatle were far, far behind.

The incident with the cherry bomb went largely unnoticed by the crowd but it had a dramatic impact on the Beatles and their party standing in the wings, or behind Ringo's drums.

At the noise there was the smallest pause as the other three Beatles looked over at John Lennon, and there was clearly the thought, and even the expectation, that Lennon would be falling to the floor, killed or at least severely wounded by a rifle bullet.

When Lennon showed no signs of a bullet the Beatles glanced round at each other, clearly believing that if the shot hadn't hit Lennon it must have hit one of the other members of the group.

The song was playing out its last notes before the realisation dawned on the group that it wasn't a rifle shot, or even a bomb. That the craziness out in the streets hadn't been carried through to the concert arena, but it was noticeable that after the cherry bomb incident the pace of the concert visibly increased, until, after the final number, the group virtually sprinted off the stage. A series of decoy cars had been set up to try to fool protestors, but it didn't work. The tour bus being used by the Beatles was surrounded by demonstrators out on the highway, and it took some swift thinking and driving from the driver to avoid a major incident.

The group and their party were driven to Memphis Metropolitan Airport, and from there they took another flight to Cincinnati in Ohio, arriving at 1.35am on Saturday August 20th. They were prepared for one open-air show at Crosley Field Stadium but the weather was incredibly bad. Torrential rain, thunder and lightning, assaulted the arena which had been set up with one flimsy canopy over a bandstand stationed in the centre. Given the amount of electrical equipment it was a lethal situation. The support acts all performed, but the really heavy rain only started after the Ronettes finished their performance.

While he was setting up the equipment for the Beatles, the long-suffering Mal Evans plugged in George Harrison's amp, and the equipment shorted and threw him several feet across the stage. Seeing this, and realising the danger that the group would be in trying to use electric guitars in those circumstances, Epstein refused to obey the promoter's demand that the concert had to proceed. In the absence of any way to guarantee the safety of the group, Epstein called off the concert, the only time that had ever happened to the Beatles.

At the moment of cancellation there were just under 35,000 fans inside the stadium, but some juggling of schedules meant that the concert was able to be re-set for noon the following day.

Given that all the support acts had played the previous day before the downpour, the Beatles were the only group to play on August 21st. As soon as the concert finished they dashed to the airport to complete the 341 mile flight to St Louis, Missouri in time for the scheduled evening concert at 8.30pm.

However, the weather problems in St.Louis were, if anything, even worse than Ohio, with the show taking place in heavy, occasionally torrential, rain. The promoter had draped a clumsy shelter over the stage as protection against the rain but, to their horror, rainwater was still able to drip onto the amplifiers. It was this incident which finally convinced Paul McCartney that the Beatles should cease touring.

They took the group away after the show in a wide, steel-lined wagon which was completely empty. There wasn't even anywhere to sit and it was that concert, the danger from the rain, the declining attendance, and the laughable transport, on top of the horrors of Memphis and Tokyo and Manilla, that convinced all of the Beatles finally and irrevocably that enough was enough.

They left St.Louis after the concert and flew directly to New York, arriving at 3.50am the following morning. Less than a dozen fans were at the airport. They stayed at the Warwick, where they held two press conferences

The first was routine, but was painfully dominated by two topics - Vietnam and religion.

Then there was then a second press conference attended just by young fans. This was an idea promoted by the Beatles in which they hoped that a different format, and different questions, might emerge. The organisation of the event involved radio station WMCA, despite their participation in the Beatle ban.

DJ Gary Stevens invited listeners to the station to send a postcard with their name, address and telephone number. Some 50,000 entries were received, with 75 winners being chosen at random. At the same time, the Official American Beatles Fan Club held a similar contest which meant that a total of 150 fans attended the conference.

Each of the children, with ages ranging from 9 to 17, was given a gift pack containing individual signed photographs of the Beatles when they arrived in the conference room. When the group finally came into the room there were screams, and wild excitement which was sustained through the event.

On August 23rd, just over a year after the historic first appearance at Shea Stadium, the Beatles returned for a second concert at the venue. Despite Sid Bernstein's efforts it was a long way short of a sell out, with almost 11,000 of the 55,600 tickets still available as the Beatles took to the stage.

Despite the fall in attendance, the Beatles took more from their appearance than in the previous year, receiving $189,000 which was 65% of the gross takings of $292,000.

Despite the reduced attendance, there was still time for a flash of the old troubles, and during the performance of 'Day Tripper' hundreds of fans broke through the temporary barriers and tried to storm the stage. They were held back by security guards and none managed to get close to the Beatles, but people like Mal Evans were standing by the defend his charges if the crowd had broken through.

There was little inclination to celebrate after the concert at Shea. It wasn't like the previous year, and it was clear to everybody in the party that some element was missing.

In the circumstances a trip to Los Angeles was a perfect restorative. The touring party flew straight to the west coast after the Shea Stadium concert, arriving in the early hours of August 24th. There was a rest day scheduled before another flight up to Seattle ahead of the next concert.

Epstein didn't bother booking a hotel for the Los Angeles period. Instead, as on previous trips, he rented a house, this time at 7655 Curson Terrace in Beverly Hills. This base allowed them time to recover from the troubles of the past month, and also, in the beautiful, warm setting, to greet old friends like Derek Taylor, Roger McGuinn and Cass Elliott.

The social highlight of the brief stay in Los Angeles was yet another show business party thrown by Alan Livingstone of Capitol Records. This had become an annual treat for the Beatles, and allowed them to interact with stellar Hollywood personalities like James Stewart, Groucho Marx, Edward G Robinson and Jack Benny.

A morning flight from LAX took the group up to Seattle for two concerts at the Coliseum in Seattle on August 25th at 3pm and 8pm. They used the Edgewater Inn as a base and held a press conference there at the hotel, where the main topic for the questions, to the evident relief of John Lennon, was whether or not Paul McCartney and Jane Asher were going to marry that night.

The Beatles had played at the Coliseum once before during their first full American tour in 1964. However, in 1966 only just over half of the 15,000 available tickets had been sold for the 3pm show, although all tickets had been taken for the evening concert. They were supposed to fly back to Los Angeles immediately after the second show but the scheduled 11pm flight was delayed by more than five hours after a serious fault was discovered on one of the plane's wheels. The airline decided that the wheel in question was worn out and had to be replaced for safety reasons before any flight could be considered. No suitable alternative plane or flight was available, and so the group and their party had to endure the waiting time at Seattle.

Eventually they returned to Curson Terrace which, as in other places in America, was not requiring superhuman efforts from police and security to keep the group safe. It was undeniably quieter and calmer than on the two previous tours, but at least in Los Angeles there seemed no possibility that they were being judged harshly, or at risk, because of the Datebook furore.

Another rest day in Los Angeles had been arranged to allow them to prepare for the concert at Dodger Stadium on August 28th. During the preparations for that LA concert Brian Epstein felt compelled to issue a statement about the stories about declining interest in the group and faltering commercial appeal.

His statement was based on the fact that they were playing to larger audiences, citing the fact that the imminent concert at Dodger Stadium was attracting 10,000 more people than had attended the Hollywood Bowls shows. He also claimed that 400,000 people would have seen the group on the American tour, and that Bernstein had already offered Shea Stadium for 1967.

No mention of Datebook, or the Ku Klux Klan, or the violence, and it was the violence which became the lasting memory of the Dodger Stadium concert.

It later emerged that the concert promoter had only arranged to have 102 security staff on duty at the concert. Whether this was complacency or cost-cutting wasn't clear, but it was obvious that all the recommendations and pleas from people like Mal Evans, and Aspinall and Tony Barrow had been wilfully ignored. The results were sadly predictable.

Over forty fans were injured and a further 25 were arrested during a charge by fans on the main gates at the end of the concert. The fans ripped up seats and wooden barricades and used them as implements against the gates: police responded with clubs to hold back the crowds, with the inevitable result that bottles and stones and sticks were hurled at the police. It took over an hour to bring the situation under control, and large parts of the audience were detained in the stadium long after the Beatles had fled from the stage.

Even the departure of the group, which had become something of a smooth process, ran into major problems. The limousine carrying the group out of the stadium was trapped by crowds, and the driver was forced to turn back when dozens of boys and girls began climbing onto the car. There were several hundred fans surrounding the car and blocking the exit path out of the stadium, and now the lack of police and security became physically dangerous.

The limousine driver took evasive action by reversing through the crowd who were forced to leap out of the way. He then raced across the field trying to find an escape route, or at least a bolt-holt in which the group could be protected. He spotted a dug-out on the far side of the field and the Beatles were dispatched into the underground safety, where they were forced to cower for almost two hours in one of the players' dressing rooms. During that period extra police reinforcements were rushed in to clear the stadium and it was those police who eventually freed the group and guided them out to safety, but even then there were major problems.

The planned escape car had been wrecked by the hordes jumping and dancing on it. The ignition key had even been stolen as a souvenir.

The authorities tried to get the group out twice more in decoy limousines but the crowds made both attempts unsuccessful. Then they were smuggled into an ambulance which set off but then crashed into a heap of broken fencing which damaged the ambulance so badly that it couldn't be driven. Eventually two squads of riot police were brought into the stadium just to ensure that the group got out of the stadium, and using an armoured car, they finally got back to the rented house in Beverley Hills.

The highlight of the stay at Los Angeles was the visit to the house by Brian Wilson and Carl Wilson of the Beach Boys, probably the only group in the world who could rival the Beatles for inventiveness. That year, to set against "Revolver" from the Beatles their Californian friends would deliver "Pet Sounds", and both albums still regularly feature in lists of the Greatest Albums ever recorded. And, given the chance to speak to the enigmatic Brian Wilson at close quarters, all the Beatles took the opportunity to discuss with him the novel idea of abandoning touring to concentrate on writing and recording.

After the siege and the mayhem at Dodger Stadium it seemed even more desirable as a prospect and a way of life.

They flew to San Francisco at 4pm on August 29th for the final concert of the tour, for which only 25,000 tickets had been sold from a capacity of 42,500. The large blocks of empty seats made a vivid picture and a stark comment on the troubled tour.

There were several pictures taken from the stage by members of the group and this, being so unprecedented, was a signal that something most unusual was happening. In addition McCartney asked the press officer to make an audio recording of the concert, and so he stood in the middle of the field holding up a hand-held cassette recorder on which he made a recording of the final show of the tour. As a performance it was as perfunctory as all those that had preceded it. Only some extra linking material plus a greater use of adlibs indicated that this show was out of the ordinary.

And so the concert at Candlestick Park finished, the final show on that tortuous 1966 tour, and quite undeniably the end of an era.

After 1400 live concerts, the four men were tired of the travel, tired of the violence, sick of the hotel rooms and the mind-numbing press conferences.

Above all, they were tired of being Beatles.

It was over. Finally over. And they could move onto the next phase of their lives, but sadly, tragically, for two of them it would also be the final phase of their lives.

Lady Madonna

I now found myself in a real quandary. I had made good progress with the project, but so much progress that I was finding it very difficult to stop. It's a fact that I had no first-hand knowledge or recollection of the Beatles. Until I got involved in this ridiculous story about the Beatles and Brian Epstein, I had never really given any thought to them. I was always much more a soul and r 'n b fan. Pop music or even beat music had no interest for me. Even my family didn't really have any history with the group. Unlike so many stories you hear I had no family who were card-carrying members at the Cavern, or in the seats at Shea Stadium, or on the adjoining rooftop one day in 1969 when some long-haired group starting playing rock music.

No history. No real knowledge of the group, and, to be honest, no real interest either. Not until Jeff's brother opened his bloody mouth that night in the pub in Fitzrovia.

But after that, the deeper I got into the whole Beatles story, the more interesting, and beguiling, and frankly wonderful I found it. The whole story, even without the alleged deaths and murders, was quite captivating, and I found it was dominating my time. In some ways, it was taking over my life.

There were things I needed to do, work that I really should have completed, and it took a very sharp email from a colleague to bring me up short. The result was that I was forced to abandon my Beatles quest to go in search of the almighty dollar, but it was while I was earning a few pounds researching for some pathetic quiz show on one of the unheralded digital channels that I had a real stroke of luck.

I was compiling quiz questions to be used in the mindless programme. It wasn't difficult work. It would have made no demands on anyone with an IQ over 10, but the programme makers were happy with my work. I fulfilled the two main requirements for people working behind the camera in television - I am reliable and I am cheap. Some, including my bank manager, would say too cheap.

Just in case you are interested, the requirements for those working in front of camera are rather different, and differ by gender. If you are female, you need to be below thirty, preferably blonde, and with an appreciably large chest. If male, you need to have a look of dogged persistence, and to know somebody who runs a production company.

I filled neither category despite the size of my moobs, so I had to concentrate on the tv equivalent of share-cropping. Poor pickings, but at least I kept my integrity!

But working in tv the overwhelming advantage is the people you can meet. It's a bit like I've always assumed the theatre would be - itinerant, casual, but full of interesting, sparky people. Maybe not people that you'd think of marrying but certainly the types you'd be happy to meet in the pub.

One afternoon I rolled up to the production house in Soho where my research material was being used. I was ostensibly there to deliver my latest bunch of material but I was also hoping to sneak in another invoice. I generally tried to supply my invoices under cover of darkness to avoid causing too much laughter in the accounts department, but that day it struck me that there was a more pleasant atmosphere than usual.

It turned out to be someone's birthday, and most of the people in the office were all going to the pub after work for a token celebration. To almost universal horror one of the accounts people asked if I fancied joining them. Not having any competing social commitments for several months I decided to go along.

I'd never been in a pub with a bunch of people from an accounts office. Perhaps foolishly I presumed it would be tedious and boring but, do you know what - I was right!

No, that's not fair. I've had worse nights in a pub but most of those didn't involve jokes about double entry bookkeeping or the merits of Macros in Excel. At one point I went to the bar to get a round and one of the accounts managers, a rather stern lady called Pamela, came with me to give me a hand with the drinks. There was a huge crush at the bar and so we were forced to make small talk while the staff worked their way round to my end of the bar. She talked about the programme on which I was working but she looked as bored or embarrassed by the topic as I was and we slumped into an embarrassed silence. She clearly felt that as a senior person in the organisation she ought to make some attempt to talk to me.

"James mentioned that you were doing a programme about the Beatles!" she started. James is a producer in the company. Self-important, condescending. He'll be a real worry when he starts shaving.

"It's not really about the Beatles", I corrected. "It's more about conspiracies, about a wild idea that Paul McCartney died and that Brian Epstein was murdered."

"Murdered?" she repeated, suddenly interested. I suppose if you are working in an accounts office even the appearance of a fresh nose hair is interesting. "Why would he be murdered?"

"Oh, various reasons. Money mainly."

"Yeah?" she murmured, as she waved trying to attract the attention of the barman. She sounded interested. I suppose it was the mention of money and her being in accounts. "What happened?"

"There was a company called Seltaeb. A lot of money that should have gone to the Beatles went missing and-"

"Seltaeb?" she repeated mysteriously. "Seltaeb?"

"Yes, Seltaeb! It's Beatles backwards."

"I know," she nodded. "My godmother used to work for them....... in New York."

"What? Your godmother?"

"Yes, that's correct." Just at that moment, in an epic of bad timing, the barman smiled on us and I was distracted for almost ten minutes by the purchase of drinks and the ferrying of them back to the tables. Only then was I able to push a chair next to Pamela's to continue the conversation.

Unfortunately, it was too sudden and obvious a gesture, and several people noticed and exchanged telling glances. I wasn't aware of the attention, but it became clear from little remarks and things that happened in the future that several of Pamela's colleagues had misinterpreted my sitting next to her as some kind of romantic move on her. Anything but. She was a handsome enough woman but rather older than me and more likely to be attracted to someone who didn't fail GCSE Maths.

"You were saying something about your godmother," I started.

"Yes," she nodded, taking a sip of her lurid purple cocktail. "A friend of my mother's. She worked and lived in New York in the early sixties. Worked for this Seltaeb thing."

"Why did you remember this?"

"It's the name. It's such an unusual word, and when I realised it was the word "Beatles" spelt backwards it stuck in my mind."

I murmured something about the Beatles. I said she didn't look old enough to remember the group. It wasn't strictly true, but it's the kind of thing you are expected to say! "And she - your godmother - worked for Seltaeb? In New York."

"I don't know what she did, I don't even know if it was a proper job. I never really spoke to her about it, but I can remember my mother mentioning her in connection with the Beatles, especially after John Lennon got shot in New York."

"And did you ever meet her in New York?"

"Just once. My sister and my mother and I went to the east coast for a holiday in oh I don't know, round-about '75."

"And?" I prompted, a little over-sharply.

"We had a very nice time."

I sighed, barely suppressing the urge to groan. "I didn't really mean your holiday. I wondered about your godmother. Did you speak to her?"

"Yes, but not about the Beatles. It was family stuff...the weather...how we were doing at school - that kind of thing! Nothing to do with the Beatles or this Epstein chap."

"And that was the last time you saw her?"

She nodded. I noticed some of the others around the table paying attention to us and our conversation but I thought it was because I had mentioned the Beatles. Wrong. I was fast on the way to becoming the butt of a number of cougar-based jokes.

"And when did she die?" I asked gently, with as much sensitivity as I could muster.

"Oh, she's not dead!" replied Pamela brightly. "She's well past seventy, but she's not dead!"

I was so excited that I spilled my drink on my trousers. It left the kind of stain that men dread.

She smiled. It was a surprisingly warm smile. "We only exchange Christmas and birthday cards now, but she's very much still with us!"

And that was how, eventually, I came to meet the remarkable Chrissie.

The visit took some weeks to set up. Pamela had to establish contact and provide some proof that I wasn't an axe murderer, or a sex predator, or even a journalist. At the end of that process, I was given an anonymous Yahoo email address and some encouragement from Pamela to use it. I sent an email within a couple of hours and waited almost three full days before getting a reply.

It didn't appear to come from Pamela's godmother, who I had learned was called Chrissie. The reply referred to Chrissie in the third person and was signed, as much as an email ever is, with the single letter "D".

I started what became a very stilted email exchange which concluded with the grand pronouncement that the Chrissie lady would meet me in the Palm Court at the Plaza at 3pm on April 7th. That gave me just under two weeks to make the arrangements, but I was so excited at the prospect of meeting her that I would have been there the following day if necessary.

On the great day, I was there twenty minutes early. In fact, I was there more than an hour early, but I had stood outside in the chill of the afternoon staring up at the exterior of the building and trying to reconstruct the excitement of when the Beatles first arrived.

Eventually I moved inside and joined the elegance of the Palm Court. You could imagine Hemingway or Rockefeller or Fitzgerald ambling past, and I felt a little out of place. For the first time in twenty years, I was conscious that I hadn't polished my shoes.

The enigmatic D had requested a description, and also my mobile number. I had expected a call as I was gazing around at the splendour of the room, but it didn't happen. The room wasn't crowded but there were enough people sitting at the beautifully finished tables to force me to look round for the object of my attention.

She saw me first. She was sitting alone at a table to the left of the entrance, a half-consumed cup of tea the proof that she had also arrived before the appointed time. I suspect that Pamela had passed on my perfunctory description, for she noticed me and raised one arm in greeting to ensure that I found her table quickly.

She was tall and slim, elegant in a British, understated way. I noticed that her cream coat was buttoned up completely despite the pleasant temperature inside the Palm Court. She wore glasses but took them off and placed them carefully on the table as I approached. I found later that she only used the glasses for reading, although she hadn't been reading anything when I came into the room.

We talked gently, absently, about Pamela and about my television work which, I was delighted to discover, sounded far more imposing the way Pamela had described it than it actually was.

I was intrigued by her accent. Still conspicuously English but just an undercurrent of Bronx or Queens. And she had an endearing habit of slipping in occasional American expressions which sounded bizarre in her cut-glass accent.

I asked about her life in New York. She gave me a very brief overview of the near half-century since she came to New York. We made small talk about the traffic, and the crime rate, and Broadway trends, but there was an elephant in the room, and it began, as Sesame Street would say, with today's letter - "B".

I started off by asking her about life for her and her friends in New York in the sixties.

"It's difficult now to recall just how breathtaking New York was in the sixties. Of course it many ways it still is but back then....." She stopped and broke into a bout of coughing, heavy coughing, and she wasn't just clearing her throat.

"It really was the capital of the world". Her voice was soft, wistful, an old lady thinking over the triumphs of youth - far-off youth. "And we were like Kings and Queens. Anybody English was, especially anybody who had any link to the Beatles - however remote."

She stopped. There was a far-off look in her eyes: I couldn't decide if it was nostalgia or some undefined pain. She took a hesitant, timid sip from a glass of still water which was the only adornment besides her spectacles on the glass-topped table. A drop lingered on her bottom lip like a tiny jewel before slipping regretfully onto her chin. She didn't seem to notice. I didn't realise then that the water helped cool the fires raging in her throat, but that even the simple act of drinking caused her pain. Severe pain.

"I didn't really know them at all."

"Them?" I ventured gently.

"The group. The Beatles. John, Paul....." Her voice tailed off. I didn't know if it was weariness or the simple shorthand once used by people of a certain vintage for whom the names "John, Paul" would always represent the greatest pop group in history.

"I met Epstein though. Brian" she continued. There was a small smile at the corner of her mouth at the mention of the name.

"And what did you think of him?"

"Oh, he was wonderful," she rasped. "It's an old-fashioned term but he was a real gentleman. Such good manners. So thoughtful. You know, I mentioned to him once that it was my mum's birthday back in England, in Hove, and that I was missing her. He didn't say anything, didn't ask any details -"

More hoarse coughing, barely concealed by the urgent jabbing of a pale yellow handkerchief over her mouth. It had small white daisies around the edge, and also several tiny red blotches. They weren't embroidery.

"And, do you know, that night, a huge basket of flowers were delivered to her. Not from him. It just said 'from all your daughter's friends in New York'."

"That's nice" I smiled.

"He was so sweet, so nice. Just wrong to be mixed up with all those crooks and gangsters"

"Gangsters?"

"He was gay, you know. He tried very hard to hide it but I could tell....all the girls could tell. Of course it was different.....easier for him in New York than London. Less what-do-they-call-it, hassle? At least he wasn't around today. The Enquirer, the other rags. What's that one in London, the Sun?"

"Yeah, that's the main tabloid back in England"

"They would crucify him now. Sad."

"I get the impression that you liked him".

"Oh yes!" she breathed softly. It had poignant echoes of "Ready for my close-up, Mr.DeMille". She looked close to tears. I couldn't tell if it was just the memories, or pain, or something else. "I liked him very much. Such a gentle...gentle person. They shouldn't have done that to him."

"What? Tormented him"" I asked, thinking she meant some kind of queer-bashing. I was wrong.

"Killed him," she stated without a trace of emotion. "They murdered him."

I couldn't help myself. I gasped in astonishment. This was the first time I had heard anybody use the word "murder" in connection with Brian Epstein.

The matron sitting at the next table with the young man she hoped would be mistaken for her nephew jerked her gaze in my direction. She clearly resented the interruption, but I didn't care.

"Killed who?" I asked, knowing the answer, but wanting some certainty and clarification.

"Brian Epstein. Killed him at his house in London in '67."

"No!" I stated firmly. "It was probably accidental, or maybe suicide,...an overdose of sleeping tablets or something."

"Okay" she bleated, even more softly. "If that's what you want to believe. Hmm" she continued. "That's what they wanted people to believe, but they killed him. I know that for a fact. Undeniably."

I was staggered, reeling from this amazing revelation from this fading flower who didn't seem like a sensationalist, or someone given to lying. And the rasps from her throat made me think that intimations of mortality might well concentrate the mind.

"Who? Who killed him?"

"The mobs, the gangsters over here. They lost millions, maybe hundreds of millions in the mid sixties because of Epstein's mistakes with Seltaeb. He made some really powerful enemies, some very, very bad people."

"It was Seltaeb that I came to talk to you about. Nicky Byrne and all that stuff."

"Yes," she replied stiffly. I noticed that her posture had suddenly grown more rigid, as though she was making a real effort to stay upright. "Yes, that's what I meant when I said we were like Kings and Queens. Nicky Byrne made millions out of the Beatles, until Epstein realised what a mistake he'd made. But during that period we absolutely ruled New York."

"And Nicky Byrne?"

"Ohhhhh, Nicky. What can you say? The most wonderful and the most terrible man I ever knew. Not an ounce of conscience or scruples in him, but a smile that could drop a pair of knickers at twenty yards!"

The mild risqué remark seemed slightly shocking coming from such a venerable, slight old lady. As if by way of apology she lapsed into another savage bout of coughing, more prolonged and maybe more severe this time. I waited patiently, nervously for her to resume. Her eyes seemed slightly glazed with moisture as she continued her tale.

"Nicky was the classic example of right place, right time. He knew various people in the Epstein organisation in London. Nams, was it?"

"NEMS" I corrected softly.

"NEMS. Nicky was a wonderful self-publicist, but to be honest, it was difficult to trust a word he said. Even his friends like Lord Pergrine and Simon and Malcolm fell out with him."

"Didn't he set everything up over here? With Seltaeb?"

"Oh no, no, no!" she laughed. "Not Nicky. It was someone called John Fenton who set up Seltaeb and...there was another company, a different name, back at home."

"Stramsact" I stated, noting, without commenting, that even though she had lived in America for decades, she still didn't call it home.

"Yes, that's right. Stramsact. People think it was all Nicky Byrne that created Seltaeb and Stramsact, but that's a crock. It was John Fenton did it all, and even over here most of the work, the proper work was done by Lord Peregrine and the other Malcolm."

I was puzzled. This totally contradicted all the accepted wisdom about Seltaeb. All the books, all the research, maintained the story, the myth, that Nicky Byrne was in charge.

"I thought Nicky Byrne negotiated a deal with David Jacobs for the merchandising?"

She shook her head vigorously. "No, no! It was John Fenton. He was married to a lovely girl called..." She struggled for the name. "Suzy - that was it! John Fenton was married to Suzy in er '63 and her father was the man who ran United Artists films in the UK then."

"Can you remember her family name, or his name?"

"I can't remember him. I never met him. Only met Suzy a few times. Name?" She thought deeply. Her brow furrowed ever so slightly. It was sweet and beguiling. "It was something like that scientist guy - E-MC squared. That guy."

"Einstein?" I offered helpfully.

"Yes, that's him. That was the name" she stated confidently.

I flipped through the list of names I had detailed in my phone. I knew there wasn't an Einstein, but there was a name that was very similar. "It couldn't have been Ornstein, could it?"

"Yes, yes. I think it was!" she confirmed brightly.

Ornstein. So John Fenton, the man who had negotiated the deal of the century from under Brian Epstein's nose, had been married to Suzy Ornstein. And she was the daughter of Bud Ornstein, head of United Artists in Britain, and the man who had signed the deal for three films with Brian Epstein. It was an amazing development.

She didn't comment but she couldn't have failed to notice that I thought it was important news. "John told me that he was at Suzy's house one night and her dad was reading a contract on the table. John sat on the other side of the table and he was able to read most of it upside down."

"Really? That's quite a trick."

"John was a very clever man, and he had a background as a writer or a journalist or something like that, so he had some unusual skills." She didn't extemporise on what those skills might have been. "And I think there was a conversation about the Beatles and Suzy's dad mentioned the problems they were having with controlling the selling of merchandise. And that was it. John got the idea for Seltaeb, and put the proposition to the Beatles lawyer in London, and that was that. Met him a number of times to discuss it."

"And where did Nicky Byrne come into the picture?"

"Oh, much later I think!" she added. "Certainly after John Fenton fixed the deal."

"So how come Nicky Byrne got all the publicity and all the credit?" I asked. It was a genuine question. I really was puzzled.

She laughed softly. It tinkled like a distant wind chime. "Have you ever met Nicky?"

"No, I've not been able to trace him."

"Not surprised. I think he will have been keeping his head down for thirty years!"

"So Nicky Byrne didn't set Seltaeb and Stramsact up?"

She must have recognised my confusion. "Did you ever see a movie, a Woody Allen movie, called "Zelig"?"

I was confused and shook my head dumbly.

"You should. It's awesome! A great treat! A movie about a guy that inserts himself into various situations and takes the limelight and the credit for things he hadn't done."

"And?" I prompted gently.

"And that's Nicky" she answered. "We all said that Woody Allen could have written the movie about Nicky Byrne."

"But it was John Fenton who got the contract for Seltaeb?"

"Yes. He knew someone at NEMS, or their attorney, and when Brian Epstein realised that he was out of his depth with the merchandising - "

"Out of his depth?" I countered more sharply than I intended.

"Yes, but that's not a criticism. Anybody would have been out of his depth in that madness. There were lots of people queuing up to knock Epstein after the Seltaeb business went so wrong, but I always thought that was so unfair. He didn't have a chance. There wasn't a blueprint or an instruction manual that Brian could refer to. All he could do was to do his best and to trust people. That's what really cost him."

"Trusting people?"

"Oh yes. In his private life, but even more in business. I think that men like Nicky saw him as a soft touch, as an easy mark."

"So Nicky Byrne or John Fenton conned Brian Epstein?"

"Oh, my god, no!" Her outrage was surprising, touching. "I would never agree with that. Nicky Byrne was asked to do a job and he did it. Brilliantly."

"I'm sorry, I don't understand. If he did such a brilliant job then what was the problem?"

She sighed, heavily and took another sip of the water. The half slice of lemon had started to curl unattractively around the corner of the glass. She removed it delicately and dropped onto the glass top of the table. I was suddenly conscious that she was visibly tiring, and I was certain that the conversation would not last much longer.

"Imagine you are the manager of the biggest pop act in the world, something like Justin Bieber or that awful Lady Gaga. And imagine that you approached someone to run a merchandising operation, to merchandise stuff relating to that pop act."

"Yes?"

"And you have an agreement for a share of 90% to 10% for the two parties. Now, in that situation, who gets the 90% - you and the pop group or the person running the merchandising operation?"

"Well me and the group. Obviously!" I answered firmly, but the look on her face told me how stupid my answer was.

"Sorry, no" she coughed. "The agreement between John Fenton and Brian Epstein gave Seltaeb 90% of all the revenues."

"That's ridiculous!" I spluttered.

"Maybe. But nobody held a gun to Epstein's head. Nobody blackmailed him, nobody swindled him. There was an agreement presented to him and he signed it. In fact John Fenton went back four or times to see Epstein's attorney, David Jacobs, to have extra codicils put into the contract, and they agreed them all. They had plenty of chances to amend or even reject the contract."

"But didn't John Fenton object? Didn't he say anything?"

My ridiculous question brought forth the only humour during our encounter. "No!" she laughed. "Would you?"

Despite the tension I grinned at the absurdity of my question. Unfortunately the effort of smiling started her coughing violently again, and this time there was no coming back. After a few seconds, during which I sat helplessly looking at her, the doorman slid across and respectfully enquired if she needed him to get her a cab. She didn't reply. The merest hint of a nod gave him the answer and less than a minute later one of the city's fleet of yellow cabs was waiting at the entrance for her.

She unfolded herself wearily out of the armchair and stood forlornly in front of me as I jumped to my feet to say goodbye. I was struck with the flash of panic that, because of her obvious illness and the overall situation, that I might not get the chance to see her again.

"If you're well enough, could we meet again?"

"Oh, I think so" she replied, a voice as thin as watery gruel. "Too few young men ask to meet me these days. I'm not going to miss another opportunity."

"I'll call you to set -"

"No!" she replied with surprising firmness. "We'll call or email you when I'm feeling up to it, when I've sorted through some papers."

I started to agree but she was gone. My last sight of her was huddled down in the back of the yellow cab as it groaned its way downtown.

But fortunately that wasn't to be my last encounter with that remarkable old lady.

It was ten days before I heard from her again. I spent part of the time worrying about what was happening, whether I'd hear from her again, but in truth I really enjoyed those precious few days in the States.

At the start I hung around New York City thinking I might get a call from her, although I knew very well that any call would be to set up a second meeting at least 24 hours later, if not longer. I spent time in Queens where I had lived for several months while working for NBC.

More poignantly I spent two or three days wandering around the Village, retreading those ancient footsteps of Bob Dylan, Phil Ochs and Tom Paxton.

But all the time - will she call? When will she call?

Although I greatly enjoyed the days in and around the Village it left me with a strange sense of loss, of emptiness. Greenwich Village had always been a tumult of strange walkways and distinctive coffee-houses, of quaint shops and idiosyncratic tenement dwellings, but much of that had gone. I was aware of the emigration, forced or willing, out to places like TriBeCa, and SoHo and Williamsburg, and this had stripped much of the life out of the Village. I greatly relished my trip back to the Village but I wasn't sorry when it ended. Washington Square was still there, still grand, and Bleecker and MacDougal were as imposing as ever, but something had gone.

The Greenwich Village experience left me feeling slightly unsettled, uncomfortable, and I decided to take a short trip away. The West Coast beckoned but another nostalgic and highly relevant trip lured me in before I left New York.

I blagged tickets from an old NBC colleague and made my way along Broadway, past the almost-forgotten magnificence of the Brill Building, until I reached 1697 Broadway. This venerable old building has an immense place in American showbiz history. It has been the location for television broadcasts from CBS since the thirties, with the primary focus being on the David Letterman talk show, The Late Show, since February 1993. In July 2009 the theatre staged a rooftop concert which featured one Paul McCartney, a strange echo of the past given that on February 9th 1964 the theatre, still under the control of the avuncular Ed Sullivan, saw the first tv appearance in America by the Beatles.

Much of my early research into the McCartney-Epstein story had revolved around that legendary show and it was a strange feeling standing on the pavement, or as Chrissie would have said, sidewalk, outside the Letterman Show building.

As it happened the David Letterman show when I visited wasn't earth-shattering. Some anonymous American movie star plugging some forgettable film, and an aggressively tuneless grunge band destroying something which slightly resembled a song. Letterman's monologue was good though, and the house band, under the timeless brilliance of Paul Shaffer, was as excellent as I expected.

I wandered out onto Broadway imbued somehow with the spirit of the Beatles, replete with memories of those far-off black and white images of them performing 'She Loves You', 'All My Loving', and 'I Want to Hold Your Hand' while giving America a collective seizure. There are many candidates for Days that Changed America - Lincoln's Assassination, Pearl Harbour, the slayings of J.F.K. and Martin Luther King and Robert Kennedy, and inevitably 9:11, but on the list, for much happier reasons, must always be that incredible first Beatles performance on Ed Sullivan. 73 million people and a country still consumed by collective grief after the Kennedy murder in Dallas and the epic pain of the Washington funeral. 73 million people receiving a communal Restorative in a five-song show that put a smile back on America's faces.

And that sense of joy stayed with me as I walked away from the theatre back to my hotel but the evening convinced me that a trip to La-La land, the West Coast, would sustain me during the wait for the phone call.

I had convinced myself that she would call when I was in the air, somewhere over the Mid-West, but it didn't happen. Instead I had three carefree days in LA and Santa Monica catching up with old friends and then took my hire car up the breathtaking expanse of Highway One. It was a journey I had made several times previously, but one that I always found exhilarating and, in a strange way, moving.

Places like the Hearst Castle at San Simeon were redolent with the history of old Hollywood in the thirties and forties, and it was difficult to drive north towards San Simeon without imagining the ghosts of Gable, and Tracy and Flynn driving in open-top splendour toward weekends hosted by William Randolph Hearst.

I didn't bother stopping at Hearst Castle. I had been there twice previously and it had no attraction for me any longer. More important by far were the two areas north of San Simeon, and one of my main reasons for making the fairly long trip by road. Approximately ninety minutes from San Simeon lies the region known as Big Sur with the magnificent forests of the Los Padres National Forest. Highway One crawls under the massive trees and exits at the Pacific paradise of Carmel, which has long been my favourite place on the planet. Just north of Carmel is the glory of Monterey, and from there it's just a beautiful leisurely drive up into San Francisco.

I wanted to stop at both Big Sur and at Carmel - Derek Taylor, Monterey Pop Festival et al - but I didn't. I had the nagging feeling at the back of my mind that I needed to be near an airport, near to the link to New York in case she rang. But as I drove along that gorgeous Pacific coast with the heady scent of San Francisco in my nostrils the phone rang, and it was her.

Thank God for mobiles. It was her and she was willing to meet again.

I had no set plans, no itinerary, so it was easy to change my arrangements. I went straight to San Francisco International Airport and booked the first flight to JFK New York. Fortunately, even with the enhanced security caused by various terrorist alerts, the transit through SFO was relatively smooth, and I was back in New York late that same night.

I had been asked to come to a house in Wainscott in East Hampton, part of the Hamptons out at the end of Long Island. Although Long Island lies some way to the south of Great Neck and Fitzgerald's fabled West Egg and East Egg, it can't be denied that parts of Long Island and the Hamptons are quintessentially Gatsby territory.

No general directions were offered, other than an address and the mention of the Hamptons, and there was certainly no offer of help with transport. I had arranged to visit Chrissie forty-eight hours after I had returned from the west coast; she seemed happy with the arrangements I offered and I made sure that I was not late.

I drove out there. There hadn't been a railway station in Wainscott since before the Second World War, and, like so many things about the Hamptons, it seemed like a slice of America long past, a serious of vignettes from Bing Crosby or Judy Garland films.

The journey, once I'd left the urban wilderness of Queens behind, was a two-hour joy. Not exactly Norman Rockwell but very pleasant all the same. I wasn't aware at that time that Wainscott included some of the most expensive property, not only in America but also in the world. The highway system seemed designed to make the best of life for the Long Islanders and so I was able to follow Highway 27 in its various incarnations all the way from Manhattan.

At various points it was two or four or even six lanes wide, sometimes called Montauk Highway, or Memorial Highway or, more prosaically, Southampton Bypass. I was oblivious to the local features. My mind was concentrated solely on the meeting to which I was hastening, and all I could think of was the dozens of questions revolving in my mind all related to Nicky Byrne and John Fenton and Lord St.Germans and Seltaeb and Brian Epstein, and even more lingering questions about James Paul McCartney.

My SatNav directions instructed me to stay on Highway 27 until I reached the pretty landmark of the US Post Office and then swing right onto Northwest Road. Another right turn onto Roxbury Lane and I was almost at my destination. I had been told to turn onto Sayre's Path and head towards the coastline, watching out for a single-plot Colonial house set back in its own grounds from Sayre's Path.

The directions couldn't be faulted. The house was all I expected with a vista imprinted on my mind from decades of American films and tv series.

In fact my first impression was that it looked like a smaller version of the property in the film, Holiday Inn - the Bing Crosby film which featured the first appearance of the timeless Irving Berlin classic, 'White Christmas'.

There was a wide, sprawling driveway in front of the house, partly occupied by a fabulous scarlet Pontiac, and behind it was a rather more demure small Renault. I parked carefully behind the green Renault, gathered my bag and papers, and walked briskly to the front door.

My arrival had been noted. I didn't even get the chance to ring the bell. The door swung open and I was faced with a young woman, dressed casually but expensively. She stared at me for a second with an expression which mixed boredom and disinterest, and then jerked her head backward and muttered "She's in there".

I presumed that this might be D, but she offered no information. Indeed I was mildly surprised that I wasn't asked for any form of identification, or that the woman offered no kind of greeting to me. She turned on her heel and walked into a spacious hallway across a burgundy carpet with a deep, thick pile. The decoration was simple but classic, and it had clearly benefitted from an unrestricted bank account.

Several doors opened off the hall which was dominated by a traditional, spacious staircase. The only doorway that allowed a glance inside showed an immense kitchen built around an island topped by impressive black marble slabs. I didn't get the chance to look any further. My taciturn guide touched my arm and guided me soundlessly into a room on the far side of the hall from the kitchen. "In here", she stated without a trace of emotion, pushing on a door which creaked slightly as it opened.

I was allowed into a wide, long room, rich in cream and brown. The far side of the room was filled with massive French windows through which I saw an undulating lawn beyond which there was a copse of trees. In the distance, past the trees, a smudge of grey and blue told me how close to the Atlantic we were.

I didn't know enough about décor to identify how ostentatious the fittings were but I could detect value. This room hadn't been assembled on the cheap. Another deep pile carpet covered half the room, giving way to a clean-lined wooden floor which drifted across to an imposing stone fireplace which was fronted by a beautiful throw rug.

Three paintings were in evidence on the walls. One was a portrait of the lady I had come to meet. Clearly she had posed for it some years earlier but the artist had captured her fine cheekbones and the quizzical, almost haughty expression which she invariably wore. The other two paintings were landscapes. I was too far away to read artist's names but neither looked like a print.

The only incongruous feature of the decor was a display cabinet constructed in some gentle and attractive rosewood. The slightly tinted glass doors made seeing the contents rather difficult but a brief glance suggested that the cabinet housed a series of dolls or models.

I didn't have time to think about this. My hostess was sprawled across one limb of a huge "L-Shaped" sofa arrangement. She had a sheaf of papers on her lap and was intently staring at one sheet as I entered and coughed gently to attract her attention. She stopped momentarily as if trying to identify the sound, then turned her head to the right and saw me hovering near the door.

"Hello again!"

Her voice sounded a little brighter than on our previous meeting but her position on the sofa seemed a little unnatural. She waved me across to a seat of the other wing of the sofa and waited for me to settle into a comfortable place.

"Would you like a beverage?" Americanisms, again. Beverage, not drink. I shook my head, perhaps a bit too vigorously. I didn't want any distractions.

"I suppose you've been thinking about what I told you, about Seltaeb and Nicky Byrne and John Fenton?"

"To be honest I've thought of little else!" was the completely truthful answer. "I've put together some questions to ask you."

"I rather thought you might!" she replied drily. "But I've been going through some papers that might help you as well." She picked up some of the papers lying casually to her left. I could see even from a few yards that most of the papers were a mix of computer print-outs, typewritten sheets and even a few handwritten notes that looked like letters. Old letters. There was also what looked like a couple of hardback books. Both had dark blue covers.

"Questions. You said you had questions?"

"Er, yeah."

"So?"

I grinned. It was a very fair question. "I suppose the first ones, the obvious ones, are Why Now? Why Me?"

She put the papers down delicately on her lap and stared intently at me. I noticed for the first time how luminous her eyes were, but I couldn't ignore the guarded, almost haunted, expression.

"Why now?" she repeated softly. "I suppose it's just time. I've sat on this stuff, the Seltaeb stuff, for so, so long. Almost half a lifetime it's been. And it's not fair. It's just not fair!"

I was confused. It wasn't the reaction, or the opening to the conversation, that I was expecting. "Well, what isn't fair? What do you mean?"

Several seconds passed during which I had to talk over another bout of coughing, again punctuated by more vigorous dabbing of the handkerchief to the lips. "It's just the fact that when there's money involved, especially really big money, then anything goes."

"Anything?" I prompted gently.

"Yes, anything. Lying, swindling, fraud......murder."

"That's a big claim!" I ventured.

"It's all in here" she retorted, patting the sheaf of papers.

"Okay, but then there was a second question - why me?"

"You?" she asked, almost flirtatiously. "Yes, why you? I suppose the simple answer, the honest answer, is that you are the first person to find me and ask the questions."

"What? Nobody has ever asked you about Seltaeb and Epstein and those things?"

"Nobody outside my immediate family and friends. It's always amazed me. I last saw Nicky Byrne in the city in 1968, the year after Brian's funeral, and after that the first time I had Seltaeb mentioned to me was when you emailed me a few weeks ago."

"And what about John Fenton?"

"I'm not sure. I think I only met him a few times. He wasn't really involved with America, with Seltaeb. I think he devoted himself to Britain and Europe, and maybe the rest of the world. I don't know. But not here. Not America. That was down to Nicky Byrne and Lord Peregrine and Malcolm, Simon and the others."

"So John Fenton didn't come across to New York much?"

"I don't know. I wasn't involved in the day to day stuff. But I think he would have stopped coming over when they all fell out with Nicky Byrne!"

"Fell out?" I queried.

"Yes, all of them. John Fenton, Lord Peregrine and the rest. It got really nasty, but it was all Nicky's own fault."

"Why? What happened?"

"Oh he was crazy. A real Belle Vue job! He was completely out of control. Spent money like he was sponsored to do it."

"And that's what caused the problems between him and the others?"

"That, and Nicky's attitude!" she scoffed. "It was lunacy. They'd been given the winning Lottery ticket with Seltaeb, and he was ripping it up and throwing away the pieces."

"You sound as though you were close to it all for a while?"

"Yes, I was. But then it went badly wrong, 'cos of Nicky Byrne's stupidity, and then the trouble started."

I had a notepad on my knee beside the tape recorder which was whirring by my left knee. On the pad I had written "TROUBLE!" in caps. She saw me do it.

"Trouble? What was that?" I asked gently.

"The group that started Seltaeb and Stramsact - John Fenton and the others - fell out. Big time! Lord Peregrine and Evans got really riled with Nicky Byrne so that they started proceedings against him. Fenton was really upset with Nicky as well but he wouldn't have anything to do with legal stuff. Then the Seltaeb group collapsed. It got really ugly."

I was busy scribbling notes on my pad and that provided a helpful little gap in the conversation.

"So when did Seltaeb fall apart?"

"I'm hazy about dates. The law suits started in '64 and that would've carried on for a couple of years. Lord Peregrine and Malcolm and Simon had gone from New York long before that, but if you want dates they're all in here."

She patted the papers which were next to her.

"And what's that....those papers?" I asked, more timidly than was necessary.

"Stuff from then. The sixties. Nothing legal. No contracts or anything. That sort of stuff was nothing to do with me. If anyone's got stuff like that it would be John Fenton. But there's some stuff I think you'll find interesting. And, of course, you've also got my diaries from that time."

She slipped some of the papers to one side, and picked up the two hardbacked books, one of which fell open. I could not read the contents, but the layout was classic A5 Diary format, with copious longhand writing on the pages that were visible.

"Your diaries? You'd entrust your diaries to me?" I breathed, scarcely trusting in the answer.

"Uh huh!"

"Why? I mean…I'm really pleased, and really grateful, but I don't understand why you'd trust me."

"Yeah." She suddenly looked and sounded tired. In the distance I was conscious of Atlantic breakers on the shore. "You asked me, Why Now and Why me? Well the real answer to the question, Why Me? was that you mentioned the magic name."

"Mal?"

"Yes, Mal Evans. One of the real unsung heroes of the Beatles story, and a really decent, unappreciated man."

"You knew him then?"

"Oh yes" she answered huskily in a way that made me wonder just how well she had known the one-time Beatles Road manager.

"How did you know him? When did you meet?"

She shuffled the papers and glanced intently at one of them. Shaking her head she looked up at me and commented, "Oh, I don't know. I think it was '64 definitely, some time during the summer. When the group came over for their first American tour."

I glanced down at my iPhone on which I'd typed various notes including some crucial dates. "That would be August '64. They'd made some appearances earlier in the year, after the Ed Sullivan appearances, but the first proper tour started in August in…..in San Francisco."

"Yes."

"Didn't you meet them, or Mal Evans on the first trip, in February?"

"No. I told you last time that I'd just met Brian. That was at the Warwick, or maybe the Drake. Nicky took a little party of us to meet Brian. He had a couple of people with him. That was before Derek Taylor. They had that pompous little prick of a Press Officer with them. I'm sure Mal wasn't there. I think Brown might have been there. Peter Brown!" The way she hissed the name made me suspect that Mr. Brown, and the unfortunate Press Officer, Brian Sommerville, weren't on her Christmas card list. A glance at my notes showed that she must have been wrong about Brown. He didn't join NEMS until 1965, but I didn't want to correct, or interrupt, her.

"But you think you met the group, possibly with Mal Evans, during that first full tour, during the summer? Where?"

"It was New York. Definitely New York. It wasn't Carnegie Hall, because it was an outdoor concert. And it couldn't have been the Shea Stadium thing because that was a year later, in '65. No, it was the tennis place - Forest Hills."

My electronic record revealed that the Beatles had performed concerts on consecutive days at Forest Hills Tennis Stadium in August 1964, on Friday 28th and Saturday 29th. There was also a sub-note showing that on the Friday the group and Epstein went to the Delmonico Hotel where the writer Al Aronowitz introduced them to his friend Bob Dylan. And August 28th would prove to be the night when the peerless Dylan was responsible for first adding marijuana to the wide range of influences operating on the Beatles.

"Yes, I'm sure it was Forest Hills because I can remember Nicky taking two limos out there about a month earlier for a Barbra Streisand show. There was some sort of Music Festival on at Forest Hills that summer -"

"You saw Barbra Streisand there?" I asked, barely hiding my admiration.

"Yes, I really loved her. We'd been to see her in Funny Girl at the Winter Garden Theatre sometime that spring, and then she was doing some outdoor dates. Forest Hills was one of the dates but that was definitely about a month before the Beatles went there."

"I can't believe you saw Streisand in Funny Girl, and then in a concert." My admiration sounded a bit sycophantic, but was entirely genuine.

"Yes" she said dreamily. "She was amazing, a real force of nature. And I heard her sing one of my favourite songs, 'My Colouring Book'. Wonderful."

Despite my jealousy that she had somehow managed to see one of the artists I most admired, this was a diversion from the subject at hand. "So you think it was the Forest Hills concert when you first met the group, and also Mal Evans?"

"Yes," she replied firmly. "That fits, although when you say "met the group" that was a bit of an exaggeration."

"Why?"

"It wasn't an introduction. It was more like the merest handshake. I don't think the group knew or cared who anyone was, but there must have been a thousand people backstage, all wanting to meet them. We were luckier because of Nicky. Seltaeb made us important so we were closer than most, but closer doesn't mean close. Not really!"

"So did you speak to any of them?"

"Just George. He was lovely. Very shy, but very funny. Really dry sense of humour. I offered to show him round New York but he said there were problems with security, and in any case he had a sister or an aunt or someone who lived over here."

"I get the impression you liked him as well?"

Her eyebrows jumped slightly at my mention of "as well" but she didn't pick me up on it. "Oh yes. I thought George was wonderful. It was him that introduced me to Mal backstage there at the Forest Hills."

"And what about Mal?"

"I didn't know what to make of him at first. He was such a big guy, you didn't know how to take him. Could come over as quite full of himself, but not when you got to know him."

"Who was there with you?"

"I er don't really recall. It was a Seltaeb party so it would have been Nicky, Malcolm and the others."

"Others?" I enquired, although I largely knew the answer.

"The others involved with Seltaeb. Mark Warman, Simon Miller. Maybe John…..John Fenton, and Lord Peregrine. There was another called Malcolm Evans, but he's completely different from Mal Evans who worked with the Beatles. I really can't remember exactly who provided the initial introduction but something tells me it was Simon who was talking to Mal when George introduced us."

"At Forest Hills? At the show?"

"Yes. Backstage. He spilled a bottle of beer on me. He bumped into me and knocked the bottle out of my hand and onto my jacket. He was mortified. It was really sweet."

"It seems a lot of trouble for George Harrison to go to - introducing you to people like Mal Evans."

"Well, I used to be quite an attractive woman" she answered sharply, then smiled at my obvious embarrassment. "No, the simple fact was that we had English accents so we stood out from all the arse-licking Americans surrounding them at that time. People like that awful Murray the K! No, it was the accent - nothing more."

"I had a drink in my hand," she continued. "George bumped into me, and some of the drink went over my top. George apologised, and Mal was standing nearby, and George called him and asked him to get a cloth and another drink for me."

"Like a servant?" I asked.

"No, no!" she corrected. "It was never like that. I always thought of Mal and the others - particularly Mal - as just being devoted to the group. He would have done anything for them, and he did! They took that for granted. In many ways they took advantage of him."

"Really?" I murmured. "I didn't realise that."

"And much as I liked Brian I thought he was one of the worst! He didn't seem to be cruel, or nasty, but he had a really old-fashioned, kind of Masters and servants attitude." She paused, thinking. "What was that British tv show, about a big house and the toffs and the servants?"

"Downton?"

Her blank look told me she wasn't a fan. "It was called Upstairs....Upstairs something."

"Upstairs Downstairs?" I suggested.

"Yes, that's it!" she confirmed. "That was the show. Full of below-stairs and above-stairs, Master and servant stuff. Brian Epstein had a touch of that about him."

"With Mal Evans?"

"Yes, with Mal and with others as well. But I never really saw that. I only ever really saw what happened with Mal."

"You saw it?"

"Only once. But Mal told me stories - like the pathetic amount that he and Neil...Neil - was it Anderton?"

"No, Aspinall. Neil Aspinall" I corrected.

"Right. Well, it was a pathetic amount that Mal and Aspinall were paid every week. There was an interview I read that George Harrison did where he said he found something that showed how much the Beatles earned at one point in 1963. They took in about £75,000 and the four Beatles each took about £4000. Brian Epstein as manager got around £2000 a week. How much do you think Neil and Mal got?"

I shook my head indicating that I didn't know. "£25 each! And when they flew overseas, Brian and the group travelled in first-class in real style. Neil and Aspinall were kept in the back in steerage."

I nodded my agreement that this was unfair, but I couldn't take my eyes off the two diaries she had offered, and effectively promised to me.

"Mal Evans did a lot for the Beatles and for Brian Epstein, and they screwed him. And he took physical beatings for them, and suffered for them, electrocuted, and he helped them do something so outlandish - so crazy that -"

She stopped suddenly and rubbed her hands across her eyes in a gesture of weariness. I was aware that she was visibly tiring and, not being a proper journalist, I was trying to be considerate about her health. But I didn't want to go, not at such a key moment. Especially when I was so keen to hear what it was that was so outlandish and crazy. I had a slight, breathtaking idea what it might be, but the moment had passed. And then a very rare brainwave hit me.

"Look" I started. I've noticed that I'm spending too much time with Australians. "I would love to carry on talking but I'm worried about tiring you out." She didn't argue. "So here's a suggestion. Why don't I take your diaries and read through them and then, when you are up to it, I'll come back with some specific questions?"

She seemed to brighten at the thought that I would be departing. It's strange how often that happens with women in my company. "That would be excellent!"

There appeared to be no movement, no gesture but almost immediately the door to the room opened and the unsmiling D stood in the doorway. She hovered like an unwelcome smell in a lift until I took the hint. Chrissie smiled at my temporary discomfort and passed the two diaries over to me with, "That sounds like a plan. Read through them and email me any questions and then we can arrange another session, either here or at the Plaza."

"Do you still go into the city, regularly?"

"Oh, if I can, I do" she smiled, brightly. "I've not lived in Manhattan for many years but it's still my most favourite place on earth."

The way she enthused the expression "most favourite" made her seem like a young girl with her life before her, and I liked her all the more.

D, still by the door, didn't make a sound, but her superpower was clearly the ability to reduce the temperature in a room. As Chrissie was talking, the temperature seemed to drop by ten degrees. I sensed I was in danger of overstaying my welcome. I stood up, pushed my pad and recorder into my bag and carefully placed the two blue books safely deep inside. I shook Chrissie's hand warmly and sincerely. She didn't get up. I turned and walked briskly to the door, avoided the real temptation to click my heels in front of the stoney-faced D, and crossed the hall to the front door.

She glided past me and had the door open before reached it. I walked through and said "Thank you. Let's do this again some time" but the door had closed firmly behind me before I got the verb out.

That didn't matter though. I had Chrissie's diaries from the sixties, and who knew what treasures they might reveal?

The diaries were revealing and puzzling and enlightening. I spent many nights poring over the scribbled notes and compiling questions I intended to submit to Chrissie. I hoped that it would not be just an email exchange. I really hoped I could meet her again. Besides being a very nice and regal lady anyway, I had the real feeling that she had been present at an important moment in history. Maybe, only a small moment, but the Beatles in America in 1964 was, by any estimation, a major event.

There were strange remarks in the diaries, references to "ME", who I took to be Mal Evans, and frequent, not always complimentary, references to "N". From the context I took "N" to be the ubiquitous Nicky Byrne, and there were plenty of other remarks about other people in and around New York at that time. I didn't know most of them, and presumed that most of them were irrelevant to the story.

In a way I thought, and perhaps hoped, that Chrissie's diary material would prove an interesting backdrop, a bit of local colour, nothing more critical than that.

As a result I threw myself back into the basic research, believing that my incisive investigation would find the answers, whatever they were. Before my trip to see Chrissie, I had just finished researching the 1966 tour of America by the Beatles, and so that was where I picked up the thread of the research and the story.

The return to Britain for the Beatles was wildly different to all those that had preceded them. For anybody who had been at Heathrow in October 1963 when the group returned from Sweden, or during those ecstatic returns from America in 1964 and 1965, the atmosphere in September 1966 was markedly and visibly different. It was Hitler's 6th army slinking battered away from Stalingrad ground into defeat, rather than the triumphant Beatles parades of years gone past.

And no wonder. Since leaving England in July for the trip to Japan the four Beatles had suffered physical pain, death threats, incarceration by over-zealous security staff and, almost inevitably, a total inability to enjoy what they were doing.

All the pent-up frustrations of the increasingly hapless performances since Beatlemania became the norm rather than something remarkable came to the fore, and exploded in the tired, sour decision that Candlestick Park would be the end. The inability to play their new material, as demonstrated so gloriously on "Revolver", was a major factor but far from the only one.

Instead it was overwhelmingly the fact that the group realised, as Ringo Starr put it so succinctly, that people were coming to see the Beatles not hear them.

There were some four thousand fans at Heathrow to welcome them home, but, whilst the pride in the group and what they had achieved was still evident in the fans, the whole Beatles experience had soured for the four young men.

And so they stopped. It wasn't communicated to the public, despite the continual presence of newspapermen and tv and radio, but the change in attitude was clear to all the inner circle.

The person who should have been most disturbed by the situation was Epstein. He had obviously detected the change in mood among the group and had communicated his fears to people like Nat Weiss about the ending of public performance. But on the plane journey home he had more immediate, painful concerns. Although he had managed, he thought, to keep the dread news of Seltaeb away from the Beatles the agony continued. The legal mess in America seemed never-ending, and several conversations with Walter Hofer while on the American tour had failed to provide relief, let alone a solution.

But a more immediate, and vicious problem had presented itself at the very end of the tour. A ghost from the past had reappeared in Los Angeles, just before the Dodgers Stadium show. Dizz Gillespie had crawled up out of the sewer, determined to extract even more from Epstein, and this was possibly the worst thing that could happen to Epstein in the opinion of many of his friends and associates.

Gillespie was the handsome and charming hustler, the Gene Pitney lookalike, with whom Epstein had become infatuated in 1965, going so far as to give him a management contract with NEMS to encourage him in his declared career as an actor. Despite the opportunity to settle down in a life of pampered domesticity with Brian Epstein, the lamentable Gillespie abused him and physically maltreated him and robbed him, until he was bought off and bribed to get out of Britain.

Although there was then 3000 miles of separation there were many of Epstein's friends who feared that Epstein's frequent American trips, both with and without the Beatles, would make it easy for Gillespie to resume contact, and sadly that had happened in August 1965 during the build-up to the Shea Stadium concert.

Fortunately that occasion didn't involve any direct contact between Epstein and Gillespie. Instead the young American, possibly fearing a less than friendly response from Epstein and his friends, made contact via a business associate of Nat Weiss.

It was common knowledge in New York entertainment circles that Nat Weiss was acting for Brian Epstein, and so it made sense for the devious Gillespie to make an approach that way. It was a simple, shameless blackmail attempt. Pay him a sum of money, in that case $3000, with which he intended to buy a car, and he would agree to disappear.

Weiss brokered the deal and made the arrangements, taking care to ensure that Epstein and Gillespie were kept well apart. Part of the agreement was that Gillespie agreed to be detained in a locked and guarded hotel room at the Warwick Hotel until the Beatles party, crucially including Epstein, had left for Toronto on the 16th. It was a risky strategy keeping Gillespie under guard in the same hotel being used by the Beatles and their party for the New York stay, but Weiss reckoned that on balance it was safer keeping him close by rather than in some distant location. It would only work if the security in the hotel room in which Gillespie was detained was absolute. And it was. Nat Weiss had access to some very powerful and intimidating friends.

During the time that Epstein and Gillespie were on the premises of the Warwick Hotel they didn't come into contact with each other. Epstein didn't even know he was there, or about the blackmail attempt, until Nat Weiss inadvertently let it slip on the night of the Shea Stadium show. It might have been suspected that Epstein would express some wish to see his beloved Dizz, but he didn't. Perhaps he had finally accepted that it was a brutal chapter that was thankfully closed. More likely the tumultuous evening at Shea provided more than enough to distract him, but some of the images from the concert show him with a wistful expression which might have meant a thousand different things, but one might well have been a longing for Dizz.

There was no contact after that. For most people in Epstein's acquaintance it was a blessed relief, and many hoped that Gillespie had been flushed out of Epstein's life for ever. Sadly that was not the case.

As the 1966 tour wound down with the LA and finally the San Francisco concerts, the shameless and disgusting Gillespie slithered back into Epstein's life. It wasn't difficult to make contact with the Beatles manager if you knew your way round the politics, and, from his period living in London with Epstein, the calculating Gillespie certainly knew what to do. He established contact, told Epstein a tale to elicit sympathy from the Beatles manager, and started the squalid process of cheating and betraying Epstein all over again.

They met in Los Angeles, had dinner and a romantic evening together, interrupted only by the unqualified mayhem at the Dodger Stadium, and it seems likely that Epstein, against all the evidence, believed that his chance for personal happiness might have returned. In less than twelve hours those illusions were shattered.

When Epstein returned to his base at the Beverly Hills Hotel the following morning it was to the shock that the briefcases belonging to Nat Weiss and himself had been stolen. It wasn't a casual burglary. It was an opportunistic theft, set up and exploited by Gillespie. The briefcase owned by Weiss was a loss, but not a major problem.

Epstein's was a very different matter. The contents included a number of items which would have caused his friends great concern to know that he was carrying them about with him. A liberal quantity and assortment of illegal substances, mainly pills, were by no means the most dangerous element.

More worrying were the number of letters from lovers in London and America, generally named and gifted with a full address. With the letters were a number of photographs of young men, usually undressed and often in highly compromising situations, in Epstein's company. A couple of the older pictures even showed Gillespie in London more than a year earlier. One graphic image showed the young man with whom Epstein had been in tryst in New York in February 1964 when Nicky Byrne and elements of the New York Mafia negotiated the problem, although Epstein was not aware of the connection.

The briefcase also contained the brown bag cash receipts from the latest concert, and almost $20,000 in ones and fives and tens were sitting inside the bag in the case.

Finally Epstein was also carrying with him various NEMS papers relating to contractual negotiations that were underway. These included future plans for Cilla Black and others on the declining NEMS roster of artists; there were also documents relating to future plans, mostly speculative for the Beatles, although vitally the documents contained some of the position papers prepared by Geoffrey Ellis on the on-going EMI negotiations on a new Beatles contract; finally, and most importantly, the briefcase contained virtually everything about the Seltaeb situation. This was not an example of lack of planning or foresight. Epstein had conducted several meetings with Walter Hofer and Nat Weiss about Seltaeb while on the 1966 tour, and for that reason, it made total sense for him to keep all the papers with him.

Unless he was going to lose the briefcase, or have it stolen.

It was a disaster of monumental proportions. Because he had been so nervous about the full extent of the Seltaeb disaster leaking out he had contrived to keep the full details from those people who thought they were his confidants. Nat Weiss knew details that Epstein kept from Geoffrey Ellis and David Jacobs; those two UK-based professionals were also only allowed to learn part of the story. The whole picture, all the sordid details, were kept in one place, with Epstein, and now everything was lost.

The party were booked to leave LA at 4pm to provide time to make the journey to San Francisco for the Candlestick Park concert. Before lunchtime Weiss received a note, a blackmail note, demanding $10,000 for the safe return of Epstein's case with its valuable contents. There was no mention in the blackmail note of the briefcase belonging to Nat Weiss but both Weiss and the writer of the note knew that Epstein's case was the valuable element.

Using other contacts in greater Los Angeles, the resourceful Weiss kept the police out of it, conscious of the illegal nature of much of the contents of Epstein's case and set up an elaborate deception to ensure the completion of the blackmail process.

Weiss made the arrangements to exchange the $10,000 in return for Epstein's case, and like a scene from a B-movie spy thriller, Weiss and his accomplice, a heavily-built private investigator from north Hollywood, met the alleged blackmailer near Macarthur Park, later to be immortalised by Jim Webb and Richard Harris.

The $10,000 blackmail fee wasn't paid; the blackmailer was indeed Gillespie, but he had sent a hapless colleague along, who didn't know the full story. He was content to hand over the case in exchange, not for the $10,000 but a promise not to involve the police and an assurance from the large man with Nat Weiss that if the case was handed over he could leave with a full complement of limbs and organs.

The case was returned to Epstein but the contents were far from complete. Only $400 remained of the money, and all the pills and tablets, and most of the letters and photographs had been removed. Most damagingly, many pieces of the Seltaeb documentation had gone.

Weiss left his private investigator colleague to have a quiet word with the emissary from Gillespie but it was clear to Weiss that the man was an innocent dupe. The meeting for the exchange of the money and goods was by the tunnel that connects Macarthur Park from the south side of Wilshire Boulevard to the north side. It was a well-chosen spot. Enough rough spots to hide out, and plenty of ways to get away quickly. Weiss had the distinct feeling that Gillespie was in hiding nearby watching to see what happened with the transaction. When it went wrong he would, in his usual cowardly fashion, have scuttled away. But, crucially, scuttled away carrying Epstein's priceless, irreplaceable things.

Weiss went back to Epstein with the near-empty case. He took it back, glanced quickly inside, and put it away, and never mentioned the subject again - to Weiss or any of the others likely to be compromised by the loss of the letters or the photographs, or the Seltaeb documents.

But it was clear to Weiss, and to the other people that saw him in San Francisco during the day before the party caught the flight back to England that this latest betrayal by Dizz had hit Epstein very, very hard.

The last day of that tour was grievous for Brian Epstein. Trying to deal with the continuing fall-out from the Jesus Christ controversy, as well as Lennon's latest raft of incendiary remarks concerning the Vietnam War.

Attempting to sort out the Seltaeb mess and struggling to keep the news away from the Beatles. Fighting to hide the bitter pain of finding the love of his life betraying him yet again and so totally. And, above all, the realisation that Candlestick Park represented the end for the Beatles as he had known them and very largely created them. He didn't know what the future held, but for such a precise, correct man that uncertainty was mortifying, crippling.

On his return to London he moved into action to try to limit the damage from the loss of the incriminating papers, but, in the absence of a means of tracing Gillespie or even receiving another blackmail note, it was difficult to take any positive steps.

Nothing seemed to help and he moved into a dangerous, damaging spiral of a greater dependency on drugs, both prescription and illegal, and a squalid insertion into a rough trade world that was extreme even by his earlier standards. There was the on-going negotiation with EMI to occupy him; there was even the struggle to reclaim the high ground from Seltaeb, especially given Walter Foley's reassuring remarks in America about the likely ending of the court proceedings within a matter of months.

What Foley had delicately omitted to tell him was the vast sweep of problems that the freezing of Seltaeb assets was creating in America. He was sitting on dozens of complex counter-suits against NEMS, and there was no easy or quick way through the morass. Because of Epstein's continuing intransigence, Hofer had taken to discussing the problems more often with Geoffrey Ellis. With his legal background, and his experience in the States, Ellis was best placed to agree a sensible route forward. Most crucially Ellis wasn't as emotionally crippled by Seltaeb as Epstein, and he was more able and ready to agree a way forward, especially during those periods when Epstein went missing. During September 1966 those periods were becoming more regular.

Paul McCartney and Ringo Starr went along to a function hosted by the editor of Melody Maker on Tuesday, September 13th, where they accepted awards for the Beatles as winners of the British and International group section in the paper's annual awards. Ringo Starr was in ebullient form, larking about in front of the camera in photographs with Dusty Springfield and Tom Jones.

His fellow Beatle, Paul McCartney, stood alongside Dusty Springfield and beamed at the camera, providing what turned out to be the last photographic image of James Paul McCartney for some three months.

There was an obvious deterioration in Epstein. Despite some flashes of the old Brian during September, such as accompanying John Lennon to Spain to commence work on "How I Won The War" he was visibly declining. The impact of the drug-taking, and the severity of the physical and emotional effects on him of Manila and Los Angeles and San Francisco, crashed in on him in the middle of the month. On September 26th he was taken into a London clinic, with the official statement claiming the need for a check-up, though most of his friends and colleagues were aware of more serious problems. Above all he was suffering from a complaint which sounds trivial but can have catastrophic effects. He was increasingly unable to get to sleep, and found himself ever more reliant on drugs to help him find release and a few hours peace in sleep. The session in the discreet private clinic south of the Thames in late September was not his only visit. There was a developing pattern of seeking seclusion and peace there when the strain of daily life in the media goldfish bowl that was Beatles management got too much. This pattern would continue, and increase in frequency and intensity, for the rest of his life.

He was released from the clinic on October 3rd, and went back to his various NEMS commitments, which included a statement confirming that there were no plans for the Beatles to tour or appear in concert again.

There was planning already well advanced for another American trip. Although the primary purpose was a promotional visit with Georgie Fame, it was also high on Epstein's agenda to hold a crucial meeting with Walter Hofer which, he hoped, would lead to a successful; resolution of the Seltaeb fiasco in 1967, if not sooner.

He flew out to New York with Georgie Fame on October 15th, and the day before the flight he received notification that in the previous year, 1965, Northern Songs had made a profit of £614,000. The new public company was going from strength to strength and, although he would not have discussed the matter with Lennon or McCartney in those terms, he really hoped that the good news from Northern Songs, plus a successful conclusion to Seltaeb, and finally a fantastic new deal with EMI for an amazing new royalty deal, might mean that a new management contract could be signed with the group in 1967.

While he was out of the country the most recent Beatles album, 'Revolver', went gold, continuing an unrivalled stretch of sales success. As an unwelcome adjunct to that welcome information, Epstein had to pass on to Sid Bernstein the unhappy news, for both of them, that there were no plans for another American tour. Neither of them used the word "never" but that was clearly the sub-text, although the indefatigable Bernstein would keep trying for another Beatles performance for many years.

To maintain the pace of NEMS activity Epstein booked the Four Tops for a British tour, plus a single show at the Saville Theatre which would go on to be one of the most successful shows ever staged at that theatre, but he had to fly back slightly early when he received the tragic news about Alma Cogan.

The loss of someone close is hard to bear even when in the best of health. For Brian Epstein, at that time, in his seriously weakened condition it was possibly the worst time to receive bad news, and this was what the death of Alma Cogan on October 26th represented.

She died, a victim of stomach cancer, at the Middlesex Hospital. In many ways she was the love of his life, the girl that, in radically different circumstances, in a different world, might have become his wife. That would have delighted his mother, Queenie, and many of their mutual friends. It wasn't to be. It never could be, and now she was dead, at the sad, young age of 34.

She had met her death in a private room. She slipped into a coma and passed away unable to recognise people in the last few hours. The cancer had ravaged her body and she had lost an enormous amount of weight, particularly in the last few weeks.

He had visited her for the last time just before his departure for America, but the visit had upset him so much that he started sobbing in the room and had to leave.

They were never lovers in the traditional, physical sense but they shared an intimacy through mutual experience that bound them like an old married couple, or a devoted brother and sister. That closeness was based particularly on the problems he suffered through trying to hide his homosexuality from the world. Like many female stars Alma Cogan was receptive and sympathetic to the gay community, and her fondness for Epstein was obvious to all. She suffered from taunts about her alleged lesbianism, and so they were soulmates, linked by the insensitive cruelty of the world.

Her death followed close on the suicide of another friend of Brian's, Kevin MacDonald, who fell, or jumped, or was pushed from a west London rooftop. MacDonald was a leading light at the time, co-owner of the major nightspot, Sibylla's, with the prominent socialite, Tara Browne. George Harrison was a minority shareholder in the club, and all four Beatles had been present at the opening of the club. Although Epstein wasn't involved in the opening, because of another brief clinic visit, he had been a regular visitor. There were a group of clubs he enjoyed visiting late at night, generally gaming establishments of which Epstein had become a frequent patron, places like the Clermont Club,

Cromwellian, Quent's, George Raft's Colony Club, and Crockford's. They enjoyed his patronage as well. Besides the obvious glamour of having the Beatles manager at the table, the clubs welcomed his visits because he very frequently lost, and lost very heavily. Among the various other characters involved with these clubs were the leading London criminals and gangsters, Ronnie and Reggie Kray, and Epstein often found himself in their company at the gaming establishments.

In the first days of November, another stage in the evolution of NEMS was reached when the company finally moved completely to the offices on Argyll Street, next to the Palladium. The offices at 13 Monmouth Street had served NEMS nobly since the earliest London days, but now even the Fan Club people, including the mythical Anne Collingham, had to join the rest of the NEMS operation on Argyll Street.

While he was out of the UK the country had suffered one of its worst ever peacetime disasters when the Welsh village of Aberfan was swamped by a moving mountain of slurry and coal debris. A period of heavy rain brought down the deposits of rock and shale which had been deposited on the hills above the village. The disaster killed 144 people of whom 116 were children under the age of 10. It was an unbelievable tragedy, partly because of the huge number of children killed, but also because, as the enquiries revealed, it was a totally avoidable disaster.

A Disaster Fund was quickly established and there were imaginative suggestions for efforts to raise money and spirits, and one of the most prominent suggestions was for the Beatles to put on a show as a benefit for the Aberfan Fund.

Of course in the contemporary world, especially after Live Aid, using pop and rock to raise awareness and funds is a popular, and very successful, strategy, but in 1966 it was an alien concept and simply didn't exist.

Epstein asked the Beatles if they wanted to put on such a benefit concert but, fresh from the horrors of Manila and Memphis, they refused, not least because it would be dragging them back into the pain of live performance.

Epstein issued a polite, respectful statement indicating that such a performance would not be possible. He later made a substantial donation to the fund on behalf of the Beatles, but the impact wasn't the same.

It struck many observers that it was a demonstration of the changing dynamic between the Beatles and their manager that he was no longer in a position to order them to do something, or even suggest that it might be a good idea and then see them fall meekly into line. As in so many other instances, those days had gone, but it would be only five years later that

George Harrison would revive the benefit event idea to miraculous effect with the Concert for Bangladesh.

Fortunately for Epstein and the Beatles, there were far more grievous worries surrounding the Aberfan Disaster than the support, or not, of the Beatles, but it was a rare uncertain step on the part of manager and group in gauging the public mood. For once, fortunately, it did not materially impact on the group or their reputation.

On the same day that Epstein issued his Aberfan Disaster Fund statement confirming that the Beatles would not be staging a benefit concert, Paul McCartney left the country to travel to France.

Such trips, any overseas trips, were detailed at the NEMS office for security reasons, and also because it was easier for the NEMS staff to make the travel and hotel arrangements on behalf of the individual Beatles.

Like modern-day footballers, the Beatles at that time existed largely like children, with everything, particularly anything involving officialdom, prepared for them in advance. For a number of years, Epstein had established a smooth-running and valuable system where NEMS artists would receive a weekly cash advance, effectively a wage packet, that would be delivered to them wherever they were in the world. Indeed, during the period when she was working as Epstein's de facto secretary, the wonderful Freda Kelly was often deputed to make these deliveries, often at the cost of some embarrassment when police and security would often refuse to believe that she was part of the Beatles management group.

McCartney's travel arrangements for France were known and set up by the NEMS office, as were similar arrangements for Lennon in Spain for his film; for Ringo and Maureen to travel to Almeira to spend time with Lennon; or George and Pattie Harrison to travel to India in September.

McCartney took his Aston Martin DB5 out to Lydd Airport in Kent, and took a flight to France. That much is certain, or at least as certain as anything can be in this mysterious and strange affair. The standard texts, which I had used exhaustively in my research over the previous few months, stated that, following the flight from Lydd, he spent a week driving the DB5 around the Loire Valley, visiting assorted chateaux and vineyards.

Several days later he allegedly met Mal Evans, the Beatles sometime roadie, in Bordeaux near the Pont de Pierre.

According to legend, McCartney and Evans then drove from Bordeaux in France across the border into Spain and then onto Seville. Accounts claim that McCartney had planned to meet John Lennon in Almeria where he was on location filming "How I Won The War". Because Lennon allegedly finished shooting his part in the film early, the claim is that McCartney decided on an African safari instead. To enable this to happen, the pair made the trip from Bordeaux to Seville, a distance of almost 600 miles. Then, abandoning the main purpose of the trip, because of Lennon's early finish on the film, they flew to Madrid and took a flight to Nairobi which involved a ten-hour Rome stopover which they occupied with St.Peter's and other tourist haunts.

Allegedly the pair reached Kenya and then spent a further week at Amboseli National Park, which sits below Mount Kilimanjaro, the highest free-standing mountain in the world. They also allegedly stayed at the Treetop Hotel, the royal family's customary Kenyan temporary residence and the place where the then Princess Elizabeth learned she had become Queen following the death of her father, George Vl in 1952.

The final leg of this alleged magical mystery tour came when McCartney and Evans, together with Jane Asher who had joined them in Kenya, flew back to London on November 19th.

To add to the air of mystery it is said that it was on this journey that McCartney came up with the concept behind the Sergeant Pepper's Lonely Hearts Club Band album. It may well be true, although it conflicts with the other popular story that Evans was bemused by the letters "S" and "P" on the salt and pepper pots being used for breakfast, and asked McCartney what they represented. The patronising and offensive image this paints of Mal Evans is beneath contempt.

This was the point in the research when I met my first major problem, and a real quandary.

If the alleged death of Paul McCartney, and his supposed replacement, was genuine and not some crazy story then this period - November 1966 - is when it happened.

I looked, but couldn't find, the single piece of dynamite evidence, the picture of the body, which would be solid proof, but I was unable to find it. However, interestingly, and most curiously, I wasn't able to find the counter-evidence, the proof that James Paul McCartney was still moving around the earth during that period.

As one of the most photographed men on the planet I couldn't comprehend why, despite strenuous efforts, I was not able to find a single piece of credible photographic evidence to validate his presence during that period.

Not one.

Curious.

The only thing to emerge, much later, was some highly suspicious home movie footage from the trip, but, even to an open-minded or even confirmed sceptic like myself, the footage was odd and highly dubious, and raised more questions than it provided answers. And the man in the video footage looked.....well - odd!

And given the alleged flight to France, and then touring round France and Spain, and a flight to Madrid, and a flight Rome, and a ten hour tourist trip round St.Peter's and other Rome landmarks, and a flight to Nairobi, and a stay at the Treetops Hotel, it struck me as very odd that I couldn't find a single photograph from an individual in France or Spain or Rome or Kenya to place McCartney in those locations at that time.

Of course, it was a different world and a different time. In those days if people wished to take a photograph they had to physically carry a camera with them. Not the irritating modern ease of smartphones with built-in cameras, and people taking photographs on every possible occasion and forwarding those images to other people.

For many people the new version of Dante's Inferno would have Eight Levels of Hell, with the deepest, hottest, most agonising level inhabited by Tumblr and Twitter and Pinterest and Facebook and the rest.

Even so, and allowing for all the stories about the staggering efficiency of the disguises adopted by McCartney, I found it hard to believe that there wasn't a single tourist who took a shot, posed or sneaky, of the Beatle, then undeniably one of the most famous faces on the planet. The fact that I was not able to trace a single such image is not proof of anything. But I tried, very, very hard, and the fact that I wasn't able to do it was curious at the very least. As I would discover, "curious" was the word I would use over and over again when considering the Beatles story during those months after November 1966.

I realised that the involvement, or participation of Mal Evans was a key factor, and this caused me to go back to my notes on the discussions I had enjoyed in New York with Chrissie. Although she did not raise the topic directly she had been fulsome in her praise for Evans, and his devotion to the group. She had waxed lyrical about the ways that he had been taken for granted by the group and Epstein, and she had also been extremely indignant about the "below-stairs" treatment meted out to him.

And I couldn't forget her statement that Mal had helped them do something outlandish and crazy. She didn't spell out what it was, but........

And she had also talked, and I remember thinking at the time that she was talking obliquely and coyly, about Mal's professional interest in the young man he and Chrissie had met in New York in 1965.

The Paul McCartney look-alike.

William Campbell.

In November 1966 Epstein was trying to maintain a Business as Usual posture at NEMS, despite all the indications of panic and chaos. He told his old promoting partner, Arthur Howes, that he would not be accepting any more bookings for live performances. Following that news the British newspapers jumped on the bandwagon of no more tours, with a fleet of pun-filled headlines. On the following day he made an announcement that although the existing Beatles contract with EMI had expired, a replacement contract was under negotiation and close to finalisation.

On Sunday November 13th the stories about the future of the Beatles came very much to the fore again when the Sunday Telegraph ran a story on its front page asserting that an American pop manager had been approached by two of the Beatles with a view to his taking over the management of the group. Epstein got a copy of the newspaper and read the story which didn't identify the two Beatles and provided precious little solid information. Klein himself, the American manager in question, happened to be in London working on his current role with the Rolling Stones, having recently taken up a co-management role with the group.

Perhaps tellingly, Klein didn't reject the story or the rumour; with uncharacteristic restraint he merely refused to comment.

In response both Harrison and Starr were said to be disturbed by the story while Lennon was described as annoyed by it. Whether he was annoyed by the story, or by its disclosure, was not made clear. Epstein dismissed it as ridiculous and absurd.

Epstein was forced into an uncomfortable position by the story and by the inevitable interest. He ridiculed the premise of the story, and used his contacts in the media to spread and emphasize his distaste for the story. At that time the fondness for the Beatles and Epstein among the media was still strong. There were a number of journalists who guarded stories about his private life in order to protect his reputation.

The fourth Beatle, Paul McCartney, was not able to comment on the story as he was out of the country. Allegedly.

Ironically, on the same day as the Sunday Telegraph story, came one of Epstein's greatest non-Beatle triumphs. The first pop production at the Saville Theatre featured the only live performance in the UK by the Four Tops that year. On every level it was a complete triumph and is even lauded today as one of the major nights in the long, glittering career of the Four Tops. Epstein sat in his box and beamed down at the joy demonstrated in the seats beneath.

Despite his growing worries he had tried to make some positive moves to contain the growing firestorms. An appearance on The David Frost Programme gave him the chance to present a polished, sophisticated front although there were a number of viewers who thought he looked tired and strained and worried. He had been adamant before the programme with the various production staff that he would not add anything about the Beatles situation and their future beyond the statements already made. This was unusually forceful on Epstein's part, and suggested concerns which hadn't yet been communicated to the public.

He hosted a party a week later at his house which was attended by Lennon and Harrison, plus many stars of the UK music scene, people like Mick Jagger, Keith Richards, Charlie Watts, Georgie Fame, Donovan and Eric Burdon. Curiously, despite allegedly being back in the country by then, and being just under three miles from Epstein's house, and having a number of friends plus the Four Tops present at the party, McCartney did not appear.

For Epstein there were two substantial pressures at that time. The negotiations with EMI towards a new contract for the Beatles were progressing smoothly, thanks mainly to the calm stewardship of Geoffrey Ellis. There were even hopeful signs from America indicating that a resolution to the Seltaeb disaster might be approaching.

In normal circumstances either or both developments would have been very welcome but it was clear that he was consumed by greater pressures. In this context his absences from the NEMS offices which had become more pronounced during 1966 proved to be a benefit. The frantic series of meetings that the Paul McCartney situation created were easy to accommodate and hide at Chapel Street, and the middle part of November saw a constant flurry of comings and goings at the house.

Inevitably it is impossible to ascertain exactly what happened in those meetings. At least six of the principals are dead. Equally it is difficult, on any objective basis to deny that something very odd happened in November 1966. Years later the remarkable Heather Mills stated, "People don't want to know what the truth is, 'cause they could never, ever handle it. They would be too devastated!"

Now, Heather Mills has been ridiculed and lampooned and denigrated but, as Michael Winner said about himself "Just because you are mad, doesn't mean that you are wrong!" The remarks by Heather Mills could mean anything, and could relate to a thousand different topics, but......

Curious.

Definitely curious.

Towards the end of 1966 Epstein tried to keep up a front of normality, attending the opening of the new club, the Bag O'Nails, and also announced several new shows at the Saville, including major American artists like Chuck Berry, Edwin Starr, The Impressions, Lee Dorsey and Billy Stewart. As part of this impressive pattern he presented Little Richard in two shows at the Saville on December 11th. The hospitality after the show was so lavish, and the atmosphere was so convivial that Epstein was moved to offer Little Richard a management contract, but that was, perhaps reluctantly, declined.

A more distressing disappointment came much closer to home. After two frantic years the wonderful Wendy Hanson had told Epstein that she was resigning from her post as his personal assistant. She had been by his side since the heady days at the Plaza in February 1964 but now, seeking other challenges and, tiring of the tempestuous life around Epstein, she declared her intention to leave. Like many others, like Derek Taylor and Neil Aspinall and Alastair Taylor, she had been angrily sacked by him on several occasions during those two and a half years.

Always though Epstein retrieved the situation with a contrite apology, and invariably flowers, but this time nothing would dissuade her. She had worked closely with Epstein at the office at Albemarle Street, separate from the NEMS office, and indeed the NEMS staff, and so she had closer access to his irritable mood swings than any of the others.

Her range of contacts and interests was so wide that a job with the management of the Beatles was never going to keep her, and the resignation went in, and was accepted with a gracious letter from Epstein a week before Christmas.

At the start of December McCartney was so impressed by The Young Rascals that he visited their Blaises concert a second time. This followed on from the huge impression the group made in America on the 1966 Beatles tour.

On December 9th 1966 the first ever compilation of Beatles music was released. 'A Collection of Beatles Oldies' was a sixteen song collection of material covering their career since 'Love me Do', with the only new track being 'Bad Boy', which had appeared on a Capitol issue in America in June 1965.

The inclusion of the Larry Williams classic represented a pivotal moment in the group's recording career, for the release of the album, including 'Bad Boy', finally saw British and American releases in balance. Thereafter both countries would release Beatles albums in exactly the same format - same track-listing, same covers, and, wherever possible, the same release dates.

It was the first Beatles album to fail to reach the number one position in the charts. At the time of release, "Revolver" was still a very strong seller, but the top UK seller over Christmas was the soundtrack to "The Sound Of Music".

A week later, on December 16th, the fourth Beatles Christmas record, "Pantomime: Everywhere It's Christmas", was distributed to the members of the Fan Club. The material for this Christmas release had been recorded late in November using facilities at the London offices of Dick James. It was very unusual, almost unprecedented for recordings to take place away from Abbey Road, but in those unusual circumstances it apparently made sense not to risk appearing at Abbey Road where questions, however vague or innocent, might be raised.

Two days later McCartney and Jane Asher attended the world premiere of the film "The Family Way" at the Warner Cinema in Cranbourn Street in London. The film had an incidental soundtrack which had been written by McCartney and arranged by George Martin, and the film also included Jane Asher in a supporting part.

Some two hours after the premier ended, a car crash happened just three miles away in Redcliffe Gardens near Earl's Court Exhibition Centre. Just before 1am Tara Browne and his friend Suki Poitier were driving from a friend's house to join up with other friends at a restaurant when their Lotus Elan crashed into a stationary van.

Browne was a friend of both McCartney and Lennon, a member of the Guinness family, and a wealthy young man. He had even been involved in a previous road accident involving McCartney when, with both men on a moped, it crashed over, leaving McCartney with a wound to his upper lip. The accident seemed to have been the result of simply driving too fast in a built up area, but the results were catastrophic. Browne swerved to avoid an oncoming Volkswagen and drove into a stationary van near the junction of Redcliffe Gardens and Redcliffe Square. Observers claimed later that Browne's car had gone through a red light, but the tragic result was that Tara Browne died of his injuries the following day. Potier survived and was almost unscathed, and indeed she claimed that Browne had deliberately swerved the car to try to avoid injuring her.

The relevance of the sad story is that allegedly John Lennon was reading a copy of the Daily Mail on January 17th. In the newspaper was a brief item reporting the verdict of the coroner to Tara Browne's death, and Beatles mythology has always claimed that it was Browne's crash which inspired the opening lines to the epic 'A Day in the Life'.

On December 20th the group, albeit in strictly individual fashion, had been booked to provide interviews to ITN, the main commercial station in the UK.

The interviews were intended for a weekly magazine programme called Reporting '66. In contrast to the staged ensemble interviews which had been their stock in trade for almost four years, the Reporting '66 interviews were snatched words with the Beatles as they arrived and hurried into Abbey Road. They all arrived separately, all now wearing conspicuous facial hair which had appeared since November. The amount of discussion was severely limited.

Indeed Harrison sprinted up the steps to the building and only provided a terse denial to a question about whether the Beatles were splitting up or not.

Starr, as ever, was the most affable and almost talkative, although Lennon, who was the first to arrive, stated firmly that the group would continue working together and also that he and McCartney would continue writing songs.

McCartney arrived accompanied by Mal Evans, the first of a succession of public appearances where Evans would stand, ever watchful, by his side. These appearances would include Evans moving into McCartney's house in St.John's Wood after dismissing the resident housekeeper and would culminate in Evans appearing as a witness in McCartney's first marriage some two years later, a ceremony to which, curiously, none of the Beatles were invited. But Mal Evans was.

The series of brief interviews was handled by John Edwards, and shown on ITN on December 28th. Given the surprising brevity of the interviews, the segment on Reporting '66 had to be padded out with archive material and even badly-researched comment pieces from the likes of Richard Lester.

The reason for the gathering at Abbey Road so close to Christmas was to have a discussion about the future, although no details of the discussion or any decisions were released to an expectant world. In addition, the group took the opportunity to work over yet another old McCartney number retrieved from the mountain of material which had been dumped upstairs at Cavendish Avenue. That song was called 'When I'm Sixty-Four' and would become a leading feature of the album which the group intended to complete and release some time in the middle of 1967.

The Christmas period saw all four Beatles remain at home. No trips back to Liverpool, which was unusual, but perhaps there were telling reasons to keep the group, particularly McCartney away from their home city. On Boxing Day there was a show at the Saville Theatre starring Georgie Fame, and Epstein both presented and attended the show which would run for three weeks under the banner "Fame in '67". A future star was on the bill with Cat Stevens, fresh from recent success with 'I Love My Dog', taking an important step towards future success.

Thursday, December 29th saw a notable day in the evolution towards the future, as a lone McCartney spent the day at Abbey Road. He worked, without the involvement of Lennon, Harrison and Starr, on a track which had been kept in the anthology of scraps and song fragments at Cavendish Avenue.

This song was listed as 'Untitled' in the Abbey Road logs for that day, but it would become known as 'Penny Lane' and McCartney had been referring to a song with that name for more than a year.

Work on 'Penny Lane' continued on December 30th, and into the following year, and on January 5th the pace of recording at Abbey Road continued with more work on 'Penny Lane' and another new song, a very odd still unreleased piece called 'Carnival of Light'. It lasted almost fourteen minutes and was a freeform, experimental piece without the melody or lyrical balance which had made Northern Songs and Dick James so wealthy.

Many of those who heard the recording were bemused, with George Martin particularly scathing, being heard to demand that the group should get their teeth into something more constructive.

'Carnival of Light' was played at various fringe events in London in 1967 but received little attention or praise. It remained ignored and unreleased as a recording for the next few years. McCartney wanted to include the piece on 'Anthology 2' in 1996, but the attempt was vetoed by George Harrison. Given the scope and scale of the Anthology series it is difficult to find anything else recorded by the Beatles in any format which was not included. 'Carnival of Light', the first fresh piece of music by Paul McCartney after November 1966, stayed unreleased and received a veto against release by one of the Beatles when the chance lay open to put out the piece along with a smorgasbord of scraps and unknown pieces.

That was the obvious chance to release it, but that possible release was denied, even to hide it away among all the rest of the alternate takes. But the inclusion of 'Carnival of Light', the release of the first new music produced by McCartney after November 1966, didn't happen, vetoed by one of his fellow Beatles.

Curious.

In the early days of January 1967 McCartney was allegedly involved in a road accident on the M1 north of London. It wasn't a major incident, and would have gone largely unreported but for its proximity to other car crashes late in 1966. In the M1 crash in January his Mini Cooper was written off after a crash when the car was actually being driven by a friend and drug acquaintance, Mohammed Chtaibi, who was part of the circle surrounding art gallery owner, Robert Fraser.

In later years this incident would become part of the swirl of rumour and nonsense and false stories which sprouted in response to the alleged death of McCartney in November 1966. But, whatever did happen with this incident in January 1967, it is clear that something curious did happen both with the event and with the way the details of a fairly unremarkable story were spun by a number of interested parties. The other curious aspect concerns the mysterious Mohammed Chtaibi, who appeared in public with various Beatles during the middle part of the year. Whatever his part in the Beatles legend, the simple fact is that he was central to the strange story of the car crash at the start of 1967.

But 1967 was replete with strange stories and unexplained incidents. The calamitous problems imploding at this point on the fragile Epstein now caused him to make another immense decision with major long-term consequences.

For a number of months he had been holding discussions with one of the new personalities of British entertainment, Robert Stigwood. The Australian had skirted around the fringes of London showbiz for a couple of years but as another Jewish entrepreneur in those circles he had a number of prominent colleagues like Lionel Bart, Joe Meek and even Brian Epstein to call on.

Stigwood had built up interests in the entertainment industry before 1967 but these had largely been unsuccessful until, fortuitously, he sublet space in his offices to two young men called Kit Lambert and Chris Stamp, who were managers of a group called The Who. It wasn't kindness or generosity on Stigwood's part. He had severe cashflow problems, and Stamp had promised to pay him cash!

Although it was an uncomfortable relationship the stability provided by Stamp's money enabled Stigwood to move forward again with his agency. During 1966 he made the astute move of becoming booking agent for The Who, using his relationship with Stamp and Lambert and a down-payment of £500 taken from the money they'd paid him for rent. This involvement with The Who allowed him to persuade them to leave their label, Decca, and their producer, Shel Talmy, to join his new label, Reaction. The first single on that label would be 'Substitute' by The Who (591 001) although it had to be re-released several times with different b-sides to circumvent legal problems caused by the group's furtive departure from Decca.

The end of 1966 saw the release of the Reaction label's first album, "Fresh Cream", from the three-piece super group compromised of three musicians from groups already represented by Stigwood.

The success in British charts made Stigwood's overtures to Epstein quite interesting, but his contacts in, and plans for, America, were particularly attractive. During the painful last few months of 1966 Epstein began to look upon a deal with Robert Stigwood as a possible answer to a number of pressing problems. It was partly the injection of fresh blood, both from Stigwood at management level but also from his growing roster of artists. And the artists were another potential benefit for Epstein who was clearly disappointed by the withering away of the NEMS roster of artists. The great days of NEMS as a stable of world-class artists had long gone, but the addition of Stigwood's artists might revive Epstein's dreams for a substantial agency crammed with world-class talent.

But in many respects the most pressing reason for Epstein to consider a merger of some kind with Stigwood was money. Despite appearances Brian Epstein was starting to experience money problems. Since his early days in Liverpool he had enjoyed the finer things in life, and his time at NEMS, particularly in London, demonstrated his belief that his work justified his need for first class travel and expensive meals and top-quality wines. Much of this spending came out of the expenses charged by NEMS as part of management fees to artists like the Beatles.

But his spending outside those areas was starting to get dangerously out of hand. Long, late nights at gambling clubs like the Clermont and the White Elephant were socially enjoyable because they passed the evening, and allowed him to spend time with like-minded individuals. He would often, and quite casually, lose thousands of pounds in an evening by playing baccarat or chemin de fer, but would stay at a single club, like Curzon House, the whole evening.

Critically he was able to relax in those places because he would not be bothered and pestered by people on the basis of his being the Beatles manager. Most people in the gaming clubs didn't care. For most of them Epstein was just another punter.

The management of the clubs had a different attitude to Epstein. They welcomed his frequent visits, partly because of the glamour he represented and presented. More tangibly though, they relished his visits, signified by the waiving of drinks and food bills, for the simple reason that that during those visits he lost, and lost heavily. And, during the second half of 1966 and the early months of the following year, those losing nights became more frequent.

He had been used to leaving notes for Joanne Newfield telling her to bank his happiness on the infrequent occasions when a night at the clubs left him holding some tangible return for the evening. But those notes, and those returns, were a rare event, and the scale of Epstein's losses was a concern to his friends and even to himself in his more lucid moments.

The need to realise capital to cover his growing losses became an issue, particularly given his commitment to cover all the costs of the Seltaeb litigation out of his own pocket. Even though the 1965 nightmare of the $5 million judgement in favour of Seltaeb had been set aside, the costs of maintaining Walter Hofer's battle against Nicky Byrne were excessive.

Added to his extravagant lifestyle and the mounting and continuing losses at the gambling clubs the situation was serious. Not surprisingly, he started to consider Stigwood's overtures not just from the business perspective but also as a possible personal salvation.

Discussions had continued during 1966 both before and after the American tour, but they had picked up pace towards the end of the year. Stigwood had made a firm offer to purchase NEMS but Epstein had rejected it, not least because any purchase offer for NEMS would expect to include the Beatles, but there were severe doubts about how the members of the group would respond.

Stigwood was in a position to make such offers because he had recovered from his early business problems thanks to an association with Polydor records where Roland Rennie was in place as managing director. Rennie and Stigwood had worked successfully together during Rennie's period with EMI and of course Rennie had played a role in the breaking of the Beatles in America by negotiating the release of the early singles via Vee-Jay and Swan.

It was the highly advantageous terms offered by Polydor that provided Stigwood with the means to fund the trips to New York for Cream and The Who, trips which impressed Epstein sufficiently to encourage him to consider Stigwood's offer seriously. It later emerged that Stigwood was in no position to pay the whole sum at once. He struggled to raise investment to meet his commitments to Epstein.

Nevertheless, on January 13th 1967 Epstein and Stigwood signed an agreement which meant the merging of their two companies. The legal work on Epstein's side was overseen by David Jacobs, who was being allowed back into the fold as the Seltaeb crisis finally began to ease. In addition it made the negotiations slightly less fractious given that Jacobs knew both men well, as prominent gay and Jewish members of British entertainment royalty.

The outcome was painful. Reaction among the NEMS staff was largely hostile, and even trusted stalwarts like Alastair Taylor and Geoffrey Ellis were nonplussed by Epstein's move, especially as there were well-documented previous offers to buy NEMS for sums considerably in excess of that paid by Stigwood. Prominent among those offers was the one made by Allen Klein some time earlier, and the discrepancy in the amounts offered to Epstein was never explained or justified.

Instead of a simple purchase the deal became a merger. Stigwood agreed to put all his company assets into NEMS whilst in return he was awarded a reciprocal shareholding in NEMS, plus a substantial salary, an executive position as co-managing director plus, importantly, direct access to all NEMS extensive financial and wider resources.

It was a major breakthrough to the top level for Robert Stigwood. It was clear that the weary Epstein was giving serious thought to abandoning his role as Beatles manager. Unfortunately the fresh independent spirit in the group reared its collective head again and thwarted any moves in that direction. Indeed this was the famous occasion when the group registered its opposition by threatening, if the move went ahead, to record 'God Save The Queen' as the A-side on every future single, and to sing the song conspicuously out of tune.

Epstein could combat the opposition within NEMS to Stigwood; he could not fight the total antipathy the Beatles expressed towards Stigwood. As a result, Epstein remained as manager of the Beatles but effective responsibility for almost all of the other acts was surrendered to Stigwood.

For the staff at NEMS, already severely disillusioned by the presence of Vic Lewis in the company, the likely arrival of Stigwood threatened to be a disaster. Lewis had not proved popular and his distinct lack of man-management skills had already caused trouble at Sutherland House. The NEMS staff, particularly those who had been loyal to Epstein from the early days saw the promised, or should it be threatened, involvement of Stigwood as yet further evidence of Epstein's abrogation of his role, and even his interest in NEMS.

Epstein had convinced himself that a merger with Stigwood would strengthen NEMS immensely, especially in the sense of providing an injection of fresh talent. Given the culling of NEMS artists in the previous few months, involving the loss of names like Tommy Quickly, the Rustiks and many more, the injection of talents like Cream and The Who couldn't help but improve the profile and performance of NEMS, but despite Stigwood's early introduction of new talent in the form of the Bee Gees, it wasn't long before Epstein was regretting the arrangement with Stigwood.

The father of the Gibb brothers had sent acetates and an album to NEMS in the hope of a contract for the group, but the material was picked up by Stigwood just after his arrival at Sutherland House. He signed the Bee Gees to a five-year management contract at the beginning of March, and took them with him when he parted from NEMS at the end of 1967. He had spent heavily trying to get the group's first Polydor single, 'Spicks and Specks', off the ground, including a substantial sum on a month's exposure on Radio Caroline.

Though the record flopped Stigwood wasn't deterred, and continued spending heavily to break the group in Britain. By some estimates he spent around £50,000 during the year just on promotion of the Bee Gees, and it appears that most, if not all, of the money came out of NEMS resources.

It obviously worked. In April 1967 their second single, 'New York Mining Disaster 1941', became a major hit and the follow-up, 'Massachusetts', was released in September 1967 and became their first number one.

There were major disagreements between the autocratic Epstein and Stigwood, generally over expenditure. The hiring of a yacht for the Bee Gees proved particularly troublesome, but there was a constant bubbling of disputes during the scant few months that Epstein and Stigwood were working together. The net result was that NEMS became a distinctly unhappy and unpleasant working environment during 1967. Brian Epstein was rarely present, preferring to work from Chapel Street during his increasingly erratic working hours. Back at NEMS both Vic Lewis and Robert Stigwood seemed to vie for the title of most disliked person in the building.

NEMS was a massively changed organisation. When Epstein moved down to London in 1964 the roster was only just over a dozen, but by 1966 the staff numbers had climbed to eighty. It provided fertile ground for empire building and office plotting, and the atmosphere was often rancid. Vic Lewis could be extremely abrasive, and many of the NEMS staff who had been working there happily before his arrival resented his attitude and behaviour. The only consolation for such long-time members of NEMS was the sight of Stigwood and Lewis conspiring against each other and working so hard to damage each other.

But that was a small and pathetic return. The overwhelming sensation as 1967 gathered pace was that NEMS had been deserted and abandoned by Epstein. Of course nobody really knew the agonies he was hiding. Only people like the loyal Joanne Newfield could see his pain at first hand, though he was often intent on hiding himself away even from her.

Epstein was seeing little of the individual Beatles. He knew they were spending significant amounts of time at Abbey Road but he was starting to feel increasingly uncomfortable at being just an onlooker at the court of the Beatles, and that was increasingly the scenario at Abbey Road.

It wasn't even like the great days of 1963-1966 where he could watch the television news and invariably catch an item about one or other of the Beatles. They were becoming nocturnal, hidden creatures flowering only inside the protected walls of Abbey Road. Curiously though he might have anticipated a rare opportunity to see one of the Beatles in daylight and outside Abbey Road in mid January when McCartney said goodbye to Jane Asher who was flying to America to tour with the Bristol Old Vic.

Curiously he did not travel to the airport to see her off, and though he would fly out to America, accompanied if not guarded by Mal Evans, the enforced separation seemed a watershed moment.

Two other significant, if trivial pieces in the Beatles tapestry came while Jane Asher's flight was heading across the Atlantic. Inside Abbey Road, as recording continued remorselessly on the new, or in some cases, old Beatles material, a man called David Mason, a prominent British classical musician, added a piccolo trumpet solo to the tracks being recorded for 'Penny Lane' and that solo would become one of the most joyful signatures for the track when it was released some weeks later. On the same day, the Daily Mail carried a piece lambasting the state of roads in Blackburn in Lancashire. John Lennon saw the piece and incorporated the story in the lyrics for 'A Day in the Life', one of the pieces on which the group were currently working.

On January 16th, Walter Shenson, starting to grow slightly apprehensive about the delay in implementing the third Beatles film, met with Joe Orton in London. Shenson had delivered a script to Orton's agent which he wanted Orton to re-work. The basic premise - four different aspects of the character of one man - was interesting to Orton in terms of what he could do with the idea.

As a result of the meeting in mid-January Orton began work on what would develop into "Up Against It". There was also a meeting with Epstein and McCartney a week later at Chapel Street which gave Orton a contract allowing him to purchase the rights to the script if Shenson and Epstein rejected it.

Epstein's miseries were compounded early in 1967 when one of the great figures in British pop music died in mysterious and tragic circumstances.

Joe Meek was arguably the first great record producer in British pop, with hits like 'Bad Penny Blues', 'Telstar', 'Johnny Remember Me' and 'Cumberland Gap'. Working from his improvised studio on the Holloway Road, he was a vital force in the early years of British pop. And, he was yet another gay man forced to keep his private life secret for fear of persecution from the ignorant or pressure from the authorities. As such it was inevitable that he would come into contact with the likes of David Jacobs, Lionel Bart and Brian Epstein. He had even worked extensively with Stigwood and it was the pair of them working in tandem who provided John Leyton with his greatest success, the unforgettable 'Johnny Remember Me'.

On February 3rd 1967, Meek took a single-barrelled shotgun that belonged to former bass player for the Tornados and 'Just Like Eddie' solo star Heinz Burt, and shot first his landlady, Violet Shenton, and then himself.

Allegedly.

The sudden death of Meek, and the continuing miseries coming out of NEMS forced Epstein into a further bout of depression which would largely dog him for the rest of his life. And of course he no longer had his perfect, ultimate antidote to depression. The Beatles were elsewhere and the opportunities for the kind of regular contact he had enjoyed so much for four years had virtually disappeared.

The pressure he felt to stay at the pinnacle of the music business was immense, made worse by the growing alienation from the Beatles and the developing civil war inside NEMS. Added to the insomnia and the money issues and the dangers posed by Seltaeb, he was growing more depressed and irritable. Drugs had been an adornment to his life for several years. In 1967 they became the one thing that kept him going.

But then, at the end of January came the day he had anticipated and dreaded and worked so hard to realise. The fabled fresh contract with EMI which had occupied Epstein, and particularly Geoffrey Ellis, in deeply intensive negotiations for many months, had reached fulfilment. January 27th was the day, and the deal provided a new contract to replace the original one signed with George Martin back in the early days with the Beatles in 1962.

The new contract was for a nine-year term, broken down as five years + four years. It contained a host of clauses relating to sales ratios, overseas sales, compilation albums and the like, and future months would throw up problems relating to overseas sales as identified by Alan Livingston of Capitol. However, the greatest problem caused by the new contract would only come to light after Epstein's death when it was realised that under the terms of the new EMI contract, a full 25% would be paid to NEMS for the duration of the contract, whether the Beatles management contract, due to expire in September 1967, was renewed or not.

This was a very surprising development, and one which would cause the Beatles no little pain and annoyance when they started to appreciate the ramifications of their NEMS deal in those dark days after Epstein's death as the group finally looked into their various contracts.

The deal signed on January 26th started afresh. Material recorded between June 3rd 1966 and the date of the new contract was covered by a series of subsidiary agreements. Capitol continued to derive its rights to manufacture and distribute in the U.S. under the Matrix Exchange Agreements, though the internal royalties override that EMI received for licensing Beatles masters to Capitol was reduced from 5% of retail price to 2.2% of retail price, payable on 90% of sales, less a fixed packaging fee; there also were several other technical nuances.

Royalties payable to the Beatles for new material were substantially increased. The 1967 agreement would later, in the coming NEMS difficulties, become the source of immense confusion. Normal expectation would be for royalty to be paid on retail price rather than a wholesale price.

In itself this wouldn't have presented a problem but for the fact that that because of Alan Livingston's faulty understanding of the terms of wholesale price, misapprehensions about the actual amount to be paid to the Beatles would dog relationships for many years. And the climate of mistrust thus created, however innocently, was ripe for exploitation by a hard, unprincipled bruiser of a manager - someone perhaps like Alan Klein.

Livingston's error was created because separate terms for Beatles product had been negotiated under the Capitol banner for the United States, Mexico and Canada, and it appears that he got the figures confused because the sales base for each of those territories was calculated and expressed differently.

The next stage in this process came on April 19th when Epstein, after discussions with tax lawyers and the newly-reinstated David Jacobs, created a company which was named The Beatles and Co. This was essentially a single umbrella company devoted to the management of all the subsidiary interests of the Beatles. Within a year the name would be changed to "Apple" which would be the name, and the label, which would linger with the group thereafter.

At the time the Beatles as a trading concern had large amounts of capital, and there was a severe danger of losing a considerable proportion to the Inland Revenue. As a means of avoiding this disaster the group were advised to invest in a business venture.

The original partnership, Beatles Ltd, had been set up by Epstein in 1963, but that company was now superseded by Beatles & Co. which gave each of the four Beatles 5% of the company with a new corporation which would be collectively owned and would control 80% of the company. This new corporation would later become Apple Corps.

The terms of the deal resembled elements of the original Northern Songs agreement in that the four Beatles would be bound to the company on an exclusive basis, under which the four Beatles became a legal partnership. All income from all group or even solo work would be shared under the terms of the partnership, with the only exception being songwriting which was a separate entity and locked away inside the edifice which was Northern Songs. All revenue earned by the group, collectively and individually, would be channelled into The Beatles & Co., and one major result would be that they would be left with a much lower corporate tax rate.

The final significant element in the agreement was the duration. The creation of The Beatles & Co. bound the four Beatles together for a period of ten years, and the initial share issue was £1 million.

EMI made the formal announcement on February 6th that the Beatles had signed the new nine-year contract.

Before the creation of The Beatles & Co. came the release in Britain and America of what many considered their finest single. The double a-side, 'Penny Lane'/'Strawberry Fields Forever' came on February 13th in America and four days later in the UK. The video clips of the Beatles performing both songs were shown on Top of the Pops on February 9th, establishing the remote performance model which would become the norm for the group for the rest of its existence.

In mid-February Vic Lewis, in his role representing NEMS, flew to America for talks about bringing the new American sensation, the Monkees, to Britain for concerts. The Monkees were a Screen Gems creation, a group shamelessly and cynically modelled on the MopTops whose memory and image was being perpetuated every week on the ABC cartoon series. That was the main reason that the Beatles disliked the series initially. Not because of the quality of the scripts or the artwork, but because it continued to represent them in a time warp, in the collarless jackets and the madcap comedians captured in "A Hard Day's Night". That wasn't them any more. That mantle had been passed, gratefully to the Monkees and the four Beatles couldn't help but delight in the fact that they were no longer Fab.

In one of his many flashes of pomposity or autocracy, Epstein had decreed that the comperes on stage at the Saville theatre were not allowed to mention his name. No justification was given. By that point in the midst of depression and insomnia and money problems and drug binges he didn't really care. This time his irritability backfired on him. There was a famous concert on February 19th at the Saville where Chuck Berry topped a bill which also included Del Shannon. The concert was a great success until two members of the audience had the effrontery to get on the stage to dance to one of Chuck Berry's numbers. At that point the heavy safety curtain was dropped down on the stage, effectively finishing the show.

There was trouble inside the theatre which then developed into a mini-riot outside on Shaftesbury Avenue. Epstein promptly sacked Michael Bullock, the manager of the theatre, and though Bullock was reinstated some days later it was further demonstration of Epstein's heavy-handed treatment of people. And it was increasingly backfiring on him.

However, it is worth remarking on what a remarkable addition to London's pop and rock life the Saville Theatre became - and it was all the brainchild of Brian Epstein.

In just a few weeks in 1967 the theatre featured shows starring Chuck Berry, Fats Domino (supported by Gerry and the Pacemakers plus the Bee Gees), Donovan, The Impressions, Bo Diddley (supported by Ben E.King plus the Alan Bown Set), Cream (supported by Jeff Beck plus John Mayall's

Bluesbreakers), Jimi Hendrix Experience (supported by Denny Laine and his Electric String Band plus Procul Harum plus the Chiffons), Edwin Starr (supported by Duane Eddy and the Wild Ones) and Lee Dorsey (supported by Pink Floyd).

March saw real progress being made on the packaging and marketing of the new album for the Beatles. Peter Blake and Jann Howarth had been approached about designing and creating the new sleeve and on March 7th McCartney met with them to discuss the concept. A week later, the process was completed with a dinner shared by Lennon and McCartney, Blake and Howarth.

With the brief clear Blake and Howarth went to work and their efforts culminated in the shooting of the cover art for Sergeant Pepper on March 30th at Michael Cooper's Manor Studios in Chelsea.

With that task completed the shackles were released and McCartney was able to fly out to keep his planned date with Jane Asher in America.

However, it still wasn't possible to trust him entirely solo so he was accompanied on the flight out of London by the faithful Mal Evans. The pair flew London to Los Angeles via Paris, and after a few hours in Los Angeles they took Frank Sinatra's personal Learjet up to San Francisco. They were only in California for twenty-four hours but that provided the opportunity to drop in on a rehearsal by the Jefferson Airplane at Fillmore West.

Although they had taken the rare opportunity to watch the Airplane, one of the golden groups of that Summer of Love at work, that was not the main reason for the trip. Mal had made arrangements for McCartney to be visited in San Francisco by several old friends from New York and Toronto. The reasoning was that such an encounter in a rented house across the bay would attract less attention than in Los Angeles or New York. That, and not the Jefferson Airplane, was the reason for the trip. After all, McCartney and Evans had boarded Frank Sinatra's plane in Los Angeles, and the plane could have taken them to Denver as easily as San Francisco.

On April 5th the hired Lear jet took the pair to Denver Airport where they were met by Bert Rosenthal from whom McCartney had arranged to borrow a house. He stayed there with Jane Asher; Mal Evans booked into the Driftwood Motel. Rosenthal came back to the house in the early evening and picked up the pair, and ferried them to the Quorum Restaurant in Denver where the Old Vic company had laid on a lavish celebration for Jane Asher's 21st birthday. Curiously the official photographs of the event were taken, and published, by Datebook Magazine, the same journal that had republished Lennon's Jesus remarks a year earlier.

The following day was spent in Denver. Given a night off from the rigours of "Romeo and Juliet" Asher went out for the day for a romantic few hours with her boyfriend and lover, Paul McCartney. Interestingly they weren't alone. Mal Evans was with them every step of the way. He hired a rental car from Hertz and chauffeured McCartney and Asher up into the Rockies.

They stopped off-road and went walking in the beauty of the Rockies, enjoying the scenery and each other's company. Fortunately, and perhaps curiously, Mal Evans was never far away.

The following day was spent idling around Denver, but the next day, April 8th, Jane Asher had two performances, a matinee and an evening show. For that reason McCartney and Evans took the opportunity to travel up into the mountains.

They drove north west to Boodle Mine, a famous historic mining settlement dating back to the middle of the 19th century. At its peak during what became known as Pike's Peak Gold Rush, Boodle Mine was at the heart of what was labelled the Richest Square Mile on Earth.

A century later, little of that industry or wealth remained and McCartney and Evans wandered around the mine and the outbuildings, and spent the afternoon exploring Central City. Then it was a leisurely return to Denver, to the theatre to watch Asher in that night's performance with the Bristol Old Vic.

The following day the Old Vic company, having finished their Denver season, flew out of the city and McCartney and Evans eventually took the Lear jet back to Los Angeles, to begin a two-day stay at the home of Derek Taylor. This culminated in the flight back home, and McCartney was back in England on April 12th.

For McCartney it then became a quiet period with Evans living at Cavendish Avenue with him, following the sudden sacking of the existing housekeepers, Mr. and Mrs.Kelly, with Evans required to ask them to leave. The skills of Mal Evans has a housekeeper hadn't figured prominently on his cv up to that point.

And to sack two housekeepers - long-standing, capable and trustworthy - without explanation, and to effectively replace them with someone like Mal Evans could be described as many things. Curious is just one of them.

But Evans was on hand and in situ when Brian Epstein came calling several days after McCartney and Evans got back from America. On one level, Epstein was making just a social call but more immediately he clearly needed reassurance from Evans that nothing had gone wrong in America.

There was an animated conversation with McCartney about a new concept called Magical Mystery Tour which briefly produced a flash of the old Brian Epstein as he excitedly started drawing up lists and diagrams of likely requirements for the planned one hour television film. In a perverse sense this was the closest Epstein had come to the planning for the major Beatles tours which had been his speciality for four years. Seasoned observers of Epstein and the Beatles believe that had he survived and kept control of Magical Mystery Tour the outcome for the group and the programme might have been very different.

And it is clear that in the weeks leading up to his death Epstein was already making preparations for Magical Mystery Tour. In the eventual programme the technical director was cinematographer Peter Theobald, and it emerged that he had been recommended to Epstein by leading film critic, Peter Wollen, after Epstein rang the British Film Institute to ask for help.

In addition Epstein registered his American company, Beatles USA Ltd, as holding the copyright of the film, which gave the distinct impression that he fully expected to be involved in the project through to completion and beyond.

On April 21st the long battle to finish the new album was finally over. The amount of studio time invested in the album's creation was reckoned at some 700 hours, but at last, at long last, "Sergeant Pepper's Lonely Hearts Club Band" was complete.

Release date was set for June 1st but unprecedented demand in the UK forced EMI to rush it out to the shops several days earlier. May had been set aside for an intensive period of promotion which caused unusual interest in the media given the fact that the Beatles had become reclusive since Candlestick Park almost a year earlier.

The first major event was scheduled for May 19th when a Press Launch had been set up at Epstein's house on Chapel Street. Four days before that, McCartney ventured out into the London social scene, perhaps pining for Jane Asher who was not scheduled to return from America for two weeks.

Prior to that, pirate station Radio London had achieved a notable scoop by playing the new album in its entirety, and this before copies had even been pressed. That news was put into relief by an announcement from EMI that since the start of their contract in 1962 the Beatles had achieved aggregate sales of 200 million!

The pressure building up to the release was intense, and it was being felt most keenly by Epstein. His medical condition was worsening and he was moving into a period where he would spend nights, or longer periods at the Priory, the private clinic in Roehampton, coming out briefly for specific appointments or functions, and then returning to the peace and safety of the clinic.

On those occasions, like a butterfly he would dazzle briefly, gloriously but then, like Cinderella at midnight, leave the glamour and return to the austerity of the Priory. He hosted a dinner party to celebrate the release of the album, and this was a private occasion for his boys. The atmosphere was allegedly convivial and exuberant, given the group's appreciation of what had been achieved with the new album.

Much of the dinner table conversation concerned the recent news from America that Capitol Records had suspended and then cancelled all work on the new Beach Boys opus, "Smile". The album had been discussed when the Beatles met various Beach Boys during the American tour in 1966 when much of the conversation revolved around Brian Wilson's retirement from touring. McCartney had even contributed to the recording of one of the intended 'Smile' tracks, 'Vegetables' during his recent West Coast visit with Mal Evans.

Given the mood, and the air of celebration it would have been quite reasonable to expect the party to go on to the early hours, but it was not to be. McCartney was the first to leave. The other Beatles stayed for quite a while after his departure, conscious in different ways of the decline in Epstein and his need for them to be there.

McCartney had a previous assignation, a plan set and laid in the private meetings in San Francisco. He was driven to the Bag O'Nails club in Soho. The official reason for the trip was to see Georgie Fame perform. The secret, actual reason was to meet an old friend, a girl called Linda Eastman, who he had arranged to meet there. She was in the company of Chas Chandler, manager of the Animals, and some members of the group. She knew them through her work as rock photographer in New York, where she had developed a close relationship with a number of musicians and bands.

She also had been the girlfriend in New York of a young man named William Campbell. A young man who had seemingly vanished in the autumn of 1966. But, as an unmarried, itinerant jobbing actor, he had no domestic ties to alert authorities that he was missing.

McCartney struck up a seemingly casual conversation with Linda Eastman in the Bag O'Nails and then invited her to join him as he moved on to the Speakeasy on Margaret Street, for an evening which was illuminated by the first playing of a new single 'A Whiter Shade Of Pale' by Procul Harum.

Though the evening with the Beatles was a joy for Epstein, the pain of the change in their relationship, of the attitude of the Beatles towards him, caused him to slip into an even deeper depression when they had all gone.

He re-admitted himself to the Priory and put himself back under the supervision of the clinicians and psychiatrists who were the only ones capable of dealing with his severe and growing depression.

On the day before the Press Launch of the new album came another Press Release demonstrating just how complete was the Beatles domination of the pop world. The group had been selected to represent the United Kingdom in the initial world-wide satellite broadcast. The arrangement was that in their segment the Beatles would be shown in Abbey Road recording a new song to be written especially for the television programme.

The show had been set for June 25th. In the new spirit of cheerful competition both Lennon and McCartney were to produce songs for the occasion. McCartney suggested 'Hello Goodbye' or 'Your Mother Should Know', both of which were sitting in the mountain of material in storage in Cavendish Avenue when he moved into the house. Both of these suggestions were rejected.

The alternative was a new song produced by John Lennon, and this was the one chosen on the basis that it best represented the ethos of the Summer of Love. The Lennon track, 'All You Need Is Love' would go on, alongside the new album, to be the anthem for the counter-culture and for that whole glorious summer. The clip of the Beatles performing the song in the studio, with Jagger, Faithfull and the rest sitting respectfully at their feet, has become a timeless representation of innocence, mainly because the sustained darkness and corruption and villainy was off-camera.

Epstein had largely managed the negotiations for the Beatles appearance on Our World which had been proceeding for many months. The sheer scale of the programme demanded it. There were fourteen countries taking part with the show transmitted to 31 countries, and the total audience was reckoned to be between 400 million and 700 million.

Inevitably there was controversy about the choice of the Beatles to represent the United Kingdom, and the row grew to remind people of the controversy generated by the award of the MBEs in 1965. Critics suggested clips from the Royal Shakespeare Company, or footage from Westminster Abbey or St.Paul's, or even film of the Queen visiting a location in Britain. These objections were set aside and in truth it is difficult to think of another image or scene that would have more truly represented Britain in the middle of 1967 than the flower-strewn Beatles singing 'All You Need Is Love'.

Once again Epstein's deft work in negotiating the Our World agreement was largely overlooked. He was in no state to notice. On May 19th he temporarily left the Priory to attend the press reception governing the release of "Sergeant Pepper's Lonely Hearts Club Band". The party had been arranged at Chapel Street, and managed by Joanne Newfield and Wendy Hanson acting in concert. Wendy Hanson had returned to Chapel Street on a temporary basis a few weeks earlier, in response to a plea from Epstein. He needed her to complete a very awkward and unique task.

There needed to be clearance and agreement from all the figures depicted on the cover of the new album, and Epstein asked the meticulous Wendy Hanson to come back and oversee the clearance procedures.

Most of the celebrities were happy to be involved, although some had slightly odd concerns about their involvement. Mae West, for example, was worried about being associated with a Lonely Hearts Club! Various original choices, such as Mahatma Gandhi, Jesus Christ and Adolf Hitler were excluded because of the various sensitivities likely to be affected by their inclusion.

Wendy Hanson worked through the list and eventually, in time for the printing of the covers, all the required permissions had been received. Only one person had his image excluded for non-sensitivity reasons. One-time Bowery Boy, Leo Gorcey, was asked to be included on the cover, but demanded a fee of $400 and so he was dropped.

Over the years there have been countless hours expended on analysis of the names and faces on the design. Was it a grave? Is it flowers in the shape of a guitar? Does the OPD patch mean Officially Pronounced Dead? In my research I read and re-read all the conspiracy theories and much of it seemed to stretch the truth, or at least credulity. Yes, the back cover of the album was red, but was that genuinely meant to represent blood? And every album from Sergeant Pepper onwards became a petri dish full of elements which can be turned over and examined and investigated ad nauseum.

But that doesn't mean that there aren't some elements which are, quite simply, odd. For example in the very centre of the Sergeant Pepper collage is an image of an American writer named Stephen Crane, who was hardly the most famous, or perhaps even the most talented American writer available for inclusion.

There are few documentary records to justify the specific selections. It appears that the choice of Stephen Crane was advocated by John Lennon although there is little in his history to suggest any great devotion to the writer's work. But a look at Crane's history throws up one interesting element. Although perhaps best known for the book "Red Badge of Courage" there are many who assert that Crane's most perceptive and challenging book is "The Open Boat" published in 1897. This is an adventure story concerning a sea voyage which culminates in a shipwreck. The relevance here is that the shipwreck sees four men thrown overboard, they fight to survive, but only three of them manage it. Four men share the adventure - only three survive.

Coincidence? Of course, but it is also curious particularly given that the largely anonymous Stephen Crane is located at the very centre of the album cover, directly behind Paul McCartney with a hand extended and palm upright precisely above the head of McCartney.

And once again the strange overlap of coincidence and curious comes to the fore. This peculiar hand signal, with the palm of the hand held up right over a person's head, is often represented as a sign of death in certain Indian religions. Whilst that appears to be true it is not universally accepted, and it seems quite likely that as a piece of symbolism it can be interpreted a dozen different ways by a dozen different people.

However, that fact doesn't overturn other facts such as this peculiar palm upright signal is never seen in a Beatles photograph before the Sergeant Pepper cover but from that point forward there are plentiful examples. That in itself is curious, but perhaps even more curious is the fact that, despite frantic research, I was totally unable to find a single such 'palm upright over the head' symbol in which the head in question was anybody but Paul McCartney.

Not Lennon; never Harrison; certainly not Starr.

Just the hand over the head symbol over the head of McCartney. Just McCartney.

Curious.

The Press launch of Sergeant Pepper was an exclusive affair. Thirteen reporters representing the major elements of the media had been invited to the event. They were presented with the obligatory lavish press pack, and treated to caviar and poached salmon and champagne. The press people were the most prominent people in the sector but there was one exception to that roster, one person who, however talented, was not a leader in the field or representing one of the major media outlets. That person was Linda Eastman who had been invited by McCartney in her role as a photographer, although she was hardly the best or best-known photographer in London that day, let alone the rest of the world.

Only thirteen members of the world's press, radio and television. Plus Linda Eastman, a woman that McCartney had allegedly met just four days earlier.

Curious.

Various people present commented on the fact that McCartney and Jane Asher stayed on separate sides of the room the entire night.

It was also noted that McCartney was conspicuously spending most of his time at the event with Linda Eastman.

And even if this were a situation where the couple had suffered a major row it is very odd for one partner to spend the whole of an evening, especially one devoted to such a prestigious album release, in the company of a near stranger, especially a member of the opposite sex.

Curious.

The gathered reporters were given the opportunity to discuss the new album with the four Beatles and a strangely nervous Epstein. Nobody attending the launch was really aware of the full extent of his physical and emotional decline. Consistent with his earlier wishes to become an actor Epstein was invariably able to summon up extremes of energy and self-assurance for a performance. In his case the show involved things like press launches and conferences, rather than appearances on stage, but just like many performers he could hit terrible depths coming down after a major event.

That was his fate after the Pepper launch. His chauffeur drove him immediately back to the Priory where he stayed overnight, before leaving temporarily in mid-afternoon on May 20th. That day saw him being picked up at the Priory and driven over to Weybridge for a civilised, nostalgic and quite jocular afternoon tea put on by Ringo Starr and his wife. It was quite like a family do back in Liverpool, and present, besides Brian Epstein, were Harrison with Pattie, and Lennon with Cynthia.

Curiously, the only member of the Beatles family absent was McCartney.

After the party Epstein was taken back to the Priory. It was becoming a regular routine, a procession across the Thames, but his deteriorating health left him little alternative. The treatment he received there was crucial to his well-being, as was the sheer peace he was able to enjoy in the tranquil surroundings. In recent years, the name, the Priory, has become synonymous with pampered celebrities and escape from self-created problems. It was different in Epstein's case. He was very ill, and his basic state of depression was being exacerbated by drink and particularly drugs, and his escalating worries were the final ingredient in the cocktail.

But by the middle of the year there was another, sinister aspect, something which caused him to seek the sanctuary of the Priory, and yet again it was a problem leaking out of Seltaeb.

Although the legal proceedings in the States were virtually over, the fall-out from the situation was still cascading on the principals like Epstein and Jacobs and Byrne. There were a large number of companies and individuals who were massively out of pocket as a result of the Seltaeb problems. Many companies had gone to the wall simply because they had large amounts of money invested in stock of Beatles memorabilia which was locked up, and stored away while the courts awaited the conclusion of the legal process.

That ending was reached in 1967 but it was a conclusion which, as ever, brought comfort to nobody except the lawyers. Final settlement in the case resulted in NEMS paying just over $100,000 to Seltaeb, a figure rather less than the millions they had claimed. David Jacobs reckoned that the $100,000 would barely cover the legal expenses for Seltaeb in America. All the legal expenses for NEMS had been paid personally by Epstein, but even this honourable gesture became a weapon to be used against him. David Jacobs had received threats and warnings from America aimed at NEMS and Epstein and himself from people who had been damaged grievously by the Seltaeb disaster. Epstein was seen as the person most responsible for the problems, and the sense of grievance many Americans felt against Epstein was inflamed when it emerged that Epstein was paying the legal costs out of his own pocket.

Not unreasonably many such people felt that if the multi-millionaire Brian Epstein could afford to pay such hefty legal bills then he could arguably make good some of the damage that he, and Seltaeb, had caused. Although it is fair to state that Jacobs was the instrument of the Seltaeb mess by agreeing the original deal with John Fenton, nobody, particularly people who felt they had been cheated out of millions, were prepared to listen to reason.

There were a number of people who had contacted NEMS requesting, even demanding, to speak to or see Epstein. The NEMS staff routinely rebuffed such enquiries, even when several unpleasant people turned up at Argyle Street looking for him. His fairly regular absences from NEMS was a benefit in those circumstances but widespread publicity over the previous few months meant that his home address was widely known.

The spring of 1967 saw the start of a series of visits to Chapel Street from people seeking Epstein, and they weren't looking for autographs.

The staff were generally capable of steering such people away but the police were called twice to persuade the unwelcome visitors to leave. Unfortunately the kind of people in question, with several coming from New York's garment industry, were not prepared to discuss the issues reasonably. They wanted their money, or restitution, and Epstein was in no position to contest the issue. But it meant that he spent months fearful, looking over his shoulder. The visits to the Priory during May and June were therapeutic, not least because of the care from psychiatrist John Flood, but there was also an undeniable aspect of safety involved.

On May 21st the usual pattern was repeated with Epstein being picked up at the Priory and taken for an afternoon soiree, this time with his parents at Chapel Street, but once it was over he was ferried back to the Priory. This time the stay was four days before he was brought back into the real, dangerous world. He was conscious, as was the staff at NEMS, that he needed to be on top form to cope with what was coming over the following week. He returned to Chapel Street on the afternoon of May 25th and spent a couple of hours resting before making a rare public appearance at the Royal Albert Hall where he enjoyed a concert by Georgie Fame with the Count Basie Orchestra.

The date was also notable as the day when Apple Music Limited was incorporated, with Brian appearing on the roster as a director. At that time the world had no idea what significance the name "Apple" would have for the Beatles in the coming years, and of course on June 1st 1967 Steve Jobs was living in California and he was just twelve years old.

That week's issue of Melody Maker featured an interview with John Lennon which, as usual, ranged over a number of topics but provided the stark, stern announcement that the group would not play live again, containing the evocative, almost Twitter-like statement, "No more tours! No more mop-tops!"

May 26th saw the surprise rush-release of the album. Excitement was building and there was very definitely the sense that the album would be indeed be something very special. To celebrate the release of the album Epstein staged a very extravagant party at his new country house, Kingsley Hill, which was located in Warbleton in East Sussex. He had purchased the house in February and this was to be the first grand occasion at the house. He had spent heavily on the event, even to the extent of having bunches of brightly coloured balloons attached to shrubbery on the roads immediately leading to the house.

As ever with Epstein, and especially with his growing need to have friends and trusted people around him, it was a truly glittering occasion with dozens of show business stars attending. Names like Lionel Bart, John Pritchard, Kenny Everett, Nat Weiss, Mick Jagger, Marianne Faithfull, Robert Stigwood, Derek Taylor and his wife Joan were present. As the event was part housewarming but mainly as celebration for the release of "Sergeant Pepper", the star attractions at the event were the Beatles who were there delighting in their accomplishments with the new album.

All the Beatles. Except Paul McCartney.

Curious.

May 27th was Cilla Black's birthday, 24 years old, and Epstein celebrated the event in lavish style by having illuminated birthday greetings shown in Piccadilly Circus in London, and also in Manchester, Birmingham and Bristol. It was a nice gesture and representative of the care he traditionally lavished on his artistes, other than the Beatles. But the slump in the artist roster at NEMS was indicative of his declining interest, and the relationship with Cilla Black was inevitably suffering.

He had tried to widen her appeal by moving her into films, but with little success. He had just concluded negotiations to provide her with her first BBC series, and he had also proposed that she should represent the UK in the Eurovision Song Contest in 1968. She refused on the reasonable grounds that as Sandie Shaw had won for the UK with 'Puppet on a String' just three months earlier the chance of a second consecutive win for the UK was remote.

In truth, despite the illuminated birthday greetings, Cilla Black was seriously contemplating leaving the management of NEMS. It emerged much later that she had been asked to appear in the iconic film, "The Italian Job", taking the role of the girlfriend of Michael Caine. It didn't happen because her then management failed to negotiate a fee with the producers. It is a perfect 'What If' moment, but it's hard to imagine that Epstein would have failed to appreciate the boost that such a film would have made to her career, or would have failed to ensure that it happened.

On May 29th McCartney was on public display, meeting Jane Asher as she returned from the triumphant Old Vic tour of America. This was a vital time in the couple's relationship, with her at the peak of the British acting world and him part of a group that on June 1st released the album that came to symbolise an era. The sales figures in Britain, America and the rest of the world were astronomic, and the awards - Grammys, Ivor Novello's and the rest - came thick and fast, and "Sergeant Pepper" would prove to be a consistently strong seller for half a century.

The American release of the album came one day later than the UK release, but within two weeks the American release had gone gold. Epstein wasn't able to bask in the reflected glory. The temporary ending of his Priory escapes left him working more on a normal basis than for several months but it was hard for him to escape the constant fear of being stalked by unknown and unnamed Americans anxious to remonstrate with him about the fall-out from the Seltaeb disaster. He tried to shake off his concerns by slipping back into the pill regime which had blighted his life for a couple of years, but that merely added to his depression. He tried yet again to divert himself in the gambling clubs but lost a considerable amount just in the first couple of weeks in June at the Clermont and the Cromwellian. And there were people grimly keeping tally of his losses.

Early June saw two important film announcements. On June 6th NEMS released some information about the possible filming of "Yellow Submarine", and two days later a NEMS press release stated that the Beatles had agreed to contribute to the "Yellow Submarine" project. The background to the situation wasn't made clear in the announcements but it was clear that NEMS and the Beatles hoped, if not thought, that the film, "Yellow Submarine", would complete their commitment to United Artists. It is equally clear that United

Artists quickly took the opposite view, despite the Beatles agreement to provide music to the film and even make a token appearance at the end.

That clear disagreement was the cause of the Beatles eventually being forced into the "Let It Be" film, with all the agony involved.

But on June 25th came possibly Epstein's proudest moment as manager of the Beatles, and there had been many. The Royal Command Performance, 73 million watching the Ed Sullivan performance, Shea Stadium - the great moments were truly magnificent, but the Our World television show was a sublime moment in the life of Brian Epstein and of the Beatles.

Our World broadcast to an expectant world with the Beatles debut performance of 'All You Need Is Love' forming the last item in the show. Even though the programme featured such major talents as Maria Callas, Pablo Picasso and the Vienna Boys Choir, it was undoubtedly the Beatles that were the highlight of the show. Dressed in peacock finery inside Studio One at Abbey Road with Jagger, Richard, Faithfull, Moon, Asher, Clapton, Nash and others sitting like disciples at their feet the Beatles performed the song which would become the anthem for London's Summer of Love.

Epstein is not immediately visible on the footage. Unusually for him he wandered around the huge spaces of Studio One without his customary tie, but with his lovely shy smile illuminating his features. Diffident and unassuming as ever, public displays were not Epstein's way, and, despite the enormous pride he must have felt at the event and what it meant for the group, he wouldn't intrude, unlike so many other lesser people who would have found some way to force themselves on camera to exercise their own self-importance.

That never was Epstein's way, and his innate modesty is perhaps best seen in a rare clip from three years earlier when he appeared on the American show What's My Line in October 1964. The panel quickly guessed who he was but he was charming and diffident even when the compere continually called him Barry Epstein. No self-inflated pomposity about Brian Epstein that night, or even the night at Abbey Road when Our World showed the Beatles, his Beatles, to the whole world.

The single of 'All You Need is Love' was released in the UK on July 7th, and, for the first time ever on a Beatles single, George Martin received a producer credit on the label. The single came out just a few days after a swish party was held at the Speakeasy for the Monkees who were appearing in London, and even though their concerts were under NEMS representation it was Vic Lewis who hosted the shindig. A sprinkling of pop royalty was present, including three Beatles with partners, all the members of The Who, Dusty Springfield, Eric Clapton, Lulu, various members of Manfred Mann, Procol

Harum, Micky Most and Vicki Wickham, Dusty Springfield. The most notable absentee was Brian Epstein, confined under sedation at the Priory.

He spent most of the next week either inside Chapel Street or inside the Priory. The only variation was the hurried chauffeur trips between the two, during which his previous calmness was replaced by a furtiveness as he stared repeatedly out of the windows to see who might be following or chasing him.

Most of the time it was drug-fuelled paranoia, but it wasn't entirely paranoia.

And then, on July 17th one of the bedrocks of his existence was snatched away. His father Harry died at the age of just 63. As the eldest son, Brian had particular responsibilities, and it is to his great credit that despite his huge problems and his state of health he did not shirk those responsibilities.

After receiving the message about their father's death from his brother, Clive, arrangements were made for Epstein to hurry back to Liverpool to be with his mother, Queenie. She naturally was distraught at the loss of her husband, and the calm presence of Brian must have been a great comfort to her during those trying days.

He stayed close to his mother's side during the week of Shiva, the seven day period of mourning in the Jewish religion. He based himself at his mother's house and ministered to her, and in a perverse way the situation was probably really good for him. He was needed again.

The Beatles had needed him during those hectic years after 1962 but that all ended at Candlestick Park in 1966 and for much of the past year he hadn't been able to find anything to fill that void. Drugs helped, but only temporarily, and his brief romantic interludes were invariably with the kind of rough trade to be found on building sites or in the shadows of Central Park or Regents Park. Even if those encounters provided physical relief they couldn't, wouldn't provide him with that essential sense of being needed. For a long, long time the Beatles had needed him, but that had ended.

Now his mother needed him and Epstein didn't let her down.

While he was in London he participated in the start of a campaign for the legalisation of cannabis. An advertisement was published in The Times on July 24th as the start of the campaign. It was sponsored by a group named Soma and was supported by 65 signatures including R.D.Laing, sixteen doctors, two Members of Parliament, four Beatles and Brian Epstein. And, separately but coincidentally, three days later Parliament passed the bill which could have had a really positive impact on his life. On July 27th homosexuality was made legal in Britain, and the door to civil partnerships and humane treatment of people was opened a crack, although it would be a generation or more before tolerance became widespread. That was too late, far too late for Brian Epstein. When the bill was passed, he had only a month left to live.

He travelled back to London after the week of Shiva, but this was just to make various arrangements for the future, although he had to attend a fairly strict meeting with Doctor John Flood, the psychiatrist, about his condition.

Then every weekend he went back home to Liverpool to be with his mother. There were quiet evenings for conversation and contemplation, and opportunities for Queenie to confirm that, despite the problems when Epstein had been a teenager, his amazing achievements in recent years had made his father very, very proud.

On the nights he was back in London he would call her every evening without fail, partly to check that she was still okay but mainly to preserve that sense of normality which was so necessary for her, and had become so valuable to him. Because of his ministrations to his mother, and the weekend trips back to Liverpool, he was forced to miss vital sessions with Doctor Flood on August 3rd and August 5th. On one level, this was not a problem as the need to look after his mother was imposing a regime and a discipline on his life which Flood and others at the Priory thought was not just beneficial but actually essential for Epstein's future well-being.

On August 14th he brought Queenie to stay with him at Chapel Street for a ten-day period. This was his chance to pamper her and he didn't stint.

They had trips out where he could show her his haunts, carefully selected, in London, and take her into the NEMS office to show her how mighty the fledgling Liverpool organisation had become. She was treated with sympathy and respect, befitting the mother of the creator of NEMS but also a woman recently-widowed. And the chance to look after her was really beneficial to him as well. The empty nest syndrome caused by the loss of the Beatles was suddenly, briefly, a thing of the past. He was needed again, needed by his mother, and it brought a last flowering of normal life for Brian Epstein. He was examined by Norman Cowan, his doctor, during her stay but he was able to reassure her that the examination was normal - overwork and a little stress. There was no mention of the pill-taking, or the insomnia, or the glandular fever, or the worries. He didn't tell her about his fears about shadows at the windows, or his growing terror about what might happen at the end of September, the day his 5 year contract with the Beatles would end.

Just before Queenie came down to London to him, he heard about the death of Joe Orton. He had been killed by his lover, Kenneth Halliwell who then killed himself, and though Epstein and Orton had never been particularly close, he was one of that inner circle of the gay men in the entertainment industry with whom Epstein had felt a kinship since coming down to London.

At another time the loss of Orton would have hit him much harder, but the need to look after Queenie was a welcome and a therapeutic distraction. Ironically, on the day after Orton's death, the bodies were discovered by a chauffeur who had been sent to take Orton to a meeting with Dick Lester to discuss the filming possibilities for "Up Against It".

While his mother was living with him at Chapel Street for that brief period, Epstein was able to maintain a regular lifestyle, totally different from the way he had lived at Chapel Street for many months. Early nights, sensible meals, fewer pills - it was just the kind of routine that the medical people like Doctor Flood had been urging on him at the Priory for months.

Epstein and his mother discussed the value of her moving down to London to be near him, and when he put her on the train at Euston on August 24th he was clearly intending to bring her back permanently. The night before her departure he had taken her to the Saville Theatre and it isn't difficult to imagine the huge pride she must have felt in her son - denied a career in the theatre by circumstance but now a theatre-owner in the West End! The day was even more significant because, squiring his mother around London on August 23rd, he wanted to take her in to meet the Beatles at a recording session they were holding that day. Unusually it wasn't Abbey Road. Instead they were working at the Chappell Studio on Maddox Street, just off New Bond Street. Feeling tired she stayed behind at Chapel Street, and Epstein went to the Chappell Studio session alone. Sadly the last sight the Beatles had of the man who had done so much for them was him standing alone, depressed and even slightly angry at the back of the control booth.

Poignantly the song on which the group were working that day was 'Your Mother Should Know'. Even more poignantly and sadly this would be the very last time Epstein would be in a recording studio with the Beatles

On the same day, some three thousand miles away in New York, around 2,000 fans gathered together at Shea Stadium, to register their protest about the fact that the Beatles had not appeared in concert in the United States during the summer of 1967.

The protests were peaceful and good-humoured, but obviously futile.

Despite all the public declarations from assorted Beatles and management, it would be quite some time and several tragic deaths before the fondly-held dream of seeing the Beatles return to the stage would fade away completely.

The return of his mother to Liverpool allowed Epstein to make a welcome return to the Priory, and receive a much-needed addition to his medication. It also allowed him some respite from what he was beginning to imagine was more unwelcome attention from Americans furious about the Seltaeb outcome. David Jacobs had expressed severe concerns during a visit within hours of Queenie getting on the train but Epstein was actually more immediately concerned with the English gambling interests who were pressing him for money. As such the Priory was a place of sanctuary as well as a medical source, and he was happy to stay inside the Priory until the imminent long weekend incorporating the August Bank Holiday. He used the time profitably by catching up on correspondence with letters to Nat Weiss and Derek Taylor about his future plans for American trips and, importantly, work in America. There was a trip already planned for early September which would include negotiations on a new tv interview series to be fronted by Brian Epstein.

While he was sequestered in Roehampton, his charges, the Beatles, were taking another step forward in their private lives. On the night that Queenie went home the Beatles, along with some friends, attended a public lecture in the Hilton Hotel on Park Lane given by an Indian mystic, Maharishi Mahesh Yogi. The stimulus for the meeting had come from Pattie Harrison who had become interested in Indian mysticism during her trip to India with George late in 1966. She saw the lecture being advertised, mentioned it to her husband, and he brought his colleagues, minus Ringo Starr, along with him.

When the lecture finished the Beatles stayed on for a private meeting with the Maharishi which had the unlikely outcome that the group hurriedly arranged to travel to Bangor in north Wales for the weekend to attend the Maharishi's summer conference of the Spiritual Regeneration Movement. This meant leaving London the following day, Saturday, from Euston Station and, because of the tight timescales, had to be a hurriedly-arranged trip.

It turned into bedlam. The press and media were in their element seeing the Beatles associated with this strange little man and talking about meditation and mantras. The scenes at Euston were reminiscent of the more shambolic days of Beatlemania. John Lennon's wife, Cynthia, became separated from the party in the frenzy and they boarded the train without her. Although she later caught up with them in Wales thanks to an emergency drive by Neil Aspinall the scene was perhaps a metaphor for the way her life with Lennon was developing.

More pertinently, the Beatles were making a trip as the four Beatles for the first time in almost four years without the care and organisation and devotion of Epstein or Aspinall or Evans. The chaos which dogged the trip from the arrival at Euston cast a shadow over the weekend. Less insular or self-obsessed people than the Beatles might have stopped to question how competent they would be to run their own affairs if one or more of their devoted support apparatus were ever to be removed.

Of course, the mood as the train pulled away from London was exuberant and excited and joyful. That collective enthusiasm was sustained as they travelled in their first-class compartment to Wales with the Maharishi in another first-class compartment on the same train.

In Bangor the Beatles were brought up short by the sudden change in the living conditions presented to them. They were given the same dormitories and bunk beds being used by the rest of the three hundred people attending the seminar, but their keenness to explore this new lifestyle made them tolerate if not ignore the various deprivations. As a break from such spartan circumstances, they went out into Bangor that night to the Senior Chinese restaurant, the only one they could find still open. Once the convivial meal was over it came time to pay the bill. Almost unbelievably none of the party had any money with them, and perhaps even more ridiculously, none of the staff at the restaurant realised that the large party included not just Mick Jagger but also the four Beatles.

Eventually the embarrassment was relieved by Harrison who discovered some currency concealed inside his shoe. But none of them recognised that this was the kind of situation that Epstein, and also Aspinall and Evans, had managed, so adroitly, on their behalf over the years.

The party returned to their small cramped rooms at the college and prepared for the meaningful insights that Sunday August 27th would bring.

Back in London Brian Epstein had spent a couple of troubled days. He had been driven to the Priory immediately after waving goodbye to David Jacobs. An appointment at the Priory had to be kept. Too many had been missed over the previous few weeks.

His driver picked him up to take him back to Chapel Street ahead of a planned trip down to Sussex, but a sudden change of plan was considered as the car pulled into Chapel Street. The intention was to stay there before going away for the weekend. His mind was changed rapidly by the sight of a dark blue Mercedes parked across the road from the Chapel Street house, a car that he thought he had noticed on more than one occasion previously.

Not for the first time in recent months he didn't feel safe and able to relax there.

Epstein had already made plans for the Bank holiday weekend. Several people had been invited out to Kingsley Hill including his assistant, Joanne Newfield, about whom he felt quite guilty because of the extra workload she had suffered in the previous weeks because of his stays in the Priory and periods in Liverpool. Newfield was asked to bring along a friend of both her and Epstein, the young Scottish singer, Lulu. In many ways her youth and sheer vivacity reminded him of his old friend Alma Cogan, who he still missed desperately since her death the previous year.

In the event neither Newfield nor Lulu could make it, as both of them had other commitments that weekend. Newfield was still working at Chapel Street as he drove away, wishing him a pleasant weekend. Epstein had also invited two long term friends and NEMS colleagues, Geoffrey Ellis and Peter Brown, plus a few friends from the gay community.

Epstein had asked his driver to pick him up on the Friday afternoon at Chapel Street but changed his plans when he spotted the dark blue Mercedes. Instead he took his own car to hurry out to Kingsley Hill.

Leaving London raised his spirits and he was even spotted in an antique shop in Uckfield en route to Sussex. At that time he had every reason to expect a really enjoyable weekend with friends at Kingsley Hill, and perhaps even a link-up with the Beatles on the Bank Holiday Monday. But once again the limitations of the then technology impacted on him. With a mobile phone he would have been able to learn minute by minute about the changes in the plans of his friends. He would have known that his hopes for a convivial weekend were falling apart. He might well have changed his mind about what he would, should do over the weekend.

He reached Kingsley Hill during the afternoon and rejoiced in the peace and beauty and the complete absence of blue Mercedes cars, and was joined later in the afternoon by Peter Brown and Geoffrey Ellis.

However, the other expected arrivals failed to appear. He already knew about Joanne and Lulu. More disappointing, his latest paramour had been invited, was fervently anticipated, but the man failed to arrive. Epstein wanted him to spend the weekend at Kingsley, partly so that they could get to know each other better, but also because he genuinely felt better, more secure with someone with him. The possible sightings of the blue Mercedes might have been coincidence, or his imagination, but the recent threats to him and David Jacobs weren't imaginary, and some strong male companionship did make him feel much better, and not just for reasons of sexual gratification.

Nobody but Brown and Ellis arrived. They had dinner, which was enlivened by conversation and scurrilous gossip about Stigwood and Vic Lewis, and Epstein, trying to hide his disappointment at the collapse of his weekend, drank far more than normal. He then decided, on a whim, that he would return to London at around 10-45pm. This was a bad move on several grounds, not least the fact that by modern standards he was well in excess of accepted drink driving limits. However, that was a different era and a different attitude to things like drink driving.

The Road Traffic Act 1967 had started the change towards a climate of penalties for the offence of driving under the influence, and indeed 1967 was the year that Britain saw the first appearance of a new device called a breathalyser.

But in August 1967 it simply wouldn't have occurred to Epstein that the amount of drink in his system might have been a problem. And, in the very unlikely event that the police should stop him in the car on the way back to London, the power and the influence and, to be brutally frank, the money of the Beatles would smooth over any temporary problems. It had happened several times previously, and, on more than one occasion in 1966, for a situation far graver than drink driving.

Despite the pleas and warnings of Brown and Ellis, he couldn't be dissuaded, and he drove back to London in his Bentley.

Comically, but tragically, he had not long driven away when a black cab turned up at Kingsley Hill with the man that Epstein had been so eagerly anticipating. He had brought with him three friends and, had Epstein still been there, it could have been a very pleasant weekend for him. The four arrivals were clearly surprised at the absence of their host, but they remained at Kingsley Hill, drinking and enjoying a few substances in the company of Brown and Ellis. And, with the simple addition of a mobile, Epstein could have been contacted en route, and he could have turned round and returned to Kingsley Hill, and how much musical history might have been changed by that simple reverse?

The next contact with Epstein came late on the afternoon of Saturday August 26th when Brown spoke to him on the telephone. Brown was concerned that Epstein was speaking in what Brown described as a "woozy voice", clearly influenced by the sleeping pills Epstein said he had taken.

Epstein was apologetic about his failure to return to East Sussex, and for causing concern to his friends. It was also clear that he felt extremely disappointed that his male friends had effectively passed him in the taxi as he drove back to London. Brown suggested that he should come back to Kingsley Hill to join the party but, by the way he sounded, it was clear that he was in no state to drive, especially with the presence of Tuinals and Preludins in his system.

Instead Brown suggested that he should travel down on the train to Uckfield, although in hindsight it seems bizarre that, with the NEMS wealth and influence, somebody, even a taxi driver, couldn't be found to drive him the fifty miles to East Sussex. Epstein told him that he would get Antonio to prepare something for him to eat, read some correspondence and watch Juke Box Jury. The plan then was to call Brown back to confirm which train he would be taking. No call was received.

It later emerged that his housekeepers, the Spanish butler Antonio Garcia and his wife Maria, had heard and seen him briefly late on the Friday evening, but that was as he was preparing to go out in London. There must have followed yet another sad, seedy night in gambling clubs, loveless conversations and the loss of significant sums of money. The difference was the eyes, the hostile eyes, that were following him.

The housekeepers had no contact from him during Saturday, and heard nothing from him, apart from a brief interlude around 5pm when Antonio took some food in to him. Given the layout of the Chapel Street house, it wasn't unusual that nothing else was heard. The use of intercoms was a means of overcoming the problems of being able to hear communications between different floors. And the distance between the outside corridor and the door to Epstein's bedroom was substantial, with the width of an imposing drawing room between the two.

But when that lack of contact stretched into Sunday August 27th they started to become worried. Once again telecommunications played an unfortunate part. The Spanish housekeeper, Antonio, had no way of contacting anybody other than Joanne Newfield who was still in London.

She tried to reassure Antonio but, feeling concern about the information relayed to her, she went to Chapel Street that afternoon. As it was a Sunday, and a Bank Holiday weekend, the traffic was light and she was able to make the journey rapidly.

She went up to Epstein's bedroom with Antonio and went through into the ante-room, the dressing room, from which a single door opened into Brian Epstein's bedroom. It had always struck her that there was a lot of space between the outside hallway and Epstein's bedroom. She knocked several times, called his name, and knocked again, without response. Then she went up onto the next floor to her office and tried the intercom connecting her office to Epstein's quarters. Still no reply, and she began to get very concerned.

The Spanish housekeepers were getting quite agitated. They had passable, but not good, English, and even with Joanne Newfield they were quite reserved and shy. She needed someone else there and so rang Peter Brown at Kingsley Hill for advice. They knew that Epstein's usual doctor, Norman Cowans, wasn't available, so Brown suggested that she should call his personal doctor, John Galway.

That call was made and when Joanne explained the unusual circumstances he agreed to come to Chapel Street immediately.

While she waited for his arrival Joanne tried calling other people who might have been helpful but, being the Bank Holiday weekend, most were unavailable. Yet again the lack of mobiles had an effect. Eventually she was able to contact Alastair Taylor and he came over without delay.

John Galway arrived and went up to Epstein's bedroom with Joanne. They tried knocking and shouting his name again, but without an answer. No alternative was left. Joanne asked Galway and Antonio to break down the doors into the bedroom.

She followed John Galway and Antonio into the Brian Epstein's bedroom.

The curtains were drawn. Epstein was lying across the bed. John Galway told her to wait outside which she did. He came out a couple of minutes later and, even if she didn't already know it, the look on his face told her that Brian Epstein was dead.

Joanne Newfield had kept the telephone line open to Peter Brown, and John Galway sadly told him about Epstein's passing. Before departing hurriedly for London, Brown rang David Jacobs who, as friend and lawyer for Epstein, needed to hear the news. Jacobs was at his house in Brighton and he left immediately to go to Chapel Street, as did Brown and Ellis.

Alastair Taylor was the first to arrive, just moments after the discovery of the body. He and Joanne consoled each other, but counselled that they should delay informing the authorities until they were sure that the house contained no illegal substances.

Then, in another curious incident, the doorbell rang and when Joanne Newfield answered she saw a reporter who she knew. He seemed surprised that she was at the house and told her that he had heard that Epstein was ill. This was less than ten minutes after John Galway had pronounced Epstein dead, and before any call had been made to police or emergency services.

She got rid of the reporter but never forgot her bewilderment that a reporter should be on the doorstep so rapidly after the tragedy was discovered.

Joanne was also bemused by the controlled reactions of both Brown and Ellis when they reached Chapel Street. She hadn't expected hysterics but the absence of emotion seemed strange, and she wondered if something else had happened at Kingsley Hill that hadn't been revealed.

Inevitably the death of such a prominent man caused a media storm. The pavements outside the Chapel street house were quickly filled with reporters plus radio and television people and equipment. Inside the house the bad news had to be transmitted to relevant parties, family and friends plus relevant business contacts. It was certain to be a major news item, especially on such a traditionally slow news day as a Bank Holiday Sunday, and the concern was to ensure that people like family members didn't get the tragic news from radio or television or, god forbid, a reporter asking that awful question "How do you feel?"

Joanne was principally concerned about Brian's mother, Queenie. It was only a matter of weeks since she had lost her husband; the death of her eldest son would be a crippling blow, and Joanne rang Clive Epstein to give him the bad news in the hope that he could pass on the awful news to her in the most sympathetic manner possible.

The other critical call was made to the Beatles, still sequestered in Bangor with their Guru. Jane Asher took the call from London and passed the phone to McCartney. His shock and sadness was quickly communicated to the rest of the group. The group immediately made preparations to return to London, and their sense of horror is almost tangible in the television interviews with the Beatles as they started their return journeys, with Lennon in particular looking shell-shocked. Curiously only three Beatles gave their views. McCartney had allegedly already left for London, leaving the other three to face the media firestorm.

A scheduled concert by Jimi Hendrix at the Saville Theatre was cancelled as a simple mark of respect that evening.

Brian Epstein was found on a single bed, dressed in pyjamas, with various pieces of correspondence spread casually over a second single bed close by. Peter Brown and Alistair Taylor carefully scoured the premises before the police arrived trying to ensure that anything potentially incriminating was found and removed. Only one joint was found.

David Jacobs arrived very quickly from Brighton, getting there just before Peter Brown and Geoffrey Ellis. Chapel Street was hideously busy, with the media milking the tragedy for all they were worth. However, Jacobs' flair for self-publicity came to the fore, and he quickly took charge of events, helped by the fact that virtually everybody knew him. Even those who didn't know who he was could hardly fail to be impressed and invariably browbeaten by Jacobs in the street. Later in the day, when things had calmed down somewhat, Peter Brown and David Jacobs went to the mortuary to identify the body.

At the statutory inquest, his death was officially ruled as accidental, probably caused by a gradual build up of Carbatrol in his system, mixed with alcohol. It was revealed that he had taken six Carbatrol pills in order to sleep, which was probably usual, but meant that his tolerance was very close to becoming lethal. Indeed the coroner commented that the barbiturate level in Epstein's blood was a "low fatal level".

In the bedroom, in a series of jars - none of which were empty - were found 30 Carbatrol capsules, 40 Librium capsules and 20 Tryptizol capsules which had been prescribed by Dr Cowan.

It emerged that Carbatrol can be used to treats different types of seizures, but is also used to treat nerve pain and bipolar disorder, which has also become known as manic-depressive illness. The nerve pain situation was also relevant because of the long-term implications of the glandular fever suffered in 1966 and also the damage caused to his back in the fall from the plane in America.

The consultant pathologist at the inquest stated that the capacity of bromide in his blood was significant, believing that it had built up over weeks rather than hours. Too much of it is likely to make someone forgetful about, for example, how many tablets had already been taken. In Epstein's case the bromide was housed within the Carbatrol, and the final verdict was that he had taken just enough, although it wasn't a massive amount, to tip him over the edge.

Despite the official verdict there were many people speculating on suicide as a likely cause of Epstein's sudden death. The fact that none of the pill jars had been emptied tends to negate that possibility. More importantly though, he was a conscientious and attentive son and, given the fact that his father had died just weeks earlier, it was frankly inconceivable that he would voluntarily expose his deeply-loved and newly widowed mother to even more grief by killing himself.

Despite all the denials of the suicide rumours, Peter Brown later claimed that he had removed a suicide note and a will from Brian's bedroom prior to the arrival of the authorities. However, Brown also admitted that the suicide note was from an earlier suicide attempt, some months earlier. Although it is curious that the will removed from Epstein's bedroom left his house and his money to his mother, Queenie, and his younger brother, Clive. Given that Brian Epstein's father, Harry, had only died just six weeks earlier, the will must have been recently updated, otherwise his father would certainly have been mentioned. It is also surely curious that a person would leave a suicide note just 'lying around'.

I was surprisingly moved to reach this point in the story. It all seemed sad, desperately sad, and I was surprised at how upset I became learning about the desolate, lonely demise of Brian Epstein.

And, as I realised, the death of Brian Epstein meant that much had changed and could never, ever be the same again. The group began to fall apart visibly, painfully, but, to be perfectly frank, by this point I didn't care.

The stories I had learned about the Beatles and McCartney and Epstein had fascinated and amazed and appalled me, but I was no further forward. I had started out on the search for the truth about the replacement …..alleged replacement Paul McCartney but I still wasn't sure.

There were a great many strange aspects to the story - things I couldn't explain - but nothing that would stand up in a court of law. In truth I was quite depressed. I had felt so close to the story and I had hoped that I could write a script that Jeff could film as a staggering, world-shaking revelation.

But I didn't know if I could do it. There were so many facts that made me suspect that something very odd had happened to Paul McCartney and also to Brian Epstein, but I was also aware that the television company's legal people would put any script of mine into a complete strait jacket. In truth I was ready to jack the whole thing in, and I went to meet Jeff for one of our occasional production meetings fully prepared and bracing myself to abandon the whole thing.

Until he dropped his bombshell.

"So what happened with the Paul McCartney thing?" was his opening gambit. We were back in the pub on Charlotte Street. Safe, familiar territory, though I had no reason to feel apprehensive.

I took a sip from my pint and breathed in, ready to verbally throw in the towel.

"Hey!" he began, again reminding me of nothing so much as Monica from Friends. "You'll never guess what happened! Strangest thing!"

"No, I probably won't!" I replied drily, in my best Oscar Wilde tone. He appeared not to notice.

"I ran into an old mate. He used to do some format transfer work for companies in the business round here." Here was Soho. Not the throbbing heart of the tv industry that it once was, but still home to a host of facilities providers. "A while ago he was doing some conversion work on a Beatles film, "Yellow Submarine"."

"Yes?" I answered blankly. "That was the third film, or so they thought, but United Artists wouldn't let them use that to get out of the contract. That's why they had to do the "Let It Be" film." I must admit feeling slightly smug that whatever the topic was I had some information to impart. I guess that's how Stephen Fry feels all the time. The difference is that he can do it about any topic. I can only do it about the Beatles.

"So he was there doing the work, running through frame by frame and comes to a section where the Beatles are inside the submarine."

"Yes? The Yellow Submarine. What about it?"

"Well the Beatles, the cartoon Beatles are there, dotted around the submarine in the frame. The Beatles. All of them."

"So?" I asked, slightly grumpily.

He was clearly enjoying my discomfort. "They were there in the frame inside the submarine. All the Beatles."

"And?"

"Only there weren't four Beatles. There were five! The cartoon Paul was there twice!"

"Never!" I scoffed. "He must be wrong."

"Well, see for yourself" he said triumphantly, pulling his iPad out of his bag. He had it primed and ready. One touch on the screen produced an image. It was the inside of the submarine, piping and tubes pre-dominating. The cartoon George Harrison occupies the left hand side of the screen with the cartoon Ringo peeking out from behind a metal structure at the front of the screen. John Lennon is dancing and waving an arm and a leg at the back of the scene. And in the bottom right the cartoon McCartney is popping up out of a hatch.

And there, in the top right, the cartoon McCartney, and it is unmistakably and undeniably him, is also there, peeking out of a hatchway.

Two Pauls. Not a mistake, or a technical glitch. When we ran through the full clip it is there - only a fraction of a second - but undoubtedly and inexplicably two Paul McCartneys. I watched it, and re-watched it. I saw it eight or nine times. Jeff was right. There were two Paul McCartneys.

Curious.

I was more than curious. I was exultant. Two Pauls - how could that be explained away? It couldn't, it simply couldn't, and I determined there and then to go back to the Hamptons and speak to one of the few surviving people who could throw some light on those remarkable events.

And In The End, The Love You Take

It took two weeks to get her to agree to see me again. I don't know the reason for her reluctance. I assumed she was just weary of the subject. I also suspected that the raising of the topic caused her some sadness and pain and not unreasonably, she wasn't keen to subject herself to the ordeal again. But, she had loaned her diaries to me, and one of those diaries contained a strange, but hugely exciting element.

The journey to the Hamptons seemed longer, harder than I remembered it. The weather didn't help. It was unseasonably cold and miserable, largely echoing my mood. The unpleasant atmosphere was typified by the unsmiling D who was even more brusque than I remembered. This time she stared soullessly at my face for around three seconds when she opened the door. Then she swivelled and walked silently across the hall before opening the door into the lounge. Chrissie was sitting on the same sofa in virtually the exact position she occupied on my previous visit.

She was wearing a loose fitting yellow dress, full length, that bubbled softly around her as she moved on the sofa.

D stood in the doorway until I shook hands with Chrissie, as though needing to be certain that I would stay within the room.

Chrissie didn't speak to welcome me. She beckoned me to sit across from her on the sofa, and waited for me to speak. I thought I would be careful and not mention the book outline immediately. As always, my enthusiasm made things happen sooner then I had intended. A few women have mentioned that to me over the years.

I took the two diaries out of my bag and held the important one facing her in my right hand. There was a piece of paper attached by sticky tape to the inside of that diary, and it was that sheet which was most interesting to me. It appeared to be the outline for a book with chapter headings which resembled the subject headings I had been pursuing in my research. There was no mention of the book in the diaries although a few oblique references did make me wonder. And I hoped beyond hope that she had written a book and that she still had it secured somewhere in the Hamptons or even under lock and key in New York.

I didn't hold back with the questions. I, rather too dramatically, opened the second diary at the back page and held it out to her. She smiled thinly. "Oh, you saw that, huh?"

"Hard to miss it!"

"I suppose so!" I hoped she would go on to talk about it, to describe what it meant, but she was silent. She just sat staring at the sheet and the elegant but slightly fading handwriting.

"Can I ask you - does that refer to a book?"

"Uh huh!" she confirmed. "After Mal died I thought I'd write a book about the whole fucking mess!"

The use of the expletive was a real surprise. It was as though someone had dropped a drinks glass on a stone cathedral floor.

"And what happened? Did you publish it?"

"Oh no. Several publishers were interested but then, for some reason, each of them seemed to lose interest once they had read it. At first I thought it was because it was no good, but then I realised that because it was sensitive - too sensitive - for some people!"

"What people?"

"You tell me. Nobody else could - or would!"

She didn't seem to want to discuss the subject any further. I thought I'd try one more attempt. "So have you got a copy I can read?"

"No. Gone. No copies left!" She spat the words out like phlegm, but it was obvious that, whatever the circumstances, the book was not or would not be available to me. I was nonplussed. I couldn't tell if she was upset or angry or both, but I couldn't afford to waste this priceless opportunity.

"Em, can I ask you about some of the topics you had listed?" She nodded slightly. I expected her to start leafing through the papers which seemed to sit permanently beside her on the sofa. That didn't happen. Whatever the background, whatever the circumstances she knew more about these topics, without any reference to notes, than I would have thought possible.

"You mention Nicky Byrne and two mysterious warnings."

"Yes. In October 1967 Nicky claimed that he'd had two phone calls during the summer of 1967 telling him that Brian Epstein was going to die shortly."

"Who from? Who called him?"

"Don't know. Always presumed it was some of the mob people he knew in New York but I didn't ask and he wasn't telling!"

"Right. Now in the same section you mention something about changing dummies."

"Do you know what happened on Marylebone Road in London in 1969?"

"No. Should I?"

"Probably not. There's a famous waxwork place there, models of famous people and so on. One of the models was altered."

"Altered? What do you mean? They alter models all the time."

"Yes. They change costumes. They change hairstyles. They don't make a dummy taller."

"Sorry, I don't get this. What do you mean - taller? How? Why would you need to make a dummy look taller? I thought they always measured the people and made a replica of the people."

"That's A1. But if a person gains four inches in height then they have to increase the height of the dummy."

"But that's stupid. Nobody but a child or a teenager can grow four inches. Certainly not a grown man or a grown woman."

"Exactly. So if one of the celebrities suddenly grows four inches in height that would be surprising?"

"It wouldn't be surprising - it would be miraculous!"

"Wanna see the proof?"

I nodded dumbly. She leafed through the pack of papers on her lap and produced a blue folder which she opened and handed to me. Inside were two large photographs, one mounted on either side of the folder. They looked to be around 8 inches by 5 inches, and they were both pictures of the four Beatles. The one on the left was a shot of them on stage at some unidentified concert, probably, from the suit styles, in 1964-1965, the classic picture - Ringo on the plinth at the back, Harrison, McCartney and Lennon side by side at the front. The photo on the opposite side was much later, around 1967-1968, and showed the four men in a posed picture in some garden situation, glowering into the camera. The older shot was black and white, the later one was colour.

I stared at them, looking from one to the other but didn't really understand what I was seeing.

"I don't get this? What am I looking at?"

"They look the same to you? The Beatles, I mean?"

"Well, apart from the ages. There's three, maybe four years gap here."

"Okay. But apart from the ageing, do the four men look the same to you?"

I was confused. Older certainly. Possibly more cynical and bitter, but I couldn't see what she was getting at. She had a small six inch wooden ruler on the arm of the sofa. She brought it across and laid it roughly in line with the tops of the heads of the four Beatles in the picture on the left, the younger version. Though it wasn't a straight line, the height of Harrison, Lennon and McCartney was quite similar and the edge of the ruler hovered close to the tops of their heads.

Without commenting she withdrew the ruler and placed it in a similar position across the heads of the four Beatles in the later picture. The heads of Lennon and Harrison were proportionately more or less the same.

The top of McCartney's head disappeared under the ruler. It wasn't possible to see the top of the head until she moved the ruler upwards, suggesting a height difference of some three inches.

I looked at the picture, then stared at her. "That's impossible! It must be a trick!"

"Want to see some more photos showing the same thing? How many - 5? Or 15? Or 50?"

"But that's crazy. It doesn't make sense!"

"Yeah. You'd think so, wouldn't you?"

Her quiet confidence was unsettling. I looked down my notes and chose another subject. "Now, you mention somebody called Terry Knight."

"Terry Knight? He was a muso and a DJ from Chicago or Detroit. He met up with the Beatles when they were recording that double album. In the middle of all that Apple nonsense when they were supposed to be signing up anyone with a vocal chord. They let him sit in on one of their recording sessions."

"Really?" I was very surprised. "That hardly ever happened!"

"True. So it makes you ask - why? Anyway, the day he was there, some row blew up and I think that was the day that Ringo Starr walked out."

"I'm sorry. I don't see the relevance."

"Terry Knight went away from the session and wrote a song called 'Saint Paul'. It's a weird song, never mentions a possible break-up, but a lot of people think it relates to Mr.McCartney being replaced in the Beatles. The interesting aspect is what happened to it after it was released. It came out on Capitol, and if you listen to it you can hear bits of 'She Loves You', 'Lucy in the Sky' and 'Hey Jude' in the performance. Nobody at Capitol seemed to notice or even care, but then the song got reissued as the only song, the only non-Beatle song, ever to be published under the MacLen banner."

"What? MacLen? That was just for Lennon and McCartney songs."

"Yes. Go figure! Only one person besides Lennon and McCartney ever had a song on MacLen, and it wasn't George Harrison or Ringo Starr or even George Martin. It was Terry Knight. And that song, 'Saint Paul', remains the only song in the entire MacLen catalogue that wasn't written by John Lennon and Paul McCartney, either together or solo. The only one!"

My only comment was "Curious!" but she obviously didn't appreciate the significance of the word.

She saw my slight discomfort and clearly thought she'd carry on making the point. "Do you know Derren Brown, the magic man, illusionist back home?"

I was strangely pleased that she still thought of Britain as home. "I don't know him personally, but of course I know his stuff."

"Do you know his 'Person Swap' piece?" I shook my head. "You can catch it on YouTube. Derren Brown is on some street in London and stops a woman and asks for directions. He's holding a map. While the woman is looking at the map a couple of guys walk down the street carrying a large image of Derren Brown. They walk between the woman and him, and another man steps in to take Derren Brown's place. Then the conversation carries on without the woman noticing that Derren Brown had been replaced by someone else."

"Wow!" was only sensible comment I could offer. But she wasn't finished.

"And where do you think he's asking directions to?"

"Dunno."

"St.Paul's! And then, once the item is finishing on the tv show, he makes a very strange comment. He says, 'I'm sure that wouldn't have worked so well if I was a super famous pop-star'!"

"Wow!" I was repeating myself, but there was little else I could say.

She smiled, clearly enjoying my slight discomfort. "I presume you have more questions" she opened.

"Just a few!" I lied. "I'm hoping you can clear away some of the clouds, some of the confusion for me."

"Fat chance! Such as?"

"Well, one of the big ones is - why should they want to cover up a major world tragedy like the death of Beatle Paul McCartney?

She took a deep breath. It wasn't as melodramatic as it sounds. "Well, that's part of the answer in itself. The sheer scale of it. Look at it this way. Just say, hypothetically, it did happen. Mr.McCartney is killed in a car crash in London - how it happened doesn't matter - the question is - what happens next? Just imagine, if Brian Epstein was desperate to hide the Seltaeb thing from the Beatles, and desperate to get them to sign the new EMI contract, and desperate to get them to sign a new management contract with him then...." She stopped speaking, allowing me to mull over the implications of her words. "Mal hinted to me that Epstein persuaded them go along with the switch as a short-term thing just to get the fortune for them that the new EMI contract would mean. They have an expression over here - do the Math! - and it really applies to this. It's all about money!"

I was confused. "But even if that's true, why keep it going afterwards?"

She smiled thinly. "Money, again! And then, of course, the small matter of major fraud. Signing contracts, pretending that the full group still exists!"

"Can you explain a bit more - you've obviously thought a lot about this."

"You could say that". She smiled, but there wasn't much humour in her eyes. "After Mal died in LA in the seventies I started thinking about it a lot. About all the crap, and the criminality, and the horrible, horrible-"

She paused. A slight glistening below her right eye betrayed the start of a tear. I was surprised. She obviously cared more about the situation than I had suspected.

"That's why I thought of writing a book about it!" she continued. She was clearly, deeply upset. Another handkerchief wiped her eyes. I felt like a swine.

"But, of course it never got published. Always a good reason, I'm sure! she concluded enigmatically. "But that's why I kept the diaries and all these other papers. For the book. If I ever did get to publish it. And that's why I held onto all that stuff."

She gestured vaguely off to her right, but what ever she was pointing at was behind my back and I didn't want to break the mood by turning round.

"Well…with this book, what did you think happened? What was the whole story?" She pulled herself to her feet, slowly and it seemed with some pain. I was suddenly conscious that it was the first time I had seen her standing since that first meeting at the Plaza. She walked slowly over to stare through the big windows which were dripping on the outside with large raindrops sweeping in from the Atlantic. Although she wasn't a heavy woman, her footsteps made visible indentations in the carpet pile. I watched absently as the pile quickly slumped back to horizontal conformity. I was impatient for her to carry on speaking.

"What happened?" she repeated slowly. "I suspect that Mr.McCartney was killed in a car crash somewhere , probably London, in the first half of November 1966, and that Brian Epstein persuaded Mal Evans to find this

McCartney double - who certainly wasn't an identical double at all - persuaded Mal to bring him back to London."

"And what happened then do you think?"

"I wish I could give you the answer" she smiled. "We live in a world where people want short, easy answers to everything, both with a big pink bow. It's not that easy."

"Yes," I agreed wearily, "but what do you think?"

She paused, and gazed dreamily out of the window. "Think? Something very strange, very curious happened. I got to know a young man in New York in the sixties, a man who bore a good resemblance to Paul McCartney. Like a lot of people in New York he was an unknown, struggling actor trying to get somewhere Off Broadway."

"That's this William you mentioned last time?"

She nodded, but clearly didn't want to be interrupted. "I only met him a handful of times, and on one of those occasions I met him with Mal Evans. I knew very little about the young man, except he was from somewhere near Toronto, he was roughly my age, and he had a girlfriend who was a photographer. Called Linda."

This was a bombshell. She hadn't mentioned this before. She carried on talking before I could come in with a question. "I last saw him in....it was probably in June 1966. He was at a party I went to in Queens, playing his guitar."

"Beatles songs?" I enquired. Her snort of derision told me I was wrong.

"No way! He didn't like the Beatles. His English favourites were the Stones and the Who and the Kinks."

I scribbled down a note though I wasn't sure what the significance of this was. "And what happened then?"

"Nothing. I never saw him again. He vanished off the face of the earth. I didn't know him well. We'd moved in similar circles so he would occasionally be at some function or other I was at. And then nothing."

"But.....what-" I started, not knowing how to proceed.

"And then the strangest thing happened. Out of the blue I got a call from Mal asking if I had a number or an address for him, for the William Campbell man."

"Weird!" I commented. She appeared not to notice. "And did you have an address or a number?"

"Of course not. I barely knew the man. How would I have those details?"

"So why did Mal Evans want to find him?" I asked, though I thought I knew the answer.

"I don't know, or rather I didn't know. Then. He didn't tell me. He was quite upset that I didn't have any contact details. He even made me look through my FiloFax, but I knew I didn't have any details."

"What happened next?"

"I don't know. We talked about how Mal might find him, and all I could suggest was that he try the Radio station that sponsored the competition at the club in the Village when Mal first met him."

"And that was it?"

"Yes. I never saw Mal again. Spoke to him several times though. There was one odd thing though. Mal told me he was ringing from London."

"So?"

"You couldn't ring direct from Britain in the sixties. I know because when my mother or my friends called me they had to book a call with the operator, and the operator would ring my number to check that I was available. Mal didn't do that."

"Curious." It was the only comment I could make.

"And there was something else. I found a contact number for the radio station so I did a dial-back to check the number that had just called. I thought it might be the Beatles office in London. I was going to call him back with the radio information."

"And wasn't he there?"

"No. He was here. In New York. At JFK!"

I stared down at the pad on which I was scribbling notes, but she hadn't finished.

"So you have a young man who looks like Mr.McCartney who lives in New York and has a girlfriend, a photographer, called Linda. He vanishes off the face of the earth. In that period Mr.McCartney and his girlfriend, Joan Asher-"

"Jane Asher. Her name was Jane!" I corrected gently.

She smiled grimly. "At that time Mr.McCartney and his girlfriend, Jane Asher, were the golden couple. William and Kate, if you like. Then one day Mr.McCartney, for some strange reason, drops Jane Asher and next thing he takes up with this girl from New York. Called Linda. Who is a photographer!"

"And then, before long, Mr.McCartney marries this woman called Linda. The photographer from New York." She paused, and took a long, slow sip from a bottle of water placed on the floor at her feet. "And who is the witness at the Register Office? Not Mr.Lennon, or Mr. Harrison or Mr.Starr. No, the witness was Mal Evans. He was the only person from the Beatles party who was there. I don't know what that means but it's very strange."

It was also very curious, but I didn't want to break the mood by making any flippant remark. Yet again I didn't know what to say. I thought it might be the moment to change tack. "You've got a lot of stuff about Kenya and November 1966?"

"Well, if it happened, that's when it took place. Something very odd happened - that's clear, and Mal hinted at that a couple of times to me."

"How?"

"Well you read the stuff at the time and the dates and times don't add up between what he said happened in the first half of November and what Mr.McCartney says happened."

"Like what?"

"Mal is talking about the trip a few weeks later and he says he met Mr.McCartney-"

I noticed that she always referred to him as 'Mr.McCartney'! No explanation for the formality, but I found it strangely affecting.

"He says that he met Mr.McCartney on November 8th at 7pm at a theatre in Bordeaux."

"So?"

"Mr. McCartney's story is that they met under the church clock at the Saint-Eloi catholic church, on Rue Saint-James in Bordeaux. At that's meant to be on November 12th."

"Okay, there's a discrepancy, but what does that matter?"

"The relevance is when they tell their stories. Mal's account appeared in one of the Beatles publications shortly afterwards. Mr.McCartney's version didn't appear for more than ten more years. So who do you trust - somebody remembering something after a few weeks or someone remembering something after more than a decade?"

"I'm sorry, I don't see the point. Is this important?"

"In itself, no. But think of it this way. You have Mel Evans who has effectively lost his family because he's so devoted to the Beatles, he's been beaten up for them, taken the blame for things for them, known where they are every minute of every day. Then suddenly, in November 1966 Mal Evans apparently had no idea where John Lennon is for six whole days! Does that make sense to you?"

"Well no, but-"

She was on a roll, and I couldn't interrupt her. "Mal Evans and Mr.McCartney disappeared for several days, and in the few papers of Mal's that survived there's one sheet in his handwriting that mentions 'they did a good job in Nairobi' and also mentions a clinic in Kenya'!"

I was baffled. "Nairobi? Kenya? What's that about?"

She sighed, and sat back on the sofa rubbing her eyes with both hands. "You want me to tell you what I think happened?"

"Oh please", I stated, trying not to sound too desperate.

"I think there was an accident in November 1966. I think Mr.McCartney was killed. I think Brian Epstein and others persuaded Mal to trace this double of Mr.McCartney-"

"Your friend, William Campbell?"

"He was not my friend!" she snapped back. "He was just someone I knew casually, someone I met a handful of times. I believe Mal found William Campbell and took him to London where they all agreed what would happen-"

"All? Who is all?"

"Brian Epstein obviously, plus the three surviving Beatles. Maybe some others - Neil Aspinall and so on."

"And where does Kenya come into it?"

"William Campbell was a lookalike for Mr. McCartney. He wasn't an identical twin."

"So?"

"So he needed some surgery, to get him closer to Mr.McCartney. In looks."

"Surgery?" I repeated. Enlightenment dawned. "In a clinic? In Kenya?"

She nodded, silently. "So what do you think?"

I waited several seconds before answering. My head was swimming with information and the possibilities, but I was suddenly deeply weary of the whole thing. And from the rigidity of her posture she was growing tired of the topic, and probably me, as well.

She didn't wait for me to answer. "It's a shock to people to realise just how seedy the business aspects of show business are. I mean the whole Seltaeb thing was mostly relatively innocent. There was no violence intended, or even threatened, on either side - until some of the gangsters over here decided to take things into their own hands."

"And you know this as fact?"

She smiles, a little firmly I thought. "Oh yes, I know. That's why I told you Brian Epstein had been murdered, when I first met you."

"But have you any proof? It's fine making statements like that, but have you-"

"Well, I wasn't in Brian Epstein's bedroom when it happened. Very few girls ever made it there!" She didn't smile, but it was a very rare moment of humour in the room where the air suddenly seemed stretched and thin. "I think….I believe various of these evil bastards caught up with him and dealt with him because of the money he had cost them."

"Who?"

"Oh, I dunno. There were fifty people and companies in New York alone that lost more than a million each because of Seltaeb. There are plenty of people in New York that would cut your throat for a lot less than that. I think a couple of these Americans or Brits got into his room and killed him, but made it look like suicide."

"Brits?" I asked in my best mystified tone. "What Brits were involved?"

She cut across me. It was unusual for her, a shade impolite. "What do you know about the Krays, or Arthur Thompson?"

It was a strange question. Everybody knew about the Krays, at least the name, and their legendary savagery as they ruled the centre of London and the East End in the sixties. Thompson was a new name to me.

She carried on without waiting for me to reply. "The Krays ruled London, extortion, protection, violence, buying off the police. Thompson did the same in Glasgow, A meeting took place in Glasgow at a place called the Cockatoo in '63 or '64. It was like a summit meeting of villains. The Krays told Thompson they were going to take over the Beatles management,"

"What? Why? How?" It was a stupid response, but I wasn't able to say anything else.

"Why? Money. It's always money! The Beatles then were making so much money that it was a real attraction for people like the Krays as a way of making money and laundering money. How? That's easy. They were blackmailing Brian Epstein. Had been for a couple of years."

"I don't really follow this? Why would they be blackmailing him?"

"Money. Again! He lost a fortune at the clubs in London, and the Krays owned some of them or bought the debts off other club owners. They also supplied him with boys, and more than one person told me that Reggie Kray and Brian had a brief relationship. I never believed that myself - I always thought....maybe I mean hoped he had more taste. I think they got hold of stuff - pictures and documents - that incriminated him."

"Where from?"

"Who knows? Maybe that Gillespie bastard!"

"So what happened to the idea of the Krays taking over the Beatles?"

"For once good sense took over. I think Thompson probably warned them off, saying that if it came out that the Krays were managing the Beatles that might be the end for them."

"But how do you know all this?

"Mal. He was very close to the centre of things. Mal always reminded me of that Indian, the Chief, in the Jack Nicholson movie, "One Flew Over the Cuckoo's Nest". 'Cos Mal was always there, and was always just a silent sort of presence, I don't think they realised he was there a lot of times. He heard a lot of things, saw a lot of things that he maybe shouldn't."

She coughed, and dabbed her eyes. There was a long, pregnant silence. "Sorry. I'm tired. I don't want to talk about this any more!" At the mention of Mal her eyes had glistened over. Something told me that the discussion was over, and so I got up slowly, respectfully, to leave. I had the clear feeling that I would not meet Chrissie again. I shook her hand and then, in a burst of emotion, I bent down and kissed her on the right cheek. Her face felt surprisingly cool, as though she was sitting in a draught, though there was no draught I could feel in the room.

As I walked away I glanced at the cabinet which had been in the corner of the room on each of my visits. For the first time I took more than a casual glance at the contents. There were four shelves behind the glass door and I realised to my genuine surprise that each was adorned with a number of items relating to the Beatles. I wasn't aware of it but I must have paused while I was staring at the memorabilia inside the glass-fronted cabinet.

She had appeared silently beside me, staring at the cabinet. "Yes", she stated quietly. "It's Seltaeb stuff. I kept it all. Those things are like first editions now."

"There was a long, heavy pause before she added, "Things like that Beatles record player are worth a fortune now!"

I didn't comment on the real incongruity of this kind of plastic crap housed in a room on which so much love, and money, had been expended.

Besides the assorted buttons and lunch boxes and faded wigs on the top shelf were a series of dolls in plastic cases. They obviously dated from the Yellow Submarine period, and were assembled with a doll representing one of the Beatles accompanied by some other figure from the film.

All of them were there, Lennon, Starr, Harrison, McCartney….and McCartney. Two dolls of Paul. Not two copies of the same one because the accompanying figures were different. But undeniably two Pauls.

Curious.

And then I noticed that on the second shelf there was a collection of the famous nodding dolls, four mannequin representations of the individual Beatles. In 1964 these were huge sellers, particularly as the heads on the dolls shook when touched - aping the head-shaking performed by the group in the early days when performing numbers like 'She Loves You'.

The four dolls were there but only three were upright. I turned back towards her intending to just point out the discrepancy, but she had anticipated my comment.

"Yes, I know. One of the Beatles is fallen."

"But why do you keep all this stuff?" I asked. "What's it for? Who's it for?"

"For?" she asked blankly, bleakly. "I don't really know. It's for no one."

The Run Out Groove

There were many things that happened in the wake of Brian Epstein's death. A series of meetings at NEMS were intended, at least in his mind, to result in Clive Epstein carrying on with Business as Usual. Unfortunately, that was simply not possible.

Although NEMS limped on for a while, it quickly lost Stigwood and his acts, who left to form the Robert Stigwood Organisation in December 1967.

The long-discussed Apple organisation became a reality but merely opened a Pandora's Box of further troubles on which a host of unpleasant and/or loathsome creatures crawled and fed - much like the fabled cockroaches.

People like Alan Klein were able to take advantage of the confusion, but his intervention, despite all the fabled prowess, cost the group a lot of money and created immense heartache for a lot of people, many of whom had nothing but the Beatles best interests at heart.

NEMS was doomed as soon as the individual Beatles began to take more than a passing interest in the various contracts they had signed over the years. It was at that point that the realisation about the ramifications of the new EMI contract signed in January 1967 hit home. They were committed to paying 25% of those earnings to NEMS for the duration of the contract, and Epstein's death had no impact.

And it was in the wake of that shock that the Northern Song walls began to collapse in on them. Dick James, wearying of all the in fighting, decided to sell his shares in the company, which opened Northern Songs up to the many predators with deep pockets and avaricious eyes. The result was perhaps inevitable. The long road which started with Epstein stumbling into Dick James' office on Charing Cross Road led inexorably to Lew Grade and characters like Robert Holmes à Court and Michael Jackson. And that road culminated in the perhaps squalid sight of Paul McCartney, whoever it might actually be, effectively having to request permission to sing 'Yesterday'.

A painful road indeed.

And there was one unexpected and unpublicised postscript to the tale. An old lag called Bradley Allardyce had spent long periods in prison, with some of that time spent sharing a cell with Reggie Kray. On one of their long evenings together Reggie Kray told Allardyce that his brother, Ronnie Kray, had murdered Reggie's wife, Frances Shea in 1967. The inquest on her death had delivered a verdict of suicide, but the conversation between Reggie Kray and his sometime lover Allardyce also produced the startling admission that the Krays had the means of committing murder but making it look like suicide.

The claim was that Frances Shea had been forced by Ronnie to take the pills that killed her, making her apparent suicide actually murder.

Then, in December 1968, came possibly the final chapter in the whole story. Brian Epstein's lawyer, David Jacobs, allegedly committed suicide at his house in Hove. He was found hanging from a two-metre length of satin secured to one of the beams of the garage at his seaside home.

He had requested police protection in the weeks leading up to his death, and indeed told a private detective, John Merry, working casually for him that he was in terrible trouble with a number of people after him. Several of his friends and associates confirmed after his death that he seemed extremely upset and worried. Indeed one of them used the word terrified to describe his state of mind.

He had been asked for legal help by Ronnie Kray in the months leading up to his death, but that request was rejected. At that stage, the Krays had been in custody for months and a message had been sent to Jacobs that the pair desperately needed his legal skills to defeat the charges against them. But Jacobs turned them down and, many believe, paid the ultimate price. In their heyday, nobody said no to Ronnie Kray or his brother and escaped without penalty. In the aftermath of the suicide verdict a close friend of David Jacobs was told by two policemen that they believed Jacobs had been murdered on the orders of the Krays for refusing to help them, but they had so many charges pending against them that another would make no real difference.

The likely connection to the Krays and through them to Brian Epstein might be nothing more than coincidence, but it is also curious.

Very curious.

I didn't make my Conspiracies tv programme. I never will. It's too messy and painful, and, being frank, I would be slightly concerned for my health. But, when people ask for my opinion about the whole McCartney and Epstein story, I just state that if you see one thing that's odd, you write it off.

If you see three or five or nine things that are odd, you put them down to coincidence.

But then, when the number of odd, inexplicable things reach twenty or thirty or fifty or ninety you surely have to reckon there is something going on!

If you didn't, then that certainly would be curious.

Lightning Source UK Ltd.
Milton Keynes UK
UKHW01f1835180718
325932UK00001B/126/P

9 781631 735400